'Film history rarely has such a deft touch.
As with so much, Korda got lucky.'
Times Literary Supplement

'In this thorough and jaunty biography,
Drazin gives us a masterly portrait.'
Sunday Times

'An engrossing exegesis of film-making in inter-war Britain and a
rounded portrait of what we'd now call an economic migrant who
lived profligately, left others poorer and occasionally
and enduringly enriched the screen.'
Evening Standard

'Wry, ruthless and expertly researched.'
Financial Times

'[Drazin] tells his story well. He has enough weapons in his armoury
to destroy a few myths. The result is an intriguing narrative.'
Observer

'Thorough and readable.'
Mail on Sunday

'An engrossing memoir with a scoop story about
the film producer's espionage activities.'
Books of the Year, Independent

For my parents

KORDA

BRITAIN'S MOVIE MOGUL

Charles Drazin

I.B. TAURIS

New paperback edition published in 2011 by I.B.Tauris & Co Ltd
6 Salem Road, London W2 4BU
175 Fifth Avenue, New York NY 10010
www.ibtauris.com

First published in hardback in 2002 by Sidgwick & Jackson Ltd

Distributed in the United States and Canada
Exclusively by Palgrave Macmillan
175 Fifth Avenue, New York NY 10010

ISBN: 978 1 84885 695 0

A full CIP record for this book is available from the British Library
A full CIP record is available from the Library of Congress

Library of Congress Catalog Card Number: available

Printed and bound in Great Britain by
CPI Antony Rowe, Chippenham

Contents

Acknowledgements

I would like to thank the following people for the often considerable help and encouragement they have given me in the course of researching and writing this book.

Angela Allen, Sandy and Kelly Anderson, Gyorgi Balogh, Beáta Barna, the late Dallas Bower, Kevin Brownlow, Jenny Cambell, Noelle Carter, Jerome Chodorov, Mary Cohen, John Cunningham, Sir Andrew Cunynghame, Teddy Darvas, André De Toth, Sabina Grinling, Luca Giuliani, Samuel Goldwyn Jr, Guy Hamilton, Sir Anthony Havelock-Allan, Peter Hopkinson, Glynis Johns, Andrew Kelly, Andrew King, David Korda, Günther Krenn, David Lewin, Russ Lloyd, Robin Lowe, Hilary Mackendrick, Brian McFarlane, Janet Moat, Colin Moffat, Howard Prouty, Tony Read, David Russell, Peter Sasdy, Jeanie Sims, Anthony Slide, Roger Smither, Norman Spencer, Hugh Stewart, Michael Thornton, Brigitte and Herbert Timmermann, Hugo Vickers, Ellen Von Kassel.

I am grateful to the following institutions for access variously to books, videos, films and documentary information: the Bibliothèque du Film, Paris; the British Film Institute Library; the British Library; the Churchill Archives Centre, Churchill College, Cambridge; the Cineteca del Friuli Library, Gemona; Film Archiv Austria, Vienna; the Harry Ransom Humanities Research Center, University of Texas at Austin; the Hungarian Film Institute, Budapest; the Imperial War Museum, London; the London Library; the Margaret Herrick Library, Academy of Motion Picture Arts and Sciences, Beverly Hills; the Prudential Archive, Prudential Assurance plc; the Public Record Office; the State Historical Society, Wisconsin; the UCLA Film and Television

Archive; the Cinema/Television Arts Library, University of Southern California, Los Angeles.

I would like to thank the Leverhulme Foundation for a research grant which enabled me to make some attempt to follow in my much-travelled subjects footsteps around the world.

List of Illustrations

Every effort has been made to contact copyright holders of material reproduced in this book. If any have been inadvertently overlooked, the publishers will be pleased to make restitution at the earliest opportunity.

Preface

The history of the British cinema over the last half century serves only to confirm the truth of the closing comments that Laurence Olivier made at Sir Alexander Korda's memorial service in 1956: 'We shall not look upon his like again.'

Korda – or 'Alex', as he was known to those who worked with him – built in Britain a film industry that dared to rival the scale and ambition of Hollywood. Indeed, often he far surpassed it. While in the 1930s Hollywood was content to make-believe on its California soundstages, Korda was sending his film-makers far across the world to the Congo, the Sudan or India. Nothing on the scale of his 1939 Technicolor epic *The Four Feathers* would be attempted until David Lean directed *Bridge on the River Kwai* for Sam Spiegel nearly two decades later. In the boldness and extravagance of his vision, Korda offered a compelling example of a British film industry punching so far above its weight that with hind-sight it seems appropriate that he should have died in a year that, with the *débâcle* of Suez, came to symbolize Britain's imperial retreat.

The first edition of this book appeared nearly ten years ago. If there is one impression I should wish to emphasise, among the thoughts that I have given to Korda in the years since, it is the interconnectedness of what he achieved. For all his personal genius, Korda was reliant on other people. This dependence began most notably with his own family. There was not one Korda but three: his brothers Zoltán and Vincent, who made immeasurable contributions to the overall Korda enterprise, deserve studies of their own. Then there was an even wider family of key contributors: the screenwriter and script advisor Lajos Biro; the cinematographer Georges Périnal; the editor William Hornbeck; and so on. The regular association of this group of film-makers is so important to the overall mood and ambience of the Korda films that Alex's true measure may be seen to lie in the skill with which he harnessed and integrated their talents. Cosmopolitan and colourful, he was easily the British cinema's most glamorous figure, yet to the extent that he also belonged to the band of creative producers who dominated Hollywood's Golden Age, his career brings out the nature of the cinema as an intrinsically collaborative and transnational medium.

Perhaps the most significant development since the first publication of this book has been the interest that Hungarians now show in the many celebrated émigré film-makers whose early years were passed in their country. The Jameson CineFest Miskolc International Film Festival provides just one of many examples. In 2009, it hosted a conference devoted to Emeric Pressburger, who was born in Miskolc; and the following year it turned its attention to the second of the Korda brothers, Zoltán, whose achievements as a director have long been hidden behind Alex's considerable shadow. Increased collaboration between researchers in the émigrés' countries of departure and arrival promises new insight into a culture and society that was so important to the formation of not only Alexander Korda but also the exotic breed of film moguls as a whole.

Charles Drazin
May 2011

1. THE PUSZTA

Mile after mile the view was the same. Vast, flat fields stretching as far as the eye could see, interrupted only by an isolated farm building or a clump of trees on the horizon. 'If you are going to get the atmosphere and "feel" of Hungary,' said a friend who worked at the university in Debrecen, 'you have to come out east, to the Puszta. This is where the Hungarian "soul" is to be found.' But it didn't seem that there was anywhere a soul could possibly hide.

Very occasionally the train would rattle through a town. You could see into people's gardens – although 'garden' was hardly the right word, for every inch had been turned over to growing vegetables. Roads between the houses were no more than dirt tracks, so that even quite sizeable settlements seemed somehow temporary, less a break from the countryside than a variation on it.

At Kisújszállás, we got on to a bus that took us to Túrkeve, a quarter of an hour's drive through the same flat landscape. In the winter's gloom the huge puddles that had gathered in the fields looked like stepping-stones through the vastness.

As we came into the town, some brightly coloured, spray-can graffiti offered a modern intrusion into a townscape that can have hardly changed in a hundred years. On the side of a house the letters A-L-E-X had been entwined within a yin–yang circle. But if this was meant as a sign, it was the first and last of the day. I had hoped we might find some memorial to Korda – perhaps a statue, or the cinema that had been named after him, or even the Jewish school he had attended as a young boy. But we found nothing.

1

Túrkeve was another town that seemed to have grown out of the surrounding fields. Peering over fences, I would see a barn or a tractor or a stack of hay. The streets we walked along were unpaved, the defining element not concrete but mud and grass. The few shops that had been sparsely scattered among the farmhouses seemed like an afterthought. Almost every dwelling possessed a dog, which would bark fiercely as we passed, making the owners look up at these strangers. The whole town was at home *en famille* that day because it was a National Holiday. The atmosphere was that of a sleepy Sunday.

It was difficult to believe that a man who had become a British knight, who had famously lived for many years in a penthouse at Claridge's, who owned a sea-going yacht and felt most at ease on the Riviera, could have come from such a place. Indeed, Sir Alexander Korda wasn't even born in a town. He may have gone to school in Túrkeve, but to visit his actual birthplace we had to take another bus journey into the depths of the countryside beyond.

About 5 miles to the south of Túrkeve, the word *Pusztatur-pásztó* was chiselled in the plaster beneath the eaves of a roadside house. Had we been looking the other way, we could easily have missed it. We had to ask the bus driver to stop to let us off.

Alex would have recognized this building, but there was little else that a hundred years had spared. His family's house featured in a BBC documentary of his life made in 1968, but had been demolished by the time a second *Omnibus* documentary was made a quarter of a century later. All there was to see in this desolate place were some barns behind the house, some distance off, low, barrack-like buildings which looked as if they had been built shortly after the war, when much of Hungary's farmland was collectivized, and, on the other side of the road, a row of farm-workers' cottages. Here, maybe, I hoped, someone might have heard of Sándor Kellner, the original name by which Alex had been known.

As we walked past a couple of haystacks, an Alsatian tied to a post began to bark, a black pulli dog ran round in circles, and three chickens – much to my town-person's amusement – crossed the road.

A woman came to her gate to see what all the fuss was about. Sándor Kellner, we asked, had she heard of him? We explained who he was. But not even a flicker of recognition. She was pained not to be able to give us an answer, and the trouble she took to find one for complete strangers was touching. She opened the gate to the cottage next door, and called her neighbour. They conferred for some time, then shook their heads in frustration.

The trail had gone cold. Pusztaturpásztó had forgotten its most famous son. We walked back to the bus stop. I looked at the house opposite with its pitched roof and the name of the village I couldn't pronounce. A blue plaque, I fancied, would fit quite snugly, tucked in between the eaves and the village name:

SIR ALEXANDER KORDA WAS BORN HERE
1893–1956

But what could that name possibly mean to the people who worked the fields here? I imagined how seeing it at the end of each day as they returned the tractors to the barns could even become an irritation. Such an exotic figure did not belong to their world, even if he had been born into it.

The sun was setting. I looked back down the road in the direction of Túrkeve, which was somewhere over the horizon. Narrowing to a pinpoint, flanked on either side by the endless plain, this was the view that would have faced the young boy, Sándor, as he set off for school every morning. Some miles down the road to the south was Mezőtúr, where Sándor went to school from the age of nine. But it was the identical view: a straight road running through an empty plain to the horizon.

Perhaps inevitably I found myself thinking of the movies – Dorothy, living on the homestead in Kansas with her Auntie Em and Uncle Henry, longing to get away to some place over the rainbow where exciting things happened. Alex's early life, I felt, must have been very similar, except that once he got away from the farm he never went back.

Alex had enjoyed a comfortable and – for the area – even privileged childhood. His parents were Ernesztina and Henrik Kellner. His father was manager of a large estate belonging to the Salgó family. It was a respectable and secure position, which would have set the family apart from the peasants who worked the land.

So too would the fact that they were Jewish, although this should not be overstated. By the late nineteenth century Hungary's Jewish citizens were integrated into the wider community and had taken advantage of increasing opportunities for advancement. In 1905, for example, there were 102 Jewish members in the Hungarian Parliament, a quarter of the total, although Jews made up only 5 per cent of the country's population. Two-thirds of Budapest's taxpaying businessmen were Jewish; there were even Jewish baronets.

This very success of course provoked a degree of anti-Semitic activity, but it was marginal. Jews in Hungary would probably have had the sense of being slightly different that most immigrant communities experience – social exclusion less an everyday occurrence than an ever-present possibility.

According to Túrkeve's register of Jewish births, Alex was born on 13 September 1893, but he would routinely claim to have been born three days later on 16 September. For someone who would demonstrate a talent for Protean, chameleon-like behaviour, it seems apt that the very first anecdote about his life should concern a switch in identity. On the day he was born – whichever date it was – his father sent a farm-worker off to register the birth in Túrkeve. He had chosen the name Sándor, but when Ernesztina learned of this name, she was furious, as she had wanted to call her son László. She sent the worker back to ask the registrar to change the name. But all the registrar could do was to add 'László' after 'Sándor'. Ernesztina persisted in calling her first-born by the preferred name, and throughout Alex's life members of his close family would call him by the diminutive of László, Laci or Lacikám. The story suggests where the balance of power lay in the Kellner family. Two more boys were born to the Kellners – Zoltán in 1895, and Vincent in 1897.

The details of Alex's early life are extremely sketchy, but the evidence suggests that although as a young child he went as a matter of course to the Jewish school in Túrkeve, he had a secular rather than a religious upbringing. In later life, when he came to regard his religion as a possible risk, it was something that he was able to hide with ease. On the few occasions that the matter was an issue, he claimed to be a member of the Hungarian Reformed Church. In his memoir of his family, *Charmed Lives*, Alex's nephew, Michael, described his surprise when in 1961 his father, Vincent, arranged for his Uncle Zoltán to have a Jewish funeral. 'The Kordas had always been reticent about religion, allowing their children to be brought up as Anglicans, in the English tradition, but taking no interest in it themselves. They always described themselves as Hungarian, which was sufficiently exotic to forestall all questions.'[1]

//

A photograph of the Kellner family, taken when Alex was ten, shows his mother Ernesztina, plump and cheerful, sitting on a garden bench with her family around her. In her lap there is an open book, to which presumably she is just about to return.

It's one of those photographs that draws you in. You want to 'read it', to know what happened before and after the click of the shutter. Zoltán stands with his father behind the bench, while Vincent and Sándor sit on either side of their mother. The two younger Kellner boys look directly at the camera, which their expressions of curiosity suggest is still a novelty for them. Father and mother and eldest son, on the other hand, look away from the camera to their right at some unseen incident – dogs scrapping in the yard maybe. While his two younger brothers have the manner of children, Sándor seems precociously grown up, closer to his parents' generation.

Henrik Kellner, who had been a sergeant in the Hussars, was recalled by his children as a gentle and generous man, but the key influence on them would be their mother Ernesztina. All three children would remember her with enormous affection and, as her grandson Michael put it, they 'never forgot her strength, courage and love'.[2] Among the fragments of family reminiscence, a recollection of Alex's first wife Maria suggests that Ernesztina went to considerable lengths to take care of her boys long after they had ceased to be children. When Alex and Maria were living in Vienna, Ernesztina would send them pots of homemade chicken goulash, which they used to eat for breakfast every morning, 'with great love in our heart to his mother Esther'.[3] She was clearly at the heart of a close and happy family, although the photograph remains the principal piece of evidence of the sort of person she was, giving the impression of someone warm and maternal but also cultivated. As the book on her lap suggests, Ernesztina loved to read, and she would pass on this passion to her eldest son. As a child, Alex devoured adventure stories, thrillers and Westerns, but above all the science fiction of Jules Verne. Many years later, when he was a successful film producer, he would form a company to acquire the rights to all Verne's stories. Although remarkably he never got round to putting any of these stories on the screen, Verne's brand of stylish fantasy was recognizable in many of the films that he did make, from H. G. Wells's *The Man Who Could Work Miracles* to *The Thief of Baghdad*.

The talent that Alex would display in later life for living out of a suitcase was cultivated from his earliest years. At the age of five he attended school in Túrkeve. It was impossible to make the 5-mile journey there every day, so he was boarded out with friends in Túrkeve during the week, every Friday evening cheerfully returning home in a horse-drawn buggy. Zoltán joined him at the school two years later.

At nine, Alex won a scholarship to a *Gymnasium* in Kisújszállás and then in Mezőtúr. Alex's first biographer, Paul Tabori, who had worked as a screenwriter for him, gave a brief description of his schooldays. The young Alex would 'refuse to stay in line or stick to any group', he wrote; 'he hated the shackles of discipline and always tried to walk alone.'[4] But an early responsibility was rescuing his younger brother Zoltán, who would often get himself into fights. Less plausibly, Tabori described Alex as 'a lively boy who loved all sports'.[5] If this was true, it was at odds with the physical indolence that he would display in later life, although it's possible that an eye infection which led to his having to wear thick glasses from an early age put paid to any such aspirations. Indeed, Alex's eyesight was so poor that to many it seemed extraordinary that he should have made his name directing films. Whenever he read a book or a script, he would push up his glasses and hold the paper so close to his eyes that it almost touched his nose.

Alex's childhood had afforded him the luxury of being able to dream and to grow up in comparative tranquillity. This came to an abrupt end in October 1906, when his father died from a ruptured appendix. The family home, which had come with the job of estate manager, had to be vacated, and the Kellners moved to Kecskemét to live with Ernesztina's father-in-law, Károly, a harsh old man who would regularly beat his grandchildren with a leather strap. Ernesztina and her children might have hoped for some comfort and support, but it was clear that they would do better to fend for themselves as soon as possible.

The tragedy propelled Alex into adult life. 'Korda told me that he became a father rather earlier in life than is usual,' recalled the actor Ralph Richardson, who would become a close friend, 'that is between the age of twelve and thirteen, because his father died, and he and his brothers, Zoli and Vincent, were left quite destitute, and he had to look after the other children and see that they went to school with their clean collars and clean behind the ears, and he was the father of the family.'[6] It was a role from which in his subsequent life Alex would never be able completely to escape.

//

Back in Kisújszállás, we sat in the sepulchral hall of the station waiting for our train to arrive. Pinned up in a window above a closed news stall was a glossy magazine called *Ez Amerika*. A Hollywood film star in black tie – George Clooney, I think – adorned the cover. In some ways, it occurred to me, not much had changed in a century. When they were growing up, Alex and Zoltán used to walk to the edge of the village at sunset – Alex always heading for the western boundary. Eventually he would get as far west as it is possible to go. But if he came to enjoy equal terms with Hollywood's film moguls, his temperament and experience gave him a deeply European outlook. The cities in which Alex first made his fortune were Budapest, Vienna and Berlin, while the Hollywood moguls could not help but associate

Europe with the disadvantage and failure they had left behind. Often poorly educated, they belonged to the 'huddled masses' in a way that Alex never truly did.

The day in Túrkeve and Pusztaturpásztó had been something of a disappointment. I had deluded myself with the fantasy of finding some wonderful relics of Alex's past – maybe his name scrawled on a school bench; or a gnarled old peasant woman who could remember running errands as a little girl for Mrs Kellner, full of stories about the mischief that Zoltán and Alex used to get up to. But no one we met had even heard of him.

Well, I reflected, Túrkeve, with its tractors and barns and haystacks, was an unpromising place to harbour such memories. That was why Sándor had left in the first place. But then some days later, leafing through the Korda file in the Hungarian Film Institute, I discovered that the citizens of Túrkeve had been doing their best. In the summer of 1979, the town held a three-week Korda festival. The various events – all free of charge – included an exhibition of Vincent Korda's paintings, a lecture on 'The Role of Sándor Korda and his Brothers in Film Art', a showing of short films by amateur film-makers from Túrkeve, and three Korda movies – *The Private Life of Henry VIII*, *Rembrandt* and *That Hamilton Woman*.

Four years later, in September 1983, to mark the ninetieth anniversary of Korda's birth, the town held another festival. In these twilight years of Communism, it was the cause of some controversy. An official from the Film Institute turned up to speak on 'The Life and Works of Sándor Korda', but he spent most of the lecture talking about other film-makers. When he finally got round to the supposed subject of his talk, he commented that Alex's main ambition had been to get rich.

The Túrkeve audience, who judged their most famous son differently, were shocked. They began to suggest ways in which he could be remembered. One person proposed erecting a statue. Another suggested that perhaps the town's new cinema could be named after him. But the lecturer argued that Alex did not deserve such memorials.

An indignant letter was written to a Budapest newspaper, which reported the debate and passed its own verdict. 'To claim that Korda's main ambition was to get rich is a slander,' it commented. 'If there was one genuine connoisseur among all the millionaire philistines of the film world, it was Korda.'[7]

Twenty years on, Túrkeve still has no statue, but there is the cinema – the Korda Sándor Mozi – which we must have missed by taking a wrong turning.

2. SÁNDOR OF THE RIVER

Eager to get away from his harsh grandfather, Alex persuaded his mother to let him stay with cousins in Budapest, where he continued his education at a *Gymnasium* in Barcsay utca. Half a century later, his nephew Michael would travel to Budapest himself and try to imagine what it was like for the young Alex 'to confront a great city for the first time'.[1] Anyone who chooses to write about Alexander Korda must address the gulf between the famous sophisticate he became, who kept the company of the rich and powerful, and Sándor Kellner, the country boy from the Puszta. How did the one become the other? We can get some idea from an autobiographical story that Alex wrote only two years after his arrival in Budapest in 1908 at the age of fifteen. It begins with his alter ego, Mihály Ság, approaching the city in a train:

> Mihály Ság leaned out of the train window and said to himself, 'Pest . . . Budapest . . .' Behind this strange, mysterious word lay new and miraculous mysteries. He was on the threshold of some great darkness that he feared to enter, but ran towards none the less. The thick, black smoke from the engine billowed into the night sky. Red and yellow sparks etched a fiery line across the darkness, racing along with the smoke before exploding into nothing.
>
> Mihály Ság then turned back into the third-class compartment. He closed his eyes so as not to see the sad, tired faces of the old women who reminded him so much of his own mother, and so as not to see anything that would hurt or disturb him.
>
> For on that misty September night he sensed that his soul,

which had so far been enveloped in greyness, would encounter marvellous new discoveries. It was a moment that Mihály Ság had long been waiting for. He had known from books that in the world beyond, there existed things other than what he had experienced and seen during his eighteen years of life in a small town, that there were secrets as strange as an Eastern tale. Sometimes it seemed to him that only by chance had his soul settled in a half-peasant family in a small town. In a small town there were no mysteries to unlock, no beauty to be born, only tranquillity. And tranquillity was boredom.

Thirsty for the unknown, Mihály Ság approached the city like a bride waiting for the moment of revelation. Its contours were lost in the darkness, but he could feel its pulse and trembled with expectancy of what it held in store for him.[2]

The impression is of someone who threw himself completely into a new experience without hesitation or reserve. I was reminded of a comment made to me by the journalist David Lewin, who, drawing on a series of interviews with Alex in the weeks before he died, was the first person to write his life story. 'Alex grew into things and they became part of him, and then he could discard that part.' In this way the young Sándor Kellner turned his back on his provincial upbringing, embracing his new city life with total commitment. Like Mihály Ság, the hero of his story, he felt that 'the murmur in which all the discordant sounds of the city merged into a harmony, ran through his blood. The music of the city was a part of him.'[3]

//

I had my first taste of Budapest in the breakfast-room of a hotel named after a famous Hungarian painter, Gyula Benczúr. At the table next to me sat a couple of American businessmen, Tom and Mike, in conversation with the Hungarian translator who was looking after them during their stay in the city.

The conversation turned to the subject of humour. 'One time I was in England,' said Tom, 'and nobody understood my jokes, but they laughed anyway.'

This mention of the duplicitous English reminded the translator of Hungary's recent Communist past. Whenever an important

Soviet politician visited Budapest, the Hungarian translator would translate word for word until he came to a joke. Then he would warn the audience: 'I'm not going to translate this next bit because it is a joke, but would you please laugh.'

The English and the Hungarians, it seemed to me, shared a lot in common.

After breakfast I began my tour of the city in the Hösok Tere, Heroes' Square, which marks the northern end of the Andrassy Ut. The centrepiece of the square is the Millennium Monument. Poised on top of a column more than 100 feet high, the Archangel Gabriel holds out the Crown of Hungary. Gathered around the base of the column, mounted on their steeds, are Prince Arpad and his chieftains. With their rugged garb and bushy moustaches they reminded me of Norsemen. In 896 they led the seven Magyar tribes from the western Ukraine into the Carpathian basin, launching Hungary's existence as a nation.

Mention of the Millennium in Budapest is as likely to refer to this event as the recent passing of the twentieth century. The monument had been erected in 1896 to mark the 1,000th anniversary of Hungary as a nation. Behind stretched a crescent-shaped colonnade, under which stood statues of Hungary's great leaders, from István, who was crowned the country's first Christian king on Christmas Day 1000, to Lajos Kossuth, leader of the 1848–9 War of Independence against the Habsburg Empire. All of them, without exception, wore moustaches, which seemed to be a *sine qua non* for Hungarian heroes. (When Alex arrived as a young director in Hollywood, he too wore a moustache.)

On the right-hand side of the square stood the neo-classical Mücsarnok, the Palace of Arts, distinctive with its gilded façade; and on the left side, the Szépmsvészeti Múzeum, an imposing building with heavy stone columns that reminded me of the British Museum. It was finished just a year before Alex came to Budapest. The fifteen-year-old would have found a bustling, prosperous metropolis – vying with Vienna for the title of first city in the Habsburg Empire, and expressing its new-found confidence in extravagant monuments and boulevards built on a scale that even a Baron Haussmann would have envied. By the turn of the century, Budapest was the sixth largest city in Europe.

A key event had been the 1867 Austro-Hungarian Compromise, according to which the Empire was to consist of two separate states, the Austrian Empire and the Kingdom of Hungary, each with its own parliament. The political stability and unprecedented economic growth that followed allowed Hungary for the first time in centuries to indulge in the unfettered expression of its separate nationhood.

The Andrassy Ut, which leads from Heroes' Square into the heart of the city, has the feel of a Champs-Elysées. It's a spectacle of dilapidated splendour now. The tall buildings are riddled with cracks, chunks of masonry have fallen from the high balconies and in several places the plaster has crumbled away, but walking down this wide boulevard, you can still sense the great release of energy with which, at the end of the nineteenth century, Hungary celebrated its millennium. This is the Budapest that Alex would have known – when the stucco was still fresh.

At the southern end of the Andrassy Ut, the Jozsef Attila Utca veers to the right, taking the shortest possible route to the Danube. There had been plenty of sights to arrest one's attention along the way, but nothing to match the hills of Buda suddenly coming into view, rising up steeply on the far side of the river's broad expanse.

Originally two separate towns, Buda and Pest were for the first time linked together in 1849 by the building of the Széchenyi chain bridge. Reminiscent of Brunel's famous suspension bridge at Clifton, the Széchenyi was actually completed fifteen years earlier. It is an early example of a British–Hungarian partnership. The Anglophile statesman Count István Széchenyi commissioned a Scottish engineer, Adam Clark, to build the bridge, and most of the iron was smelted in English foundries.

Clark, who would also build a tunnel beneath Buda's Várhegy hill on the far side of the bridge, settled in Budapest and married a Hungarian wife. Virtually unknown in England, he became something of a celebrity in Hungary. During the 1848–9 War of Independence he intervened personally to save the bridge from destruction. Books have been written about him and there is even a statue of him in Budapest. He was, I suppose, as important to Hungarian engineering as Alex would later become to British films.

I crossed Adam Clark Square. Two massive stone lions flanked the threshold to the bridge. On the Buda side, there were two more. Had Adam Clark been thinking of Trafalgar Square, I wondered, when he put these lions here? So many of Budapest's public monuments seem to have been built in the grand Victorian style. On the Buda side, I looked back across the Danube to the neo-Gothic spires of Hungary's Parliament. Finished in 1902, it had taken the Palace of Westminster as its model. When Alex, newly arrived in England, chose Big Ben as the trademark of his new company, which with unashamed directness he called London Films, he wasn't the first Hungarian to pay such a tribute.

If the Parliament building itself was every bit the equal of its Thames-side inspiration, the nascent democracy it was intended to house lagged some way behind. The sovereign of the Habsburg Empire retained sweeping powers with which to over-rule its decisions and the 413 members of the House of Representatives were elected by just a quarter of the country's adult male population, who had to meet a minimum requirement in wealth or education. But the Compromise had none the less ushered in a genuine age of social and political reform.

The progressive atmosphere nurtured an increasingly sophisticated urban populace that caused Budapest to stand out in stark contrast to the rest of Hungary. Ferenc Herczeg, the editor of *Uz Idok* (*New Times*), one of the many new literary reviews that were springing up in the early years of the new century, would comment on the speed with which Budapest was breaking away from the traditions of what was otherwise a largely rural country, so that it had 'no organic link at all with the nation which dwells in the surrounding provinces'.[4] The great storyteller of nineteenth-century Hungary was Mór Jókai, whose novels were set against key episodes in the country's history and struck a consistent tone of patriotic heroism. But his death in 1904 seemed to symbolize the mood of change and coincided with an eagerness among a new generation of Hungarian writers to look further afield. One of them was Endre Ady. Today regarded as the most significant figure in early twentieth-century Hungarian literature, he would cause a furore with the publication of *Új versek* (*New Verses*) in 1906 and *Vér és arany* (*Blood and Gold*) in the following year. These 'new verses of a new era', as Ady called them, challenged Hungary's provincialism and social backwardness. Hugo Veigelsberg, who under the pseudonym of Ignotus would contribute to a celebrated literary magazine called *Nyugat* (*West*) took up the cry: 'We should not enclose ourselves within stone walls,' he declared, 'but throw the gate wide open to all trends which come from the West, using them to develop our minds and sharpen our eyes.'[5] This was the sort of sentiment that must have appealed enormously to a boy from the country who always used to walk to the western edge of his village. Launched in 1908, the same year that Alex arrived in Budapest, *Nyugat* became a flagship for literary and cultural progress in Hungary. Alex would come to know many of its writers, and grew up in the atmosphere of intellectual curiosity that the periodical fostered.

//

'We Hungarians feel we can cross any line,' said Beáta, who had been helping me with translations. We had spent the morning at the Film Institute watching Alex's only surviving Hungarian film, an adaptation of Mór Jókai's classic novel, *The Golden Man*. Now we were exchanging our impressions of the Hungarians and the English over lunch. Beáta had been commenting on how class-ridden England was – she had recently spent some months in London and Birmingham. I remembered her words because they seemed to sum up Alex so well. He would cross a succession of lines in his life, geographical, social and cultural.

It occurred to me that what might often appear to an outsider to be some immense gulf was not nearly so immense for a Hungarian. Budapest might have been a metropolis that dwarfed all other Hungarian towns, yet, as Beáta told me, many people in the city had country connections. So perhaps it worked the other way round too. Túrkeve, which seemed to be just a collection of farmhouses, was actually a sizeable town of 10,000 people, with a flourishing cultural life. The relationship between the metropolis and the countryside, it seemed, was more one of symbiotic co-existence than the stark opposition I had imagined.

Later that day I set off for Hungary's National Gallery, perched high above the Danube on top of the Várhegy, Castle Hill. A huge canvas, about 12 by 18 feet, faces you as you climb the central staircase. The *Recapture of Buda Castle* depicts a famous victory in 1686 over the Turks, who had occupied Hungary for over 150 years. Through an arch behind the soldiers fighting hand to hand, the Danube curves into the distance. By looking out of a gallery window, I could see the same view.

At first I thought the canvas was the work of some eighteenth-century master, but it had actually been painted by Gyula Benczúr in 1896, the year of Hungary's millennium. It quickly became clear from the gallery's other rooms that there was a whole school of such historical art, which complemented the grandiose monuments put up all over turn-of-the-century Budapest. Its chief purpose was to glorify Hungary as an independent nation.

I stood before the *Self-sacrifice of Titusz Dugovics*, painted by Sándor Wagner in 1859. Titusz – moustachioed of course – valiantly fights off the marauding Turks as his comrades set the Hungarian flag flying above the citadel tower. Down below in the distance flows the ever-present Danube, virtually a watermark of authenticity in these paintings.

The leading Turk in the assault, with his supercilious manner and his crimson cloak and turban, reminded me of Conrad Veidt as the evil Vizier Jaffar in Alex's *The Thief of Baghdad*. Indeed, I couldn't help wondering if this painting had in some way been an inspiration. Alex, in his wanderings through Budapest, must often have come up to the Gallery on the hill. Even if he never consciously considered the parallels himself, all these triumphalist paintings – and the general mood of bravado in early twentieth-century Hungary – offered a precedent for the celebration of British history that Alex the film producer would attempt in films such as *Fire over England*, *That Hamilton Woman* or *The Four Feathers*.

While Alex's attendance in Budapest's art galleries may be a matter of speculation, the significance of the city's coffee houses in his early development is indisputable. 'When I was a boy in Budapest,' he would comment in later life, 'I learned the most important thing of all – how to be a good talker.'[6] The coffee houses were his teacher.

'Your intellectual, social, political status could be pegged by knowing which coffee house you called home away from home,' observed the Hollywood director André De Toth who had grown up in Hungary and worked for Alex in the 1930s.[7] Korda's home from home was the Café New York. A favourite haunt of writers and artists, it was, in Paul Tabori's description, run by 'a most understanding head-waiter who acted as pawnbroker, money-lender, father confessor and agent to his large, varied clientèle'.[8] It was a place both to meet people and also to work. You could spend hours at a time here nursing just a cup of coffee. The most indigent person could swell with confidence in its palatial sur-roundings. 'They sent you off to face the day not thinking, but knowing you are the king,' recalled De Toth. But there were niceties to observe. 'It all depended, of course, on how well you tipped.'[9]

The Café New York still survives today. It is a tall, castle-like building with a mass of stony pinnacles. It was built in 1894 with all the extravagance of the age. Flights of steps leading to different levels pass through a gauntlet of candelabras and twisting col-umns that reminded me of the Bernini altar in St Peter's. Sculpted reliefs of fawns and half-naked girls frame paintings with pastoral themes on the ceiling. The tables on the ground floor gather around an open basement which in Alex's day was known as 'deep water'. Above, more tables stand in balconies like boxes at the theatre, which of course in a sense this place is. It reminded me of a London picture palace and I found it no surprise to learn that the first film show ever to be put on in Hungary should have taken place in a coffee house.* For the commodity it was meant chiefly to offer – like the picture palaces that would follow just a few years afterwards – was escapism.

André De Toth remembered the Café New York as 'a marble

---

* At the café of the Somossy Orfeum, on 29 April 1896 (Erzsebet Pongrácz, *The Cinemas of Budapest*, City Hall, Budapest, 1998).

and mahogany, crystal-chandeliered, burgundy and gilt depository',[10] but the intervening age of the proletariat and mass tourism have wrought some changes. The crystal chandeliers have given way to crude clusters of white globes on iron stalks, and the red plush seats have been replaced by plain wooden chairs. The menu is in several languages, and on the day visited only the waiters and the piano player seemed Hungarian.

Every now and then a camera would flash as yet another tourist photographed the splendid décor – although there was no need for this really, as you could buy postcards of the place as you collected your coat from the cloakroom on the way out. Here a solitary, unused stack of newspapers served as a reminder of what the place once was. Café life is a fragile thing, no sooner celebrated than threatened. The Café New York that Korda or De Toth would have known had been killed by its fame. It was no longer a haunt for writers and artists, but a city sight for one-time visitors from far away.

The pianist's repertoire had perfectly caught the idiom of international entertainment. With his black tie and easy smile, he could have been performing in any gin joint in any town in the world. And he improvised brilliantly. When he saw a little girl at a nearby table wearing a bib stitched with the word 'Eva', he launched into the opening bars of 'Don't Cry for Me, Argentina'. Everyone applauded. The people here, I felt sure, would have been as unlikely to have heard of Sándor Kellner or Sándor Korda or Sir Alexander Korda as the farm-workers in Pusztaturpásztó.

//

The Kellner family followed Alex to Budapest in 1909. To bring in an income, Ernesztina had to take in lodgers. The apartment was small and living conditions were uncomfortable. As the eldest son, Sándor had a tiny room of his own, but Vincent and Zoltán had to sleep in the living-room or the hallway.

Alex had by this time transferred to a commercial school in Mester utca. Here he would become president of the school literary club. He made his début with a short story, in which a landlord ejects a poor family for not paying the rent. Its unhappy ending – the family are left sitting on the pavement with their heap of furniture in the rain – had a note of sad realism that many people who knew Alex in his later life would have recognized, although publicly he would always cloak it in a determined optimism.

He found a mentor at the school in his history and literature teacher, Oskár Fabér. An ex-Catholic priest, Fabér was a progressive socialist active in politics. He encouraged in Alex a youthful idealism which would eventually bring him into open conflict with authority. In the autumn of 1909 one of Fabér's political heroes, Guardia Ferrer, was sentenced to death by the reactionary Spanish Government. Alex led a demonstration through the streets of Budapest to denounce the sentence. At the Octogon, he climbed on to a café table and addressed a crowd of several hundred people, denouncing the Spanish Government. The police turned up, dragged him from the table and dispersed the crowd.

'He was deeply dejected,' wrote Tabori of Alex's first and only political protest. 'He knew nothing could save Ferrer. But he wondered how such judicial murders could be prevented in the future; what he and his friends could do to shape a better and happier world.'[11]

Descriptions of the young Sándor Kellner in Budapest are as likely to conjure up the picture of a revolutionary with a round black bomb as that of a future film producer. His passions were politics and literature. If someone had asked him then what he wanted to do with his life, probably he would have said, 'Go into politics or be a writer.' Oskár Fabér helped him with the latter ambition by persuading Budapest's liberal daily newspaper, the *Független Magyarország* (*Independent Hungary*), to publish some of his articles and stories.

Sándor began to contribute pieces while he was still at school. He wrote under a pseudonym, 'Sursum Corda', a phrase that Catholics will recognize from the old Latin mass: 'Lift up your hearts . . .' The 'Corda' would soon be changed to 'Korda', perhaps an attempt to root the new identity in his old name, Kellner; or possibly for reasons of pronunciation, the initial 'c', in Hungarian, being pronounced as a 'ts'. The choice of such a pseudonym may have owed something to his mentor, Oskár Fabér, the ex-Catholic priest. According to Paul Tabori, Sándor had to adopt it 'lest his headmaster discover that he was breaking the school rules'. But one might have thought that the school would have been proud to see the articles of one of its pupils published in a newspaper. The real significance of the chosen name lay in its philosophy. In the years to come, Sándor would undergo many changes of fortune and circumstance, become famed for his unpredictable, Protean nature, but those two words, 'Sursum Corda', represented a bedrock conviction, an attitude to the world that he would embrace until his dying day. The Korda legend would be built on boundless ambition and faith in the future regardless of the odds. If in the years to come there would often seem to be something about Alex's achievements that defied any rational account, those two words always offered the best explanation.

Certainly, Sándor's straitened family circumstances meant that he could have done with an anthem of encouragement. His mother couldn't make ends meet by taking in lodgers, and Sándor had to do what he could to supplement the family income. While he was still at school he gave lessons to his fellow pupils, and the extra money from journalism would have been welcome.

Some idea of Alex's youthful idealism is reflected in his friends of the time, who, like his close family, knew him not as Sándor, but Laci. Alex's close friend at school was Simon Darvas, the son of a poor Jewish cobbler. 'Alex arrived the year after my father,' Darvas's son, Teddy, told me. 'Father was standing to become president of the students' union when he suddenly found someone canvassing against him, and that was Korda. But they became the greatest friends.'[12] Darvas was a Socialist, who would become secretary of the Hungarian equivalent of the Fabian Society, and an aide to Count Mihályi Károlyi, briefly Hungary's Prime Minister after the First World War.

Another friend was Ödön Pajzs, who would become editor of one of Hungary's largest newspapers. Indeed, Pajzs, Darvas and Alex all began their working lives as journalists. They were 'like a triumvirate of friends' who were always together, said Teddy Darvas. Their regular meeting-place was the Café New York. 'Alex was always beautifully dressed with a big cigar, but had no money at all. Father was earning money by that time and so was

Pajzs, and Pajzs told the head waiter that when Mr Korda comes in and orders a coffee put it on his bill, on Pajzs's bill.'[13]

It was Simon Darvas who first introduced Alex to the cinema. He took him along to the Café Venice, which, like many cafés in Budapest at that time, put on several short shows a day. The programme would have been a compendium of primitive travelogues, news items and comic sketches, but as Teddy Darvas recalled his father saying, Alex recognized the potential of the new medium instantly. 'Father said that when the lights went up, Alex said, "That's for me." He was fascinated by it.'[14]

Years later Alex himself would claim that his youthful ambitions had been literary. 'When I was eighteen,' he said in a 1953 interview, 'I wanted to write a big novel – a novel as great and big as *War and Peace*. Or if that wouldn't go, a very slender volume of wonderful poetry, about a dozen sonnets.'[15] Recalling such musings in *Charmed Lives*, Alex's nephew Michael considered it likely that his uncle's 'wistful references to a lost career as a literary figure were simply another manifestation of the Kordas' notorious inability to be content with their own fate'.[16]

But the evidence suggests that on leaving school in 1909, however excited he may have been by the crude new medium of the cinema, Alex's principal aspiration was indeed literary. While working as a junior reporter with the *Független Magyarország*, he wrote several short stories, four of which were published in an anthology called *Kórborlások* (*Travels*) in 1911. Alex's literary œuvre amounted to a lot less than *War and Peace* but considerably more than a dozen sonnets. Another contributor to the collection was Simon Darvas.

Of Alex's stories it is the one called *Este* ('Evening'),[17] quoted at the beginning of this chapter, that gives the most insight into the kind of young man he was. Mihály Ság is a musician who finds inspiration in the night life of Budapest. His burning desire is to capture the 'music of the city'. The quest requires him to embrace solitude and sadness, for the 'people of the night streets follow the bitter roads of life'. Beauty therefore is to be found in sorrow, which is the key to his happiness.

But there are days when he is tortured by self-doubt and

dismisses the artist's life he has chosen for himself as a conceit, a 'fantasy that I make up in my boredom'. He thinks back to his previous simple life, when he was spared the unfathomable dilemmas that now disturb him. He detests the blinkered security of that life, but longs for it too.

One beautiful sunny afternoon he meets a girl. She takes his hand and they kiss. They enjoy the simple pleasure of just being together. It is a day of perfect happiness. But then the evening comes, and, gripped by its melancholy calling, he finds that ordinary contentment is not enough. When the girl offers her cheek, he kisses her. 'But when he looked into the girl's eyes, he wanted to weep. Her desire and happiness tortured him. He wanted to run into the night and dash himself against something that would destroy the pain he felt.'

Mihály Ság says goodbye and their parting is cold because 'the Evening was already in his soul, the pain-weaving girl who is everything to us: our wife, lover and mother; the pale girl whose look is secretive and suffering, whose secrets are always new, whose sufferings are always fresh, whose beauty is always triumphant.'

He wanders through the night-time streets towards the Danube. He sits down on a step by the river and looks at 'the shadow-palaces' on the opposite shore. 'From behind came the whispering of the city, and a sad melody issued from the soul of Mihály Ság, which embraced the whole town and then flew with wings up to the summit of the Gellèrt Hill, a melody so beautiful that he wanted to die.'

Getting up from the steps, Mihály Ság returns to his tiny room where he transforms the 'hymn of the evening' into notes on a score. When he is finished, he falls asleep by his piano on this 'happiest night of his life'.

The following day he sets off to show his composition to a friend. 'He knew that he was doing something wrong, that it was a sin to show off beauty, that it remains only so long as it is hidden, but we never do what we want.' He plays the melody to his friend, Peter, and then asks him what he thinks. 'It is very good,' replies Peter, but such is the look of puzzlement in his expression that Mihály Ság presses him to be completely honest:

Peter looked at him and asked abruptly, 'Have you heard of István Föld?'

On hearing this name, Mihály Ság recalled a whole range of forgotten yet once familiar melodies. He realized that his music was somebody else's music. He ran down the stairs and the pain was so unbearable that he wanted to scream that all is in vain, all beauty is lost and his life worthless, because what is life if he cannot create something new? What is beauty if he cannot possess it? And all the time he kept repeating the tragic name: István Föld . . . István Föld . . .

'Evening' is a brooding story about an artist's vocation that brings to mind not the adventure stories of Jules Verne that Alex would devour as a child, but Oscar Wilde. 'It is through Art, and through Art only, that we can realize our perfection':[18] Mihály Ság, wandering through the streets of Budapest, is Dorian Gray's kindred spirit, who lives according to this precept. Alex's story is so accomplished that it is easy to forget that he was only seventeen when he wrote it. Its intensity leaves one with no doubt that a literary career was what, at seventeen, Alex prized above all else.

Getting a job on a national newspaper was an exceptional achievement for the seventeen-year-old. Most people would have buckled down to make the most of the opportunity, to do what was necessary to progress within their new career. But Alex was determined to follow his own star.

//

At about the same time as the anthology of stories was being published in Budapest, Alex asked his editor if he could be sent to Paris as a correspondent of the paper. It must have seemed a presumptuous demand for a junior reporter to make, even in spite of Alex's precociousness. The editor told him that the paper could not afford it. He would try to publish any articles Alex might write, but could offer no regular commitment. Defying security like Mihály Ság, Alex decided to make the trip none the less. Paris had become a key destination for any young Hungarian artist or writer with progressive aspirations. The leading poet of the time, Endre Ady – whose verses were strongly influenced by

Baudelaire and Verlaine – had just spent several years there. But Ady, who like Alex had also worked as a journalist, had had a rich mistress to support his foreign travels. Not so lucky, Alex had to write a begging letter to one of his relatives, which Paul Tabori quotes in his biography:

> I would like to go to Paris and study at the Journalists' Academy. But as you know, I am poor. Would you lend me two hundred crowns? I'm sure that I'll pay you back and I guarantee to become a great man.[19]

The letter is the first recorded instance of Alex attempting to borrow money. Although his talent in this field would one day reach the level of genius, this attempt was unsuccessful. The relative refused the request and his mother, Ernesztina, had to scrape together what she could, which wasn't much.

If Alex's trip to Paris has the quality of legend, it is principally because the accounts of it are so confused. According to Paul Tabori, the young Korda left Budapest in June 1911, confident that he would soon become 'somebody in films'. Before the First World War, when Hollywood hadn't even been heard of, Paris was certainly the place to go if you had such an aspiration. The Pathé company, which had studios at Vincennes, was the largest film-making concern in the world. This was a time when Charlie Chaplin had yet to step before a movie camera and the most popular international film star was Pathé's Max Linder. France was responsible for 60–70 per cent of the world's film exports.[20] According to Tabori, after hanging around the Pathé studios for some time, Alex managed to get occasional employment. Even when there was no work for him to do, he would sneak on to the floor and stand quietly in the background watching films being made. 'He soaked up knowledge; often he itched to take over from a bungling director, set a scene, change the position of the actors – for he felt already that he could do better.'[21] But in later life Alex himself does not seem to have mentioned this early apprenticeship in the Pathé studios. His nephew Michael, presumably on the basis of Tabori's account, would suggest only that his uncle 'may have discovered the way to the Pathé Film Studio'.[22] Whether he did or not, the overriding motive of the Paris trip was less the narrow one of getting into films that Tabori suggests than to learn about culture in the city that had long been a magnet for writers and artists. In an otherwise extremely fanciful account of his life, written soon after he had died in 1956, Alex's first wife Maria describes the trip as a 'pilgrimage to knowledge' which Alex embarked upon with five friends.[23]

In Paris the young Hungarians were too poor to attend university, but were allowed to study by themselves in the Bibliothèque Nationale. Maria's account contains so many dollops of fantasy that it has to be regarded with extreme care, but none the less it rings true in essence. She writes about the experiences of Alex and his friends in terms that the seventeen-year-old writer of 'Evening' would have instantly recognized: 'They watched the beating heart of Paris which when the sun went down started to rise and live. They wanted to be in every part of it, in every night club, everywhere where is beauty.'[24]

The one thing that all the accounts agree upon is that in the year or so he spent in Paris Alex was completely penniless. He told his nephew Michael that he had once cried as he watched someone eat through the window of a restaurant, and had suffered so badly from the cold that he had wrapped his feet in old newspapers before putting his shoes on. According to Maria, he used to eat in a soup kitchen, where the forks and knives were chained to the table: 'Alexander Korda told me that himself.'[25] But Alex covered up the hardship with glowing letters home, so that when he finally returned to Budapest – at the expense of the Hungarian consulate, according to Tabori – his family were astonished by how thin he had become.

Alex's year in Paris, wrote Maria, was 'the most important trip in his life. It changed the story and destiny completely of that young man.'[26] Whatever he may have learned in the Bibliothèque Nationale, we can speculate that one of the most important lessons was that he could not afford the luxury of becoming a great writer, as he had dreamed of doing. For all the very real affinity that Alex may have had with Wilde the writer, they were in other respects a world apart. Wilde's was a talent cushioned and nurtured by the sort of prosperity that Alex had never known and could only hope to attain with a modification of his artistic aspirations. It was a matter of what would 'go' – certainly not the intense, self-conscious stories he was writing before he set off on his trip to Paris.

The cinema must have appealed as a more materially rewarding avenue to follow. None the less he was genuinely fascinated by the new medium, indeed had written about it before he had even set off for Paris. He would have regarded a film career not as an abandonment of his literary ambitions, but rather as their continuation along a more profitable path. In Hungary there was not the sharp divide between literature and film that existed in other countries, with intellectuals looking down on the cinema as a rather vulgar new medium. On the contrary, Hungary's most progressive writers, who had gathered around the journal *Nyugat*, embraced it as an exciting new art form to which they sought to contribute.

Back in Budapest, Alex wrote for the *Független Magyarország* again. He also began to contribute pieces to other periodicals. His articles would increasingly focus on film. This had as much to do with what was happening in Budapest in 1912 as anything he might have experienced in Paris. 'If any date can be determined to mark the birth of Hungarian cinema,' the film historian István Nemeskürty would comment, 'it was this year'.[27] There had been newsreels and crude comedies before, but now film-makers were vying with each other to produce the first Hungarian film drama. A photographer called Ödön Uher won the race with a film called *Sisters* (*Nővérek*), presented on 14 September 1912. But exactly a month later, on 14 October, the company Projectograph, exploiting a subtle distinction, proclaimed its production *Today and Tomorrow* (*Ma és holnap*) to be the 'First Hungarian Dramatic Art Film'. Its director, Mihály Kertész, would subsequently enjoy world fame as the Hollywood director Michael Curtiz.

Alex himself had already become the first Hungarian film critic, when he reviewed *Sisters* in the daily *Világ*, having persuaded the paper a month earlier to let him write a regular film column. In October, together with a journalist called István Varnai, he launched a regular film magazine, *Pesti Mozi* (*Budapest Cinema*). It not only published articles on the cinema but also commented on current affairs and the politics of the day. Its contributors included famous writers such as Zsigmond Móricz, Zoltán Ambrus and Frigyes Karinthy.

In 1912 Korda was also film editor of a Hungarian weekly called *Szinházi Elet* (*Theatre Life*) and contributing articles to a trade paper called *Mozgófénykép Hiradó* (*Moving Picture News*). Alex wrote a series of pieces on the theory of film, in which he stressed the visual – as opposed to literary – nature of the medium, and argued for the director as the key creative artist. Forty years later the young critics of *Cahiers du Cinéma* would say pretty much the same thing, as if it were a new idea. The Truffaut of his time, Alex wanted to make films as well as write about them. Soon after his return from France, Lajos Biro, a famous Hungarian playwright and novelist, whom he had interviewed for the *Független Magyarország*, introduced him to Mór Ungerleider, the founder of Projectograph, and Alex got a job editing a weekly programme that advertised Projectograph's films, and subtitling the foreign films that the company imported into Hungary. As he had to watch each film several times, it was an excellent training, but it was also an opportunity to become conversant with the languages of the major film-producing countries.

//

Perhaps the thing that most strikes one about the young Alex is his colossal energy. When he got back from Paris, he really hit the ground running. He was only eighteen, but his name was everywhere. He was a journalist working for numerous papers, but also had a foot in the film industry. His two brothers, by contrast, were leading much more ordinary lives. After a difficult time at school, where he had often got into trouble with his teachers, Zoltán had left to work as a freight clerk for a firm of coal merchants; and Vincent began to study at the College of Industrial Art, while working during the day in an architect's office.

But the First World War would change everything. Zoltán was drafted into the army at once and Vincent two years later, while Alex, unfit for military service because of his poor eyesight, was free to pursue his career. Left at home with his mother to worry over the safety of his two younger brothers, he was being eased ever more firmly into the role of surrogate father. Zoltán served in the Galician campaign and, after being wounded and gassed, returned home to convalesce. After six months in an infantry regiment, Vincent was saved from immediate danger when his talent for painting was discovered and he was given the job of painting his regiment's colonel's portrait.

As part of the Habsburg Empire, Hungary had come into the war on the side of the Central Powers. At first there had been almost universal support for the war. Even the Social Democratic Party, Hungary's most progressive political grouping, was in favour. But as the fighting dragged on and the catastrophic consequences became apparent – over half a million Hungarian soldiers would lose their lives – the early patriotism gave way to a sense of futility and despair.

For Alex, however, the war offered a tremendous opportunity. The cinema was regarded as a valuable instrument of propaganda and attempts to increase film production were hampered by an acute labour shortage. So as one of the few young men exempt from military service, he soon found himself in demand. Towards the end of 1914 the actor Gyula Zilahy produced and starred in three films for a company he had formed called Tricolor. Alex helped him to direct at least two of them, *The Duped Journalist* (*A becsapott újságíró*), a curiously apposite title for a newspaper-man's first film; and *Tutyu and Totyó*.

Pesti Mozi had by this time folded, only to be replaced in February 1915 by another film magazine, which Alex called *Cine-Weekly* (*Mozihét*) and edited by himself. Through this magazine, he met a wealthy film enthusiast called Miklós Pásztory, who had in 1914 founded his own production company, Nemzeti (National). Together they co-directed *Lyon Lea*, an adaptation of a play by Sándor Bródy. Soon afterwards Alex directed his first solo effort, *The Officer's Swordknot* (*A tiszti kardbojt*), for the Korona Company, with Gabor Rajnay, a member of Hungary's National Theatre, in the leading role.

Korona had been started the previous year by Jozef Neumann, who had once been a partner of Mór Ungerleider, Alex's boss at Projectograph. As Neumann and Ungerleider had fallen out, Alex asked Neumann not to mention his participation and so the film was credited to Neumann. The reminiscences of Gabor Rajnay suggest an improvised enterprise calculated to capture the mood of the moment. Alex spotted Gabor Rajnay in the Café New York. He walked up to his table and made his first successful story pitch. The film, he told Rajnay, would be about a captain of the Hussars dishonourably discharged because of his gambling debts. When the war breaks out, he re-enlists as a sergeant and is promoted for heroism. He is wounded in battle and falls in love with his nurse.

The very next day Alex, with his cameraman Béla Zsitkovszky, began to shoot the film at Kelenfold, a railway station on the south side of Budapest. A company of Hussars was setting off for the front. Rajnay, dressed in his sergeant's uniform, slipped into the ranks. Day Two was spent at a military training ground, where Rajnay indulged in some hand-to-hand fighting and trench warfare with the cadet officers. On Day Three the interiors were shot – the Captain losing his fortune at a gaming-table; and falling in love with the nurse in hospital. And that was it. The shooting schedule had been completed. Alex would later acquire a reputation for extravagance, but when necessary, he could act with impressive economy and speed.

According to Paul Tabori, *The Officer's Swordknot* was a great success and turned Rajnay into a star,[28] but it would be a whole year before Alex got another chance to direct. One day, Jenő Janovics, director of the National Theatre of Kolozsvár (today known as Cluj, Romania), walked into the Café New York. In Kolozsvár, Janovics had established a thriving film production unit which drew on the cast and productions of his National Theatre company. Between fifteen and twenty films were made each year. Initially these films were made for Projectograph, but in early 1916 Janovics set up his own company, which he called Corvin after the sixteenth-century king of Hungary, Mátyás Corvinus.

'There was more and more to do,' Janovics would recall twenty years later. 'I had to write the script myself, and also direct. I wanted to find an assistant.'[29] He had come to the Café New York to discuss story rights with the Hungarian writer

István Szomaházy. When he asked if the writer knew anyone who might be able to help him at his studios, Szomaházy pointed towards a 'thin, blond boy' sitting at a marble table with a cigar in his mouth 'as if the whole person was hanging on it'. Janovics introduced himself. The boy told Janovics about the film journal he was editing, how every week he struggled to pay the printing costs. 'Then he talked about his ambitions,' recalled Janovics, 'which far exceeded the horizons of the Hungarian cinema.' They seemed a complete fantasy, but Janovics warmed to 'this enthusiastic, day-dreaming boy' and invited him to come to Kolozsvár.

The first film Alex directed, in June 1916, was an adaptation of Victorien Sardou's *Fedora*, which was retitled *White Nights*. Janovics remembered that it was something of an ordeal for his young protégé. 'He was delicate, kind and helpful, but the actors did not like this.' One difficulty was his youth. The veteran actors of the distinguished National Theatre resented being told what to do by a twenty-three-year-old. He angered them by suggesting that the cinema required a different style of acting from what they were used to on the stage. 'He lost his enthusiasm a bit,' remembered Janovics, 'but I did not let him lose it totally. And slowly his skill and inventiveness won over the old actors.'

Alex made a successful début. Released in August 1916, *White Nights* was praised as 'a milestone in Hungarian films'.[30] *Tales of a Typewriter* (*Mesék az írógépről*) from a novel by István Szomaházy, *The Grandmother* (*A nagymama*), based on a Hungarian stage classic and featuring the country's most famous *chanteuse* Lujza Blaha, and *The Million Pound Note* (*Az egymillió fontos banko*), from the Mark Twain story, would quickly follow. All in all Alex would direct seven films for Janovics in 1916, each about twenty minutes long.

In early 1917 Jenő Janovics switched production to Budapest, where a studio was built on Dózsa György Street, near the City Park, and Alex was put in charge of it. The move represented not an expansion of Janovics's film ambitions but a recognition that Alex had eclipsed him. Very soon afterwards Alex would buy Corvin in partnership with Miklós Pásztory, who had secured backing from a rich factory owner called Richard Strasser. Janovics would afterwards claim that he had sold the studios because by that stage of the war 'communication between Budapest and Kolozsvár had become so bad'.[31] But his real communication difficulties, suggests Paul Tabori, were with his young protégé. When Janovics sought to restrain the escalating costs, Alex insisted that he should be allowed to make the films in his own way. 'Janovics realized that while Korda was the king-pin of his organization, he himself couldn't remain its chief. Korda wouldn't work under him.'[32]

In April 1917 *Mozihét*, of which Alex was still the editor, reported his new role. 'Corvin starts the new season with the greatest ambitions,' an unsigned editorial declared.[33] The following October the studio announced that it had become a share company with a capital of 1 million crowns. Offices were opened at 76 Rákóczi Avenue, one of Budapest's main boulevards, and in spite of wartime shortages, a new, larger studio was built in Zugló, a north-eastern suburb of the city, at 39 Gyarmat Street. Lili Berky, Oszkár Beregi and Mihály Várkonyi were among the studio's contract players, boasted an advertisement in *Mozihét* – Hungary's top stars, who would be appearing in films based on works by Hungary's top writers, Ferenc Molnár, Sándor Bródy, Jenő Heltai, Ferenc Herczeg.

'We are no longer going to make ordinary films,' the 'director-ial board'* told *Mozihét*. 'Henceforth we shall make large-scale, prestige productions after the model of film studios abroad. Both in subject matter and cast, all Corvin films will be characterized by their quality.'[34] The plan was to 're-create Hungarian literature on the screen' for a world market. The ambitious new programme would commence at the beginning of December with an adaptation of Imre Madach's novel, *The Tragedy of Man*, with a budget of 300,000 kronen.

Alex's whole approach was based on a conception of the cinema as a development of – rather than a rival to – literature. At Corvin he gathered around him some of Hungary's leading literary figures, who worked under the guidance of the company's scenario editors, Frigyes Karinthy – a regular contributor to

---

* Presumably a rather elaborate title for Alex himself, who of course had two hats as the studio's managing director and the paper's editor.

Nyugat – and László Vajda. Their role was to guide writers, who might have no direct experience of the cinema, into expressing themselves in a manner appropriate to the new medium. The aim was not just simple adaptation, but the forging of a distinct literary–visual style.

In little more than a year, with the sort of lightning progress that today we might associate with an Internet entrepreneur, Alex had become by far the most important figure in the Hungarian film industry. With his new-found wealth he moved out of the family home and took up residence in the plush Hotel Royal. He was just twenty-four. In a portrait for *Mozihét*, published towards the end of 1917, the writer Ernö Gál described him as 'a strange child who only yesterday had hesitated to venture into the world of adults'.[35] His unique feat, wrote Gál, was to have directed Hungary's best films, yet at the same time to be an excellent businessman capable of organizing a large company.

When Zoltán was invalided out of the army, Alex brought him into the business as a film editor and assistant director. Vincent would also join Alex as a designer of film posters.

Over a year and a half Corvin Studios produced sixteen films. Of the seven that Alex directed, the only one to have been preserved is *The Golden Man* (*Az aranyember*), based on a classic novel by Mór Jókai.* Originally three hours long, it was by far the most ambitious film to have been made in Hungary up to that time.

The film follows the exploits of Mihály Timár, a ship's captain who helps Ali, a rich Turkish merchant on the run from the police, to escape to Hungary with his daughter. Eventually Ali is cornered by a Turkish agent and kills himself to avoid capture. Timár takes Ali's money and marries his daughter. He uses the money to build a huge fortune. But unhappy with both his

---

* The other six films Alex made for Corvin were *The Stork Caliph* (*A gólyakalifa*), from a novel by Mihály Babits; *Magic* (*Mágia*), from a script by Frigyes Karinthy; *Saint Peter's Umbrella* (*Szent Péter esernyője*), from a novel by Kálmán Mikszáth; *Harrison and Barrison*, from a script by Gyula Kőváry and Richárd Falk; *Faun*, from the play by Edward Knoblock; and *Marian*, from the novel by Israel Zaûgwill.

material success and his marriage, he leads a double life with a young woman, Noémi, who lives on an island in the Danube. There are many plot twists and adventures which, as I watched the film at the Hungarian Film Institute, I struggled to follow without the benefit of subtitles. But I couldn't help thinking of Alex's declaration that his youthful ambition was to write 'a novel as great and as big as *War and Peace*'.[36] *The Golden Man* seemed to be the celluloid equivalent of such an aspiration. The elaborate plot and characterization, lavishly decorated sets, dramatic location scenes of storms and shipwrecks at sea all suggested someone who believed passionately in the cinema as the great art form of the future.

The achievement of *The Golden Man* seems all the greater when one realizes the circumstances in which it was made. The First World War was coming to an end. The Central Powers were under blockade and facing defeat. There were shortages of everything. 'I was unable to get ten pounds of plaster of paris in the whole of Budapest,' Alex complained in an interview. 'The public, of course, cares little if one scene of the film, passing through the hands of sixty smugglers, is spoiled and it is hard to obtain a substitute; the main thing is that it should be a good picture and stand comparison with the foreign produce . . .'[37]

The question of 'foreign produce' was something that Alex, stuck in wartime Budapest, often gave thought to. In an article for *Mozihét*, which somehow he still found the time both to edit and write for, he looked forward to the end of the war with the question, 'I wonder what is happening *over there*? What is happening in the capitals of culture and the cinema, where film-making, in comparison to our ambitious but poor industry, has made extraordinary advances? What is happening in the studios of Paris, New York and Rome? What is the *world* doing?'[38]

He had felt a similar hankering for knowledge when he first came to Budapest, then again when he set off for Paris as a seventeen-year-old. Always the desire to see over the horizon. But in the summer of 1918, the world was beyond his reach. A friend recalled him complaining of his difficulties in Hungary and talking of accepting an invitation to make films in Stockholm. It was a sign of his desperation as Hungary slid into increasing chaos during the last months of the war. It was impossible to remain aloof.

On 31 October 1918 the liberal Count Mihályi Károlyi, in an uneasy alliance with the Socialists, became Hungary's premier in a revolution which effectively marked the birth of an independent republic and the end of the war. According to the Hungarian film historian István Nemeskürty, the Károlyi Government appointed Alex 'commissioner of film production with authorization to organize progressive bourgeois film production'.[39] It's hard to know what this mysterious phrase amounted to in practice. Was it just an impressive title or did Alex have real responsibilities?

What Alex clearly did do was to continue to speak out on issues that affected the industry, as he long had done both as Hungary's leading film producer and editor of its most influential film magazine. The most pressing need in these revolutionary times was to keep in tune with the volatile politics of the country. Under the influence of his mentor Oskár Fabér and his close friend Simon Darvas, Alex's political views had been broadly left wing. But the experience of the war had forged an increasingly pragmatic attitude. In April 1917 Alex's magazine *Mozihét* had criticized as absurd a proposal for the public ownership of cinemas, but by December 1918 had sufficiently repositioned itself to be able to comment, 'Those who still represent the ruling classes would do well to examine themselves and desist from defending their precarious positions so desperately.' The conclusion was that 'no one should struggle against socialism'.[40] In the weeks to come Alex would lead an increasingly vocal campaign against film distributors, whom he accused of undermining the quality of Hungarian films for the sake of profit.

Károlyi's Government was short-lived. In February 1919 the victorious powers at the Versailles peace conference reached the decision to allow Romanian forces to advance westwards to a line that marks the present-day border between the two countries. With Franco-Serbian forces occupying a swathe of land in the south, Hungary had in effect lost two-thirds of its territory. Károlyi was toppled on 21 March in a second revolution to be replaced by the Communist Béla Kun, a thirty-two-year-old journalist who had become a Bolshevik while a prisoner in Russia.

A week later, a meeting of the film industry at a cinema in Budapest, which Alex addressed, resolved to press the new Government into a re-organization of the film industry that would limit the profits of the distributors. The Kun regime, which had set about implementing a Soviet-style dictatorship of the proletariat, lost no time in making a radical response. Just two weeks later, on 12 April 1919, it issued the following decree:

> The Hungarian Soviet Republic places under public ownership all film-producing studios, film laboratories, film-distributing companies, related factories and picture theatres – regardless of the number of employees – as well as their moveables and real estate with all their equipment, and the finances required for carrying on production.[41]

The nationalization was quickly put into effect. A central department was set up to plan future productions, and Alex himself was appointed to a 'Film Directorate' – an administrative board with responsibility for the film industry as a whole. It is not clear whether Alex lost any money in the upheaval, but even after the nationalization he continued to draw a handsome monthly salary and to stay in his luxurious suite at the Hotel Royal.

As the Communists set about transforming Hungarian society, he would have felt that he had little choice but to go with the flow. A comment by Alex, quoted in Michael Korda's *Charmed Lives*, best sums up his attitude. 'Film people must make films if they're going to earn their bread, whatever the government.'[42]

But he would have found much to welcome about the new regime. Most importantly, it took the cinema seriously, sponsoring a highly edifying production programme that conformed with – and possibly reflected – Alex's own literary approach. A 'central literary board' planned screen versions of several world classics, including works by Tolstoy, Gogol, Stendhal, Shaw, Verne and Ibsen. There were also to be adaptations of works by contemporary Hungarian writers, including many with whom Alex had worked, such as Sándor Bródy, Ferenc Molnár and Jenő Heltai.

The programme amounted to a fantasy list of projects that Alex would never have dared to announce in the days before the revolution when he had to worry about such mundane matters as box-office appeal.

Alex's cooperative attitude towards the revolution was typical of the arts world in general. The leadership of the Literary Directorate, for example, included not just committed Socialists and Communists, but also such established figures as Frigyes Karinthy and Mihály Babits.

Alex would make three films during the short existence of the Béla Kun Government. The first, *White Rose* (*Fehér rózsa*), was based on a Mór Jókai story which he had been working on before the Communist take-over. The other two had subjects which were calculated to support the values of the Communist regime: *Ave Caesar!* told the story of a profligate Habsburg prince who has a beautiful gypsy girl kidnapped for his pleasure; and *Yamata* was about a black slave who rebels against his cruel master. Whether they were 'overtly propagandistic', as Michael Korda suggests, is hard to judge, since the two films have not been preserved. But it is doubtful that they could have matched the revolutionary fervour of Comrade Mihály Kertész, who in the spring of 1919 would direct one of the world's first agit-prop films, *My Brother Comes*. 'Workers of the world unite!' urged a subtitle. Kertész would become better known as Michael Curtiz, the Hollywood director of such concoctions as *The Adventures of Robin Hood*, *Casablanca* and *Yankee Doodle Dandy*.

//

Ave Caesar! brought to the screen a beautiful new leading lady, whom a review in *Mozihét* would make a point of singling out. 'Antonia Farkas has come from out of the blue, but today half of Budapest is talking about this actress with her perfect figure and arresting beauty, who has won the hearts of the public with her outstanding talent.'[43]

Most smitten of all was Alex himself. At twenty-five, he had been far too busy making films and building up his company to form any long-lasting romantic liaisons, but as he was not only rich and powerful, but also tall and handsome with blond hair and piercing blue-grey eyes, he must have been one of the most sought-after bachelors in Budapest. His brother Vincent would maintain that he had allowed himself to be 'trapped by the first beautiful woman to make a play for him',[44] but this does not do justice to the larger-than-life character of Alex's new discovery. Antonia Farkas was stunning to look at, but also bold, intelligent and extravagantly romantic.

After their marriage in 1919, Antonia, who was fond of name changes, adopted the name Maria, and as Maria Corda – pointedly spelt with a C and not a K – was built up by Alex into one of Europe's top film stars. According to Paul Tabori, she had begun her career in show business and then married a rich amateur composer. She would meet Alex in 1917 and marry him as soon as her divorce came through. But Tabori does not give the first husband's name and no other account mentions his existence.

Maria herself would provide an even more colourful account of how she entered Alex's life. According to her 'biography' of Alex, they met each other while she was still at school. Alex had then sent her love letters from Paris, where he remained for seven years. Meanwhile she attended the dancing academy in Budapest and joined the Hungarian Royal Opera. Alex, on his return to Hungary, became a famous film director, saw her dance one night, and announced his intention to make her his wife and star. They married in 1919 when she was just sixteen.

This fantasy amounted to a mission by Maria to weave herself into Alex's life as completely as possible. The one certainty is that she was madly and obsessively in love with Alex from pretty much the moment they first met. Full of high-flown notions about art and beauty, she complemented Alex's own tendency to dream, and had the kind of fierce ambition for fame and fortune that could match up to his own. Usually described by members of Alex's family as a 'mistake' or a 'tragedy', their marriage was none the less somehow inevitable. One has only to read the 'Beauty is all' short stories that Alex was writing as a young man to appreciate how he would have been attracted to Antonia's bohemian spirit. The difference between the two was that Alex would grow up, while Antonia, a kind of eternal teenager, refused to budge from a wilfully romantic conception of the world.

//

On 1 August 1919, the Hungarian Soviet Republic collapsed. Béla Kun and the commissars of the revolution fled to Vienna. A Social Democratic Government ruled for five days before power was snatched away by a group of counter-revolutionaries, known as the 'White House'. This in turn split into two factions when the new Minister of Defence, Admiral Miklós Horthy, announced to his Cabinet colleagues that the army would henceforth report directly to him. The struggle for power between the two factions would last for months, but the two sides were at least able to agree on their hatred of the Communists, as they issued summary justice to thousands of individuals associated with the Béla Kun regime, whether they had been Communist or not. Broadly Christian–Nationalist in character, the Counter-Revolution reserved a special hatred for the Jews.

Alex was arrested in late October by a sergeant in Horthy's army and taken to the Hotel Gellert, the headquarters of the White terrorists. When Zoltán and Maria learned what had happened, they rushed to the hotel, where in the lift they overheard two officers talking about a film producer whom they intended beating up that night. Zoltán and Maria then got an appointment with Horthy's aide-de-camp, who promised to do what he could. The writer Jenő Heltai, an old friend of Alex, also made representations on his behalf. At this point in the story the two chief accounts of Alex's arrest diverge.

'Actually, a mistake had been made,' writes Paul Tabori. 'Alex had a namesake, an obscure actor who had been a prominent Communist; the misunderstanding was cleared up and he was released in less than twenty-four hours.'[45]

But according to Michael Korda, after their visit to the aide-de-camp, Zoltán and Maria then approached a Brigadier Maurice, who it is 'altogether possible' was the secret link between the British Government and Admiral Horthy. 'In return for money to support his troops and the promise of Allied non-interference, the Admiral and Regent was expected not only to secure order in Hungary, but to offer exceptionally attractive opportunities to foreign investors and banks.'[46] When Maria made it clear to Maurice that she would do her utmost to turn Alex's arrest into an international scandal, the Brigadier went off and returned a few hours later with Alex:

> Taking him aside, Maurice advised him in French to get out of Hungary. 'It will be announced,' he said, 'that they picked the wrong man, that they were looking for an actor named Korda, but the fact is, the Regent can't always control his own men, and most of them are *plus royalistes que le roi*, so the next time you may not be so lucky.'[47]

The story of the mysterious Brigadier Maurice raises more questions than it really answers. One difficulty in accepting it at face value is that at the time of Alex's arrest in late October 1919 the struggle for power in Hungary was far from over and Admiral Horthy did not become Regent until 1 March 1920.

Nor can Tabori's more simple explanation of mistaken identity be so easily dismissed. Alex really did have a namesake who, as Tabori puts it, 'had been a prominent Communist', although he wasn't an actor: Sándor Kellner was a printer and a founding member of the Hungarian Communist Party. During the Hungarian Soviet Republic, he was a commissioner for the Sopron region. In the autumn of 1919, at about the same time as Alex was taken to the Gellert Hotel, he was arrested by a White terrorist unit and executed.

Maria Corda is the only individual involved in the incident to give a written version of what happened. The historical value of her account, which was set down on paper some two years before the appearance of Paul Tabori's biography, is prejudiced by her tendency to fictionalize reality, but none the less there are some truths to be deciphered.

In the following passage, the key to unravelling the code is to appreciate that in her imagination Maria, with a disturbing but also rather touching readiness to appropriate Alex's life, has swapped places with him, so that it is she who lies imprisoned in its dungeons, and Alex who turns up at the Gellert Hotel to seek her release:

In his own consciousness an invisible voice talks to him when he walks towards the hotel. 'And if they find out that I am her husband two months already?'

Then the invisible voice replies to him: 'Be brave. And so always tell she is your sister. Go to the General and ask about her. Perhaps she is in jail. Perhaps she is on the dead list. They will tell you.'

'But I am afraid,' he said, 'they will execute me too.'

Then the invisible voice became stronger and said to him: 'Be brave, Alexander Korda. God is with you. Go and find your wife, Antonia. It is your great love. You won't let her down.'

And he said to himself: 'No, I won't.'

And he steps courageously in the hotel asking for the chief. In the general headquarters where only soldiers are and nothing else. But he was not trembling any more. For God was with him.

And the angels lead him to the right direction. And they let him know what to say and how to say it. He said to the chief officer: 'She never was a Jewish girl. She is my sister and I make pictures with her. I am her brother.'

And they led him down to the cellar near to the Danube where she was condemned to death. As every night all the Jews were drown[ed] [in] the water and executed.

Risking his life he brought her up in his arms half dead.

They [got] on the next train and they left for Vienna.[48]

3. WESTWARD BOUND

Looking out of the window of the train, it was the same flat landscape. But at some imperceptible point I had just crossed the border. The Hungarian police and passport officials, burly men in military green, had got off the train at the last town. Their departure made me feel rather sad. During my stay in the Puszta and then Budapest, a capital of open-hearted, chaotic grandeur, I had become very fond of Hungary, a homely, generous country. The Austrian passport officials, dressed in their dapper black uniforms and with their neatly tonsored moustaches, belonged to a more orderly, affluent world. I had crossed not just a border, but a faultline between two cultures – one that all the wiles of the Habsburg Empire had failed to close.

Alex, who made the same journey as a fugitive in the aftermath of the Empire's collapse, would have felt the severance keenly, but none the less, I imagine, he stepped off the train in Vienna with the same kind of exhilaration he had felt as a fifteen-year-old arriving in Budapest from the country. It was a journey that sooner or later, Horthy or no Horthy, he would have made anyway. His thirst for experience, his ambition drove him on.

//

In *Charmed Lives* Michael Korda describes Alex checking into Vienna's Grand Hotel and living there for two weeks in ostentatious luxury while the unpaid bills mounted up. Every night, according to this account, Alex and Maria would dine in the most expensive restaurants and return to their hotel in a chauffeur-driven Daimler-Benz, with the hope of attracting the attention of a rich benefactor. Just as they were considering a move to Berlin and starting all over again in the Adlon Hotel, 'Alex's faith in his own approach to life was finally saved by a telephone call from a man who shared his own lavish tastes, but could afford them'.[1]

While the details of Alex's expensive life-style ring true – although his new home was actually the Imperial, not the Grand – there would have been no need for him to wait two weeks for the telephone call. The man in question was already very well known to him. Count Alexander 'Sascha' Kolowrat-Krakowsky, an Austrian–Czech aristocrat who had been born in New York in 1886, was a man whom Alex had long regarded as something of a mentor.

The Count was a keen motorcyclist, racing driver and balloon-ist, whose interest in moving things took in the cinema as well after he saw some Pathé films in France in 1909. With his considerable private fortune, he began producing films himself. He made some documentaries, a series of comedy shorts and, during the First World War, turned to making newsreels. In 1916, he built Austria's first dedicated film studio in Sievering, a suburb of Vienna, and there, in the following year, produced twelve full-length features. By far the most ambitious producer in Austria, he often used to feature in the pages of Alex's magazine, *Mozihét*, sometimes as a contributor.

An article Alex wrote for *Mozihét* in November 1917 reveals the depths of his admiration for Kolowrat:

> Count Alexander Kolowrat has used every possible occasion to help the Hungarian industry in these terrible times. Without Count Kolowrat there would hardly be any Hungarian films. This prominent Austrian Count, who leads his studios with the passion and ambition of an amateur and a sportsman, has helped many Hungarian film-makers with his professional expertise . . . Anyone writing about the Hungarian cinema must take account of his contribution. The fact that the Hungarian film industry has managed to keep going in spite of its shortage of equipment and raw materials, is in large meas-ure due to Count Kolowrat.[2]

Alex's generous words reflected the fellow feeling of one enthusiast for another. But quite apart from their past associations, Count Kolowrat's company would have been an obvious place for Alex to work. After a series of mergers, it had become by the end of the First World War the biggest film company in Austria. While the rest of Vienna was still suffering the trauma of defeat, Kolowrat looked forward to the future with a breathtaking confidence. In the spring of 1919 he travelled to America to study the Hollywood film industry. There he saw Griffith's *Intolerance* and, inspired by its spectacle, returned to Austria determined that his company should make films on the same scale.

His expansionist plans conveniently coincided with the Hungarian Counter-Revolution, as a sudden influx of the Hungarian film industry's leading writers, directors and actors arrived from Budapest on the run from the White terrorists. By the time Alex and Maria came to Vienna, Michael Curtiz and his film star wife Lucy Doraine were already working for Sascha-Film, as the Count's company was called. Indeed, the gleaming Daimler-Benz that Michael Korda describes might well have taken his uncle to the première of Curtiz's first Austrian film, *The Lady with the Black Glove* (*Die Dame mit dem schwarzen Handschuh*), which opened in Vienna on 21 November. The likelihood is that Kolowrat had invited Alex to work for him before Alex had even left Budapest, as Karl Hartl, an assistant director at Sascha-Film, would later claim.[3]

Alex himself would play down any suggestion that his sojourn in Vienna was an enforced exile. In articles that he continued to contribute to *Mozihét*, he wrote as if it were just a career choice which could easily be temporary. Alex's first film for Kolowrat was a version of Mark Twain's *The Prince and the Pauper*, a subject calculated to be of international appeal. The only hitch in the production occurred when the gargantuan Count, who weighed 22 stone, borrowed a dwarf who had an important role in the film, without telling anybody. Determined to win a prestigious two-man motor race, the Count realized that with such a tiny passenger his car would be close to the average weight in the competition. Michael Curtiz recalled how it was sometimes difficult to know if you were in a car factory or a film studio. The Count's office was filled with miniature models of the latest racing cars and on the walls were enormous maps of Austria pinned with small flags to mark the routes of the various race-courses.[4]

A truncated version of *The Prince and the Pauper* survives. Heavily laden with subtitles, it suggests a director determined to re-create the Mark Twain novel as faithfully as possible. Alex's literary approach to the cinema would only truly come into its own with the advent of the talkies, but none the less the flair for social satire and observation that would become such a distinctive feature of his later films is noticeable. There's a scene in which the pauper, disguised as the Prince of Wales, dines in the palace. The courtiers look on shocked as he drinks from the finger-bowl and scoffs his food voraciously. Alex cuts to a courtier frowning with disapproval and then to a princess daintily rinsing her fingers according to the proper form. A further cut might have taken the audience effortlessly into a famous scene that Alex shot ten years later, when Charles Laughton as Henry VIII tears apart bits of chicken and tosses them behind him, proclaiming, 'Manners are dead!' *The Private Life of Henry VIII* was the film that would launch Alex as a leading film producer in Britain, but it was made according to an already tested formula.

The Prince and the Pauper had its première in Vienna on 3 December 1920. After some delay owing to copyright problems, it was eventually released in the United States through the Herz Film Corporation, a distribution company that the indefatigable Count Kolowrat had established in America after a visit there in the late summer of 1920. It was a considerable success and Alex would later comment that the film's reception in America was the first thing to cause him to 'give conscious thought to the problem of international films'.[5]

His new career in Vienna was progressing well, but otherwise it was an unsettling time. Alex became a father in late 1921, but any joy he might have had from the birth of his son Peter Vincent was snatched away by the death of his mother Ernesztina soon afterwards. She had come to Vienna with Zoltán in the spring of 1920 and fallen seriously ill within weeks of her arrival. As his nephew Michael commented, Alex was 'deeply shaken and depressed. He had loved his mother as he would never love anyone else.'

Alex followed *The Prince and the Pauper* with two films in quick succession, a modern-day pirate story called *Masters of the Sea (Herren der Meere)* and *A Vanished World (Eine Versunkene Welt)*. A version of the latter survives in the Austrian Film Archive. Obviously pieced together from several incomplete prints, at first the film had no subtitles and when they suddenly began about halfway through they were in a language I neither understood nor even recognized. ('Zálezi jen na mné a bude má!') But the story unfolded with such visual clarity that it was easy to follow. A naval captain of noble birth is ostracized when he falls in love with a show-girl. Forced to make a choice, he puts the girl before his career and resigns from the navy. He sets off on a long voyage in his sea-going yacht with the girl and a crew of thirty sailors. As the girl flirts with one of them and is ogled by the other twenty-nine, the subtitle '*30 muza, 1 zena*' sets the scene for the tale of mutiny and cuckoldry that follows.

A Vanished World is an impressive film. Alex skilfully builds up an atmosphere of illicit eroticism, which he counterpoints with the Captain's gradual realization that he is being deceived to create considerable pathos. Notably absent from the film were the melodramatic gestures that are so often associated with the silent cinema. Alex worked well with actors, knew how to draw from them performances of subtlety.

The film was an intimate study of a man who has made a futile sacrifice, but also an allegory. The 'vanished world' was that of the great Habsburg Empire which had just fallen. The dilemma of the Captain caught between the cruel hypocrisy of his own class and the mindless malice of the mob turns the film into a kind of revisionist version of *Battleship Potemkin* – although in 1922 *Potemkin* had yet to be made.

The image of the noble-born captain who turns his back on his troubles by taking to the high seas must have had poignancy for a people that had become so recently land-locked. Brought up on Hungary's Great Plains, Alex himself was particularly sensitive to the lure of the sea. He would return to it repeatedly in both his film career and his private life. One day, when he too owned a yacht, *Elsewhere*, he would have some cause to identify with the troubled captain of *A Vanished World*.

The well-observed but understated performances give *A Vanished World* a modern, or rather a timeless quality. Alex's best films would have this feel – *The Private Life of Henry VIII* would be the story less of a king than of a lonely man. Transcending its historical setting, it offered a portrait of loneliness for all ages.

It's hard to be definitive when so few of Alex's early films survive, but *A Vanished World* has the feel of an important turning-point in his development as a film-maker. *The Golden Man* and *The Prince and the Pauper* were marred by his too faithful rendering of his source material. But here the simplicity of Lajos Biro's story allowed him to focus on character over narrative. Its blend of detached irony and lyrical sadness, its extravagance in both setting and cast (the thirty sailors) were pointers to the kind of film-maker that Alex would become.

A Vanished World, adapted from Biro's own novel *Serpolette*, was a characteristic example of a creative partnership that would last for over a quarter of a century. Alex had discovered a writer with whom he was on the same wavelength, and henceforward he would work with Biro as often as he could. Formerly a well-known liberal journalist in Budapest, Biro had briefly held an official position in Károlyi's Government. When Béla Kun came to power, he fled to Vienna, where he already had a substantial reputation as a playwright and novelist. A gentle and modest man, he would describe his life's wish as to retire to the country with his family and to devote himself to his writing. Over ten years older than Alex, he was important to him not just as a collaborator but as a mentor, one of the very few people Alex could trust to offer disinterested advice.

After *A Vanished World*, Alex left Kolowrat to set up a company called Corda Film Consortium. In partnership with Vita Film, which was run by a Hungarian film distributor called Dr No Szucs, he then produced and directed *Samson and Delilah*. The switch to Corda with a C indicated the increasing importance that Maria Corda the film star was beginning to have in his plans.

Karol Kulik writes that Alex's 'relationship with Kolowrat

steadily deteriorated as the Count insisted on interfering with the production side of Korda's work'.[6] But there's no direct evidence that this was true. The much more plausible reason for Alex's departure is that in 1922 Count Kolowrat was spending a fortune on the production of Michael Curtiz's biblical epic, *Sodom and Gomorrah*, and simply could not spare the resources to finance another production on the same scale. In any case, Alex had always intended to set up his own film company just as soon as he could, and, having been Hungary's leading film producer, probably regarded his association with Kolowrat as no more than a temporary arrangement until he could get back on his own feet. Soon after the release of *The Prince and the Pauper* a letter from Alex, published in *Mozihét*, outlined his future commitments. He mentioned two assignments for Kolowrat, and another for a film studio in Rome. But after that, 'I have no further plans. Perhaps I'll stay in Vienna, perhaps I won't. I had offers to work in Rome and Berlin but it's a little difficult to get used to such a gypsy existence.'[7] He was clearly keeping his options open and wanted people to know it.

Samson and Delilah, after the model of *Intolerance*, weaves a biblical story into the framework of a modern one. A famous opera singer, Julia Sorel, refuses to play the role of Delilah opposite Ettore Ricco, an inexperienced young tenor. A Russian prince, who has long courted Julia, tricks her aboard his yacht and then sets sail, threatening to remain on the open sea until she agrees to become his wife. Meanwhile Rico, the tenor, has smuggled himself on board disguised as an anarchist. When he tells the Prince that he has planted a bomb that will blow up the yacht, Julia seduces him into revealing its whereabouts. Rico then reveals the hoax and his true identity. 'You refused to act with me on the stage,' he declares, 'so I made you play Delilah to my Samson in real life!' The Prince unhappily yields to this new rival for Julia's affections and orders the captain of the yacht to return to port.

The rather forced parallels between modern-day events and the biblical story resulted in an extremely far-fetched film. While Alex was at home in the sophisticated setting of the yacht, and well able to depict the modern philistine that its owner represented, he struggled to cope with the ancient ones. His talent was for the intimate rather than the spectacular. But Alex was determined to make a big film that would augment not only his own reputation but Maria's. As her status grew, Alex came under pressure to pass over the literary subjects to which he had previously been inclined in favour of the star vehicle.

Maria's success as a prima donna in *Samson and Delilah*, which had its première in Vienna on Christmas Day 1922, only encouraged her to become even more of one in real life. Among the writers Alex commissioned to write his next film was the poet and critic Béla Balázs – one of the many Hungarian exiles to be found in Vienna during the early 1920s. Balázs, who had long wanted to work with Alex, spent the spring of 1923 trying to come up with a suitable idea. 'Every day I invented a new story. Two of them I drew up in detail.'[8] But all his efforts proved fruitless as Maria turned down everything he suggested. Balázs, who no doubt had studied *Samson and Delilah* closely, must have felt some fellow feeling with the young tenor Ettore Ricco, spurned by the famous opera singer.

At last Maria settled for an original screenplay by Ernst Vajda, who had written *Samson and Delilah*. By this time she and Alex had moved on to Berlin, which, in spite of an economy racked by hyper-inflation, had become the film capital of Europe. Here they moved with Peter and a nanny into a large and luxurious apartment on the Kurfürstendamm. Alex set up a new company and quickly established himself in Berlin as a leading independent producer and director. Zoltán joined him there and worked as a film editor, while Vincent remained in Hungary pursuing his vocation to be a painter in an artists' colony at Nagybánya.

The presence of Werner Krauss in Alex's first German film, *Das unbekannte Morgen*, was a measure of the steep upward path that Alex and Maria had taken. Ever since his appearance in *The Cabinet of Dr Caligari* four years previously, Krauss had been one of the biggest stars in the German cinema. In *Das unbekannte Morgen* he played the evil Muradoch, who is infatuated with Stella Manners, the wife of a famous astronomer. When she spurns his advances, he tricks her husband into believing that she has committed adultery. Flung out of her home, Stella meets an Indian mystic who in a crystal ball shows her the divorce and coerced marriage that await her unless she can cheat the future. As Stella Manners, Maria enjoyed what was becoming a familiar role for her of fending off yet another crazed admirer. Muradoch was an obvious variation of the Russian prince who had abducted Julia Sorel aboard his yacht in *Samson and Delilah*.

For crazed admirers, it would have been difficult to beat Crown Prince Rudolph, who in 1889 died with his young lover Baroness Maria Vetsera in a suicide pact at Mayerling. Maria clearly regarded *A Tragedy in the House of Habsburg* (*Tragödie im Hause Habsburg*) as a highlight of her career. Determined to establish a realistic ambiance, Alex took the production to Vienna over the winter of 1923/4, where he shot scenes in many of the original settings, including the Hofburg and Schönbrunn palaces. According to Maria, she and Alex stayed at the Imperial Hotel in the royal apartment of Elisabeth and Franz Josef. She also had the use of the Empress Elisabeth's original carriage, which would whisk her every day through the Prater to the Schönbrunn, drawn by four black horses that flew 'as if they were eagles'.[9] Whether or not Maria's recollection was entirely accurate, this would certainly have been in Alex's style. In the pursuit of the authentic, he would have done whatever he could to encourage her delusions of grandeur.

But we must be careful not to allow Maria's inflated sense of herself to delude us. She swanned around with such a self-important air that Alex, who preferred to adopt a more modest manner, would have seemed somewhat in her shadow. But behind the scenes he was still the key half of the partnership. Even Maria realized this. To some degree, her displays of ego were an attempt to assert herself in the face of the very dominance of Alex's quiet authority.

In *Charmed Lives* Michael Korda writes of the backers in Germany 'who were eager to hire Maria and willing to let Alex direct if that was part of the deal. To his distress, he was known as "Maria Corda's director".'[10] But other than Maria's own reminiscences, there's no independent evidence that this was true.

Maria was certainly very successful, but it was Alex who had built her up. Her success was his success. He would have been delighted and pleased with himself to have nurtured a major star.

But if Maria's stardom was a cause for satisfaction, he would have liked her to behave a little better, and there were many stories about Maria's temper and Alex's long-suffering attempts to mollify her. On one occasion, recalled the director André De Toth, Maria was required to play an angel and to be pulled up by a rope 20 feet above the studio floor. Refusing to be an angel in bare feet, she demanded silver shoes. So everyone waited while a props assistant went off to town to fetch them. But when the silver shoes arrived, Maria had a change of mind. 'Gold is what an angel should wear!' she declared. 'Yes, dear, you're right,' conceded Alex, and more time was wasted while a pair of golden shoes was fetched. Next Maria argued over the safety of her harness. Alex managed to reassure her and finally she was hauled up into the ether. 'You look wonderful!' he shouted. But just as the camera began to roll, the rope jumped its pulley and Maria was left stuck up in the air under the hot lights. A predictable tirade of abuse followed. 'So here is the little angel up there: "You fucking shit, I'll cut your balls off." Typical Alex – without a word to anybody, he got up, walked out and went to have dinner.'[11] In this way Alex would usually have the last word.

Away from the studio, their life together was just as stormy. Zoltán would describe to his son David some of the scenes he had witnessed.

> If they went to a restaurant together . . . if she was served something she didn't like or soup she didn't think was correct, she would literally pick it up and throw it on Alex, and say, 'How can you?' He'd book the best theatre seats and they'd go to the theatre together, and for some perverse reason she would decide she didn't want to sit where he had booked, trying to force him to get other people to leave their seats. I suppose it was all an attempt to humiliate him, I don't know, but I know that she made his life a misery.[12]

'Sex is blind,' commented André De Toth in an attempt to explain why Alex put up with her. But the fact that Alex and

Maria had had a child together and that her status as an important star made him to some extent dependent on her also deferred a split which otherwise might have come much sooner.

After *A Tragedy in the House of Habsburg*, Alex and Maria stayed on in Austria long enough to make *Everyman's Wife* (*Jedermanns Frau*), which was about a Viennese aristocrat who bets a friend that he can turn a flower-girl into a lady. The idea of such a thing must have seemed all the more implausible to Alex after his experiences with Maria, but the Pygmalion and Galatea story offers an apt reflection of their partnership in the early 1920s. As both producer and director, Alex devoted his energies to putting Maria on a pedestal. She features in the titles of all of his last three films in Germany, *My Wife's Dancing Partner* (*Der Tänzer meiner Frau*), *A Dubarry of Today* (*Eine Dubarry von heute*) and *Madame Does Not Want Children* (*Madame wünscht keine Kinder*). The fact that she was also much in demand by other film companies further swelled her ego,* making her still more difficult to work with.

Reminiscences suggest that she had become not only difficult but dangerous. The future film star John Loder made his début as a dress extra in *Madame Does Not Want Children*. He recalled Alex kindly warning him to think seriously about the career he had chosen. 'Film-making', he advised him, 'is not for you. It is an awful business. Anyone who gets a raw deal in a film studio is no more deserving of pity than someone who gets beaten up in a whore-house. A gentleman has no business in either place.'[13]

A few days later Loder was among the actors and technicians who found themselves waiting interminably for their director and leading lady to turn up on the set. 'Just a little dis-Korda,' he was told when he asked what was causing the hold-up. Eventually Alex came on to the set holding a blood-stained handkerchief to

---

* In 1924 she appeared in Sascha-Film's *Die Sklavenkönigin* (*Moon of Israel*), directed by Michael Curtiz. It received wide international distribution. The following year she made a film for the director of *Caligari*, Robert Wiene, and also appeared in two big Italian films: *L'uomo più allegro di Vienna* (Amleto Palermi) and *Gli ultimi giorni di Pompei* (Amleto Palermi and Carmine Gallone).

his face. Maria, Loder learned later, had found Alex talking to a young actress in his office. 'Finally Maria appeared on the set muttering Magyar obscenities, and I was reminded of the advice Alex had given me when I first met him.'[14]

In public Alex suffered in silence the indignities that Maria heaped on him, but he knew the depths of her self-deception, that her importance amounted only to what other people chose to allow her, that every tantrum she threw was less an assertion of her power than a sure sign that it would quickly diminish. Many years later, long after she had ceased to be a star, Maria would reflect: 'When I was twenty-three he told me I was dead only I did not know it. It took me a long time to understand this, but now I know.'[15]

The story of *Madame Does Not Want Children* concerns a newly wed husband who wants to settle down to a quiet family life with children, but his wife is interested only in giving parties, dancing and buying clothes. When the husband shows an interest in another woman, the wife becomes madly jealous and the sparks fly. As usual the gulf between Maria herself and her screen personality was extremely narrow. The script was by Béla Balázs, who had at last managed to win Maria's favour. No doubt the previous frustrating experience of working with her had helped him to appreciate how closely the story had to be tailored.

That had been Alex's lesson too. In Hungary the literary work had come first in Alex's thinking, whether it was a classic novel or an original screenplay. Once the subject had been chosen, then the most suitable actors and actresses were selected. But in Vienna and Berlin, the practical experience of working with Maria and adjusting to her growing fame taught him the power of the screen personality, that it was the star who breathed life into the subject, and that therefore there had to be an organic relationship between the two. 'I must confess that the greatest thrill for a producer, no matter how often one has failed and been through bitter experience, is the discovery of somebody who really is good star material,' he would comment years later.[16] But it was Alex's understanding of this star system, rather than the star he had groomed, that would bring him to Hollywood towards the end of 1926.

Like many other European directors at that time (as today) Alex would naturally have been drawn to Hollywood. It had become the undisputed film capital of the world, the best place in which to achieve international success. But one of the myths of Alex's film career is that he somehow got there on the back of Maria's reputation. In *Charmed Lives* Michael Korda writes that *Madame Does Not Want Children* 'brought the Kordas the offer they had been waiting for', that they left for America 'under contract to First National, which had acquired Maria as MGM had bought Garbo, Alex filling much the same unwelcome role that Mauritz Stiller had played in Garbo's contract. She was to be the star; he was to be given a few films to direct as part of the deal.'[17]

Karol Kulik expresses the same view in her biography of Alex, although she suggests that the film that persuaded First National was not *Madame Does Not Want Children*, but the one that Alex and Maria made just before, *A Dubarry of Today*, which was 'obviously a showpiece for the talents and charms of Maria Corda and may have been made with the express design of capturing the attention of a Hollywood producer'.[18] When Richard Rowland, the general manager of First National, offered a contract to Alex and Maria, 'he and the studio obviously hoped to groom Maria into another Pola Negri'.[19]

But First National's own files suggest that from the outset they showed little interest in Maria, regarding her simply as a part of the price they had to pay to secure her husband's services. While Alex signed his contract with the Hollywood studio on 11 March 1926 – well before either *A Dubarry of Today* or *Madame Does Not Want Children* had been made – Maria had no contract at all with First National before she came to Hollywood. There was just an understanding with Richard Rowland that the studio would try to find a suitable story for her within three months of her arrival, and that then she would be paid $5,000 per week for this one picture. In the event, when the three months elapsed with no story being found, the agreement was modified substantially in the studio's favour. First National 'had the right but not the obligation'[20] to employ Maria Corda in two films. In place of the guarantee of $5,000 for one picture, Maria was to receive only

$7,500 even if two pictures were made. Desperate for an opportunity to become a star in Hollywood, she was being forced into an uncharacteristic compromise.

Alex's close friend and collaborator Lajos Biro preceded him to Hollywood. Biro's 1912 play *The Czarina* had in 1924 been turned into a successful film by Ernst Lubitsch, *Forbidden Paradise*, and in February 1926 Biro went over to write screenplays for Paramount and First National. As Alex's Hollywood deal would be negotiated through Biro's New York agent, it's possible that it was Biro who recommended Alex to First National.

The move to Hollywood was an important landmark in Alex's career, but one the evidence suggests he contemplated with some hesitation. Before signing his contract, he asked the German head of publicity at First National, Heinrich Fraenkel, to translate the salient points. He wanted to know if he could live on the starting wage of $350 a week.* 'In Vienna,' he explained to Fraenkel, 'I lived in the Imperial, ate at Sacher's and had my suits made at Knicze's. Here I live in the Eden, eat in the Bristol and go to Stavropoulos. Can I do that in Hollywood as well – with this contract?'

Fraenkel said no, but explained that living conditions in Hollywood were completely different, and that Korda should regard the contract as simply a springboard.

'All right then,' answered Korda. 'I'll sign. If they don't let me do what I want over there, I'll simply come back.'[21]

The contract was to have commenced on 1 June 1926, but in the interim Alex took on more commitments in Germany and didn't leave for America until the autumn. It was as if he was putting off an evil moment.

---

* Alex's financial position was characteristically not quite as straightforward as this figure in isolation suggests. According to his contract with First National, he was actually entitled to $500 a week. But he was given a sizeable advance, which First National then deducted from his pay cheques at the rate of $150 a week.

4. THE GILDED CAGE

In the course of his life Alex would visit Hollywood many times, but it was a place that he was never fond of. On two occasions he lived there over extended periods – when he first arrived towards the end of 1926, and during the Second World War. I had expected that a short visit to Los Angeles would make the nature of his dislike instantly apparent. I was full of all the jaded tales that the place seems to attract and I expected not to like the town either. But slightly to my disappointment I found it wonderful. By some extraordinary feat a bustling city had been poured like a sauce over a vast but cosy suburb. At any point you could retire from the traffic-packed boulevards to stroll up quiet roads past the luxuriant lawns of spacious, welcoming houses. Then there was the glorious weather, which was a cheeringly pointless thing to discuss since it was continuously sunny with a clean, energizing heat. All in all, the town was the sort of place where it seemed entirely routine to have your cake and to eat it, which ought to have appealed to Alex enormously.

Then I went to my first Hollywood party. Several faces looked vaguely familiar. In a corner, nursing a glass of white wine and a canapé, stood a man with sunken cheekbones and haunted eyes who I was sure I had seen in an old black-and-white episode of *The Twilight Zone.*

The question that came most readily to mind whenever I started a new conversation was, 'Haven't I seen you in something recently?'

'Oh, you may have done,' replied a grey-haired man of about seventy. A few weeks previously he had made a guest appearance in *ER* as a man who had given some of his pills to his wife, with terrible consequences. The *ER* team was so professional, he said, that it had been rather like going into a well-run Emergency Room. Before he had even had time to be aware of it, they had whipped out his performance and he was able to go home again.

Afterwards, I spoke to an even older man who had written gags for Bob Hope, Jimmy Durante and Groucho Marx. He was quietly spoken and serious. He might have been an insurance executive. There didn't seem to be anything funny about him at all, but perhaps that was the secret of Hollywood. It wasn't the decadent place that you read about or saw in the movies, but a hard-working, conventional town – the town, after all, that dictates our conventions.

The day after the party I glided past Alex's old house on the Capo d'Oro, Bel-Air, in a 1970s sky-blue Rolls Royce Corniche with chromium bumpers. My driver was an old producer who had begun movie-making in Hollywood's Golden Age. With the kindness that I found everywhere I went in Hollywood, he had offered to show me around and invited me that day to dinner.

As we drew up outside his palatial house, he told me that his next-door neighbour was the head of production at Warner Brothers. 'My friends tell me I should work out a deal. Maybe I will.' Gesturing towards some trees and a high hedge, he pointed to a house that it was quite impossible to see – Bel-Air was the sort of estate where there was no reason why you should ever be aware that you had next-door neighbours.

'We were lucky,' said the producer. 'We bought in a dip in the market. We couldn't possibly afford this house now.' Recently widowed, he now lived there alone, looked after by Anna, a Guatemalan maid.

After Anna brought us our dinner, he turned on a television and, as we ate our salad and grilled chicken, we watched the Biography Channel. The programme was about Candice Bergen, whose father, I learned for the first time, was a famous ventrilo-quist.

'What? You never heard of Charlie McCarthy?' he said in a tone of surprise.

As we looked at the television in silence, I imagined the head of Warner Brothers' production next door and countless other movie executives scattered across the vast expanse of Los Angeles, all hunched in the same silence over their TV dinners.

'You can imagine how bored I am with these truly kind people,' Alex wrote to a friend after he had been in the town for a couple of years. The reason for that boredom was easier to understand now.

//

North Rodeo Drive runs from Santa Monica Boulevard up to Sunset. It is one of the plusher streets in Beverly Hills. Just north of the Santa Monica Boulevard, a brightly painted art deco house with fat, bulging walls and chimneys in the shape of toadstools announces that you have entered Dreamland. As you stroll onwards, you pass a gleaming white Southern mansion that might have featured in *Gone with the Wind*, a Spanish mission, a French château – 517 rue Rodéo, says a discreet china-blue plate by the entrance – a Jacobean manor and so on in every conceivable style. It is a street that seems to have been built not by architects but art directors.

Alex, who could not have had any idea that one day he would become an English knight, by some strange serendipity chose a house built in the shape of a castle, at Number 730. Here he settled down with Maria, Peter and their German governess, Clara Korke.

Just a short walk up the road on Sunset Boulevard was the Beverly Hills Hotel. A stroll into the bar was the closest Alex could have hoped to get to the café life he had known in Budapest, Vienna and Berlin. Los Angeles' vast suburb, sandwiched between the desert and the ocean, would have caused his metropolitan heart to sink.

After a few weeks to familiarize himself with a new language, he began his first Hollywood assignment in the spring of 1927. *The Stolen Bride* was the story of Sari, a Hungarian countess, and Franz, a cobbler's son. After a childhood encounter the two meet again many years later in America, where they fall in love. Back in Hungary Sari's father hears the news and furiously summons his daughter home, where she is forced to become the fiancée of a wicked baron.

Sari would have been a wonderful part for Maria, who spent most of her time behaving like a Hungarian countess anyway, but the role went to First National's leading contract star Billie Dove. The breakfast-table conversation at Number 730 Rodeo Drive must have been more than usually animated in those few weeks, and Maria's suppressed fury can be detected in an interview she gave during the making of the film to the fan magazine *Motion Picture Classic*. The title of the piece, 'Should Husbands Direct Wives?', must have seemed unpleasantly ironic given her then state of inactivity but she made the most of the opportunity to explain who ruled at home. 'When it is dinner-time, or time to go somewhere, then Mr Korda takes direction from me. He does it agreeably. We do not argue the matter, for he recognizes that in the home – I am the director.'[1]

The Stolen Bride was released in August 1927 to lacklustre reviews. The critic for *Variety*, making no effort to be kind to a director new to Hollywood, wrote:

> Painstakingly woven with close attention to geographical detail, this is but another variation of the princess-and-peasant theme. The director wastes too much time getting the opening planted, detracts from the atmospheric appeal by too much explanation in titles, and fails to handle the mush scenes with convincing delicacy when he finally does get down to work.[2]

By now Alex would have had enough English at his command to be upset by such a verdict, but the review provided a useful insight into film-making in Hollywood, where lavish detail came a poor second to a fast-paced, convincing story. Nevertheless, the box-office returns brought some solace. Costing $228,000, *The Stolen Bride* grossed $577,000.[3] In the manner that most counted – the bottom line – Alex had made a successful start to his Hollywood career.

By the time *The Stolen Bride* was released, Alex was on the floor shooting his next assignment, *The Private Life of Helen of Troy*. Based on a best-selling novel by John Erskine, it was in essence a satirical comedy of manners, deriving its humour from social observation and the contrast between then and now. It was the sort of thing that Alex had tackled a few years before when he made *The Prince and the Pauper* for Sascha-Film. Helen is portrayed as a bored, fashion-conscious housewife, who causes a crisis in Sparta when she decides to buy her clothes in Troy.

As First National had gone to great lengths to promote Billie Dove as 'The Screen's Most Beautiful Star', everyone in Hollywood had naturally expected that she would be cast as the most beautiful woman in the world. So Alex's successful insistence that Maria should play the part was a considerable feat, although the 'Director in the Home' had probably applied considerable behind-the-scenes pressure to bolster his resolve.

Years later Billie Dove would comment: 'There was a little controversy by other people because I didn't play it. I just shrugged. My philosophy was that it wasn't for me.'[4] Of Alex, who would direct her in four pictures for First National, she simply commented: '[He] was a good director; he was excellent.'

The part of the coquettish Helen suited Maria to a tee, requiring very little adjustment to the life she was already leading as one of the most bored and fashion-conscious wives in Hollywood. 'Helen wished to go to the theatre,' reads one title. 'Menelaus did not. So they went to the theatre.' This was a fair representation of the domestic life of the Kordas in 1927.

They were also both spending heavily. 'Mr Korda has pestered me almost daily for an additional advance which I have steadfastly refused because of the condition of his account,' wrote the studio's general business manager in June 1927.[5] But just in time the skill and assurance with which Alex directed *The Private Life of Helen of Troy* helped to get him out of his financial hole. Pleased with his progress, in September 1927 First National renewed his contract at an increased salary of $800, and agreed to pay him an extra $400 a week as a bonus.

The Private Life of Helen of Troy was released in December 1927. Costing $432,000, it had been an unusually expensive production, but returned what was then a colossal $717,000 at the box-office.[6] The critics too were pleased. 'Korda deserves laurel branch for fine job,' wrote the reviewer of the *Los Angeles Daily News*. The *Los Angeles Times* thought it 'something unique', congratulating the Hungarian husband-and-wife team for the 'piquant paprika of delightful burlesque'.[7] Even *Variety*, which, as a trade paper, tended to give the most hard-boiled, down-to-earth reviews, commented: 'A corking program release that figures to particularly delight what is currently smart in picturegoers.'[8]

But in spite of Maria's success, First National were still reluctant to give her a long-term contract, and with nothing to do in Hollywood, she made arrangements to star in a British film in the New Year.*

In the course of 1928, Alex directed two more Billie Dove star vehicles and *The Night Watch*, both written by Lajos Biro. Both made money and were well reviewed, but they gave Alex little personal satisfaction. He realized that his chief job at First National was not to attempt anything artistically ambitious but to build the Billie Dove brand.

Joseph Kennedy, who enjoyed a brief interlude as the new head of First National, saw *Night Watch* in August 1928. He congratulated Alex on his 'masterly hand', but Alex was too much of a realist to take such praise seriously. 'It has turned out to be quite a good film,' he wrote to Lajos Biro, who had recently returned to Europe, 'though there is nothing of a masterly hand about it – but I always say, it isn't worthwhile to make a better film than I'm making.'[9]

Yet being an efficient company man did have some rewards. In September 1928 First National rewrote Alex's contract greatly in his favour. He was to be engaged for a further period of two years, from 1 October 1928, at a salary of $1,750 per week for the first year and $2,250 for the second. The studio then had an option on his services for another year at a salary of $2,500 a week.[10] It also agreed to promote his films as 'AN ALEXANDER KORDA PRODUCTION', the sort of billing that only the very top Hollywood directors enjoyed.

The signature of this contract was the high point of Alex's time in Hollywood. Confident of his future there, he even applied for American citizenship. Exhorting the First National legal department to do everything they could to help him with his

---

* *Tesha*, directed by Victor Saville.

application, Al Rockett, the head of the West Coast studio, described him as 'one of our most valuable directors'.[11]

Maria, on the other hand, was struggling. On 14 September 1928, the studio gave her a six-month contract, but its far from generous terms made it clear how doubtful they were about her prospects.* When the contract expired in March 1929, it was not renewed. No reasons can be found in the studio files, but Maria's notorious temperament cannot have helped her case, and perhaps an even bigger hurdle for an actress with a thick Hungarian accent was the onset of the talkies. If Maria had been difficult beforehand, this final blow to her Hollywood hopes unleashed ever more bitter recrimination. Her resulting jealousy, she admitted, would lead to the eventual break-up of her marriage.

In October 1928, Alex began to shoot *Love and the Devil*, starring Milton Sills and Maria in the second of the only two films she would make in Hollywood. But Alex thought of it not as a 'Maria Korda' picture, as he would have done once, but as a Sills picture. 'We've put together quite a good story for him,' he wrote to Biro with a casual tone that gave a sense of the conveyor belt he was attending.[12]

Alex had made huge progress in 1928, consolidating his position as one of First National's top directors. Yet the letters he exchanged with Biro in the last few months of the year make it clear that he derived little contentment from his activities. 'Slowly but surely I am being bored to death. I begin to realize that apart from a raise nothing else interests me.' He was resigned to staying on in Hollywood, yet homesick for Europe. 'You can imagine how much I envy you for Switzerland and Austria,' he confided to Biro.[13] In Hollywood he found the people with whom he worked dull, pleasant though they were, and missed his friends. 'Do not think that I've grown melancholy,' he wrote. 'Only it's a terribly empty feeling to be without a single human being to whom I can talk – and who can talk to me.'[14]

The letters illustrated Alex's contrary nature. On the one hand he indulged in the incessant shop-talk of a workaholic, yet on the

---

* Maria was to receive a salary of $500 a week; the agreement was for six months only, with an option for an additional six months.

other fantasized about a life of contemplation and leisure. His dream, he confided to Biro, was of 'a motor tour in Europe and life somewhere on the Mediterranean – after all, that is the real world, the rest is just colonies'. He was too intelligent not to have some sense of his inconsistency, but the awareness afforded him little solace. 'My life passes as usual. I read it in Swift, at the beginning of one of the Gulliver chapters: "Having been condemned by nature and fortune to an active and restless life . . ." And in this accursedly active and even more accursedly restless life, you can imagine in what terrible loneliness I'm living.'[15]

Alex had a tremendous desire, as he put it, 'to be a more important personage',[16] yet at the same time felt such an aspiration to be futile. It was a contradiction that the gilded cage of Hollywood, where you were paid a fortune to follow orders, easily fostered. 'But are you at all interested in deals?' he questioned Biro at the end of one letter that had been devoted to giving an account of them. 'Maybe among the mountains of Pertisau and Switzerland one loses one's taste for business. I wish I'd reached that state.'[17]

The one constant in his correspondence was a desire to put by as much money as possible. And there was no better place than Hollywood to do that. He also tried to persuade Biro to return. 'I think if you came over for three or four months, maybe five,' he wrote in September 1928, 'you could easily do three scripts and this would still be more comfortable than work for a whole year for some European studio . . . I know that it isn't pleasant even to spend four months here – though, after all, Hollywood is still considerably better than the Siberian lead-mines.'[18] The notion of going down a mine would become a favourite, often repeated metaphor of Alex's for the activity of making films.

Biro responded to Alex's prompting by opening negotiations with First National, and with the hope that his friend would indeed return to Hollywood and that they would work together again, Alex contemplated his next film, *The Squall*, with an unusual degree of enthusiasm. 'I'm very much interested in the genuine Hungarian atmosphere,' he wrote. 'A farm – like the one on which I was raised . . . I think it'll be interesting and original.'[19] But the negotiations eventually broke down, and Alex's attitude to the project instantly changed. 'Story: awful. Cast: awful.'

He was also upset because he was told that *The Squall* had to be a talking picture. First National had just been taken over by Warner Brothers, which after its success with *The Jazz Singer* quickly converted all its productions to sound. With his taste for the literary, Alex might have been expected to take to this new medium, but in those early days it was still a crude device that required an abrupt departure from the sophisticated visual language of the silent cinema. Recalling his first talking picture many years later, Alex would comment: 'As a craftsman I was interested in this new tool, just as I was interested when I saw for the first time the gadget we now use in the cutting rooms for hanging or viewing film, but I disliked it very much indeed.' None the less, with the sort of pragmatic approach that had led him to keep in favour with Béla Kun, he buckled down. 'Whatever my artistic beliefs may have been, one has to eat and the weekly pay cheques certainly wouldn't have come if I had said to the powers who ruled the vast studios that I did not believe in this new gadget.'[20]

It was only in his letters to Biro that he was able to be frank. 'Eighty per cent talkie and the screenplay itself is terrible. But Wednesday is lovely.* I'm saving money. And everything else is unimportant.'[21] This letter, written on 28 December 1928, marked a turning-point in Alex's thinking. Before, he was discontented but resigned to the gilded cage. Now, prompted by the news that Biro was going to remain in Europe, he contemplated an alternative. 'You're telling me you're thinking of producing a picture yourself,' he wrote. 'You must know how happy I'd be if I could work with you in the future. If you find something or have some serious combination, think of me. In a year or eighteen months I'd be happy to return to Europe if we could make a picture or two together every year.'[22] In the meantime he asked Biro to do what he could to persuade Zoltán, who was still working in Berlin, to come out to Hollywood. 'Here he'll learn

---

* Wednesday was pay-day.

about talkies, special effects, model shots; and if later we do something and he can't find a good job here, I'm sure he'll become an outstanding associate of ours.'[23]

Alex's plan was to stay in Hollywood long enough to make enough money with which to establish himself once again as an independent producer in Europe. In a novel departure from his financial extravagance and usual state of indebtedness, he had begun to hoard his earnings, piling his investments into the New York stock exchange, which was powering along nicely at the start of 1929. He became an expert at playing the market, which he found far more diverting than the tedious chore of directing films.

Speculation was in his blood. He made frequent forays into the front office with various inventive but unorthodox financial proposals. It irked him, for example, that every week the studio took 5 per cent from his pay packet for 'non-resident alien income tax'. He suggested that it would be simpler if, instead of making this weekly deduction, the studio accepted bonds from him to the value of $6,000, and then sold them at the end of the year to offset the amount owed in tax. The proposal was turned down. After explaining in detail why it was not practical, the official responsible ended his note with the rather weary comment: 'Mr Korda has a different story to tell every couple of months. So let the matter rest as it is. Let's make motion pictures!'[24]

Zoltán Korda's son David recalled his father saying that 'Alex's attention span was much too short for him ever to have been a great film-maker.'[25] Hyper-active and hyper-intelligent and with a very low boredom threshold, Alex's need for constant stimulus would be the author of both his triumphs and his troubles.

The Squall told the story of a gypsy girl who seeks shelter at a farmhouse in the middle of a storm, then seduces the male members of the household one by one, bringing, as a subtitle put it, 'discord until a house once content was divided among itself'. It was pretty crude stuff, but, as the Variety reviewer pointed out, was bound to do well 'for it's full of make and hay'.[26] Released in May 1929, it turned out to be the most profitable film that Alex had yet made in Hollywood. Costing $305,000, it grossed

$696,000.[27] Whatever the frustrations of the story, Alex was at least able to learn about sound even if he didn't like it – a great gaggle of clucking geese and ducks waddling about the farmyard suggested some attempt to engage with the new technology.

Alex's next film was *Her Private Life*, with Billie Dove as an English aristocrat, Lady Helen Haden, and a young Walter Pidgeon as the American card-player with whom she falls in love. Hollywood's new craze for sound can only have made it even more difficult than it already was to produce artistically coherent work. It was a time when just about every film had to have a song, no matter how inappropriate. 'I found love when roses were red / And skies were blue above,' sings Walter Pidgeon in a rather pleasing baritone that you would never have suspected from his performance in *Mrs Miniver*. Costing $255,000, it too did well, grossing $538,000.[28]

Alex's last film for First National, shot in the late summer of 1929, was *Lilies of the Field*, with Corinne Griffith. She plays a mother whose child is taken away from her on trumped-up evidence when she is divorced from her husband. Forced to fend for herself, she becomes a chorus-girl – a plot turn that made it possible to introduce the obligatory musical numbers into what was otherwise a rather downbeat story of a blameless woman's descent into poverty and disgrace.

Alex had been slated to direct an operetta by Vivienne Segal called *Lady in Ermine* next, but when the head of production at First National, Al Rockett, and Alex's producer, Ned Marin, left to join Fox, he followed them there although his First National contract still had a year to run.

Whatever the financial terms that Alex had reached with Winfield Sheehan, Fox's then head of production, they were presumably a considerable advance on the roughly $100,000 a year he had been making at First National. But he must also have viewed the deal as an opportunity to end the tedium of the largely undistinguished programme pictures he was making for First National – the move to the prestigious Fox studio affording him the opportunity to work on more ambitious projects. The arrival of his brother Zoltán that autumn would have further raised his morale.

Looking back on his Hollywood years in a 1936 interview with the journalist Philip Johnson, Alex described his greatest accomplishment there as learning to say yes. As long as he said yes, he went on making pictures. 'They were neither good nor bad. The only thing that can be said of them was that Korda knew that he could do far better if he were left to himself.'[29] If he had hoped to find such conditions at Fox, he was soon to be disappointed. On the contrary, the reality was one of continual intervention, by which any aspect of a particular project could be changed at any moment, depending upon the whim of the studio.

His first film was to have been a version of the musical play, *The Dollar Princess*. The British comedian and playwright George Grossmith, who was engaged to write it, recalled its progress. 'We want it to be a flying story,' the film's producer Ned Marin advised him.[30] There had been a string of hugely successful flying films such as *Hell's Angels* and *The Dawn Patrol*, and the studio hoped to cash in.* So the hero of *The Dollar Princess*, who had originally been the Princess's secretary, became her private pilot. But just as the new story had been completed, two planes crashed over Santa Monica Bay in the course of filming another Fox picture. The order went out that there should be no more flying pictures, and Grossmith was asked to write a Foreign Legion story instead.

'Don't let anything worry you,' Alex advised him. 'Our story may take place in Russia or China before we've finished.'[31]

By the time they had finished, '*The Dollar Princess* music evaporated with the rest of the story',[32] and the new script, now called *Women Everywhere*, had become in effect a vehicle for the studio's newly acquired star, Fifi D'Orsay. The story, about a cabaret singer in Casablanca who hides a gun-runner from the police, was no more than an excuse to showcase her talents. Known in her day as the 'French bombshell' – although she had been born in Quebec and had never once set foot in France – she had made her name with her suggestive songs and earthy humour. Her famous catch-phrases were 'Ooh-là-là!' and 'Allo! Beeg Boy!'

---

* The film was originally going to be called *Hell's Belles*.

The essential requirement for the director of a D'Orsay film was cheerfully to embrace every vulgarity. 'Don't think I'm afraid of you,' exclaims 'Good-time Fifi' when she discovers the gun-runner Charlie Jackson in her dressing-room. 'One scream from me and fifty legionnaires will be in here.' Firmly pitched at such a 'Carry On' level, the film was a waste of time for a director of Alex's subtlety and sophistication. The move to Fox, he now realized, had been a retrograde step.

But there were compensations. As well as Zoltán, Lajos Biro was now finally back in Hollywood, and Alex had managed to get work for both of them on the story of *Women Everywhere*. Grossmith too, who would remember Alex as 'the best friend I made in Hollywood', proved to be extremely congenial company, and as they laughed at the absurdity of the production in which they were engaged, they began to discuss their own ambitions.

Grossmith, who was an important West End impresario, had come out to Hollywood with the express purpose of learning about film-making. The recent arrival of the talkies, it seemed to him, offered a new opportunity for the theatre to shape the cinema's future. He recalled in his memoirs:

I had my own ideas of what I liked and did not like on the screen, and some very concrete notions of the manner and direction in which pictures might be improved – especially in England. I even dared to imagine that with the acquisition of some technical knowledge on the subject I might even be able to produce a better picture than one or two emanations from Hollywood itself.[33]

This being so, Paul Tabori's account of the following conversation, even if not literally true, seems an accurate representation of the sort of discussions Grossmith and Alex would have been having:

'England ought to be making the best pictures in the world,' Korda told Grossmith.

'We-ell,' replied G.G., displaying his teeth and sucking in air at the corners of his mouth in the Grossmith manner, 'why can't we three – you and Biro and I – go to England and make them?'[34]

After the completion of *Women Everywhere*, Alex spent a few weeks in Europe. He discussed the possibility of directing a picture in Germany with a Hungarian producer in Berlin, Andor Zsoldos. When a specific project was eventually proposed, he turned it down for financial reasons, but it was clear that he now longed to return to Europe as soon as the conditions were favourable.

'I'm working very seriously on a plan', he wrote to Biro in September 1930, 'to get some money together ($250,000) and start in Europe. I'm convinced that the European market is a good one and is going to get better. And to earn real money, to save, is only possible through independent production.'[35]

In his disenchantment with Hollywood he had finally decided to stop saying yes. His next project after *Women Everywhere* was to have been a film called *Basquerie*, but, as he explained to Biro, 'they gave me such an awful script you can't imagine. I told them so – whereupon there was a terrific row. If I hadn't a contract, they'd have kicked me out.'[36]

Instead, Sol Wurtzel, Fox's head of production, told him to make a film called *The Princess and the Plumber*, although Alex thought it was a bad story. 'From the frying pan into the fire! . . . I'm starting the picture next Monday. Don't care a damn.'

The final break was now just a matter of time, with Alex almost willing a confrontation. The most plausible account of what happened next is to be found in the interview piece with Alex by Philip Johnson: 'Korda made *The Princess and the Plumber*. The big Panjandrums saw it and decided that they wanted "menace" put into it. Korda didn't think that menace was essential. He thought it would spoil it – if it was good enough to be spoiled. He argued. Next morning he found that he had lost his job.'[37]

In Paul Tabori's more colourful account Sol Wurtzel ordered a private showing of the film and brought along his eleven-year-old son. When, at the end of the showing, Alex asked Wurtzel what he thought of the film, Wurtzel took his cigar out of his mouth and told him to ask his son. Alex did so, to receive the verdict, 'It stinks.' Wurtzel then told him he was fired. But as instant dismissal would involve giving Alex a substantial pay-off under his contract, Wurtzel set about humiliating him into resignation. He was relieved of his duties as a director and told to work in the story department, reading synopses. When he refused, his contract was cancelled for alleged disobedience and his remaining salary withheld.

Everything one reads about Wurtzel suggests he was just about the very last person in Hollywood you would want to have as your enemy. Even his son Paul commented: 'He had a short fuse. He would blow up at anybody, and what a temper he had – awful, really profane. He embarrassed me. He would take over at meals, and he talked with his mouth full. I couldn't stand his goddamn cigars. He was a crude, rough guy.'[38] A facial tic meant that it was impossible to tell whether he was smiling or furious, but it was always a mistake to smile back. Even when he was away, it was impossible to forget him, as he had given jobs at the studio to most of his relatives. At one time there were nine Wurtzels working on the Fox lot. The often-heard utterance was 'Things are getting Wurtzel and Wurtzel around here.'[39]

Alex stayed at home while he waited for the outcome of a lawsuit against the studio. 'How is it when bad luck climbs on your back?' he wrote to Biro in November 1930. 'That's how it is with me now.'[40] There was not only the 'outrageous, swinish behaviour' of Fox, but also the collapse of his marriage with Maria. Her appearance in *Love and the Devil*, in the autumn of 1928, far from bringing them together, seemed only to bring home to Alex how impossible she was to deal with, and at his instigation a separation soon followed. 'You can imagine in what terrible loneliness I am living,' Alex wrote soon after shooting on the film had finished, 'I haven't even a family.'[41]

After a lengthy holiday at the El Mirador in Palm Springs, in 1929 Maria moved with Peter to 'a new and inferior home', as Peter would later recall it, 'somewhere in Cannon Drive or Canyon Drive or some such place'.[42]

It is perhaps Peter for whom one feels most sorry. Alex's rather self-pitying letters to Biro were full of his own ambitions and his loneliness but made not one mention of his son. The photographs in Peter's family album give some idea of the sort of life he would have been leading at the time. For his schooling he was sent to the Pacific Heights and then the Black Foxe military academies. Under a picture of him in his Black Foxe cadet's uniform is the rather endearing caption: 'P.K. as cadet at B.F. academy. He was a B.F. cadet. Now he is only a B.F.'[43] At home he had had plenty of friends who would visit him, and expensive toys to play with. He was fond of animals and had several dogs. A cause of particular excitement must have been when John Loder got a supporting role in Rin-Tin-Tin's first 'barkie', and there is a signed photograph from the two stars in the album. The overall impression the pictures give is of a prosperous and fun-filled childhood, but one which Peter's father, engrossed in his frustrations with the studio or his plans for the future, made little effort to be part of.

The familiar presences in Peter's life included Maria, his nanny Miss Miller and Miss Ida Fischer, the secretary who travelled with the Korda family from Germany to Hollywood. Alex himself features in just a handful of photographs. The antics of a small child were of little interest to him. There's one photograph in Peter's album of Alex and Maria together on the set of *The Private Life of Helen of Troy*, which is captioned: 'Mother and AK. He is annoyed about something. He always is.' Home life was more an irritation to Alex than a pleasure, an unwelcome distraction from the grand plans that he preferred to pursue. In the coming years he would play the role of father for many people, but he found it hard to be one to the person for whom it most mattered.

Maria went to considerable lengths to resist the impending divorce. 'There was a law that if you had sexual relations with a wife you had left within a year of having left her, separation was null and void,' said David Korda. 'She arrived in the house once with a battery of photographers wearing her fur coat with nothing underneath and ran into the house to try and incriminate Alex to take her back. She always regretted that he divorced her.'[44] In her anger she spread false stories in the gossip columns that Alex was having homosexual relationships. One of Zoltán's first tasks upon arriving in Hollywood was to help scotch such rumours by moving in with his brother.

The various accounts of Alex's last year in Hollywood illustrated a curious talent he had for courting disaster. When things went badly in his life, they tended to do so in a spectacular way.

He had to contend with not just the divorce from Maria, finally granted on 25 January 1930, and the loss of his job at Fox, but also the aftermath of the Wall Street Crash, which wiped out whatever he had managed to save from his salary. A graph of his fortunes would be a mad zig-zag. 'I have had my upsies and downsies in the showbusiness,'[45] Alex would once comment, and it was some sense of the intimate relationship between success and failure that would enable him throughout his life to bounce back from reverses that would have broken many other men. 'You need to have the courage to fail. People should not be afraid of failure. They should have the courage to nurse a success and then forget it, and move on to something else. Never think of what's done – think of what's to do.'[46]

So in Alex's last letter to Biro from Hollywood he could write of his misfortunes but also plot a path to recovery:

> In my opinion (1) you can make a great deal of money in Europe with a good picture; (2) a good English-speaking film has a tremendous market over here; (3) if one makes a good picture in Europe, one can get a new contract in America just as easily as if one made it here; and finally (4) if one earns good money in Europe, why the hell should one come back to this accursed Hollywood?[47]

It amounted to a blueprint for his future.

//

So what are we to make of Alex's years in 'accursed Hollywood'? Calling them 'The Best Forgotten Years', Karol Kulik concluded that 'Hollywood was too big for Korda in those years. Continental film directors, many with more talent than Korda, over-ran the studios, and Korda was simply unable to distinguish himself above the "flock".'[48]

The First National files expose this verdict as untenable. In three years at the studio Alex successfully served his Hollywood apprenticeship and established himself as one of the studio's leading directors. Only one of the nine films he made for First National – *Lilies of the Field*, released after his departure for Fox – failed to make a profit. Whatever subsequent fame he might achieve, in strictly commercial terms he had already enjoyed his most successful years.

The great frustration was the lack of freedom to make films in the way he wished to make them. While in Europe he had invariably been his own producer, in Hollywood he had to work within a system that had all the rigidity of an assembly line. But if he had lost his independence as a film-maker, there were compensations. As Alex put it himself: 'There were lots of things that Hollywood could teach me, and there were lots of things I wanted to learn. They weren't the things that the great Panjandrums thought they were teaching me, but they didn't know that. It pays to say "Yes" at times.'[49]

Perhaps the greatest lesson was 'the showmanship'. It was in this department that the Hollywood producers of the day came closest to genius. Even at Fox, where he would see his Hollywood career finally explode, Alex had reason to take his hat off to Sheenan and Wurtzel on the publicity front. One example was Fifi D'Orsay, the 'French bombshell' – her real name was Yvonne Lussier, but Sheenan and Wurtzel wanted something that sounded more glamorous, so she called herself Fifi after the stage name she had used in Vaudeville, and D'Orsay after her favourite brand of perfume. The fact that she had never even crossed the Atlantic, let alone lived in France, was of course suppressed. According to the Fox studio biography, she was born in Asnières, a suburb of Paris, and educated in a convent – her parents wanted her to become a nun – but she left for the United States, determined to become an actress. In this fantasy lay the seeds of the fiction that Alex would concoct a few years later in England for Estelle Thompson O'Brien, who would become known to the world as Merle Oberon. Alex, Maria recalled, 'laughed and amused himself terribly about the unbelievable crookedness of American publicity. If they decided that you have a hole in your stomach they talk you in until you believe that you have it . . . making from chambermaids goddesses and from goddesses chambermaids. Everything through publicity.'[50]

Hollywood may have kicked Alex out for failing to toe the line, but long after he had gone they would still recognize him as one of their own.

5. 'SOMEWHERE ON THE MEDITERRANEAN'

At the Vieux Port in Marseille not far from where the 'service régulier' departs on the fifteen-minute journey to the Château d'If, there's an inscription on a stone tablet set into the tarmac:

ICI
VERS L'AN 600 AVANT JC
DES MARINS GRECS ONT ABORDÉ
VENANT DE PHOCÉE
CITÉ GRECQUE D'ASIE MINEURE
ILS FONDÈRENT MARSEILLE
D'OU RAYONNA EN OCCIDENT
LA CIVILISATION

After his recent experiences in Hollywood, Alex might have been forgiven for feeling that civilization had yet to make it across the Atlantic, and it would certainly have been with a sense of enormous relief that he returned from what he had described as 'the colonies' to 'the real world'.

If in the real world the South of France was just about Alex's favourite place, then that plaque by the Vieux Port suggests the reason why. It wasn't as if there were any more yachts on the Riviera than there were in California or that the women there were any more beautiful, but the pursuit of pleasure was rooted in a tradition, there was a timeless quality – a sense of life continuing as it had for centuries. Alex cared little for oceans on which Ulysses never sailed or mountains uncrossed by Hannibal and Napoleon. Like Nancy Mitford's Valhubert, he had to 'live and die a European'.

Moored on the north side of the Vieux Port is *Le Marseillais*, a beautiful wooden schooner that has been converted into a restaurant. César's Bar de la Marine, the setting for Marcel Pagnol's *Marius*, the film version of which Alex would direct soon after his return to Europe, might easily have been across the way. The rectangular expanse of the harbour, fanned by the Mistral, encourages you to stay outdoors, to sit on a bench, or to watch the passers-by in a way that would seem absurd in Hollywood or Beverly Hills, with their endless multi-laned boulevards swathed in exhaust fumes and relentlessly going somewhere.

Marius went nowhere in the Hollywood sense. The tyranny of narrative was cast off in favour of character and the kind of relaxed observation that Mediterranean life seemed to encourage. One of the first great classics of the French sound cinema owed much to the inspiration Alex drew from a return to the world that he loved.

//

Alex's first port of call on his return from Hollywood was Berlin, where in late 1930 he joined his friend Lajos Biro. They met the theatre producer Max Reinhardt, who had wanted Alex to exploit his company of actors and theatrical properties in the cinema. But Alex's experiences in Hollywood had left him with little appetite for deferring to someone else. Nor would he have derived any comfort from the political situation in Germany, where the Nazi Party had become an increasingly powerful and ugly presence. Berlin, which was fast shedding its reputation as Europe's most cosmopolitan and liberal city, was hardly a promising place to start a new enterprise.

There was one obvious place for a Hungarian ex-Hollywood director to find his feet. In common with several other European countries, France had introduced regulations to encourage foreign countries to invest in home film production. In April 1930, just a few months before Alex's return to Europe, Paramount had opened studios at Joinville and Saint-Maurice on the outskirts of Paris. Dubbed 'Hollywood européen', the original concept had been to remake American films in different European languages. Alex, who besides having worked in Hollywood was multilingual, would have seemed a valuable asset, and in early 1931 the

American in charge of the studio, Robert Kane, gave him a contract. It's possible that the head of Paramount, Adolph Zukor, whom Alex had known in Hollywood, put in a word for him. Lajos Biro, who had associations with Paramount that went back a long way,* also began to work for the studio. Alex's first assignment was to direct German and French versions of a film Paramount had made in Hollywood called *Laughter*.†

As a director who had already worked in Hollywood, Alex might have found remaking Hollywood films in Europe something of a come-down. But a change in Paramount's policy soon provided him with an opportunity to stand out.

The studio's new European venture had not had a successful start. Too often the American stories seemed absurd once they had been translated into a European context. In the studio bar 'One heard nothing but comments condemning the script,' the cameraman Osmond Borradaile recalled. ' "It is impossible." "There are no such people in my country." "Something like that would never happen where I come from." '[1] Therefore, the studio began a programme of original productions instead of remakes of American films. But these rushed productions, which were shot in two weeks and corralled different language casts into short, inflexible schedules, were scarcely any better.

One of the interested observers of Paramount's early experiments was the French playwright Marcel Pagnol. His play *Marius*, about a *garçon de bar* who works in his father's harbourside café and dreams of going to sea, had opened at the Théâtre du Paris in March 1929 and was still playing to packed houses two years later. Early in 1930, when the talkies had yet to reach France, Pagnol had travelled, on the enthusiastic recommendation of a friend, all the way to London to watch Bessie Love in *Broadway Melody* at the Palladium. He recalled a voice that sounded like 'a dog barking in a storm',[2] but none the less recognized a revolutionary new art.

Back in Paris, he approached Bob Kane soon after the opening

---

* He wrote Ernst Lubitsch's first big Hollywood success, *Forbidden Paradise*, in 1923.
† *Die Männer um Lucie* and *Rive Gauche* (1931).

of Paramount's new studios. Determined to learn all he could about the cinema, Pagnol asked if he could go along and watch what was going on. But once he had acquainted himself with the basic principles of film-making, all there was left to marvel at was the routine mediocrity of the films that rolled off the Paramount conveyor belt, where any merit that the original story might have possessed seemed to be stripped away in the production process. When he put it to Kane that the author, who seemed to be the least important person in the hierarchy of film-making, should be the most important, Kane replied, 'In heaven the first may be last, but not here on earth.'[3]

Pagnol lamented Kane's refusal to 'betray the spirit of Hollywood',[4] but would soon have an opportunity to challenge the system. After the initial novelty of talking pictures had worn off, Paramount's box-office receipts began to plummet. Matters reached a head when, after a showing of a film called *Night at the Hotel* (*Nuit à l'Hôtel*), the audience began to hurl abuse at the screen and to rip up the seats. A further change of approach was clearly required, and soon afterwards Kane offered to buy the rights to *Marius*. Expressing his willingness to abandon Paramount's cheap production-line methods, he declared that in this case he would lavish the care required to produce a film with the potential to be an international success.

But at first Kane insisted that the actors in the film should be Paramount players already familiar to the cinema-going public, and Pagnol turned him down. The proposal was an absurdity. The play had grown organically around its stage cast, so that the two were inseparable. This was particularly true of the great French music-hall star Raimu, who played César, the owner of the Bar de la Marine. Pagnol had originally offered him the role of Marius, but reworked the play when Raimu insisted that César was closer to his own character. It was also Raimu who would direct the play, with countless adjustments bringing it to life on the stage.*

---

* Pierre Fresnay, who played Marius, would write: 'La part de Raimu, metteur en scène, a été considérable dans le succès de *Marius*, autant peut-être que sa part de comédien, et non seulement par ce qu'il apportait aux comédiens, mais

Kane finally relented when some months later a film version of a play by Marcel Achard, *Jean de la Lune*, which had the original stage cast, became a big success. Not only would he allow Pagnol to supervise a film version of *Marius* with the actors who had appeared in the play, but Pagnol would also effectively have 'final cut'. Kane stipulated only that Alexander Korda should be the director and that Swedish and German-language versions should be made at the same time.*

At first Pagnol was sceptical that a Hungarian could capture the idiom of a play set in Marseilles, but he was quickly won over. Meeting Alex for the first time in Bob Kane's office, he had expected the usual tedious process he had experienced with film people of having to explain a play that all of Paris seemed familiar with. But Alex cut him short and in perfect French confided that he had already seen the play twice and was going to go again that evening.

'What did you think of the actors?' Pagnol inquired, rather taken aback.

'It's absolutely essential that they should all appear in the film.'

There was a pause while one of them translated what had been said for the head of Paramount France, who did not speak French.

'But no one's heard of them!' protested Kane.

'After this film,' Alex replied, '*everyone* will have heard of them. And as for that fellow called Raimu, he's clearly one of the greatest actors in the world . . .'

'But how will they stand up before a camera?' asked Kane.

'The question you should be asking,' replied Alex, 'is how will the camera stand up before them!'[5]

If Pagnol had really been looking for someone ready 'to betray

par ce qu'il apportait à Pagnol lui-même. De toutes les pièces écrites par Marcel Pagnol, si *Marius* est la plus achevée, la plus ronde, la mieux en proportions, c'est en grande partie à Raimu qu'il le doit.' Fresnay and Possot, *Pierre Fresnay* (Editions de la Table Ronde, 1975), p. 40.

* Alex would direct both the French and the German versions, John Brunius the Swedish version.

the spirit of Hollywood', he couldn't possibly have found a better accomplice. Everything Pagnol had criticized as an observer at Paramount France, Alex had personally suffered as a director in Hollywood. In 1931 there was perhaps no one more ready to challenge the assembly-line approach to the cinema. Alex's experiences in America had left him with the strong conviction that Hollywood films 'didn't approach near enough to life. They were too artificial. To that extent they sacrificed the higher appeal of which they were capable.'[6] He believed that the moguls for whom he had worked had 'confused reality with sensationalism'. And it was when he had pointed this out that they fired him. *Marius* was an opportunity to prove – albeit in a small way, for it could never achieve the global reach of a Hollywood release – that he had been right all along.

But beyond this, of course, the play suited Alex perfectly. He loved its setting in the South of France and, with his impeccable upbringing in the cafés of Mitteleuropa, he would have had a feel for the ambience of the Bar de la Marine. He must also have identified hugely with Marius, torn between his love for Fanny and his desire to go to sea. To be torn between ordinary happiness and the fulfilment of a dream was a familiar dilemma for Alex, who might easily have wondered at the uncanny manner in which Pagnol's play seemed to capture so much of his recent experience. When it came to the movies, Escartefigue, the ferry-boat captain, content to pilot his craft back and forth across the Vieux Port and never once feeling the slightest desire to turn its bows towards the open sea, offered a pretty accurate representation of his bosses back in Hollywood. Now at last with Pagnol's help he had a chance to grab the wheel, and to take this particular vehicle in the direction he felt it ought to go.

But it would not be plain sailing. Raimu, who was prone to irrational bouts of anger and mistrustful of strangers, had originally objected to Pierre Fresnay playing the role of Marius on the grounds that he came from Alsace and not Marseilles. Now he was dismayed to find that the film version should be in the hands of a 'Tartar from Hollywood'. So it was a considerable achievement of Alex's to win him over on the first day of shooting.

A sound engineer from Hollywood complained that Raimu's voice would not register properly on his recording equipment.

'What a pity,' Alex replied. 'Because we can't replace Raimu. But we can replace you.'[7]

Raimu, jumping with rage, was soon upon the 'telephonist', hurling abuse down his microphone. But just as he seemed on the point of violence, he lowered his voice and said quietly: 'Sir, when I make a telephone call, everyone can understand me, but your American machines still haven't bothered to learn French.'[8] As it was lunchtime, he then treated the soundman to an apéritif, and they became the best of friends.

The unlikely *entente cordiale* of Raimu and the soundman summed up the nature of the production as a whole. A French story was shot with Hollywood technicians in an American-owned studio. It was fitting that Alex, who would do more than just about anyone else in the history of the cinema to bridge the gulf between Hollywood scale and European intimacy, should have been at its helm.

Recalling a '*collaboration fraternelle*', Pagnol remembered a director who never shot a scene without first explaining what he intended to do and why. Pierre Fresnay, who recalled Alex permanently puffing on a huge cigar and presiding over the production with a 'sovereign calm', felt that his importance to the success of the film was as significant as Raimu's had been to the play. 'Il a été l'homme nécessaire, indispensable et discret.'[9] Recognizing the camaraderie and understanding that the cast had developed in two years together on the stage, Alex sought to preserve this spirit. He also went to considerable lengths to capture the genuine atmosphere of a Mediterranean port. He filmed location shots in Marseilles and enlisted the aid of his brother Vincent, who by this time had long since moved on from the artists' colony in Hungary and was eking out a living as a painter in the South of France. He had him sketch the Vieux Port, then come to Joinville to help the ex-UFA art director Alfred Junge design the sets.

When it was screened, *Marius* ran over two hours. The Paramount executives were horrified by the lengthy dialogue scenes and insisted that it should be cut by at least forty minutes.

Kane probably shared their reservations, but kept his word that the French version should be exactly as Pagnol intended.

'It was obvious,' recalled Pagnol, 'that everyone thought the real *Marius* films were the German and Swedish versions, which had had proper film stars, a proper "treatment" – i.e., the "scenario department" had made the play unrecognizable – proper editing – no sequence lasted longer than thirty seconds – and proper direction – the camera was constantly roving around the set.'[10]

The French version of *Marius* amounted to a revolution. It was unheard of for the cinema to bring a play to the screen without wholesale bowdlerization. Alex showed that the film and theatre traditions did not have to be at war, that they could complement and draw on each other with mutual benefit. The film did not just record a play, as inevitably several of the more myopic critics would object, but brought a new level of reality, creating a real world for the characters to inhabit, giving them the space and time to be more themselves. Alex used the technique of the cinema to enhance, rather than cut across, the actors' performances. Seventy years on, *Marius* still stands as one of the great examples of the cinema's ability to capture the texture of life. It represents a kind of cinema that Hollywood has always had little patience for, where the narrative does not have to push relentlessly on but gently flows forward in a spontaneous fashion from the characters.

Marius opened in Paris on 3 October 1931. All over the French-speaking world massive audiences turned out to see it. By comparison, the German and Swedish versions disappeared without trace.

Paramount were so pleased with their success that they held a celebration party at the studios. After a splendid dinner Bob Kane led Pagnol and Raimu out into the studio gardens, where a bright lamp lit up a model of the Paramount mountain. Raimu was the greatest actor in the world, Kane declared, and he wanted to give him a long-term contract. But first he wanted Raimu to choose a present for himself. Pagnol translated Kane's offer into French. 'You know how generous Americans are,' he said to Raimu. 'You can choose whatever you want, a luxury pen, a watch, a car, and I bet he'll give it to you.'[11]

Raimu explained that for months the Paramount mountain had been driving him mad. What he would like more than anything else would be to kick it to pieces. On a symbolic level, that was what he and Pagnol and Alex had already done.

6. 'THE LONDON VENTURE'

Marius was just one example of a wider attempt by Paramount to improve the quality of its European production. At the same time as Alex began to work with Pagnol, a young English production manager, David Cunynghame, was sent over to London to set up a production unit at the British & Dominions studio in Elstree. As in France, the British Government had passed legislation to compel the big American film companies to distribute a percentage of British-made films.* These had to meet a low minimum cost, but over the following year Paramount would exceed the quota requirements, producing a programme of more expensive films intended to provide genuine box-office appeal.

Cunynghame, who had been the production manager for the three versions of Alex's first film for Paramount, *Rive Gauche*, must have had some sense that exciting times were ahead for he marked the occasion by buying a leather-bound diary. 'Wild rumours about the London venture,' reads the first entry, for Tuesday, 7 April 1931. Arriving in London two days later, he hurriedly engaged staff, and on Tuesday, 14 April, the first Paramount-British production, *These Charming People*, went on the floor, directed by Louis Mercanton, and starring Cyril Maude, Godfrey Tearle, Norah Swinburne and Anne Todd.

Over the next twenty-five years Cunynghame would keep his diaries with unusual care, scarcely missing a day. They are an invaluable resource because over this long period no one else would work with Alex more closely. Their significance is perhaps

---

* The Cinematograph Films Act 1927, commonly known as the Quota Act.

all the greater because they were not written with any pretension to style. They were a record of events, an *aide-mémoire*, and perhaps chiefly an attempt to impose some order on the strange and chaotic new world in which this heir to a baronetcy found himself. Conscientious and imbued with a deep sense of responsibility, Cunynghame would act as a counterbalance to Alex's more mercurial nature.

II

Paramount sent Alex to England to make a film for their new British production unit in September 1931, immediately after he had finished work on *Marius*. On Thursday, 24 September Alex began filming *Service for Ladies*, a remake of a 1927 Paramount film starring Adolph Menjou. A romantic comedy, it featured Leslie Howard in the Menjou role as a top head waiter who falls in love with a society girl. He hides his identity and, masquerading as a society figure, travels to an exclusive Alpine hotel where the girl has gone on holiday. Here he makes friends with a king, an old customer of his, who helps him to get over his difficulties and marry the girl.

It was a lightweight fantasy, but Alex, who had a talent for presenting make-believe with total conviction (both on and away from a film set) went to as much trouble to get the background details correct as he had in the case of the far more realistic *Marius*. On the Saturday after the production had begun, he invited Cunynghame to dine with him at the Savoy, where he had been staying, so that they might note the authentic ambience of a grand hotel. Then on the Monday he had the film's restaurant set re-dressed under the supervision of the Savoy's head waiter, a Signor Santarelli.

Alex was equally exacting when it came to the script. As its weaknesses became apparent in the course of production, he held a number of story conferences to rework it. Leslie Howard commented shortly afterwards: 'He would make a scene, then throw the whole thing in the ashbin because he did not like it, and do it over again quite differently and very much better. That is why his work is so good.'[1]

Alex finished shooting *Service for Ladies* on 4 November

1931. It was more than a week over schedule. The delays were caused not only by the amendments to the script, but also by Alex's busy social diary. Often he would arrive on the set late in the morning as the result of attending some engagement the previous night. One of the more notable occasions was the first night of Noël Coward's *Cavalcade* on 13 October at the Theatre Royal, Drury Lane. Alex's old Hollywood friend George Grossmith was the theatre's managing director. A prominent figure in London showbusiness and society, he was well placed to introduce Alex to influential people.

Neither Grossmith nor Alex had forgotten their conversation in Hollywood about going into independent film production together. Indeed, earlier that year, together with Lajos Biro and Stephen Pallos, a Hungarian who worked for a French distributor, Alex had already set up a company in France called Pallas Film to acquire story rights. In one of Alex's last letters to Biro from Hollywood, after his dismissal from Fox, he had written: 'In my view the inferiority of Hollywood film production is so marked today that a half-way decent European (English-speaking) picture which fulfils certain American requirements, starts with a tremendous chance on the American market, too.'[2] London may have lacked the attractions of the Mediterranean, but, as Alex was discovering on his nights out to the theatre, it was the perfect place to test this conviction.

Plans had been made for Alex to go to Khartoum with David Cunynghame to shoot location footage for a film version of Rudyard Kipling's novel *The Light That Failed*. But just days after his return to Paris on 5 November, the production was suspended. It's hard to imagine that after a pleasant few weeks in London Alex would have taken well to the Sudan's dusty emptiness. So perhaps the amenable Bob Kane – who would have been delighted with the recent successful opening of *Marius* in Paris – agreed to prolong the stay in England a little longer.

Previous accounts suggest that Alex was now keen to break away from Paramount, but in fact it had been a fruitful relationship which he was anxious to continue – although on his own terms. His next assignment was to direct a film version of a play by Frederick Lonsdale called *Spring Cleaning*, which would finally be released under the title *Women Who Play*. 'But Korda was not to direct the film,' wrote Karol Kulik in her 1975 biography, quoting from a newspaper report for an account of the events:

> He was not happy with it, and could see only failure ahead.
> One night he was riding home from Elstree along the Barnet by-pass when his car, a Paramount car with a Paramount chauffeur, crashed. Korda escaped with injuries just serious enough to make it impossible for him to work for a few weeks. Paramount paid him damages and released him from his contract, and he was free.[3]

The crash did take place – on 9 December – but according to the cameraman Osmond Borradaile, who was one of the other passengers in the car, the only injury Alex suffered was a 'state of shock'.[4] He was well enough to begin directing *Women Who Play* five days later on 14 December. Alex continued to work on the film until he became ill in the new year – probably with flu, which affected several other members of the production. On 4 January 1932, he got up from his sickbed to finish a scene before a new director, Arthur Rosson, took over the rest of the shooting. As Alex had already directed well over half the film and it finished shooting only two weeks later, there seems no compelling reason why he should have wanted to get out of the production, as the newspaper article Kulik quotes suggests. So probably on this occasion he really was just ill.

A much more important event in deciding his future would be the successful opening of his first British-made film at Paramount's Plaza Theatre on 17 January. The trade magazine *Today's Cinema* reported on the 'barrage of high-powered press praise' which hailed the film as an 'all-round triumph of film production'.[5] It was held over at the Plaza for an extended record-breaking season and, in a rare departure from usual practice Paramount were sufficiently pleased to give it an American release.*

Having made his mark in England, Alex now had the confidence to go ahead with plans for his own company. He moved into a flat in Duchess Street, and he summoned his two brothers

---

* The American title was *Reserved for Ladies*.

to join him. Vincent, once again putting down his paint brush at Alex's request, came reluctantly from Paris, and Zoltán from California – suffering from TB, he had stayed out there, hoping to recover his health in the desert air. London Film Productions was founded in February 1932. The chairman of the company was George Grossmith, the managing director was Alex, and the other directors were Lajos Biro, Lord Lurgan, an associate of Grossmith at the Theatre Royal, Drury Lane, J. S. Cerf of the French film company Pathé, John Sutro, and Alex's solicitor, Captain A. S. N. Dixie.

Paramount, who had decided to reduce their own film-making activity in Britain, gave the new company a contract to make five Quota pictures. To this extent London Film Productions was less a break from Paramount than a continuation of it. David Cunyng-hame resigned in March 1932 with Bob Kane's blessing, and began work at London Film Productions the following month. Other Paramount-British staff who joined at about the same time included cameraman Osmond Borradaile, editor Harold Young, sound supervisor A. W. Watkins and assistant director Geoff Boothby.

In spite of their divorce, Maria was still a regular presence in Alex's life, dividing her time between Paris and London. She had hoped that Alex might change his mind about the divorce and that they might remarry. Indeed, Alex's colleagues at London Films' new headquarters at 22 Grosvenor Street, where she was often to be heard arguing in his office, assumed that they were married. Difficult as she was to live with, Alex was still fond of her and valued her advice.

Maria would later claim that in the early years of London Films she had given Alex financial support. Seventy years on, this claim is hard to verify, but as Alex borrowed from just about everyone it could well be true. The undisputed piece of assistance that Maria gave is the one that she would most regret. Estelle Thompson O'Brien was, in Maria's words, 'a little black half-caste Indian girl'[6] whom she happened to spot in the British & Dominions canteen during the shooting of *Women Can Play*.[7] Estelle was a dance hostess at the Café de Paris who wanted to break into the movies and was working as a bit-part player. Maria pointed her out to Alex for her star quality, not knowing that the girl would one day eclipse her in Alex's estimation and dash her hopes of remarriage. The daughter of a British railway engineer and an Indian mother, Estelle had been brought up in India and came to England when she was seventeen. With a new name and some inventive publicity *à la* Fifi D'Orsay she became Merle Oberon, the girl from Tasmania, daughter of an English army officer and a French–Dutch schoolteacher.

Merle would be one of four starlets that Alex would sign to his new company. The others were Wendy Barrie, Joan Gardner and Diana Napier.

The Quota films for Paramount provided the new company with its bread and butter. But Alex, who was determined to move upmarket, had also concluded a much more ambitious deal with the producer Michael Balcon to make six first features for the country's largest film company, Gaumont-British, which would be distributed through its subsidiary, Ideal Films.

If Gaumont-British had been impressed by Alex's past achievements, they did little to show it, closely scrutinizing his every move. Their agreement with London Films gave them final approval over the story, the leading players and even the choice of studio. Alex's fast-moving, cavalier style soon came up against the more tortoise-like pace of the managing director of Ideal Films, Simon Rowson, a man who took pains to dot every 'i'.

It was agreed that the first film of the partnership should be a comedy based on a story by Lajos Biro, *Wedding Rehearsal*. But soon afterwards, Alex received a gentle rap over the knuckles for purchasing the rights to *Manci*, a German novel by Lili Brodi, on the basis only of Rowson's verbal assent. Rowson chided:

> May I say, as a general proposition, that I hope you will not ask me to give approval at any time to a subject on the basis of a verbal communication to me of the contents of a story. It is only fair that I should have in my files a record of the subject to which my agreement is required. This can be in the form of a book or a synopsis prepared in your own office.[8]

But even when a book or a synopsis was provided, Rowson was forever reserving his consent. In his anxiety to make the right decision, he found it hard to make any decisions at all without first referring them for endless discussion to his colleagues at Gaumont-British or to Alex himself. The result was that London Films' inaugural production, *Wedding Rehearsal*, went on the floor at Wembley Studios on 2 May 1932 with Alex still having no idea what his next film for Gaumont-British would be.

Wedding Rehearsal was a sophisticated comedy, starring Roland Young, about a bachelor who defies his mother's matrimonial plans for him by marrying off the girls she proposes to his friends. Much of the first week's work had to be reshot because of poor photography, and there were further long delays when Alex summoned Lajos Biro back from Hungary to rewrite the script. After shooting was over, Cunynghame rather quaintly compiled a report called 'unjustified studio expenditure', as if the confusion and sudden changes of plan that characterized the new company's production were just teething problems. He discovered in the years to come that London Films was routinely besieged by intractable troubles, which usually Alex contrived to dispel only at the eleventh hour.

Eleven o'clock was the hour that Big Ben struck when it was photographed by a London Films camera unit on Wednesday, 6 July 1932 – Alex would later claim that this just happened to be when the sun had come out. The day before, filming had begun on the first of the Quota films for Paramount. Alex embarked on the programme with typically high ideals. It would not be the usual collection of cheaply produced second-feature thrillers and comedies, but a nursery for the future. His growing company of young actors and actresses would gain the experience that would help to build them into stars; and new film-making talent would be provided with a route into the mainstream. That was the theory, but things turned out very differently in practice.

The signing of Leontine Sagan to direct the first Quota production was a bold statement of intent. The former actress and stage director, who had worked with Max Reinhardt in Berlin, had just made a name for herself around the world with her controversial first film, *Mädchen in Uniform*. Set in a Prussian girls' school, it told the story of a girl who falls in love with a schoolmistress. But once Sagan began to work for Alex, it quickly became clear that she would not enjoy the same scope for boldness. Alex invited her to choose a suitable story, but when she suggested Rosamund Lehmann's novel *Dusty Answer*, he turned it down as 'too lesbian'. He explained that in England audiences looked for 'the same healthy spirit that they seek in the family'.[9]

Sagan suggested instead a film about undergraduates set in Oxford. Alex approved the idea, but, as Sagan recalled many years later, warned her that 'such a film must not be burdened with exacting psychology and morbid sexuality. It must be an innocent love affair, featuring fresh and simple youth.'[10]

Sagan might have expected Alex of all producers to show a more broad-minded attitude. One of the memorable scenes in *Marius* is when Fanny's mother discovers Marius's belt on her kitchen table and then is furious when she opens her daughter's bedroom door to see the two lovers in bed together. But in 1932 censorship made such frankness impossible in England. So, straying away from lesbians, Sagan immersed herself in stories about Oxford instead, and eventually chose a novel by a young Oxford graduate, Anthony Gibbs, called *Young Apollo*. The rights were purchased, Anthony Gibbs was employed to write a screenplay under the supervision of Lajos Biro, and Zoltán was appointed to be the producer. The story concerned an undergraduate hero who loves books and poetry more than sport and is ragged by the 'athlete' members of his college.

Intense and serious, Sagan found it easy to identify with the hero of the story, but, neglecting to follow Alex's advice about the need for carefree innocence, asked Gibbs whether there was a well-known brothel in Oxford that the undergraduates would attend and 'was there much homosexuality among the boys'. Gibbs remembered her as 'clever', 'imaginative', but 'above all, emotional'.[11]

Lacking confidence, Sagan struggled from the very beginning to impose herself on the production. After seeing the first few days' rushes, Alex summoned her to a meeting and demanded that she make changes in the script. There was a row at first, but she eventually relented. The endless conferences with Biro and

Zoltán Korda that followed turned out to be less a collaboration than a war of attrition in which bit by bit she completely surrendered her conception of the story.

> My suggestions were politely turned down for being too redolent of the stage or for being too psychological and therefore unsuited to the medium of the cinema. I had promised myself to behave quietly and not become temperamental and be branded the 'female producer'. Accordingly, I often acquiesced when I wanted to argue, and agreed when I felt about to revolt.[12]

Sagan fared little better at the casting stage. Her method during the screen tests was to chat with the actors about the scene beforehand and then to ask them to improvise before the camera. But Alex, she recalled, 'in his fatherly and slightly sarcastic way' took her to task her for not letting them memorize their lines.[13]

One of the young actors to be auditioned would write down an account of the experience:

> [The] woman director . . . is fuming. She thinks I am 'ham'; she doesn't want me in the picture anyway. She has no intention of the test being a good one. The camera begins to turn. The lights flicker but the test goes on. I sit there mumbling my words. The lady director interrupts me. I fluff, I stammer, I splutter. She splutters. The lights splutter. The lady director screams, 'Cut!', but before they have time to stop the film I sit back in my chair and laugh. And laugh. I make up my mind to become a waiter. Two days later the lady director sees the test. It is atrocious; but during the last moments of the screening a Hungarian genius happens to look into the theatre and sees a bewildered young actor expressing his opinion of the film industry in terms of laughter. The lights go up. 'Well,' says the lady director triumphantly, 'what do you think of him?' 'Marvellous!' says Alexander Korda.[14]

So began the film career of Robert Donat.

Although Sagan believed that 'the film should have been kept free of women because they detract from the atmosphere of a men's college',[15] the story that eventually emerged, as one of the stars, Emlyn Williams recalled, concerned 'two undergraduates in love with two undergraduettes, in itself – at that time – a formidable improbability'.[16]

Unhappy with the script, Sagan tried to compensate during the film's shooting by improvising scenes 'out of the spirit of the moment', then lost her temper when Zoltán sought to intervene. 'I began to hate poor Zoltán and to behave very badly indeed by spluttering sarcastic remarks, so that the atmosphere between us became unbearable.'[17]

It was really made impossible for Sagan to develop her idea of the story. But then Alex had warned her, and, in spite of his warnings, she made little effort to work within the limitations of the commercial British cinema that he had outlined, and finally shunned any spirit of constructive compromise. 'Somehow or other they finished that film, but not before Zoli had locked Leontine Sagan for three days solid in the ladies' loo while he retook all the homosexual bits,' recalled Anthony Gibbs.[18] Sagan herself, in a comment that tests the reader's sympathy, would later write:

> I might have won Zoltán and his brother round to my ideas had I exercised more tact and amiability but, much as I admire these virtues in private life, I consider them a waste of time at work and I maintain that it is better to ruin a project and take the responsibility than to make a hodgepodge by compromise.[19]

Alex's biggest mistake really was to have employed Leontine Sagan in the first place. It was an example of a conflict in him that over the next twenty years would never be completely resolved. Alex the connoisseur admired talented individuals who made bold and original films of genuine artistry; but Alex the film producer, in spite of what he had suffered himself as a director in Hollywood, expected his directors to observe the rules of mainstream popular cinema. If the boldest and most talented of them often turned out to lack the necessary flexibility, it was not something that Alex had a lot of patience with, since he himself had become used to adapting to prevailing circumstances with protean ease.

The immediate impact of the difficulties with Sagan was that Alex fell back on a more prudent conservatism. The remaining Quota pictures for Paramount were filmed in quick succession over the next six months. *That Night in London, Strange Evidence* and *Counsel's Opinion* were directed by the experienced Hollywood directors Rowland V. Lee, Robert Milton and Allan Dwan; and *Cash* by Alex's brother Zoltán, who may have been making his directorial début but at least was a known quantity and so comparatively easy to guide.

//

Paramount was happy to have London Films continue to provide its Quota production. In the autumn of 1932 they were even proposing a programme of twelve to fourteen films for the following year at a total cost of £200,000.[20] But Alex's attempts to produce his more ambitious programme of first features with Gaumont-British were dogged by endless trouble. He had hoped to share the responsibility of directing these films with the top German director Paul Czinner, who had signed a contract dated 18 February 1932 to make 'two pictures simultaneously in English and German' with his wife Elisabeth Bergner, then one of Germany's leading stars.[21]

But from the outset Alex struggled to find an acceptable subject for Czinner and Bergner. There were just too many people to disagree. Soon after the contract had been signed, Alex urged Czinner to read Feuchtwanger's *Calcutta Fourth of May*: 'I am told great part for Bergner.'[22] But Czinner didn't think so.

By June Alex had their consent to two subjects, which he then put forward to Rowson: a drama called *Melo*, and Shaw's *St Joan* – Bergner had appeared in the title role on the German stage, to enormous acclaim. Rowson approved the first, but – after the usual lengthy consideration – turned down the second. 'I am sorry to say that, knowing how keen you are upon it, I am quite unable to agree with you that this would prove anything but a *succès d'estime*. We should all lose money on it – although we should get wonderful appreciative notices everywhere.'[23]

A few weeks later *Melo* had also fallen by the wayside and

Alex had to think again. As Bergner had been a great success in a German production of *The Constant Nymph*, he turned to its author, Margaret Kennedy. 'Miss Bergner', he wrote to her in August, 'would be delighted to play in a picture written by you. We would regard it a great honour to have a story from your pen in our production.'[24]

Kennedy wrote a draft for an original story, which was approved, then met Bergner and Czinner in Switzerland to discuss the idea. A contract was signed in October, and at the end of the month, with the deal agreed by everyone concerned, Alex went to Paris to direct his next film for Gaumont-British, *The Girl from Maxim's*, based on a play by Georges Feydeau. Here he passed into a kind of 'radio silence' that would in years to come become all too familiar to the various directors, writers and actors clamouring for his attention.

On 21 December 1932, Kennedy's agent at Curtis Brown, Mary Buxton, wrote a rather testy note to Lajos Biro:

> I have written twice to Mr Korda, but since I understand he is in Paris, probably the letters have not reached him. Is it possible for you to get in touch with Mr Korda about Miss Margaret Kennedy's story for Elisabeth Bergner? She has been kept absolutely in the dark about your intentions and she is very disturbed and not a little hurt. I should much appreciate it if you would give us some indication as to the present position.[25]

Biro wrote back a week later. He explained that he had been under the impression that Paul Czinner had talked to Margaret Kennedy directly, and had not been in touch for that reason.

> The situation is that we all think that the so-called Bergner story has many charming qualities but that it is not suitable to be the basis for a film. My friend Korda as well as I have the deepest respect and admiration for Miss Kennedy's genius, but this is an added reason to state frankly that it would be a mistake to try and produce this story or – to express myself cautiously – the story in its present state.[26]

He suggested, however, that Miss Kennedy might like to meet Alex when he was back in Paris in three weeks' time as 'a conversation together with him might better lead to a satisfactory arrangement'.

But the real situation wasn't quite as Kennedy's agent had been led to believe, and Biro – who was after all a writer, not a businessman, and would as soon as possible retreat back into his writer's study – must have found it extremely unpleasant to have to send such a disingenuous letter. The much more important reason for not proceeding with Margaret Kennedy's story – whatever its flaws – was the fact that Gaumont-British had just cancelled its contract with London Film Productions.

Alex, desperately short of money, had requested Gaumont-British to forward cash advances for London Films' programme of films earlier than the contract had provided. Gaumont-British agreed to consider the matter only in relation to the one film, *The Girl from Maxim's*, which was then in production, but an impasse was reached when Alex insisted on discussing the programme as a whole. A Gaumont-British representative was sent out to Paris, but failed to resolve the matter.

Gaumont-British, which had clearly regarded London Films as on probation, took exception not only to Alex's unbecoming lack of humility but also to his continuing 'on the hoof' attitude. In a letter, dated 16 December 1932, that gave formal notice of Gaumont-British's intention to cancel the agreement, Michael Balcon wrote:

> I have been very concerned with the way in which the position, as regards the Bergner–Czinner pictures, has developed. I have been asked to approve for acceptance a story for the first of these pictures which has not even been submitted to me in any sort of manuscript form; all that has happened is that Mr Biro and Dr Czinner visited the studios and verbally outlined a story. This procedure is entirely contrary to the provisions of the contract.[27]

The specific and rather legalistic reason that Balcon gave for cancelling the agreement was that London Film Productions had failed to provide a copy of its contract with Czinner and Bergner for Gaumont-British's approval by a stipulated date.

Balcon's response offers some clue as to why the British

cinema had up until then failed to offer any serious competition to Hollywood. It is hard to imagine Thalberg or Goldwyn or Mayer refusing to listen to an idea because it had not been set down on paper. Some basic absence of showmanship, some habitual clinging to prudence, had resulted in an anaemic industry incapable of making movies that would capture the imagination of the whole world.

January 1933 was a grim time for London Films. The pull-out of Gaumont-British had left Alex to finish *The Lady from Maxim's* without any finance or any obvious distributor. A particularly virulent flu epidemic that had gripped the whole of Britain only further contributed to the sense of crisis. Work on the two Paramount films then in production, *Counsel's Opinion* and *Cash*, was stopped for several days with so many of the cast and crew away ill. David Cunynghame despaired of the situation to such an extent that at the end of January he told Alex that he wanted to quit and go to America. Alex only managed to persuade him to stay by telling him that he had signed up Britain's leading director, Alfred Hitchcock.[28]

The following month *Wedding Rehearsal* was released, but performed poorly at the box-office. *Men of Tomorrow* and *Bright Lights of London* followed in March and April, but did little better. 'The three films are over-valued in your books,'[29] the auditor would comment a few months later in London Films' first set of accounts – an observation which down the years auditors of London Films would come to make *de rigueur*. Then there were the future projects – an expensive staff had been gathered together to work on a programme of films that now had no obvious means of being made.

A more prudent person – Michael Balcon, for example – might have chosen this moment to admit defeat, but Alex struggled on, looking for new backers and continuing to pay his employees with IOUs and charm instead of cash. The trick, he had learned, was always to smile and to pretend that everything was all right. *Sursum corda!* Only confidence could keep the enterprise moving, and so long as it was moving there was always the hope that help might be found.

7. SUCCESS

London Film Productions came perilously close to collapse at the beginning of 1933, although outwardly it was business as usual. Paul Czinner and Elisabeth Bergner, who still had not chosen a subject, were encouraged to carry on looking for ideas; production on the Quota films for Paramount continued; and Alex began to cast a long-planned production of *A Gust of Wind*, based on a play by Giovacchino Forzano, even though Gaumont-British were no longer around to support it. He was keen to use a young British actor who was just beginning to make a name for himself in Hollywood. Back in May 1931 Charles Laughton had done a test for Paramount-British, which led to the American company signing him.* Alex hoped that his own association with Paramount would enable him to secure Laughton's services on better terms than he would have done otherwise.

He broached the subject first with Laughton's wife Elsa Lanchester, who had returned to England some weeks ahead of her husband. She was hoping that Alex might have a part for her, she recalled later, but 'in his witty, delightful, persuasive Hungarian way he led the subject around to Charles'.[1] At that first meeting, he 'immediately suggested a delicious script called *A Gust of Wind*, in which he wanted Charles to play the leading role', but a few days later he suggested a film about Henry VIII.

There would be many stories about how Alex came by the

---

* Laughton acted out a scene from *The Man with Red Hair*, in which he had appeared on the West End stage in 1928. Based on the novel by Hugh Walpole, the writer of the play, Benn Levy, scripted Laughton's first film for Paramount, *The Devil and the Deep*.

idea of *The Private Life of Henry VIII*,* but as Elsa Lanchester observed in her memoirs it was really rather obvious. 'For many years people have taken one look at Charles and said: "You know, you ought to do Henry VIII." It is rather like saying when there is a blue sky: "Isn't it a lovely blue sky?"'†2 The much more remarkable thing was the speed with which Alex, ready to make the most of any opportunity, could suddenly abandon *A Gust of Wind*.

Laughton agreed in principle to appear in the film, but Alex still had to find backing. When the British film companies he approached turned the project down, he dismissed all but his most essential staff and set off in February 1933 on a money-raising mission to Italy. In Rome he met Ludovico Toeplitz, director of the Cines Studios, whom Maria had known when she was making films in Italy. Toeplitz was a friend of the flamboyant Italian writer Gabriele D'Annunzio and a connoisseur of literature who had himself written several books. Much more importantly, his father was Giuseppe Toeplitz, president of the Banca Commerciale d'Italia, which had two years previously saved Cines from liquidation.

On the point of retirement, Giuseppe seems to have shown an enthusiasm for the cinema that often strayed beyond strict business prudence. The screenwriter Ettore Margadonna recalled turning up at the Toeplitz home in Milan with a script that he wanted to sell to the son and finding the father instead. 'Sit down, sit down,' Giuseppe insisted. 'Read your story.' When Margadonna had finished, Giuseppe asked him how much he wanted. 'Eighty thousand lire,' said Margadonna, naming an absurdly exaggerated price. 'Far too high!' said Giuseppe Toeplitz, who then suggested 50,000, but just for an option on the subject.3

---

* 'I rather think I have told some of them myself,' remarked Alex, whose favourite story was that he had got the idea in the back of a London taxi when he overheard the driver singing the old music-hall number 'I'm Enery the Eighth I Am'.

† Indeed, when Lanchester met Alex, Laughton was already planning 'to do Henry VIII' – at the Old Vic, where he was going to appear in Shakespeare's play at the end of the year.

This was plainly the sort of man with whom Alex would have been anxious to do business.

A few touch-and-go weeks followed. Further dismissals of staff followed Alex's return to London, but at least the Toeplitzes were interested. On 20 March an all-day meeting took place at 22 Grosvenor Street as the two sides attempted to hammer out a deal. The day afterwards Cunynghame discovered that London Films had ceased to pay his salary into his account. When he took up the issue, Alex assured him that even if the talks with the Toeplitzes hadn't yet reached a successful conclusion they were going well and he also had certain 'distribution hopes'. But two weeks later still nothing had been resolved, and on 10 April Cunynghame had yet another meeting with Alex about the company's financial situation. More people were fired or had their salaries withheld, while those who were left carried on planning the Laughton picture as best they could. Alex made several visits to Hampton Court with Laughton and began to work on the script with Lajos Biro and the playwright Arthur Wimperis.

A scene from a Marx Brothers film in which Chico, Groucho and Harpo chop up a train and feed it into the engine to keep it going gives a pretty good idea of the state of London Films in the spring of 1933. But at last, on 21 April, after another big meeting with the Toeplitzes, Cunynghame was able to write in his diary, 'All reported settled.' The uncertainty was resolved. Giuseppe Toeplitz agreed to provide financial backing for *Henry VIII* and, as part of the deal, Ludovico became joint managing director of London Films. Tall and fat with a big black beard, he would inevitably be dubbed by the press as Henry IX.

With its light satire on domestic life at court, *The Private Life of Henry VIII* was a calculated attempt to repeat Alex's previous box-office hit, *The Private Life of Helen of Troy*. Ludovico Toeplitz recalled that Alex would often mention *Helen* in their protracted negotiations, jokingly admitting that its original success had been a complete accident. There was a town called Troy on the banks of the River Hudson famous for its cardboard box factories. The audience turned out in droves to see the film because they were convinced that it was going to be a touching story about a beautiful American box-maker.[4] It appealed to their sense of the familiar in a way that a story about a princess in Ancient Greece would not have done. Alex argued that *The Private Life of Henry VIII* would succeed for a similar reason. In America Henry VIII was by far the best-known English king. Everyone had heard of him, especially in the Midwest, where a large beer factory had recently featured the king in a massive publicity campaign. He was depicted on posters as he had appeared in the famous Holbein painting, but with a glass of beer in his hand.[5]

Soon after the Toeplitz deal, Alex's distribution hopes were also settled. He met Richard Norton, who was a friend of George Grossmith and responsible for the production of Quota films at United Artists. Instantly impressed, Norton would later write, 'After five minutes I was determined to try and get his work for United Artists distribution. This was my chance to stop fiddling around with ninth-rate pictures.'[6] The American managing director of United Artists' London office, Murray Silverstone, was equally impressed and began to negotiate a contract for five films, two of which would be 'first features'.

Ninth-rate pictures had been the peculiar result of the 1927 Quota Act, whose purpose had been to keep the British film industry alive in the face of overwhelming competition from Hollywood. Most of the big American distributors, faced with the necessity of having to finance British productions in order to offset their imports of Hollywood pictures, took the attitude that these films should be made as cheaply as possible. Anything more ambitious or costly would only provide unwelcome competition to films that could be produced much more effectively in Hollywood. The result was a flood of mediocre films made simply to fulfil the terms of the Act, and never seriously intended to earn any money at the box-office. Alex's films for Paramount had proved a notable exception.

United Artists, which traded on prestige releases, had not wanted to distribute British films at all. But as long as they had to do so under the Act, they preferred to distribute British films of quality which might boost their general reputation for excellence. Until the arrival of Alex, a British-based producer with the unique experience of having worked in Hollywood, the right sort of quality had always been hard to find.

Having re-engaged the staff that had been steadily sacked over the last few months, Alex began to direct *The Private Life of Henry VIII* at British & Dominions Studios on 17 May 1933. On the same day the five-picture distribution deal with United Artists was signed. The financial crisis for London Films was over – at least for a while.

Yet *The Private Life of Henry VIII*, would be remembered by those involved in its production and writers since as a film somehow made against the odds on a tiny budget. 'Those were the days when one did the best one could with a piece of string and a drawing-pin,' commented Elsa Lanchester.[7] 'Korda was faced with an inadequately financed project,' wrote Karol Kulik.[8] Alex 'knew better than anyone', claimed Michael Korda, 'that the film was a hasty attempt to put together all the elements that were available to him on a shoestring budget'.[9] Laughton himself would recall agreeing to work on a cooperative basis because there was so little money. This notion of the flung-together film that would eventually trounce the Hollywood giants at the box-office is an appealing myth, but not true. *The Private Life of Henry VIII* was one of the most expensive British productions of its time. The budget, as set out in the United Artists contract, was between £55,000 and £60,000, 'which to us,' recalled Richard Norton, 'was colossal'[10] – it was about the amount a Hollywood studio would spend on a production. Whatever initial arrangement Laughton may have agreed, by a contract dated 29 April 1933 he was entitled to a payment of £5,555 plus 10 per cent of the American box-office receipts. On 14 October 1933, eager to retain his services, London Films added to the agreement 10 per cent of the British and Commonwealth receipts.[11]

The sets were modest in size, but lavishly decorated. Alex did not stint on eye-catching detail. Henry may have had only six wives, but Alex made sure he was surrounded by many more attractive ladies-in-waiting,* all dressed in expensive costumes

---

* *Variety* would comment approvingly on the 'bevy of good-looking girls, and

designed by John Armstrong. The food for Henry's banquets was brought in every day from Claridge's. 'You make good films, you do real stuff,' Alex commented when Binnie Barnes, who was playing Catherine Howard, once asked why he didn't just use pretend food like everyone else.[12]

So far from being a 'hasty attempt', every effort was made to make the film as good as it could possibly be. The single most expensive item was almost certainly the indulgence of Charles Laughton. Elsa Lanchester recalled 'such a lot of alterations and hold-ups that in the end Charles was called back to Hollywood before *Henry VIII* was finished . . . and we did the rest after he left'.*[13] Usually the hold-ups were due to Laughton. Many times, just as the camera was about to run, he would wave a hand and declare himself no longer to be 'in the mood'. On one occasion, just as Laughton had finally signalled that he was ready, the camera operator, Osmond Borradaile, swung the camera from side to side and declared that *he* was no longer in the mood.

Laughton used his influence to ensure that his wife was cast as Anne of Cleves. 'I hadn't seen her before,' recalled Ludovico Toeplitz. 'When Laughton introduced her, he noticed my disappointment. She was well known for her intelligence, but she certainly wasn't pretty. "Don't worry, Toeplitz," he said. "Anne of Cleves was Henry's ugliest wife." '[14]

Alex handled the eccentricities of both cast and crew with infinite patience. Borradaile recalled a director who 'trusted his technicians and gave them freedom to operate as they saw fit, praising and criticizing as warranted'.[15] Binnie Barnes spoke of a 'gentleman director' who 'never shouted, never screamed. He directed you, and told you exactly in a very quiet way how to do it. And if you made a mistake, there was no problem with that. We would cut, and do it again.'[16]

The overall impression is of a director going to every length – and expense – to get an important project absolutely as he wanted

this from England, where one attractive femme screen face to a picture has been a novelty and two a full cargo'.

* Laughton departed for Hollywood on 27 June, and the last full shooting day was 3 July.

it to be. 'It cost £50,000 because that was all the money we had,'[17] Alex would claim many years later, but London Films' own records give the less conveniently round sum of £93,710.[18] He had exceeded his budget by well over 50 per cent.

Virtually all the accounts of Alex's early years in England suggest – as of course he did himself – that he had staked everything on just one film. 'Korda had put his shirt, coat, hat, and everything he had, on Henry,' Lajos Biro would comment. 'If it had failed, he would have been cleaned out.'[19] The truth was more complicated. *The Private Life of Henry VIII* was certainly very important, but it was part of a much larger production effort. With the United Artists contract Alex had committed himself to making not just one film but a programme of five, all of which, at varying stages of development, entailed varying degrees of expenditure.

There were also other commitments. When *The Private Life of Henry VIII* finished shooting on 3 July, a London Films unit switched over to working on a Columbia production called *The Lady Is Willing*, starring Leslie Howard and Binnie Barnes. And at about the same time Zoltán began to direct the first of two advertising shorts for the Daimler motor company. All this was useful bread-and-butter work.

The Columbia film had been arranged at the last moment with the Hollywood mogul Harry Cohn. He appeared suddenly at the Grosvenor Street office and explained to Alex that he was in London 'absolutely *in*-cognito' and begged them to keep his visit a secret. He had decided to have a go at directing, he explained, but so that he should not be a laughing-stock in Hollywood if the film was a failure, he wanted to make it quietly in England. Alex agreed to provide him with a film crew and any spare actors he had on contract. The experiment did not go well. After a week, Cohn watched the footage, declared the film to be 'lousy' and, suspending the production, returned to America. The film would eventually be completed by the stage director Gilbert Miller.

The next big production for London Films was *The Rise of Catherine the Great*, which Paul Czinner began to shoot on 12 September with his wife Elisabeth Bergner in the title role. Karol Kulik describes the film as an attempt 'to repeat the success of

Henry VIII',[20] but it actually went into production long before anyone could have known what sort of success *Henry VIII* would be – and, costing £127,868,[21] was much more expensive to produce.

//

Alex's efforts to get *The Private Life of Henry VIII* just right paid off. United Artists were delighted. 'It will be a tremendous sensation in the United States and should gross phenomenal money,'[22] predicted Murray Silverstone. Suddenly, there was a buzz about the film. It was something genuinely special that United Artists could promote as such long before the public had a chance to show whether or not it agreed. There was a trade showing in London on 17 August 1933, more than two months before the official première, and word of mouth helped to whet appetites.

But there wasn't just one first night, there were three. On 1 October there was the 'World Première', held at the Lord Byron Cinema in Paris. On 12 October the film had its American première at Radio City Music Hall in New York. And finally, on 24 October, came the London première at the Leicester Square Theatre. Laughton sat in the front row of the dress circle surrounded by his six 'queens', who all took a curtain-call to rapturous applause after the film had finished. The reviews were uniform in their praise. 'Really brilliant,' declared *The New York Times*.[23] 'Just as good as it was reputed to be, and a little better,' wrote C. A. Lejeune in the *Observer*.

Seventy years on, *The Private Life of Henry VIII* still stands up. Beneath the surface satire there is a genuine pathos. Certainly much of this was due to an extraordinary performance by Charles Laughton, who would win an Oscar that has rarely been better deserved, but Alex, who facilitated that performance, also deserves his share of the credit. Henry is a man who rules over an entire kingdom, but finds that however supreme his authority over his subjects may be in all other respects, he is powerless to command their affections. In the course of the film, the protective layers of youth, privilege and authority are peeled away, leaving exposed a vulnerable, tragic figure. Simple and spare, *The Private Life of of*

Henry VIII managed to render its period with fidelity, yet on another level operated as an extremely effective study in unrequited love. In the way of great films it achieved a universality.

C. A. Lejeune commented that the film was 'more likely to bring prestige to the British Film Industry, both at home and abroad, than anything we have done in the whole history of film-making'.[24] But the use of the word 'we' was deeply debatable. The excellent cast may have been English, but few of the major contributors on the other side of the camera were. The director, screenwriter and production designer were all Hungarian; the cameraman was French, the editor American. While the newspapers naturally preferred to crow over a great British success, the film was really much more an example of a British failure to back a talented outsider. Gaumont-British's decision to pull out of its contract with London Films on a technicality nearly destroyed Alex. None of the other British companies he approached showed any interest in supporting him. It finally took an Italian banker and an American distributor to bring *The Private Life of Henry VIII* to the screen.

It is hard to escape the impression that at the beginning of the 1930s British film producers were as backward as the English executioners *Henry VIII* satirized. 'It's a crying shame,' complains the English axeman forced to stand idly by as the job of cutting off the Queen's head goes to a French swordsman, 'half the English executioners out of work as it is.' 'And why are they out of work?' retorts the French swordsman. 'Because they are only fit to sever the bull necks of their countrymen with a butcher's cleaver. But a woman's neck, a queen's neck, that calls for finesse, for delicacy, for chivalry. In one word, a Frenchman.' Once again the 'Tartar from Hollywood' had come to the rescue.

The Private Life of Henry VIII was such a landmark in the history of the British cinema that it was easy to exaggerate the scale of the triumph. It 'made Alex over half a million pounds on its first run', wrote Michael Korda, repeating the standard figure that had first begun to make its appearance in London Films' press releases.[25]

The real figure is to be found in the files of the Prudential Assurance Company, which by 1938 had become the effective owner of London Films. A box-office report cites the total world receipts up to September of that year as £214,360.[26] It was an impressive sum, but not quite as sensational as Alex would have liked to pretend. And by the time the various individuals involved had taken their share of the profits – Ludovico Toeplitz and Alex 20 per cent each, for example – a very modest amount was left over for London Films' coffers.

It was always unwise to trust Alex when it came to figures, but no one could really dispute his summing-up of *Henry VIII*'s significance: 'For the first time a picture was made in England which was popular all over the world and this gave people the confidence that it could be done.'[27]

8. ALEXANDER THE GREAT

At the end of 1933, the chairman of United Artists, Joe Schenck, visited Britain to consolidate the achievements of an extraordinary year. In a glowing letter to his colleagues back in New York, he made no attempt to conceal his euphoria.

> *The Private Life of Henry VIII* is a terrific hit. *Catherine the Great* is Korda's second picture, is great entertainment, lavishly produced, with two great performances by Elisabeth Bergner and Douglas Fairbanks Jr, and no doubt will be a hit here and should do as well in the States as *Henry VIII* and may do better.[1]

United Artists, he felt, had pulled off a great coup over their American competitors, who in England continued to distribute poor-quality Quota pictures. '[I]n the high-class theatres they hiss these pictures off and in the rough theatres they throw bottles at the screen – we sell them pictures that are great box-office pictures.'[2]

Early in the new year Schenck signed a long-term agreement with London Films. In place of the old distribution contract for five films was a new one for sixteen. While under the old contract United Artists had agreed to give worldwide distribution to only two of five films, they now agreed to give it to 'all future films'. Furthermore, London Films would receive 75 per cent of the American box-office takings instead of the previous 50 per cent. Effectively, Alex had *carte blanche*. For the first time he was free to choose film subjects without having first to secure someone else's approval. These extremely favourable terms were a sign of how potentially valuable United Artists considered their new producer to be. Alex's investors in London Films also showed their appreciation of his importance. By a new service agreement, he was to receive a salary of £9,000 per annum tax-free (over £200,000 in today's money), £1,500 per film delivered and a £3,000 personal entertainment allowance. In addition, he enjoyed varying percentages on the films he produced.

Alex turned first to Ludovico and Giuseppe Toeplitz to finance the enormously extended production programme called for by the agreement, but made a sharp about-turn when it became clear that they would seek to use the new financial arrangements to increase their influence over the company. A power struggle ended with London Films buying out Ludovico Toeplitz for £100,000. Toeplitz recalled that the news of this extraordinary event spread around the European film industry like wildfire. At the UFA studios in Berlin, he even came across a framed photograph of himself with the caption underneath: 'The man who got his money back from Korda'.[3]

Bowrings agreed to support Alex's new film-making programme. In the aftermath of *The Private Life of Henry VIII*, it was not a difficult negotiation. The insurance company was 'highly enthusiastic over Korda', wrote Murray Silverstone jubilantly to Joseph Schenck, and were 'desirous placing Korda on sound financial basis'.[4]

Aware that Toeplitz had active production plans of his own, and would seek separate backing from United Artists, Alex asked that such a request should not be treated sympathetically. Toeplitz, he told Silverstone, had 'walked out on promises he made ... to put up additional capital'.[5] It's impossible to say how much justification Alex had for such a stance, but in the future he would display a consistently possessive attitude to his relationship with United Artists. When it came to other British-based producers, he did not want any competitors.

Alex's ambitions swelled with his success. One of the five films he had agreed to make for United Artists under the original distribution contract had been *Congo Raid*, based on an Edgar Wallace story. It had been conceived as a British Quota film, which, costing about £30,000, was not intended to have worldwide distribution. But after the new agreement, it was transformed into a super-production. Zoltán Korda, the cinematographer Osmond Borradaile and a camera crew set off for Africa in December 1933, where they spent much of the following year. It was a 'trail-blazer', recalled Borradaile, 'the first Korda production to include footage of remote, spectacular and inaccessible locations largely unknown to motion-picture audiences of the day'.[6] Eventually released in 1935 as *Sanders of the River*, its final cost was £149,789.[7] Were it possible to represent a film producer's ambition in terms of production cost, then Alex's had increased by 500 per cent, although the takings failed to rocket in similar fashion, the film doing little more than to break even at the box-office.*

If there was a touch of madness about the *Sanders* expedition – which, in those days before portable film equipment, involved the film-makers driving their 5-ton trucks along dirt tracks – it reflected a new grandeur of conception about London Films. As Alex planned his new programme, he seemed determined to outdo Hollywood. This boldness manifested itself not only in the despatch of camera crews around the world but also in his willingness to tackle adventurous and original themes. Side by side with planned productions that fitted comfortably within the Hollywood mould – a Maurice Chevalier musical, a couple of Douglas Fairbanks swashbucklers – were others that challenged Hollywood's notions of conventional entertainment. Alex commissioned the novelist H. G. Wells to write and assist in a feature production that would attempt no less than to predict the future of mankind, or, as the film would eventually be called, 'the shape of things to come'. He ventured into documentaries. When the zoologist Julian Huxley asked him to back a film about the breeding habits of gannets on a remote island off Wales, he assented, stipulating only that the film should be called *The Private Life of the Gannet*. Most notably of all, he began what would be a life-long association with Winston Churchill.

Alex took care almost as a matter of policy to seek out the titled, the rich and the powerful, but at this time Churchill was none of these things. He had resigned from the Conservative

---

* By September 1938 the receipts were £153,584.

Shadow Cabinet in 1931 and had sailed well into his wilderness years. Alex would have been hard put to find a more unfashionable collaborator. 'He's a little on his uppers at the moment,' he told Toeplitz, 'but he's made of cork and he's bound to bounce up again.' At the time the appointment would have seemed a Quixotic gesture, but Alex had his hidden reasons.

After initial discussions in February, the future Prime Minister was engaged by a contract dated 14 April 1934 as 'an Editor, Associate Producer and Adviser' at a salary of £4,000 per annum.[8] His role was to conceive and supervise a series of five short films that would address the important issues of the day.

At first there was very little for Churchill to do. Two days after the contract date, on 16 April, Alex began to direct *The Private Life of Don Juan*, and he suggested that any substantial work on the short films be put off until the autumn when he would have more time to devote to the series. Churchill did offer to make some comments on outlines of the various ideas, but essentially he was free for the next few months to enjoy his salary without responsibility. It was an example both of the casual way in which Alex ran London Films and the fact that no creative decision could be taken without his full involvement.

The writer Eric Siepmann, who arrived to work at London Films at about this time, was just one of many to feel that, in spite of Alex's gentle manner, he 'was working under a dictatorship . . . and there was the usual curse of dictatorships, the lack of information from the bottom to the top'.[9] Siepmann, who was assigned to the H. G. Wells film with no clear sense of what he was expected to do, recalled sitting outside Alex's office with Fernand Léger, who had been hired by Alex to paint the designs for the Wells film. Both were determined to get from Alex a precise explanation of their roles. 'Il faut voir clair là-dedans,' declared the painter, with a clenched fist.[10] But the resolve as usual proved futile. It wasn't a brutal dictatorship – 'he would disappear into a cloud rather than make it plain that you were useless, idle or a misfit' – but no one was under any doubt that it was Alex who decided everything.

The Scarlet Pimpernel, which began shooting on Tuesday, 7 August 1934, was an example of the total degree of his control.

As soon as he saw the first set of rushes, Alex expressed his dissatisfaction with the sequences that the American director Rowland Brown had shot. Still dissatisfied several days later, he demanded that Brown do some retakes. But when these were done, he was still unhappy. The actor Raymond Massey, who had the role of Chauvelin, recalled that 'Brown announced he would direct the way he liked or walk out. Alex said very sweetly, "Please walk." And he did. Alex himself directed the scene and by two o'clock that afternoon a new director, Harold Young, was watching Alex carry on.'[11]

At the end of the week Alex decided that the script needed to be rewritten, which he did himself over the Saturday and the Sunday. 'The script now all to pieces,' remarked David Cunynghame in his diary.[12] Alex persisted until he had got it right, but in the weeks to come several shooting days were lost as the actors and actresses waited around for yet-to-be-written pages. On Thursday, 30 August, Harold Young, who had previously been London Films' supervising editor, having had his few days' on-the-job training, was considered ready to make his début as a director, but, as Massey recalled, 'the direction throughout the months of shooting remained an unofficial but smooth collaboration', with Alex of course having the last word.[13] Always happy to play the role of *éminence grise*, Alex generously allowed Harold Young to take sole credit for the direction, and the film would launch Young's career as a director in Hollywood.

Alex's triple role as producer, director and scriptwriter seems all the more remarkable when it is appreciated that over the same period, as chief executive of London Films, he was conducting crucial negotiations with the Prudential Assurance Company for financial support. Not only that, but about halfway through the production, Zoltán began filming the interior scenes of *Sanders of the River* on a neighbouring stage; somehow Alex found the time to monitor the progress of this production as well. 'ZK', wrote Cunynghame in his diary when *Sanders* had been on the floor for four weeks, 'had animated discussion in the evening with AK concerning quality of the film shot to date,'[14] and two days later: 'ZK, somewhat shot to pieces by AK, is making very slow progress.'[15]

Alex's authority may have been unquestioned, but in ruling his fiefdom he depended heavily on his two brothers. He counted on their loyalty to undertake any task at a moment's notice, and they were essential pillars in what amounted to a family concern. Perhaps inevitably in articles of the time and in reminiscences since, they were often compared to another famous film trio. Raymond Massey commented:

> Vincent was pretty close to genius, but his artistic skills were sometimes overshadowed by his resemblance to Harpo Marx, both in character and appearance. As Zollie looked like Chico, it was natural to consider how Alex stacked up against the immortal Groucho. I thought there was common ground. The ten-inch Havana cigar, the outsize walking stick, the wavy hair, the elegant but crumpled clothes and the wry humour did suggest Groucho Marx, Hungarian style.[16]

The big difference lay in the leadership that Alex assumed. While it would have been futile for Groucho to attempt to rein in his brothers' anarchic temperaments, even if he had wanted to, Alex was always conscious of the role he had inherited, with the death of their parents, as head of the family. His personal ambition shaded imperceptibly into a determination that the family as a whole should make its way in the world. He habitually made plans for his brothers, even fussing over their appearance like the mother they no longer had, although it was something of an uphill struggle. Zoltán was 'the second worst dressed man in the world', his son David recalled, 'Vincent being the worst dressed'. Once Alex sent Zoltán to Lobb to get a pair of expensive custom-made shoes. He returned home, remembered David, complaining of their discomfort, and took a hammer to them to make the leather soft for his feet. 'They looked like hell, but he didn't care. Alex on the other hand was always impeccable.'

Close as the brothers were, Zoltán would often rail against Alex's pervasive influence and with the passing years seek to strike out on his own. Vincent never similarly challenged Alex. As the youngest child, he was more accepting of the paternal role his eldest brother had assumed, and his position as London Films' art director further encouraged an emotional dependence. For, overseeing the set design of all Alex's productions, he dealt with him on a daily basis.

The producer Norman Spencer, who began to work for the Kordas in the 1930s, recalled a typical day at the studios:

> Vincent would build a set. Alex would then come along and look at it, and he'd say, 'Why have you put a window there?' And the more and more he criticized, the more Vincent became terrified. Alex used to 'kick his arse' all the time and complain and complain. I remember one set where Alex came on and said, 'That's good, Vincent. Listen, that set's very good.' And Vincent, because he was masochistic, said, 'Well, do you think the window should be a little bit more like this – or that?' 'Well, yes, maybe,' said Alex. And before you knew where you were, Vincent had turned him into an angry man again from praising the set to 'Why the hell have you put up a *fooking* set like this?' And then they lapsed into angry Hungarian, and you couldn't follow.[17]

Part of Vincent's masochism lay in his having allowed himself to be hauled away from the South of France in the first place. Over the years he would often complain that he should have remained a painter, but he never took active steps to return to his former life. Alex excused him from the need to grow up. Together, they were able to continue a semblance of the secure family existence they had known as children.

Norman Spencer recalled:

> Vincent was a very simple man. He wore one suit until it wore out, and Alex would say, 'Vincent, you must get another suit,' and he'd send him out to Savile Row to get a lovely tailored suit and in a couple of days it was stained and baggy. I remember a book that Vincent had, a lovely art book I saw at his house. When you opened it, he'd marked a page absent-mindedly with a rind of bacon. Vincent was sloppy-looking, amiable, slow-talking, slow-thinking, under the thumb of his brother, but a great artistic talent.[18]

//

On 5 September 1934 an impatient Churchill invited Alex to lunch at the Savoy to discuss the series of film shorts. It was a meeting that Alex, who was still immersed in *The Scarlet Pimpernel*, might have wished postponed a few weeks, but none the less he agreed that the time had come to launch the series. 'Films of an educational value have long been in demand by the cinema public,' announced a press release on 21 September. 'Mr Alexander Korda, the Managing Director of London Films, hopes in these forthcoming features to make an altogether fresh departure in this important sphere of film production.'[19]

The following topics were provisionally decided upon: 'Will Monarchies Return?', 'The Rise of Japan', 'Marriage Laws and Customs', 'Unemployment' and 'Gold'. London Films, the press release announced, had engaged a special staff of technical experts 'to ensure that Mr Churchill's ideas will be presented in the most vivid, novel and entertaining fashion'. Churchill, for his part, commented: 'I believe that with the pregnant word, illustrated by the compelling picture, it will be possible to bring home to a vast audience the basic truths about many questions of public importance which everyone discusses, with which all are brought in contact, but about which many carelessly take too much for granted.'[20]

But soon afterwards Alex would receive a dispiriting indication of Churchill's box-office value when he was visited by a deputation representing the big cinema circuits. The public, they told him, wanted entertainment, not education; and they, as exhibitors, had a duty to provide entertainment. If Alex persisted with his plan for the shorts, they would refuse to show them.[21] On 24 September, he met Churchill for lunch and suggested that they put the short films on hold for a while, suggesting instead that Churchill could write a feature-length scenario of 'The Reign of George V' to mark the following year's Silver Jubilee. It was a typical Korda somersault in which an initial undertaking turned into an even bolder one. The idea was that Churchill would look back on the significant events in the last twenty-five years of the British Empire. He would provide a historical narrative, and comment on the key social and scientific changes of the period, such as the emancipation of women and the advent of the motor car. It would be a contemporary record for the present generation, but also explain 'to future times the antagonisms and the dominating achievements which have preserved the British people and the British Empire'.[22]

Over lunch Alex and Churchill worked out the basic idea. They then went on to discuss terms which – probably after much brandy and wine had been consumed – were agreed in principle. Churchill would receive an advance of £10,000 against 25 per cent of the net profits. It was an extraordinary bit of impromptu business. In a trice Alex had committed London Films to a costly project, without anyone else in the company even knowing.

Although Churchill had set off on holiday the day after their lunch, a little more than a week later – working on board a yacht somewhere in the Mediterranean – he had finished and sent off a 7,000-word outline to Alex, who cabled back:

> Preliminary outline really splendid and I am most happy about it. Only criticism [is] that in this version politics play too big a part, not leaving enough for technical, industrial and other developments in these twenty-five years. But no doubt this can be easily corrected in final and more detailed version ... Interest in picture tremendous.[23]

With the eye of an expert host organizing the seating arrangements of a dinner party so that his guests should be compatible, Alex appointed as director of the film Anthony Asquith, who was son of the Prime Minister in whose Cabinet Churchill had served during the Great War. When Churchill got back to England, Alex despatched the ever-faithful Lajos Biro off to Chartwell to discuss the script, and also assigned Eric Siepmann to the project. 'I am ashamed to say,' commented Siepmann, 'that many of us scuttled about wondering if Korda realized 'how far Mr Churchill's views had become discredited.'[24]

At the end of November 1934 a crisis materialized that threatened to derail the whole project. As minds turned increasingly to the Jubilee celebrations, the Government proposed commissioning a 'National' film to mark the anniversary year. Worried that official backing for a rival firm would effectively scupper London Films' proposed production, Alex arranged a meeting to discover precisely what the Government had in mind.

Churchill used the occasion to give him a masterclass in

political strategy. 'Personally I think the first step is to produce what the French call a *mise en demeure*,' he advised. 'After a few days' deadlock new possibilities may develop.'

He went on:

> I am quite sure that they would not in all the circumstances do so unfair a thing as to ruin our work at this late hour. If they want to have a National 'Government film' they ought to have thought of it themselves and thought of it long before private enterprise was launched. You should therefore not be at all discouraged if the meeting ends in a complete deadlock, and you should not be in a hurry at this stage to give anything away. If the meeting ends in a complete disagreement with you declaring your intention to proceed on the largest scale, I think that would be quite satisfactory for tomorrow.[25]

The Government eventually agreed to stand aside, but there were other difficulties. Since Alex's lunch with Churchill over two months previously, London Films had become a public company, and the new board couldn't help but notice the extremely risky nature of the venture. The Jubilee year had almost arrived and yet the production hadn't advanced beyond the script stage.

'I am rather embarrassed in writing you this letter,'[26] confessed Alex, as he went on to explain that his 'financial friends' felt that it was unfair, in the event of a financial loss, that London Films should have to guarantee an advance of more than £5,000. Churchill, keen to make the film, accepted considerably reduced terms.

It was an example of Alex's standard approach to business negotiations. First he would clinch a deal with generous terms and then, long after the contract had been signed and the parties fully engaged, proceed to whittle down its provisions as circumstances dictated. Everything was geared to action, to getting films made, but it was a risky strategy which occasionally ended in disaster.

Racing to make up for lost time, Churchill worked on the scenario through December with an intimidating energy. On Boxing Day a finished draft was delivered to the London Films scriptwriter Arthur Wimperis, whom Alex had recently assigned to the project. 'He seemed put out that you should expect him to work at Christmastime,' commented Churchill's private secretary.[27]

On 28 December Wimperis and Anthony Asquith went to Chartwell to discuss the script with Churchill. Another meeting followed in the New Year, and the written summary of the discussions that took place on that day give a sense of the extremely ambitious film that was taking shape. It was to combine a spoken narrative by Churchill with newsreel and dramatic reconstructions of events, of which the following were to form the framework of the story: the Accession; the Irish Problem; Suffragettes; the rise of Labour; the Great War; social advance; inventions and changes. Colour, which was still a largely experimental process reserved for the most expensive and prestigious productions, was to be used wherever suitable, and the essential statistics of the reign were to be expressed by animated cartoons.

Churchill embarked on a second draft of the script, which was ready in time for a meeting with Biro and Asquith on 15 January 1935. He also sent a copy to Alex. 'I look forward to your greatly desired help,' he wrote in an accompanying note. 'I shall be deeply interested to know what you think of the progress made in your absence.'[28] He was more than ever convinced that the Jubilee film could be of great commercial and historic value 'if we all work at it without being distracted by other matters'.

But it was really only because Alex was continually distracted by other matters that the project had progressed as far as it had. Now the second draft script caused him at last to face the fact that Churchill's rather lofty concept of drama was ill suited to the demands of the modern screen. It was Eric Siepmann's task to note down Churchill's ideas for dialogue:

> I remember that the son of a 'nobleman' was involved, and that just before he 'went off to the wars', he became engaged to a young woman of good family. His father, who was, I think, a duke, congratulated him on becoming 'affianced' to a young lady who was beautiful 'and virtuous withal'; and my despair, because we aimed at a popular film![29]

Above. Pusztatúrpászto, a tiny farming village, easily missed, on the Great Plain of Hungary. The house where Sir Alexander Korda was born and lived out his childhood as Sándor László Kellner has long since been demolished.

Right. The Kellner family.

A front yard in the near-by town of Túrkeve, where Alex went to school.
More than a hundred years after his birth, little seems to have changed.

The road west . . .

. . . to Budapest, as spectacular a city as any in Europe.
It was the sort of contrast to encourage a fifteen-year-old boy from
the country to dream on the grandest of scales.

Left. Alex in Budapest, 1916. He had already begun to direct films and was the founding editor of *Mozihét*, Hungary's leading film magazine.

Below. Antonia Fargas, whom Alex would make his wife and, as Maria Corda, build into a big star of the European silent cinema.

Count Alexander Kolowrat-Krakowsky (left) shows off his latest acquisition. As keen a cinephile as he was a motorcyclist, in 1919 he invited Alex and Maria to Vienna to make films for his company, Sascha-Film.

In 1926, the Kordas arrived in Hollywood. Here Maria stands proudly outside the future English knight's castle, at 730 North Rodeo Drive, Beverly Hills.

Mr and Mrs Alexander Korda at home.

Maria's movie career foundered in Hollywood, where she made only two films. The star that Alex would direct most often was Billie Dove. In this photograph he is sitting in Dove's chair, no doubt hoping that Maria won't notice the name.

Alex and Maria together on the set of *The Private Life of Helen of Troy* (1927). The increasing strains between the couple seem all too apparent.

In 1930, Alex returned to Europe, having divorced both Maria and Hollywood – although, in each case, the separation was far from final. This photograph of Alex, Maria and their only son, Peter, was taken during a rare family holiday in Switzerland.

Alex quickly found work directing films for Paramount in France and in 1931 achieved a notable success with Marcel Pagnol's *Marius*. Shown here in front of the Bar de la Marine are (from left to right) Fernand Charpin, Robert Vattier, Raimu, Pierre Fresnay and Orane Demazis.

Alex invited Churchill to dinner on 22 January and, tactfully saying nothing about the script difficulties, told him that it would be impossible to finish such an ambitious film in time for the Jubilee, now only three and a half months away on 6 May. And even if the film were ready, he pointed out, it would in any case have to face the competition of several rival productions.

More saddened than cross, Churchill made some attempt to persuade Alex to change his mind. On 28 January, he wrote:

> Have we not attached an undue importance to the condition that a film on the reign of King George V must be produced in time for the Silver Jubilee in May, and otherwise it has no chance? No doubt it would have been better if we could have produced our film at that date in spite of the many competitors. But if the film were a work of art and a real appreciation of the reign and of the life and history of the nation during these twenty-five eventful years, I believe that it would have a permanent value throughout the British Empire independent of the actual celebrations of the Jubilee.[30]

He wrote again three days later. 'The more I ponder, the more I am sure that you will lose a fine opportunity if you throw away all the work that has been done upon our film simply because it cannot be produced until November.' He went on to argue that Alex would be rendering a 'valuable public service' to go ahead with the film and even hinted that it might be possible to arrange some official help.

His persistence was a measure of the respect he felt for Alex. He believed a really first-rate film could emerge from such a collaboration. But none the less he knew where the line had to be drawn and ended the letter with this final comment: 'I have now said all I shall ever say upon this subject because I am anxious not to press you to decide against your own judgement or do what you think is injudicious out of any consideration for me.'[31]

At the end of March 1935 Churchill's six-month contract to work on the series of short films came to an end. He was free to end his association with London Films. 'However,' as he wrote to his lawyer, 'I like them, and particularly Mr Korda, and hope for a future fruitful collaboration.'[32] The extraordinarily generous

terms he had enjoyed would certainly have sweetened the sentiment. He had continued to be paid under his contract for the
short films after he had stopped working on them and he was
also entitled to £5,000 for the Jubilee film even though it had
been abandoned. In the event the contract for the short films was
renewed and, in place of the Jubilee film, he was invited to advise
on another film about the development of flight. Alex sent him a
script in June 1935. 'I think it admirable,' Churchill replied.
'Indeed it is its excellence which makes criticism and supplement-
ing so difficult.'[33]

This was probably what Alex had intended. He had learned
that it was much safer that Churchill should merely respond to
what others had already done rather than make any serious
efforts of his own. While he admired Churchill enormously and
continued to foster the association, he ceased to regard it as a
seriously productive one. The air film commenced shooting on 25
June 1935, and, after many difficulties and postponements, it
would eventually be released in 1939 as *Conquest of the Air*.
Every significant attempt at flight from ancient times to the
twentieth century was dramatically reconstructed. It was an
extraordinarily ambitious venture in itself, but also in its factual
approach gives some idea of what a Churchill film might have
been like.

Churchill was just one example of how much money Alex
could waste in his fondness for grand projects. In 1934 Alex
would also begin a lengthy and expensive struggle to make
Lawrence of Arabia. Lawrence, who was himself implacably
opposed to the venture, met Alex in early 1935. 'He was quite
unexpectedly sensitive,' he wrote to a friend, 'seemed to understand at once when I put to him the inconveniences his proposed
film of *Revolt* would set in my path.'[34] In spite of having already
paid £3,000 for the rights, Alex agreed not to make the film while
Lawrence was still alive. Very soon after their meeting Lawrence
died, but the project eventually foundered due to a combination
of political objections and financial difficulties.

'My greatest films are those I announced and never made,'[35]
Alex would comment years later, and, besides *Lawrence*, there
were quite a few other such films in 1934: *Young Mr Disraeli* by

Elizabeth Thane; *The Broken Road* by A. E. W. Mason; *Fregoli*, with Charles Laughton and John Barrymore; *The Marshal*, with Maurice Chevalier; *Gordon and the Mahdi*, with Leslie Banks and Paul Robeson; *Pocahontas*, with Merle Oberon; *Joan of Arc*, with Elisabeth Bergner; and, in Alex's words, 'maybe one of the best . . . which I started and never finished',[36] *Claudius the God*, starring Charles Laughton.

No other film company in Britain came close to matching such production plans. Yet London Films was still a tenant, renting space in British & Dominions Studios. It was time to find a home.

9. THE FOXY WHISKERED GENTLEMAN

'To get an overdraft, you do not go to your bank manager for £1,000. You send for your bank manager and say you're considering allowing him to loan you £10,000.'

– Alexander Korda

Alex's great coup of the year 1934 was to gain the backing of the giant Prudential Assurance Company. It was with their millions that he proceeded to build a film empire. It is at this point in Alex's story that the gulf between myth and reality opens up. One version of events is related in Paul Tabori's biography of Alex, as follows.

An Australian businessman called Montagu Marks arrived in London representing the American producers of a film version of *Pagliacci*. He went round to see Alex at his home, where they talked into the early hours. By the time Marks left, he had become an employee of London Films. Having had business dealings with the Prudential Assurance Company on a previous occasion, Marks approached them on behalf of London Films and asked whether they would be interested in investing in the company. The Prudential referred him to their 'expert who knows all about films'.[1] If the expert thought the proposition a sound one, then the Prudential would consider it. A week later Marks met the 'expert', Sir Connop Guthrie, a director of the Prudential Board whose sole experience of the film business turned out to be that he had once arranged a loan for a cinema circuit. Guthrie listened to the proposition and approved. 'He told the Prudential that Korda was an up-and-coming young man and that British films had a fine chance of competing with Hollywood.'[2] After a number of meetings, a deal was finally signed: for the first time in its history, the Prudential had agreed to back British film production.

In his note on sources, Paul Tabori wrote that 'the most important material' concerning the Prudential deal was supplied by Marks himself, 'the architect of the Korda–Prudential cooperation'.[3] But Marks would give a completely different account in a report that survives in the Prudential Archives. Dated 19 July 1934, it is addressed to the 'camera committee' of a company called Gerrard Industries. Gerrard Industries, in which the Prudential had a substantial investment, was developing a new 'Hillman' colour process:

I came to England about three months ago actuated by a desire to ascertain the exact situation with regard to the position of your camera for taking colour pictures, as the information my friends had in America was somewhat meagre. I at once learned of the difficulties you were then having with the Inventor, which difficulties have since been overcome.

Knowing a good deal of the moving picture business in America, I thought I might make that knowledge useful to you on this side, as I immediately perceived that your invention was in its infancy and that in order to make the best that could be gotten out of it, a good deal of time and money would have to be spent on experimental and development work if the invention was to be sold for any large sum of money.

I learned that Gerrard Industries Ltd could not find any such sum as I anticipated necessary to do the business satisfactorily, and after careful study I concluded that experiments to perfect the process would probably occupy two years and would cost at least £150,000.

You must understand that colour photography as applied to moving pictures is an entirely new science, and as such, no person in the world could tell exactly what is required; in fact, such information could only be ascertained by experiments carried out by the best living experts in conjunction with the best living producers. I therefore set myself the problem to find out who was the best man in England to approach on this matter. In examining the situation I started with the fact that up to a year or so ago, moving pictures made in England were not generally accepted internationally. However, there was one man, a comparative newcomer to English films, who had rescued the British film industry from the slough of despond into which it had fallen. That man was Mr Alexander Korda of London Film Productions Ltd. I may say that Mr Korda is the producer of *The Private Life of Henry VIII* (one of the greatest, if not the greatest, worldwide successes the cinema has ever seen), *Catherine the Great* and other films all of which have been a success. Indeed, so high has the star of Mr Korda risen that his new picture *The Private Life of Don Juan*, the taking of which has only been completed in the last week or so and which no one has yet seen, has already secured large advance bookings.

I obtained an introduction to Mr Korda, and by dint of carefully preparing his mind to receive my proposals, I eventually brought him to the point of getting him to pay a visit to the Studio at St John's Wood to see what you had accomplished. Although he did not enthuse over your efforts, I am glad to say he was far-seeing enough to visualize the potential value of your process, and admired certain of the pictures which you had taken. In fact, he was impressed sufficiently to continue the conversations with me.[4]

The report, which went on to outline the terms on which Alex would be prepared to take over the development of the colour process, amounted to an elaborate scam. Far from being an independent agent, Montagu Marks was actually the brother of Kay Harrison, the director of Gerrard Industries chiefly concerned with developing the colour process.

Keen to explore the potential of colour, Alex had examined several rival systems in the early summer of 1934. When Marks visited him in June 1934 to explain the colour process that Gerrard Industries were developing, whatever he may have thought of that process, Alex would have been far more interested to learn that the chief investor in Gerrard Industries was the Prudential Assurance Company. Here, he realized, was an opportunity to obtain finance on a larger scale than ever before. The key was to present London Films to the Prudential not as a supplicant, but as a disinterested party able to offer assistance.

Behind Marks's report lay Alex's hidden hand. It's possible that he even drafted it himself. 'You must understand that colour photography as applied to moving pictures is an entirely new science': that phrase, 'You must understand . . .', was a form of words that Alex himself used repeatedly in written documents.

In a letter dated the same day as the report, Marks wrote to Percy Crump, Secretary of the Prudential, updating him on his negotiations with London Films. He suggested that, with the appropriate reallocation of shares and increase of capital, London Films should take over the development of the colour process, which if brought to a successful conclusion would reap huge rewards. 'I would point out,' Marks concluded,

> that should, for any reason, the colour process prove a failure you would have an equity in a Company which is probably the most successful undertaking in the film industry at the present time, and you would still retain your interest in Gerrard Industries Ltd exactly as at present.[5]

The following day Marks wrote to Crump again. He explained that he had had a further talk with Alex, and 'in order to get his mind on the matter discussed with you last evening, I induced him to put his thoughts down on paper'. The words were carefully chosen to suggest that Alex had far more important things to think about than the prospect of receiving a huge lump of capital from the Prudential, and with his letter, Marks enclosed Alex's notes, which had the tone of a kindly but firm professor:

> [T]he assets of a successful motion picture producing company are and always can be only of two natures: (a) Cash in hand. (b) Films produced or in production.
>
> These films are the real assets and income of the company, as prints drawn from them are circulating all over the globe in about 30,000 cinema-theatres of the world, where the pictures are played either for flat rentals or for a percentage of the takings of the theatre.
>
> I do not think that a motion picture producing company acquires, during its production activities, assets of any other nature. A studio may be built, as we intend to do, machinery and various sorts of equipment are acquired but although

these things represent closer the general idea of the assets, I consider that the real property of a motion picture producing company, or at any rate a great part of its value, must lie in its pictures.

Full of prudence, the letter is couched in the language of the men Alex knew would be looking over Marks's shoulder. Making money out of movies, he wanted to suggest, was as dependable an affair as organizing a share portfolio:

Now it is true that one picture may make less than others, and one country may have worse economical conditions or smaller spending power than another, but as our business is an essentially international business, the risk is always distributed over an immense territory.

The concluding paragraph evoked the image of the care-worn and conscientious chief executive seeking only to secure the future of a great enterprise before allowing other men to bear the burden:

You must understand that so far London Film Productions have been working under very difficult financial conditions. Besides, we have had only two years to form the organization of our production unit. Two years is by no means enough to raise new producers, and so far our financial conditions have not allowed me to burden the company with the salaries of producers or directors of pictures of first quality. However, as soon as finance permits, I intend to endeavour to obtain men of the best reputation and worth to work with me, so that I can then lead a more human life than I have done during the last two years, and in order not to endanger the company's fate with the risk of my temporary or permanent incapacity.[6]

Sir Connop Guthrie, who was a director of Gerrard Industries as well as of the Prudential, became an enthusiastic proponent of the scheme. Alex was 'the outstanding man in British film production', he declared in a memo setting out the reasons for investing in London Films. 'Mr Korda has been good enough to place at our disposal certain facts and figures in regard to his profits,' he continued. 'Quite briefly it may be stated that in the figures given to us it would seem that the profits for the current year are not likely to be less than £125,000 and that figure is likely to be very considerably exceeded during the next two years.' The reason for this, he explained, was the recent agreement with United Artists that provided worldwide distribution for all Alex's films.

In light of such excellent prospects, Alex's request for £250,000 capital to expand London Films was rather modest. Sir Connop Guthrie concluded:

> To summarize the position, it would seem difficult to handle the colour process by itself, and if we have to associate it with an existing firm of producers we could not do better than obtain the practical assistance of Mr Korda. And then if the London Films Limited proves to be as successful as seems likely to be the case, we should merely be underwriting £250,000 of new Capital to obtain a valuable equity in London Films.[7]

Prudential officials began to negotiate with Alex directly. The tone of their memoranda suggest that they regarded the potential association with London Films as a fantastic new way of making money. It was the dot.com investment of its day. One memo assessed the potential profit of the newly capitalized company. It explained that Alex

> thinks in terms of the American Producing Companies and takes Twentieth Century as his model. These people have earned £800,000 in their first year, producing 8 to 10 pictures. It must be remembered that Twentieth Century commenced with all the capital they required. Korda therefore thinks that with adequate capital London Films could do as well in a year when he could produce 8 to 10 pictures, because he has the same distributing agency as Twentieth Century, viz: United Artists.

Without the slightest trace of scepticism, the writer of the memo forecast an annual profit of £840,000 once London Films had achieved a production target of fourteen films a year.[8]

In their haste to do a deal, the Prudential brushed aside any reservations they might have had. When their accountants conducted an investigation of London Films' books, Percy Crump confessed himself to be baffled by the estimate of probable earnings. He wrote to Alex:

There appears to be such a long lag between payments and receipts, that it is very difficult to get beyond intelligent estimates. However, I realize that your business has not been in existence long enough to provide me with such figures as I am used to dealing with in a case where my Company is taking a financial interest, and the figures given to my accountant were the best that could be produced at this time.[9]

So the negotiations continued on to the inevitable cheque for £250,000, which was finally paid out to London Films in October 1934. Sir Connop Guthrie and Montagu Marks duly received a reward for their indispensable support when they were, at Alex's request, both appointed to the board of the reorganized London Films to 'relieve him of a great deal of work which is incompatible with his duty as a producer'.[10]

In Beatrix Potter's *The Tale of Jemima Puddle-Duck*, Jemima falls for the wiles of an elegantly dressed gentleman with a long bushy tail. He was so 'mighty civil and handsome' that she even fetched him sage and onions, only to discover, nearly too late, that she herself was to be the fox's dinner. It was a predicament that the directors of the Prudential would come to have some experience of. On 5 September 1934 they were among the guests of honour when, in the midst of their negotiations with London Films, *The Private Life of Don Juan* opened at the London Pavilion. Costing approximately £115,000, it would take little more than £50,000 at the box-office. It was a sign of the shape of things to come.

10. THE PLAYER

In the autumn of 1934 a series of tests were conducted at British & Dominions Studios on the 'Hillman' colour process. They did not go well. 'Yesterday's tests showed under-development although 60 per cent more light was used than on B&W film,' wrote David Cunynghame in his diary on 19 October. There were also problems of space and time parallax caused by the design of the custom-built camera. So the following summer Alex suggested that London Films should buy into a competing process, Technicolor, and he asked the Prudential to loan the capital necessary to purchase the shares. The original reason for investing in London Films may have just evaporated, but none the less the Prudential readily assented. After all, Alex's personal record had for some time now been one of consistent commercial success.

The year 1934 had ended well, with the success of *The Scarlet Pimpernel*. Costing £143,521 to make, it had been London Films' most expensive production, but the receipts were well over £200,000.[1] After the disappointment of *The Private Life of Don Juan*, London Films seemed to be back on track.

The grand project for 1935 – with a little help from the Prudential – was the building of a studio at Denham in Buckinghamshire. With seven sound stages, it would be the largest and best equipped in Europe. One day, Alex imagined, London Films would be making not a handful of films a year, but ten or fifteen. In the interim, he planned to let out studio space to other production companies. When Alex told the Prudential that he took Twentieth Century as his model he wasn't exaggerating. There were obvious parallels. The production chief at Twentieth Century was Darryl Zanuck. Like Alex, he had started out on the creative side of picture-making and had displayed just as fierce a spirit of independence. Previously a screenwriter for Warner Brothers, he rose to become their head of production, but left after a dispute in 1933. He formed Twentieth Century in partnership with Joseph Schenck and released his pictures, as Alex did, through United Artists. In 1934, Zanuck and Korda were the film industry's most notable success stories, their box-office fortunes seeming to prove the value of the creative and dynamic producer. Denham would in later years come to be regarded as Alex's *folie de grandeur*, but it was the size it had to be to accommodate the expansion of a successful company. If it subsequently seemed a mistake, this was because London Films quickly ceased to be a successful company. But no one anticipated this in 1935.

//

A development that Alex would have watched with as much alarm as satisfaction was Merle Oberon's rocket-like progress to stardom. Her status as a Hollywood star of the first order would make her a powerful asset for London Films, but one extremely difficult to control. Alex felt most comfortable when he could guide his charges along the perilous path of their careers with a paternal hand – both in their interests, which he was wise enough to be able to decide for them, and of course his own. But Merle had neither the necessary deference nor patience to cooperate for long. In *The Private Life of Henry VIII*, as Anne Boleyn, she had appeared on the screen for barely ninety seconds, but, as Ludovico Toeplitz recalled, easily eclipsed the other wives.

> We had placed our money on Binnie Barnes, convinced that her role as the third wife, the most important of the five that appear in the film, would establish her as a star. But the critics talked only of Merle Oberon. More cunning than Binnie Barnes, she had worked hard to win them over.[2]

Dubbed 'the woman who launched a thousand tears', she became almost overnight Britain's biggest film star. Alex quickly loaned her out to appear opposite Charles Boyer in a French film called *The Battle*, then gave her a starring role opposite Douglas Fairbanks Sr in *The Private Life of Don Juan*.

Maria must have had some sixth sense when she first picked her out in the studio canteen, for Merle possessed the intelligence and fierce ambition that Alex had so admired in Maria herself, with the important difference that she also had a sense of restraint, a poise and reserve that Maria would have found difficult to sustain for more than five minutes.

Merle's life was moulded by her determination to bury her impoverished background and to move in the highest society. There's no evidence that at this stage Alex was in love with the woman who would become the future Lady Korda, but his own path from humble beginnings provided the sort of shared experience that would one day draw them closer. With her highly elocuted voice straying somewhere towards the mid-Atlantic, and her rather plastic beauty, she was too manufactured to be considered a natural actress, but she was the perfect material of screen stardom.

Merle was remembered by many people who knew her for her sense of fun, her thoughtfulness and generosity, but these qualities would be suppressed by a ruthless determination to advance her career – a battle in which she realized that sex was an important weapon. During the making of *Don Juan*, she was a regular visitor to North Mimms Park, where Douglas Fairbanks held court during his stay in England. She began to meet the rich and powerful not under Alex's wing but on her own terms. When Joe Schenck, the Chairman of United Artists, visited England in the summer of 1934, he and Merle were soon an item in the gossip columns. As Schenck was the nearest thing Alex had to a boss, the romance would have served as a veiled warning that he was not indispensable. There were others who could advance Merle's career.

The engagement to Schenck was soon broken off, but not until after Merle had secured his agreement that she should come to Hollywood to star opposite Maurice Chevalier in the Twentieth Century film, *Folies Bergère*. 'Europe Sends Us New Vamp,' announced Louella Parsons's column in the *Los Angeles Examiner*. By this time Merle, who had just finished shooting *The Scarlet Pimpernel* in England, was in the middle of an affair with Leslie Howard. 'Both of us scrupulously avoided the subject,' reported Louella Parsons, but she did venture to ask whether the engagement with Schenck had been a publicity stunt. 'We were engaged,' replied Merle, 'but I felt there was too great a difference in our ages, although Joe is a dear and I shall always look upon him as my friend.'[3]

Folies Bergère, on which Merle began work in December 1934, turned out to be an unpleasant ordeal, but an even better opportunity soon presented itself. Samuel Goldwyn, one of the owner-members of United Artists, wanted to cast an English girl in the title role of *Dark Angel*. It was the story of an English soldier who is blinded in the First World War and pretends to be dead so that his fiancée should not have the burden of looking after him; on her wedding day the girl discovers that he is alive and searches for him. Goldwyn's first thought for the part of the fiancée, Kitty Vane, had been the English film actress Madeleine Carroll, and on 18 December 1934 he cabled Murray Silverstone in the United Artists office in London with the request that he should find out if Carroll was interested. 'Ask if she has seen picture and tell her I think it greatest role ever written for a girl. That it made star out of Vilma Banky . . . Please treat this strictly confidential and advise.'[4]

In spite of Goldwyn's request for confidentiality, Merle had soon learned of his plans. Determined to get the 'greatest role ever written for a girl', Merle, who was conveniently on hand making *Folies Bergère* in the Goldwyn studios, began some energetic lobbying. Suddenly she remembered that the whole reason why she had wanted to be an actress in the first place was because she had seen Vilma Banky in the original silent movie when she was growing up in Calcutta.

Goldwyn was won over, but before giving her the part wanted Alex to give him the right to star her in other films as well. He cabled Alex on 11 January 1935:

Because of importance of *Dark Angel*, and the type of productions I would make with Oberon, I feel certain the arrangement would be of great assistance to you in the creation of an important lucrative market for the pictures you will be producing with her in England. While you would be watching her career in England, I would be watching it here and [we] would both benefit through the fact that all her pictures would be released through one company.

A few days later Alex replied that he was unable to accept this proposal. He also asked Goldwyn in future to talk to *him* about any plans he might have for his contract players. 'Your direct dealing makes them very difficult for me to handle.'[5]

Alex had his own plans for Merle. He had agreed with Joseph Schenck that she could appear in a picture a year for Twentieth Century, and other Hollywood producers were making offers. But his reluctance to deal with Goldwyn made Merle only more difficult to handle. Rather than accept his decision as the last word on the matter, she redoubled her campaign. After *Folies Bergère* had finished shooting in February 1935, she set off for New York, where Leslie Howard was appearing on stage in *The Petrified Forest*. In offering Merle the part in *Dark Angel*, Goldwyn had hoped that she might be able to persuade Howard to appear in the film with her. On 13 February, Merle cabled that she had found Leslie 'very keen'. She also took advantage of her sojourn in New York to visit Joe Schenck. 'He seems to be waiting for some reason before settling anything with Alex,' she reported back to Goldwyn. 'Why don't you talk to him?'[6]

Merle's campaign suffered a setback when soon afterwards Leslie Howard broke off his affair with her and returned to his wife. At about the same time *Folies Bergère* opened in New York. Her performance was poor, thought Sidney Franklin, who was to direct *Dark Angel*. He also felt that 'she was too oriental to portray [a] typical English girl'. Making these points in a cable to Goldwyn, he commented: 'The sole reason I thought you were negotiating with Oberon was in order to get the other person with her.'[7]

But Goldwyn waved these objections aside. Somehow the sheer force of Merle's personality and her determination made it inevitable that she would get the part. Even Alex had begun to come around. 'Fully understand your ambition and desire [to] play *Dark Angel*,' Alex cabled her on 5 March. 'Because you insist so strongly I don't want [to] resist, but I don't want to do anything without Joe Schenck whose friendship I value too highly and whose friendship is too important for yourself to do him bad turn.'[8]

The following day Merle cabled back: 'Am sure we would not lose Joe's friendship. He would realize it's for my best.' She added: 'Know Sam has to settle cast very soon. I would die if Carroll got part. So please don't keep him waiting.'[9]

Ten days later, a contract was agreed. Merle would appear in *Dark Angel*, and, in a deal smaller than the long-term arrangement Goldwyn had originally envisaged, Alex agreed to give him the option to use Merle in two more films. Merle had won. Alex wasn't used to people who didn't do what he asked them to do. Merle must have infuriated him with her scheming, but earned his respect. Eventually that respect would turn into love.

Merle impressed everyone with her hard work when shooting on *Dark Angel* began in May 1935. Goldwyn became more and more sure of his initial hunch that he could build her into a big star. And Merle, for her part, admired the smooth efficiency of a first-class Hollywood organization, which contrasted so markedly with the unpredictable progress of London Films. She had, for example, expected to star with Charles Laughton in *Cyrano de Bergerac*, but the starting date kept being put back. Laughton was having trouble with his noses and the scriptwriter was tripping up over the rhyming verse. Alex's productions, through their very novelty and ambition, tended to contain an element of built-in trouble.

Having no starring role that he could immediately offer Merle after *Dark Angel*, Alex had planned to loan her out to Columbia, but Goldwyn objected that to do so would damage her prestige. 'If you have not enough work for her I would be glad to buy the contract from you,' he suggested on 12 June. On the same day Merle sent her own cable. It would be a pity, she felt, to do the Columbia film 'after such a big picture with Goldwyn'. She also expressed her wish, if Alex still had no work for her by then, to make another picture with Goldwyn in November. She was therefore furious when in July Alex loaned her out to Douglas Fairbanks Jr for his first independent production in London, *The*

Amateur Gentleman. The starting date made it unlikely that she would be free in time for the Goldwyn picture.

Her response was promptly to fall ill, although everyone knew what kind of illness it was, and that Goldwyn was the only doctor who might possibly be able to find a cure. Douglas Fairbanks Jr begged Goldwyn to ask her to 'bend every possible effort' as the story had been specially written for her.[10] But Merle's illness suited Goldwyn as much as it did Merle. He cabled back:

Spoke to Oberon. She evidently not in very good health. Insists she must have holiday between now and time she starts next picture. Confidentially she has worked very hard on *Dark Angel* and we had to stop at one time for two days on account of her health and picture not finished yet. Would gladly cooperate with you and do everything I can, but I am afraid I am helpless in this matter.[11]

A week later Douglas Fairbanks Sr approached Goldwyn on behalf of his son, but the answer was still the same. Ever thoughtful, Merle sent a cable to Fairbanks Sr herself:

Thank you for your interest. Sam has talked to me about doing picture for Douglas and for your sake would really like to do it, but doctor has definitely ordered me to rest for next two months. I could not do justice to any picture in my present state and when *Dark Angel* completed will leave immediately for mountains as rest is absolutely essential.[12]

It was a measure of how high her star had risen that she felt confident enough to resist the combined influence of both the Fairbankses.

Alex must have wondered whether he would ever get her back to London, and chose this moment to add to the pile of coded telegrams that had lately been winging their way to Goldwyn in Hollywood:

We are preparing for British market publicity studio news reel. Would be very grateful if you would make with Merle about one hundred feet for this picture. She should speak about the picture she is making for you and then her plans to come back to London and make here an Anne Boleyn picture. Would be greatly obliged if you would personally talk over with her what to do best.[13]

Ever since *The Private Life of Henry VIII* Merle had longed to make a full-length film about Anne Boleyn, but after the wonderful time she had been having in Hollywood, she did not find this particular carrot as appetizing as it had once been. All she really wanted to do was to have a holiday and then to work for Goldwyn.

Goldwyn's response on 24 July was to offer once again to buy Merle's contract, which made Alex only more determined to hold on to it for the time being. Now that her work on *Dark Angel* had finally finished, he made a point of reminding Merle that she was still contracted to London Films, something she had clearly forgotten long ago: 'If you are really ill,' he cabled, 'I absolutely insist your coming back to London immediately.'[14]

Merle's obvious desire to stay in Hollywood was annoying, but none the less the impact she had clearly made there was proof that London Films could groom stars of international appeal. It added to a general sense in 1935 that London Films was about to become a major player. It was already an indispensable part of the United Artists' operation in Britain.

//

All Alex's efforts in 1935 were devoted to building up a big Hollywood-style company. He was convinced that the golden years of London Films were yet to come. The most pressing matter was a new studio. Alex didn't like having to share one, and at the start of the year, after a dispute, had moved from the British & Dominions Studios to the Worton Hall Studio in Isleworth. As he was the exclusive tenant, he could make pictures here as and when he chose. He had found it hard to fit in with B&D's strict schedules, since his 'trial-and-error' method was to work and work away at something until it was right. The first film on the floor at Isleworth was an example. Dissatisfied with *Sanders of the River*, which Zoltán had finished shooting at B&D, Alex had viewed the film over and over again with Zoltán ('the usual acrimonious routine', Cunynghame noted after one such session)[15] and then insisted that several scenes should be reshot and others added.

No expense was spared in adapting Worton Hall to London Films' requirements – a new silent stage was even built – but it was only ever intended as a temporary arrangement. On 14 January, just a week after the move to Isleworth, Cunynghame noted in his diary 'a trip with Marks to Denham to see an interesting suggested studio site'. Three days later, they returned there with Alex and his American architect, Jack Okey, who had designed several studios in Hollywood. Just a forty-minute train ride from Central London, 'The Fisheries' comprised a house and 165 acres of meadows and woodland, but perhaps it was the river snaking through the property that more than anything else sold it to the water-loving Alex. The following month it was announced that Denham would be the site of the new London Films Studios.

At the beginning of June, even before construction of the studios themselves had begun, a set was erected in the grounds at Denham for *Whither Mankind*, as *Things to Come* was at first called. On 7 June a high wind tore through the structure and blew it down. A man was killed and several others injured. With hindsight, it would come to seem like an ill omen.

The American director William Cameron Menzies began filming *Whither Mankind* at Isleworth on 26 March. H. G. Wells's vision of mankind's future after the destruction of civilization in a massive air war had been in pre-production all the previous year, and although Menzies could not have known it then, he would be working on the film well into the next year. It was the super-production of its age, its progress being followed with as much interest as, say, the making of *Titanic* sixty years later. With *Things to Come* Alex planned to take the whole world by storm. He had such faith in Wells that he also put into production another script that Wells had written a few months earlier while he was on holiday in Nice, *The Man Who Could Work Miracles*, the story of a draper's assistant who is given the power to work miracles, but finds that the gift is more trouble than it is worth. The director Lothar Mendes began filming it at Isleworth on 16 April. To do trick shots for both these films, Alex imported a special effects team from Hollywood under the supervision of Ned Mann – who would perhaps inevitably become known as 'The Mann Who Can Work Miracles'. Wells, whose son Frank worked with Vincent as an assistant art director, took a meddling interest in both productions. He was such a familiar sight around the studio in 1935 that a casual observer might have been forgiven for thinking that he ran it, not Alex – which, given the degree to which Alex was ready to defer to a writer he revered, was in a sense true. It was a regard that baffled many people. Richard Norton remembered 'a horrid little man' with 'a small high voice', although he took himself to task for such a low opinion because, he observed anyone Alex regarded so highly had to be of considerable worth.[16]

There were a few people Alex admired so much that he would do practically anything for them. It was his Achilles' heel. On *Things to Come* Wells had effectively taken the role of leading luminary that Churchill had enjoyed the previous year on the ill-fated *The Reign of George V*. Not only did he write the script, he also oversaw every other sphere from the design to the music. But while Churchill displayed a humility in his dealings with Alex and his team of film-makers, constantly seeking their advice on what was practical, Wells behaved with a breath-taking conceit. In a letter to the composer Arthur Bliss, he complained of the film-makers' conventional attitude to music: 'They say – it is the Hollywood tradition – "We make the film right up to cutting. Then *when* we have cut, the musician comes in and *puts on his music.*" I say "Balls!" '[17]

But such arrogance had its place in the brave new world Alex was building in 1935. London Films was now a magnet for the very best film-makers in the world. As a Hollywood producer observed a few months later,

Alexander Korda can stand on the corner of Hollywood Boulevard and Vine Street and wave a checkbook and all our actors and actresses, stars and featured players, and cameramen and technicians and writers and directors would desert our studios and pour around him from all over town and follow him just like the way the rats of Hamelin ran after the Pied Piper.[18]

The difficulty Alex was having in getting Merle to return to London suggests that this was something of an exaggeration, but none the less it was an indication of Alex's standing.

The only thing that was really capable of humbling him that year was the English weather. For much of August and September thick clouds blotted out the sun, and many shooting days on the huge *Things to Come* set at Denham were lost. The air documentary *Conquest of the Air* was similarly blighted, the weather occasionally making not only filming but also flight impossible. On 14 September high winds grounded the Wright Brothers' Kitty Hawk. Zoltán was told to shelve the film and get on with planning *Lawrence of Arabia* instead.

It was a good time to be out of the country and for much of these two months Alex was in Hollywood, his first visit there since he was sacked by Fox five years previously.

A little bit of good fortune that summer had immeasurably strengthened Alex's position. In June Joe Schenck merged Twentieth Century Pictures, with the Fox Film Corporation, resigned as chairman of United Artists and sold his stock in the company. No longer able to distribute Twentieth Century films, United Artists were in desperate need of product, and also anxious that Alex, who was receiving attractive offers from elsewhere, should not switch to a competitor once he had completed his sixteen-film contract. Alex did what he could to suggest that this might be soon, exaggerating the number of films he expected to complete in the course of 1935. He also made a point of keeping on good terms with Joe Schenck, since United Artists' fears that he might join Twentieth Century-Fox made him seem all the more valuable.*

Precisely how valuable became clear when United Artists began negotiations for Alex to become an owner-member of the company. The new chairman of United Artists, Dr A. H. Giannini

---

* Goldwyn, who was in the middle of a long-running feud with Schenck, was particularly worried about this possibility. 'Don't believe Korda would do deal with Fox as he anxious be in big league and practically expressed himself to that effect,' Murray Silverstone reassured him in a telegram dated 29 July 1935.

(known to his colleagues as just 'the Doctor') negotiated a deal that required Alex to distribute his films exclusively through United Artists for a ten-year period, a minimum of twenty films to be made during the first five years. At the same time Alex was given a unit of stock for $650,000, which he was allowed to pay for by annual instalments over the next three years.

The trip to Hollywood was for the public announcement of this extraordinarily generous deal. The return of the conquering hero was an irresistible story for the press. 'This summer Alex revisited Hollywood for the first time since his disgrace,' wrote W. B. Courtney in a long article for Collier's, 'and there were genuflections by the greatest and hosannas from the highest . . . They're calling this fellow Alexander the Great – but he's Napoleon, too, if you ask me. He's just about the czar of the international film business today.'[19]

With what would have seemed a stylish touch then, Alex arrived in Los Angeles by aeroplane, to be met by Merle Oberon and his host during his Hollywood stay, Samuel Goldwyn.

On 2 September he attended a dinner held in his honour by the Academy of Motion Picture Arts and Sciences. All the leading producers, directors and writers were there. Darryl Zanuck, who gave the address, joked that Alex was proof that most of the assembled company were unnecessary. 'You had producers, supervisors, and all possible assistance when you were here five years ago and ended up without a job. You went to England without any of them, and now come back five years later and get a testimonial dinner.'[20]

On 3 September Alex attended the opening of *Dark Angel* at Grauman's Chinese Theatre. Merle herself was travelling on the *Santa Fe Chief*, on her way to the première in New York and then – at last – London. The following day Goldwyn cabled her aboard the train:

> The reviews this morning are triumphant . . . It is acclaimed as the great picture of the year. Korda told me last night in the presence of Lubitsch and Chaplin and a number of others that he did not expect a performance from you like last night for at least two or three years. The talk about the change in your screen personality is something that will make history.[21]

Alex sent his own cable back to his publicity chief, John Myers, in London:

> Merle Oberon's success in *Dark Angel* is tremendous. After this film she ranks with first four stars in America which is marvellous considering how few pictures and what a short time she did this magnificent career. I want you to make for her the greatest possible reception. We all have to be very proud of her achievement as she was with us from the very beginning.[22]

On the afternoon of Thursday, 5 September 1935, a special meeting of the United Artists board was convened to ratify the agreement with Alex that had been signed two days previously and to elect him to the board. Afterwards, an official statement was released to the press:

> The board of directors of the United Artists Distributing Corporation announced that Alexander Korda, chairman of London Films of England, has been elected a member of the board.
>
> It was also announced that Korda has been made an equal partner in United Artists and an owner-producer, joining Miss Pickford, Chaplin, Fairbanks and Goldwyn in the ownership of the corporation.[23]

If you had to choose one moment as representing the pinnacle of Alex's fortunes, then perhaps that Thursday teatime in Hollywood was it. Never again would he seem so full of fantastic promise, his record so unblemished by failure. 'British capital', reported the *Los Angeles Herald and Express*, 'had made its first invasion of the United States.'[24]

On Thursday, 26 September, Alex arrived in Southampton aboard the *Berengaria* to find the press waiting for him on the quayside (no doubt summoned there by his publicity chief John Myers). He proceeded to regale them with delicious plums. 'As a result of this deal we shall get more money from America for our pictures,' he told them. Mary Pickford, Samuel Goldwyn, Charlie Chaplin and other United Artists producers were all planning to produce films at the new studios in Denham, where twenty films would be made a year. Marlene Dietrich had been signed to make a film there the following spring, and Alex had also engaged several famous Hollywood directors. 'We found the atmosphere in Hollywood rather different from what we expected. We were very welcome, and there was a genuine desire on the part of all the big executives to help British pictures.'[25] On Saturday, 28 September, the staff of London Films held a 'welcome home' party for Alex at the Savoy and a special presentation was made to celebrate his triumph. The following day David Cunynghame went into the Grosvenor Street office to find Alex there running a rough cut of *The Ghost Goes West* and a sequence from *Things to Come*. It was perhaps some attempt to return to earth after the glories of the last few weeks, but he seemed 'well satisfied'.[26]

A few days later, choosing the psychological moment perfectly, Alex asked the Prudential for extra finance. The Denham studios, he explained, would probably cost £375,000 instead of the original estimate of £250,000, and, as a result of the visit to Hollywood, the programme of films to be made in the course of the following year would be considerably expanded. With things going so well, the Prudential could hardly have refused – everything seemed set fair for a bonanza once Alex was properly set up in his new studio. Rarely could they have granted what was then a huge loan of £500,000 with such lack of concern.

11. THE BUBBLE BURSTS

At the beginning of 1936 Britain was in the grip of a particularly severe winter. The building of the new studio at Denham was considerably held up. Then, just as the weather began to improve, in the early hours of 17 March a fire tore through two of the newly erected sound stages, destroying the roofs and sound-proofing. Over ten fire engines battled to stop the flames from spreading. The opening of the studio, which had been scheduled for the spring, was delayed by four months.

Alex was never one for half-measures, so perhaps it was inevitable that when bad luck came it did so in one unending stream.

First there was *Things to Come*. Only the deadline of a première at the Leicester Square Theatre on 21 February seemed to provide the necessary incentive to bring shooting to a close within a calendar year of it having commenced, but two units working every day including Sunday were required to achieve this feat. By the last day of the production, on 13 February, the budget had swelled to £240,000, making it easily Britain's most expensive film.

Its opening was regarded as a major landmark for the cinema. Never before had such a bold attempt been made to turn the medium to serious purpose. A seasoned professional, Murray Silverstone, sent the reviews to Alex's United Artists' colleagues in two separate telegrams. First the good news:

Picture shown last night press ... *Daily Herald* says is astounding piece of work, paralysing in its prophecies, noble in conception, magnificent in achievement. In many respects most momentous thing camera ever done. Acting brilliant.

Its thrilling force takes breath away. Not for fraction second is it possible take eyes from screen and only of great films can this be said. *Daily Express* says screen's most remarkable wizardry. Acting of high order. Film amazing technical curiosity everyone will want to see. *Daily Telegraph* says Alexander Korda has once again made film history. *Things to Come* makes stories of future such as *Metropolis* look like quota quickies . . .[1]

Then the bad news:

Have cabled you separately for sales executives. To get complete analysis press reviews, take other cable, which absolutely correct, and add following: *Daily Herald* says is not entertainment in accepted fan sense. *Daily Express* says women in cast cold, do not arouse sympathy. *Daily Telegraph* says Wells' moral lessons shade too thoroughly rubbed in and may affect chances at box-office. *Morning Post* says as entertainment is vulnerable at number points. *Evening News* says women will deride *Things to Come*. Men will like it because its appeal is more to intellect than to emotions. *Evening Standard* says not in ordinary meaning an entertaining film.[2]

On the same day, Alex's head of publicity, John Myers, also sent a telegram to Alex's United Artists partners, which naturally gave just the good news: '*Things to Come* received greatest critical rave since talkies,' he began.[3]

Given the extraordinary coverage the film had received, it would have been surprising if *Things to Come* hadn't attracted a large audience, and the box-office receipts of £130,000 would have been a bonanza for most British films of the time, but it was a disaster for a film that cost nearly twice as much to make.[4]

Things to Come was an example of Alex allowing personal enthusiasm to overwhelm his common sense. He believed that the success of a film ultimately depended upon the creative vision of a writer. From this it was an easy step to imagine that a great writer equipped with the necessary technical assistance would produce a great film. Beneath all Alex's sophistication and worldliness lay this naiveté, which had caused him, with a touching faith, to give H. G. Wells virtual *carte blanche*.

'Alexander Korda offered to make a film which was, as far as humanly possible, exactly as I dictated,' recalled Wells soon after the film came out. 'The film has emerged spiritually correct, despite the fact that it now embodies many alterations suggested by Alexander Korda, William Cameron Menzies, and a score of other people.'[5]

Things to Come can seem rather comic today, perhaps because nothing dates quite so quickly as an earlier age's vision of the future. It contains many extraordinary sequences, including a depiction of the Blitz five years before it actually happened. But the overall impression is of a pretentious and dull film.

Raymond Massey, who had agreed to play the dual leading roles of John and Oswald Passworthy, had admired Wells's original book, but was appalled when he read the script. 'Every trace of wit, humour and emotion, everything which had made the novel so enthralling, had been cut and replaced with large gobs of socialist theory ... The novel's realism had vanished from the screenplay in which we delivered heavy-handed speeches instead of carrying on conversation. Emotion had no place in Wells's new world.'[6]

Even Wells would soon come to recognize its failings, although with bad grace – considering the lengths to which Alex had gone to please him – he would blame them on his collaborators. '*Things to Come* isn't right,' Wells admitted in a letter to a friend. 'It's confused, incoherent, hurried at the end, muddled and badly directed.'[7] While he admitted that he was partly to blame, he considered that he had been 'considerably let down in the production'. Still, he concluded wrongly, 'it looks like being a box-office success, I've learned a lot from it and please God (or not) I'll do better next time.'

This turned out to be one of his less accurate prophecies. *The Man Who Could Work Miracles* had actually been completed many months previously, but when Alex viewed a rough cut in July 1935 he was 'manifestly disappointed'.[8] He ordered retakes, directing many of them himself, but still he was dissatisfied. Worried that its early release might have a detrimental effect on the much more important *Things to Come*, he shelved it for a while.

This shelving of films was a practice to which Alex would often resort. In *Charmed Lives* Michael Korda suggests that it was an accounting trick:

> Unfinished films, finished films that were too bad to be released, and scripts and literary properties that would never be made could all be carried on the book as 'assets'. Thus every disaster could be used to improve the balance sheet, and the larger the disasters, the rosier the prospects of the company would seem.[9]

But the principal motivation was the much more laudable desire to make a film as good as it could possibly be. As long as it was on the shelf, there was always the chance of improving it.

So, in the case of *The Man Who Could Work Miracles*, once the première of *Things to Come* was safely out of the way, Alex took it off the shelf and looked at it once more in March 1936.* He was even more despondent about it in the light of the mixed notices for *Things to Come*, but none the less struggled to redeem the film. On 4 April he ran it with H. G. Wells, then on 22 April began to direct some retakes and added scenes, soon afterwards delegating the task to his assistant director Geoffrey Boothby. On 4 July a preview was held in Southend. Alex was pleased with the response and the film opened the following month, only to receive bad reviews and to fare extremely poorly at the box-office. But at least Alex had done everything he could to give it a chance of success.

'I am more than a little disillusioned with films,' wrote Wells of his recent experiences with the medium.

> They *could* be magnificent art, but all the art has still to be learnt and the temptation to go back to writing books with nothing between you and your reader but the printer – no

---

* Another film to come off the shelf that year, although it would go back on it again, was *Conquest of the Air*. In April, Alex hired the documentary producer Cavalcanti to prepare some new sequences for the film. But the two men soon fell out, and so *Conquest of the Air* went back on the shelf again.

producers, directors, art directors, camera men, actors and actresses, cutters and editors – is almost irresistible.[10]

As far as Alex was concerned, Wells would have no choice. Never again would he allow a writer to have the authority over a production that Wells had enjoyed; it had been an expensive lesson to learn.

//

In a difficult year, perhaps the worst shock was the company balance sheet of 2 May, which revealed a loss of £330,842. London Films needed an immediate loan of £250,000 if it was to continue. But in a letter dated 14 May 1936, the Prudential refused to advance any more money unless the company was reorganized to their satisfaction. There was no sensible system of financial control and accountability. Alex had been left free to do more or less whatever he wanted. Henceforward, any important decisions would have to receive the approval of an executive committee. Alex's role was to be clearly defined as that of chief of production, with the responsibility for administration and finance left in the hands of C. H. Brand, a director nominated by the Prudential.

In a letter dated 18 May, Alex wrote to express his agreement with the Prudential's suggestions but also his disappointment at the criticisms which he felt had been levelled against him personally. Defending London Films' record, he wrote:

I realize that being the head of the company means that I must accept full responsibility for whatever may happen, but I am sure that with your wide business experience, you would not overlook the tremendous and overwhelming difficulties with which we have had to contend in the building up of a company like L.F.P. Ltd. In the short space of two years, to have built Studios such as we are in the process of building now and at the same time to produce motion pictures, to fight against keen foreign and domestic competition and to lay the foundation of a new industry in this country has been no easy task.

I must again impress upon you that however difficult the position has been and however dejected I might sometimes feel about things, I cannot feel ashamed of the job I have tackled in the last two years. We have a Studio which is as good, if not better, than any Studios in the world. The reputation of this company, artistically, is as high as any Company, not only in Great Britain but in the world. It has been a great struggle for the last two years but now I feel that in our new Studios, we are working under circumstances which, although far from easy, are at least as good as those under which other companies are producing their pictures.[11]

Alex then addressed the conditions that the Prudential had laid down. He challenged just one of them. While he was only too pleased to be relieved of the burden of finance and administration, he could not fulfil the duties of chairman and managing director by confining himself strictly to production matters. It was an issue of such importance that he threatened to resign over it:

What you have asked me to do now, as I see it, is something like this – to carry on as Chairman and Managing Director of the Company but denying me, at the same time, every means of discharging this responsibility. It has come as a great surprise to me that my function in London Film Productions Limited is not, in your opinion, clearly defined. I have always thought that the building up of this company, to be not only the nominal, but the actual head of this Company, is the job which I have always been required to undertake . . .

I started this undertaking from little or nothing and if you will disregard or set aside the momentary difficulties of the Company, I hope you will agree that I have accomplished a task of which nobody need feel ashamed. Nobody knows better than I, however, that the job is only half completed, that my chance to finish it must be given me *now*; that only now can I say that in the next few months, with hard work and endurance, I will be able to achieve from London Film Productions Limited and our Studios a real and proud goal . . . Now, with our object almost achieved, with success almost within our grasp, after putting every demand of yours into effect, you ask me to become only the nominal head of the Company, but nevertheless, to carry the responsibilities of Chairman and Managing Director. To this, I am afraid, I cannot agree. If it be your desire, I am willing to resign my Chairmanship and

Managing Directorship and so give you an opportunity to appoint a person who has your confidence as without this I am unable to discharge the duties connected with these or to remain with the Company in any capacity whatsoever. You must realize how difficult it is for me to tender my resignation after years of hard struggle just before my aim has been achieved and just at the time when I am absolutely sure that a few more months' work, and the finishing of this year's programme will put the Company in an unquestionably strong position.[12]

But otherwise Alex behaved as if resignation was the remotest possibility. Two days later, on 20 May, after what David Cunynghame described as a stormy board meeting, he signed the official response of London Films' Board of Directors to the conditions that the Prudential had outlined for a further loan:

We are pleased to assure you that the company will in future be run on ordinary business lines, and in view of the reorganization which has already taken place and the adoption of the various conditions now laid down by you, we are confident that any errors and omissions of the past will not recur . . .[13]

On 3 June, the Joint Secretaries of the Prudential, Ernest Lever and Percy Crump, wrote to inform the London Films' Board of Directors that the £250,000 loan would be granted. They followed it up with a delicately phrased letter to Alex himself which was intended to be a diplomatic rap over the knuckles but also an assurance of continued support. While they held all the directors of London Films to be responsible for the company's parlous financial state, 'naturally any criticism directed towards the Board as a whole must fall in large measure on the Chairman and Managing Director'. None the less, their wish that he should continue 'to be actively engaged as the leading personality in the Company was proof of their confidence in him'.[14]

The reality, which the Prudential sensed but couldn't quite bring themselves to grasp was that, whatever the niceties of company protocol, of board meetings and collective decision-making, finally Alex *was* the company. At almost every was impossible to disentangle the company and the individual. When United Artists, for example, signed a distribution contract level, it with London Film Productions, it was a condition of the contract that Alex should personally supervise all the films to be made under the agreement. When United Artists sold a unit of stock to London Films, it was sold to 'London Film Productions *and* Alexander Korda'. In the cinema, the famous Big Ben trademark of London Film Productions may have come first, but immediately afterwards followed 'Alexander Korda Presents . . .' Audiences didn't go to see films made by London Film Productions, they went to see films made by Alexander Korda. It was why he knew that the Prudential would not ask for his resignation.

Alex was renowned for his powers of persuasion, but in deciding to bail out London Films on this occasion, the Prudential were simply responding to cold reality. To withhold extra finance would have been to pull the plug on an investment just as the structural changes that they had agreed as necessary to build a prosperous, profitable company had been put into place. Indeed, the official letter accepting the Prudential's conditions for extra finance was one of the last Alex signed in London Films' old offices in Grosvenor Street. Just a few days later, on 25 May 1936, the company moved into its new home at Denham Film Studios.

One of the Prudential's conditions had been that the new Executive Committee of the company should hold regular minuted meetings. The first such meeting took place at Denham on 27 May. As Alex, the chairman and managing director, looked down the length of the boardroom table, he would have encountered a formidable trio of watchdogs ready to bark their disapproval – C. H. Brand, the new finance director appointed by the Prudential; Ray Mortimer, an observer of the proceedings on behalf of the Prudential; and Sir Connop Guthrie, the Prudential's original nominee on London Films' board. Alex had little choice but to play the part of a man who had turned over a new leaf, and in the weeks that followed he adopted the manner of the most over-zealous executive that one could hope to meet, circulating efficiency charts and announcing ever more radical economy drives. But somehow subsequent events always seemed to render these plans meaningless.

The first London Films production to go on the floor at Denham was an example. At the third executive meeting, on 10 June, Alex estimated the budget for *Rembrandt* at £112,200, although he 'thought it would be possible to reduce the total figure by £4000 in which case the actual cost of the picture would be reduced to £108,200'.[15] It eventually cost £142,888. It was some time before it became obvious, but the reorganization that the Prudential had demanded amounted to little more than rearranging the deck-chairs on the *Titanic*.

II

The trouble with film production, as Alex knew but refrained from telling the Prudential, was that it was a fundamentally unpredictable business. Alex had announced that he *might* go ahead with *Rembrandt* only in March 1936, just a few weeks before the production went on the floor. In his diary Cunynghame would criticize 'this lack of a definite plan',[16] but Alex's hesitation was to a large extent caused by the difficulty of coping with his extremely nervous star, Charles Laughton. His original plan had been to begin production at Denham with Laughton in *Cyrano*. The previous year the actor had worked closely with the scriptwriter, Humbert Wolfe, and made prodigious efforts to get into the character, but – as was always a terrible risk with Laughton – eventually succumbed to a crisis of self-doubt. Alex had hoped that after a break in Hollywood to make *Mutiny on the Bounty* for MGM, Laughton would return to London with renewed confidence. He had even gone to the lengths of making a short film especially for Laughton's wife Elsa Lanchester called *Miss Bracegirdle Does Her Duty*, which the American cameraman Lee Garmes directed in January 1936. The idea was to make Laughton feel at home. As Lanchester put it, 'I was just a human shoe horn.'[17] But the actor felt no more confident, and

Alex finally bowed to the inevitable. 'Last night AK decided with Laughton to release him from *Cyrano*,' noted Cunynghame on 5 February. 'Cannot say that I was surprised!'

Alex's respect for Laughton's talent had caused him to put up with his notoriously difficult temperament far beyond the point at which other producers would have run out of patience, but rather than waste any more months on *Cyrano*, he decided to switch to another subject with which Laughton would feel more comfortable. He was duly reassured to find that *Rembrandt* did indeed capture Laughton's imagination, but it was not something that could possibly have been predicted in a business plan.

While Carl Zuckmayer wrote the script, the actor embarked upon his usual exhaustive research, buying 'an endless number of books and reproductions of the paintings . . . in an effort to find out just one more little detail about Rembrandt's life'.[18] Alex encouraged the obsession. On 8 May 1936 he travelled to Paris to watch Laughton appear in a gala performance for the Comédie Française. The day afterwards, on the spur of the moment, the two drove off in Alex's car to Holland, where they spent a couple of days soaking up the atmosphere.

But good relations evaporated shortly before filming began on 2 June 1936, when Laughton suddenly presented a last-minute ultimatum that he would not appear in the film unless his wife Elsa Lanchester could play the part of Rembrandt's mistress Hendrickje Stoffels.

As filming proceeded, there were the usual delays occasioned by Laughton's painstaking efforts to pin down his character. The presence in the cast of Gertrude Lawrence, who played Rembrandt's housekeeper, Geertje Dirx, did not help. While Laughton solemnly rehearsed his lines over and over again, the set rang with laughter as the comedienne entertained the other actors and the film crew with an inexhaustible supply of funny stories and anecdotes. Elsa Lanchester recalled:

> It was very painful for Charles. He had a screen put around the set to keep away the chattering and flittering of her voice. But Korda hadn't much respect for needed peace and quiet. He preferred to be on the other side of the screen with

Gertrude Lawrence most of the time, except when the camera was rolling or near rolling.[19]

Lanchester's recollections have the rather sad tone of someone who was never told the straight truth by either her husband or Alex, but none the less knew that she was unwanted:

> Charles and I wanted to be together and the only way seemed to be acting in the same picture. Korda fought quite hard *not* to help us and, indeed, the situation activated his fairly open criticism of me. So when Charles and Korda were together planning *Rembrandt*, I could only wonder what they said about me. Okay, she can play Hendrickje Stoffels – after all, she doesn't come on until the second half.[20]

The bad feeling perhaps led to – and was certainly intensified by – Laughton's declaration that, in defiance of his contract, *Rembrandt* would be the last film he would make for Alex. For most of the production Alex was in the awkward situation of having to coax a performance out of Laughton while at the same time contemplating whether to sue him for breach of contract.* No wonder he preferred to listen to Gertrude Lawrence's jokes.

'Feeling between Laughton and AK is running pretty high,' noted Cunynghame on 15 August. But this tension between director and star, which could so easily have been destructive, seemed instead to galvanize their efforts. *Rembrandt* represented the high point in their short partnership, even if this was not much appreciated at the time.

The film received generally respectful reviews, but the one that over the years has carried the most authority was written by Graham Greene in the *Spectator*:

---

* Minutes of the London Film Productions Executive Committee for 3 July 1936: 'The Chairman reported on conversations which he had had with the Solicitor acting for Mr Charles Laughton from which it would appear that Mr Laughton intended to leave the service of the Company as soon as REMBRANDT was finished and the Chairman felt that if the Company was to restrain Mr Laughton from so acting it would be necessary to commence proceedings.' (Prudential Archive, Box 2354.)

[The] film is ruined by lack of story and continuity: it has no drive. Like *The Private Life of Henry the Eighth*, it is a series of unrelated tableaux. Tableau One (a far too emotional beginning): wife of famous painter dies while he is being feasted by the burghers. Tableau Two: famous painter loses, by his artistic experiments, his bourgeois clients. Tableau Three: but already I begin to forget how these unrelated scenes follow one another. From the dramatic point of view the first might just as well be the last and the last first. Nothing is led up to, nothing is led away from.[21]

In this rather dogmatic criticism, Greene was applying the standards of the well-constructed thrillers for which he had begun to make a name. *Rembrandt* certainly does take the form of a series of tableaux, but they are not unrelated. They depict the artist at different stages on a path from fame to obscurity. The 'drive' and 'continuity' of the film lie in Rembrandt's struggle to be true to himself as an artist. His step-by-step retirement from the world is reflected in the canvases on which we see him work. At the beginning of the film, he reluctantly accepts a commission to paint the officers of the Civic Guard; it is this sort of engagement with worldly affairs that has made the painter famous. In the middle, he paints David playing music for King Saul; the future king's melody soothes the soul of a man who has taken his fill of worldly pleasures and found only torment. The sequence marks a transition from the material world to the spiritual. At the end, Rembrandt paints only himself. He is an artist, a human being in isolation; all adornment has been stripped away.

As in the case of *The Private Life of Henry VIII*, a particular historical figure becomes representative of a general human dilemma. *Rembrandt* depicts the struggle that any artist, writer, actor and – perhaps above all – film-maker must face. The film was both allegorical and deeply personal. The artist, who follows his star and resolves to make no compromises, was the sort of person that Alex would have liked to have been, if only he could have renounced his worldliness. He never did, but he was none the less intimately acquainted with what Rembrandt must have suffered in his attempts to do so.

'You know how an artist has to beg at court,' rails Rembrandt. 'An artist has to smile and smile and keep on smiling. "May I humbly crave the honour of being presented to His Royal Highness. I am Rembrandt van Rijn." "Oh, yes. I remember you now. Wasn't there some scandal about the picture you painted for the civic guards. I hope you have learned how to behave properly."'

Alex's own refusal to behave properly dated back to when he stopped saying yes in Hollywood. The whole of his subsequent career had been an attempt to go his own way, rather as Rembrandt had done.

At moments in the film Alex seems consciously to rub away at the allegorical line between Rembrandt's situation and his own. 'Paint the sort of pictures people want nowadays,' Rembrandt's housekeeper urges him. 'Look at Flink,' she continues, mentioning a successful painter who had once been an apprentice of Rembrandt. 'Now he owns a carriage and pair. Why? Because he paints high-class pictures and gives the people what they want for their money.'

But a picture about a painter turned out to be not what the people wanted for their money. With receipts of only £92,168, *Rembrandt* was yet another box-office failure.[22] Was Alex really that surprised? It was an extraordinarily brave subject that most producers would have shunned as incapable of ever being more than a profitless *succès d'estime*. But the opening of Denham marked the moment when Alex was above all going to resist compromise. The worldly film producer was once again the young man from the country who had come to the city longing to be a great writer.

II

Weary of the town, Rembrandt van Rijn returns to the mill in the country where he grew up. If he cannot make his way as a painter, at least here he might find some peace and live his life properly. Trudging across snow-covered fields, he arrives to be greeted by his father and brother, and sits down with the words, 'Black bread, peasant's bread, I am home.' But he discovers that he has become a stranger. Unable to slip back into its way of life, he no longer belongs in his little village, and reluctantly he returns to the city.

Alex had already imagined such a scene long before he filmed it at Denham. One of the stories he had written as a seventeen-year-old in Budapest began:

> One day I found myself at home. It was snowing peacefully and everything was quiet. My family were sitting in the large dining-room when I entered. My mother – a peaceful, meek old woman – sat by the fireplace knitting. My aunt sang as she wove a tapestry. My father was writing a letter to me, his grown-up son. And I, a pale little boy, sat at my aunt's feet listening to her sad songs.
>
> Only my child self, at home with his little life, seemed to notice that I had entered the room. He sensed that the sad man who had opened the door so quietly and looked at them with tears in his eyes would be his adult self. Outside it went on snowing, concealing the blackness just as the peace within covered up the blackness of life.
>
> I wanted to cry because everything was so perfect here . . .[23]

After painting an idyll of a contented family life, the story ends with the shattering of the dream:

> I would stay there for ever and nor would I ever tire, in that quiet house, among those quiet people, of saying every lunch-time, 'Give us this day our daily bread . . .'
>
> But now a waiter shakes my shoulder. I raise my tear-stained eyes and look around with dread at having to return to my cheap and mean little rented room.[24]

A quarter of a century later, Alex was still tormented by conflicting impulses, a fierce ambition struggling with a desire for tranquillity. The great difference for the adult Alex was that like Rembrandt he had come to know fantastic success, but still there was a sense of emptiness. Like the old painter standing before his self-portrait, he recognized all his achievements as just one more conceit: 'Vanity of vanities – all is vanity.'

12. TWENTY-FOUR HOURS A DAY

When the writer Humbert Wolfe was commissioned by Alex to translate Edmond Rostand's play *Cyrano de Bergerac* into English, he was bemused to meet a man who, apart from continuously smoking a cigar, did nothing that could be identified as typical of the film world.

'I cannot believe that Benes is right in supposing that the Germans will go off gold. What do you think?' asked Alex as Wolfe stepped into his office for the first time.[1]

In the weeks to come the translator would find himself even more surprised by the continuous respect that Alex would show for the writer's craft. Never before had he been treated with such generosity. 'Advice, praise and conferences were lavishly at my disposal,' he recalled.[2] His assignment turned out to be an extremely difficult one, as he struggled both to render the rhyming couplets of the French into natural English and to adapt himself to the demands of the new film medium. Yet Alex continued to show a 'habitual gentleness', with any criticism always couched in as positive and as encouraging terms as possible. The sympathy perhaps stemmed from the fact that Alex had been a writer himself.

Alex was a rather startling combination of artist, workaholic businessman and *bon viveur*. His whole attitude to life was based on lavish consumption. Just as he had to dine in the most expensive restaurants or wear the most expensive suits, so he had to employ the most expensive writers, directors, actors and so on. It was a reflection of the high plain on which he chose to live his life – a life in which there was little discernible line between his business and his private interests.

In the wake of *The Private Life of Henry VIII* Alex bought a large house in Avenue Road, near Regent's Park. Evenings there would often evolve into lengthy meetings at which future plans would be discussed into the early hours. 'Korda had a habit of working day and night,' recalled Richard Norton.[3]

In doing so, he made little allowance for the frailties of his colleagues. 'His extraordinary energy often prevented me from getting the sleep I physically needed,' commented Ludovico Toeplitz.[4] One morning, at about three, Alex rang him with an idea for a film in which Mae West would play the goddess Circe. Hardly awake, Toeplitz questioned whether this particular star was beautiful enough to play such a role.

Alex argued that the most important thing was that she should be convincing as a sorceress who could change men into pigs, and as far as this was concerned he could think of no one better.

'OK,' replied Toeplitz, just a little bit more awake. 'But how much will she cost?'

Alex said that he would find out and that was the end of the conversation. Slowly Toeplitz drifted off to sleep again only to be awoken three hours later.

'She wants three hundred thousand dollars.'

'It's too much,' yawned Toeplitz.

'I agree,' said Alex. 'A pity, because it was a great idea.'

'Korda throws all sorts of ideas up at the ceiling,' observed Ralph Richardson, who from the 1930s through to the 1950s would appear in more of Alex's films than just about any other actor. 'They don't always stick, but every now and then some of them do.'[5]

In Alex's head, ideas and schemes were constantly bubbling. He was a man of considerable physical indolence, but mentally found it quite impossible to stay still. His habitual restlessness caused him to blend his considerable appetite for pleasure into his working life. Richard Norton recalled going on a business trip with him to Paris. 'Richard, have you ever tasted that blerdy stuff *ratatouille*?'[6] Alex asked him one afternoon. Norton hadn't, so Alex whisked him off to a restaurant. They then spent the rest of the trip looking for new types of *ratatouille*.

Whether it was a business appointment or a social engagement, it was always on to the next thing and the next thing and the next thing. When David Cunynghame's first child, Andrew, was born, he asked Alex to be the godfather. One Sunday Cunynghame invited Alex to tea as an opportunity to see his godson for the first time. Alex arrived early – with Vincent in tow as usual – and kept the taxi outside with the meter running while he waited to see the child. Ten minutes later he was gone.

As far as being a father to his own son Peter was concerned, Alex expected nannies and schools to do the job for him. The actress Joan Gardner, whom Zoltán would marry in 1936, recalled attending a dinner party at which 'Peter would crawl around underneath the table and bite people on the legs and Alex wouldn't say anything to him'.[7] As Joan Gardner only met the Kordas in 1932, Peter can't have been less than eleven when this happened. In 1933 the task of taming the child would be handed over to Westminster School.

The stormy relations between Alex and Maria can't have made Peter's home life any easier. The volatile Maria spent much of 1932 and 1933 living with Alex and Peter in London, but after one bust-up too many flew off in a rage to the Continent, thenceforth spending most of her time in Italy.

Every now and then she would return to London. In 1935 Ludovico Toeplitz received a visit from her soon after he had started his own separate company. His memory of the occasion captures the highly dramatic – and often embarrassing – person that Maria could be. Entering his office, she let a spectacular fur coat fall to her feet and stood before him, 'like Venus emerging from her shell', dressed in a tight-fitting girdle of black satin.[8]

'Now that we're both divorced from Alex,' she declared, 'wouldn't it make sense if we worked together?'

She then dropped a folder on his desk together with a script based on the life of the great turn-of-the-century Italian actress Eleonora Duse. In the folder Maria had interspersed photographs of herself with those of Duse in such a way that it was impossible to tell them apart.

There were reasons why Maria thought that such a project might appeal to Toeplitz. Eleonora Duse had been the great muse of Gabriele D'Annunzio, whom Toeplitz revered. A decade and a half previously, when D'Annunzio had seized the Yugoslav town of Fiume and held it for many months in the name of Italy, Toeplitz had been one of the young disciples who helped the poet to rule over the city.

With ill-concealed triumph, Maria told Toeplitz that her private secretary was his friend Eugenio Casagrande, who had been D'Annunzio's air force chief. The news, however, had the opposite effect to the one she had intended. Furious at the thought that his old comrade should have become Maria's lap-dog, Toeplitz showed her the door.

Maria could not come to terms with the fact that her life as a movie star was over. She still believed that she could make a splendid comeback, and the idea that she might star as Eleonora Duse was her great dream in the 1930s.

In her memoir of Alex, she even fantasized that he had helped her. In this mythical but ultimately rather sad recollection of the past, she and Alex visited D'Annunzio in his home at the Lago di Garda, and sought his permission to make a film of Eleonora Duse's life. They then even began the production:

> Alex wrote everything which would make a woman great. But not Antonia. She was just an empty shell. After playing [a] couple of scenes from *The Life of Eleonora Duse* they stopped the whole production, as she proved herself not to be an actress. [In] the meantime Korda went back to London and made one success after the other. She blamed everything on Korda. Even that the public did not want her.[9]

None of this may have happened, but Maria's misery at her own failing career and her jealousy of Alex help to explain the great rift that opened up between the couple in the 1930s.

Although her memoir suggests that she came to have a sense of her own shortcomings as an actress, at the time she felt abandoned. She was still beautiful and extremely intelligent. Rather than be left to moulder away, she wanted the support for a film career that Alex would not give. The severance was all the more painful because she had imagined herself to be as much Alex's muse as Eleonora Duse had been D'Annunzio's.

Maria's way of coping with the sense of rejection was to assert her own independence in a manner calculated to cause Alex the maximum embarrassment. The overture to Toeplitz was one example. Then, in 1935, she announced her engagement to Count Teleki. As Hungarian Prime Minister under the regency of Admiral Horthy, Teleki had been responsible in 1920 for introducing the notorious 'Numerus Clausus', a law which openly discriminated against the country's Jewish population. He would become Prime Minister of Hungary again in 1939 and commit suicide in 1941 after an uneasy alliance with Hitler. The romance with Teleki would be short-lived, but soon afterwards Maria began to live with the Duke of Agostino in Sicily.

Alex must have looked on with considerable dismay as Maria made herself at home in Fascist society, but at least her absence from London allowed him to indulge in the occasional romance himself without having to fear the violent retribution of which she was fully capable, even in spite of their divorce.

As the country's top film producer, he enjoyed an excellent choice of young starlets, but his desire was often frustrated by his artistic conscience. During the shooting of *Henry VIII* the actor John Loder recalled sitting next to him while the crew lit the scene in which Jane Seymour's ladies-in-waiting make her bed ready for the king:

> One of the young ladies was the pretty, blonde daughter of Sir Bernard Spilsbury, the famous Home Office pathologist. Korda, who had been watching her appreciatively, remarked, 'You know, John, I would like to sleep with that Spilsbury girl, but maybe she would not like to sleep with me, and if she did she would expect me to give her a big part and that I cannot do – so what the hell . . .'[10]

There were no such scruples, however, to prevent a brief affair with Vivien Leigh. Eve Phillips, an actress and fashion model who had worked as Vivien Leigh's stand-in, told Thomas Kiernan, the biographer of Laurence Olivier, that she lent her flat to the pair on two or three separate occasions soon after Alex had signed Vivien Leigh to a five-year contract with London Films.[11]

According to Kiernan, Leigh's schoolfriend Maureen O'Sullivan warned her that Alex tried to sleep with every actress he put under contract. O'Sullivan, who had become a film star at Fox Studios in Hollywood, starred in Alex's last film there, *The Princess and the Plumber*. 'It's something he feels they owe him,' Maureen had told her. 'He claims it's good for business – it's the only way he can decide which actress is best for which part. He must know an actress completely before he can really use her in films. At least that's what he says.'[12]

As Alex was having acrimonous disputes with Fox over *The Princess and the Plumber* and had just been divorced from his wife, it is not unlikely that he would have sought any solace that an available actress could offer. But this account of a rather crude Lothario is at odds with the correct image he sought to cultivate once he had settled in London. It was at about this time that, according to Ludovico Toeplitz, he was posing the vexed question to his friends of whether it was possible for a film producer to be considered a gentleman. Although he came to the conclusion that it probably wasn't, none the less he strove hard to maintain the appearance of one. His seductions and assignations would have been above all discreet.

After his brief affair with Vivien Leigh Alex resumed his customary paternal attitude. Their relationship was much more significant as an example of the extraordinary calculation and care with which he would seek to manufacture a screen personality.

Vivien Leigh's iconic status has hidden the far from certain start to her career. She was less a jewel discovered than one painstakingly moulded in Pygmalion fashion. She left drama school early to marry her first husband, Leigh Holman, and had virtually no stage experience when in 1934 she appeared in a Quota quickie called *Things Are Looking Up*. She almost certainly got the part on account of her extraordinary beauty, rather than her acting ability. Shortly afterwards, the producer Anthony Havelock-Allan cast her in two Quota films for Paramount, *The Village Squire* and *Gentleman's Agreement*. But he was unimpressed.

I thought that her neck was too long, and she was out of proportion ... You had to be careful that you didn't put her in a dress with a low collar, which in real life she was inclined to wear, and you saw this tiny head perched like a sort of pea on top of a long neck.[13]

With hindsight Havelock-Allan realized that he had made a mistake, that as a then inexperienced producer he had overlooked the way in which careful lighting and costume design could hide such a defect. The same was true of acting ability. Leigh, he felt, was not a natural actress, but on film an acting performance could be manufactured.

Alex understood this essential trickery of the movies perfectly. When he first saw Vivien, probably in one of the Quota quickies, her performance as an actress seemed to him amateurish, but he was struck by her great beauty. There was potential here to be explored.

On 15 May 1935, Alex attended the first night of *Mask of Virtue* at the Ambassadors Theatre, the play that turned Vivien Leigh into an 'instant star'.[14] According to Anthony Havelock-Allan, it was actually Alex who put on the production in the first place. He chose a director and a play which he knew could be easily and quickly staged, then gave Vivien Leigh the starring role. 'He wanted to see if she could carry it through, and she did. She looked very good. But nobody said what a wonderful actress; they said what a pretty little girl.'[15]

On a wave of carefully orchestrated publicity, Alex announced that he was giving his new discovery a £50,000 contract, but with much less publicity had her carefully coached. It was not until over a year had passed that he deemed her polished enough and – just as importantly – the circumstances favourable enough for her first appearance.

Alex had a reputation for keeping actors and actresses idling away their time on long-term contracts without using them. But however annoying this practice may have been for those concerned, it was an intrinsic part of the star-making process. A star, Alex realized, was a peculiar combination of personality, talent and, not least, happenstance. You had to wait for the right moment.

In the early summer of 1936 happenstance took the form of Laurence Olivier, with whom Vivien Leigh had fallen in love. There is an implausible-sounding story that Alex lent his house to the two stars – who were both married to other people at the time – so that they could consummate their affair. Whether or not this is true, he certainly did everything he could to encourage the relationship by casting them as two lovers at the court of Queen Elizabeth in *Fire over England*, which went into production at Denham soon after *Rembrandt*.

Flora Robson, who in the part of the Queen had thought herself to be the star, was dismayed to discover that this romance was taking over the picture. With all her years of treading the boards, she was also jealous of the attention that was being given to a young girl who had hardly any acting experience at all. 'Resentment burrowed through her mind,' wrote her biographer, as hour after hour she sat in her heavy Elizabeth costume, 'feeling the sweat coursing its subtly torturous way down the inside of her putty nose'.[16]

Olivier and Leigh did not bother to hide their rapture. Everyone connected with the production was aware of their off-screen romance. Olivier, who had impressed everybody with his athleticism, confessed that his habitual look of exhaustion was due not to performing his own stunts but to Vivien. 'It's every day, two, three times. She's bloody wearing me out.'[17] And in the background, Alex the matchmaker looked on with approval. 'We went to him with every little problem we had,' Vivien later recalled. 'We usually left convinced that he had solved it – or that we'd got our way, even when we hadn't.'[18]

The real-life romance added lustre to Vivien Leigh's début, and soon after the film's heavily promoted release in early 1937, word of her performance even got as far Hollywood. 'Miss Vivien Leigh in Korda's *Fire over England* is as fine a prospect for stardom as any girl I have seen in a long while,' a talent scout, Charles Morrison, cabled his boss David Selznick in February. 'I strongly urge that you make an effort to secure this girl for one or two pictures a year.'[19]

The opportunity to build up Vivien Leigh a little more occurred soon afterwards when the producer/director Basil Dean sought

Alex's backing for *Twenty-one Days*, a film version of John Galsworthy's play *First and Last*. Alex seemed very pleased with Dean's wish that Laurence Olivier should play the leading male role and happily accepted most of his other casting suggestions.

It was only when it came to the question of who should play Olivier's lover that Dean suddenly found Alex digging his heels in. He insisted that Vivien Leigh should play the part.

> I had my doubts about this because of her obvious lack of experience, but Alex was adamant. Slowly I was learning to appreciate his admirable technique in business negotiations, namely to allow others to have their way in inessential matters, and then by firm decision to disclose his ultimate purpose, which in this case was to build Vivien into an international film star.[20]

By this time both Leigh and Olivier were separated from their partners and living together in the same house. Basil Dean was put out to find the set ringing out with their fond, carefree laughter, which he thought created the wrong mood for what was supposed to be a melodrama about a man who had killed his mistress's husband. He would be even more cross when he was summoned to Alex's office just as he was about to shoot the film's big court scene on a huge set that Vincent had spent a whole week building. In his memoirs he recalled the conversation:

> 'Come in Baazil, I must talk to you. Have a cigar?'
> 'What is it, Alex?
> 'Life is so difficult for me, I have too much to do and the blaady Prudential – they worry me so.'
> 'What do you want to see me about, Alex?'
> 'The blaady Prudential. They worry too much . . . Have you finished your court scenes yet?'
> 'Alex, the set was only finished this morning. However, I've just managed the opening shot.'
> 'I am sorry, very sorry, Baazil, but I have to take down your set tonight.'
> 'What?!'
> 'I have some retakes for another picture.'
> 'But we've got four days there!'
> 'Sorry. It is so difficult for me. I must have some retakes.'

'Well, what do I do?'

'You must do something else. Take some exteriors. You have exteriors, yes?'[21]

The following day Dean discovered the hidden motive that Alex nearly always had. His two stars were going to be away for a week in Denmark, where Leigh was going to play Ophelia to Olivier's Hamlet in a special Old Vic production at Elsinore. It was an excellent opportunity to publicize the two young lovers.

Another publicity exercise was Vivien Leigh's ostentatious brandishing on set of the latest bestseller from America: 'I'm reading *Gone with the Wind*,' she told the film correspondent of the *Evening News*.

> If I brought it here I shouldn't be able to start working. I've never been so gripped by anything in my life. It's the finest book I've ever read. What a grand film it would make! I've cast myself for Scarlett O'Hara. What do you think?[22]

Vivien spoke the lines, but Alex told her what to say. Since he must have known that she had already been pointed out to David Selznick, it amounted to a gentle reminder to Selznick that he ought to take her seriously. The casting of Scarlett O'Hara had been a huge publicity circus ever since Selznick first announced that he had bought the rights to *Gone with the Wind*. Even top Hollywood stars were auditioning. Alex realized that to have Vivien in the race was an excellent way to build up her profile even if she didn't get the part. But the extraordinary determination with which she then pursued her goal must have encouraged him in the hope that she might.

He helped to pave the way by loaning her out to appear in *A Yank at Oxford*, a film that Hollywood's biggest studio, MGM, were conveniently making at Denham, where Alex could keep a discreet eye on Vivien's progress. She had a secondary role, but with the guarantee of a big American release the film effectively served as a shop window. 'Her entire characterization in *A Yank at Oxford* was worked out as a kind of screen test for Scarlett O'Hara,' recalled Eve Phillips. 'Larry helped her some, but it was Korda who really coached her. Her part was that of an English-woman, yes, but really an atypical Englishwoman . . . She had this vision that she had to do an English version of Scarlett O'Hara.'[23] At about the same time Alex also decided to shelve the now completed but indifferent *Twenty-one Days*, which he feared would not show Vivien Leigh in her best light.*

David Selznick would see *A Yank at Oxford* in February 1938. 'I think Vivien Leigh gave an excellent performance and was very well cast,' he commented to colleagues.[24] Bit by bit, he was being won over. Another important move, which no doubt Alex had some hand in, was when David Selznick's brother, Myron, became her American agent. At the end of the year Vivien Leigh finally travelled out to meet David Selznick in person.

The legend of their meeting was first set out in the *Gone with the Wind* souvenir programme. On a cold night in December 1938 the studio back lot was set on fire for the film's first scene, the Burning of Atlanta. Selznick had turned out to witness this historic moment. As he watched the flames, his brother emerged from out of the shadows. 'David,' he said, 'I want you to meet Scarlett O'Hara.'

Vivien Leigh would have a screen test a few days later but from that moment, Selznick would maintain, he knew that the part would be hers. Alex was soon in Hollywood to sign an extremely lucrative seven-year contract by which each year Selznick would be entitled to make two films with Vivien Leigh, and London Films one.

'The lucky Hungarian has fallen into something,' Selznick wrote to his business partner Jock Whitney, 'and we're going to make a fortune for him.'[25] But Alex had made his luck. Ever since putting Vivien Leigh on stage in the *Mask of Virtue*, he had done everything possible to weight the chances in her favour. Her road to stardom was one more example of the very long game that he played.

---

* The film would finally be trade-shown in April 1939, a few months after Vivien Leigh's contract with Selznick had been safely signed. 'To my surprise [I] found it quite an acceptable little picture,' commented a colleague of Selznick.

13. FALLING WITH STYLE

'Every man has a destined path. If it leads him into the wilderness, he's got to follow it with his head high and a smile on his lips.'

– Rembrandt

In its depiction of an artist stubbornly refusing to conform, becoming bankrupt and then resorting to stratagems to escape his creditors, *Rembrandt* offered a pretty accurate depiction of what lay in store for Alex. Perhaps his obvious identification with the poverty-stricken painter ought to have alarmed the burghers at the Prudential. The situation might have made a good question in one of their staff accountancy exams. 'If you employ Rembrandt to run a studio, is he going to make a profit?' But with their reorganization and watchdogs and cost-cutting schemes, they thought they had done enough to rescue matters. And however much Alex may have admired the Dutch painter, his own continuing hunger for material success was obvious. All may have been vanity, but *he* had no intention of renouncing the ways of the world.

It has always been difficult for businessmen to understand artists, but it was particularly so in the case of an artist like Alex because he went to such lengths to appear to be a businessman. So it would take some months for Alex's backers to realize that the new studio at Denham was the expensive toy of a man who wasn't now flying but rather falling with style.

//

That summer of 1936 Denham became one huge Vanity Fair. For the Prudential executives the studio offered a break from the mundane routine of their headquarters at Holborn Bars and they came to regard it for a short time as a rather wonderful form of corporate hospitality. On 13 July 1936, the chairman, Sir Edgar Horne, held a private party there for about 300 guests, much to the annoyance of the actors and technicians of the *Rembrandt* unit, who had to put up with their continual intrusions. Other visitors included a Parliamentary committee, the Maharajah of Mysore and Winston Churchill.

A visitor to Denham in those months would have found a bustling, confident place. Alex took great pride in showing the various dignitaries around. The vast studio became a sort of star itself, a Xanadu shown off in newsreels and magazine features. There were the usual statistics. The extensive grounds boasted stables, a boathouse and the Fisheries. The seven sound stages with their electrically controlled doors occupied 118,800 square feet of floor space. There were two projection theatres and eighteen cutting-rooms. The power-plant generated enough electricity to supply a town the size of York. Over 2,000 staff worked there, and each week the restaurant – known by the workers as 'Snobs' because of the glamorous people you could see eating there – cooked 50,000 sausages.

People who worked there recall the place with enormous fondness. 'It was a terribly grand and original sort of place,' remembered Norman Spencer. 'We all thought it was beating Hollywood.'[1] It had the spirit of an atelier on an industrial scale where great pictures could be made. But it wasn't very practical. Sandwiched between the Uxbridge Road on one side and the River Colne on the other, the buildings had been strung out in a line. It meant that everywhere was a long way away from everywhere else. If you were working in the furthest sound stage from the restaurant, you faced a good quarter of a mile walk to have your lunch. A long corridor, with different-coloured lines directing people to the various departments, ran along the backs of the sound stages. Richard Norton, who at the time was supervising the construction of the much better organized and more compact Pinewood Studios, once teased Alex by riding into his office on a bicycle 'puffing and panting as though I had just done a marathon'.[2]

The positioning of the stores and workshops so far away from the stages was 'most unpracticable and uneconomical',[3] as a report published some years later pointed out. Next to the stages, where the stores and workshops ought to have been, was the power-plant: extra precautions had to be taken to ensure that its loud humming couldn't be heard on the stages. Denham was really a model of how not to build an efficient film studio. Much as they all loved the place, the general view of film technicians was that it had been laid out on the 'thoughtless, ramshackle, it-just-growed, Hollywood pattern'.[4]

This of course was part of its charm. Its generous use of space contributed to the sense of grandeur and embodied the scale of Alex's ambitions. The trouble was that, like the enormous one-sided sets that began to spring up on the lot, there was very little support behind.

The key prop was Alex's vanity. The enterprise was driven forward by his unflagging belief in his own importance. Most people who worked for him were happy to be part of the splendid show, but few dared to peer behind the façade.

In the early 1930s, André De Toth, who would years later become a well-known director in Hollywood, was embarking on the sort of path in Hungary that Alex himself had taken as a young man before the First World War. He had a stint in journalism and began to write plays; he frequented the Café New York, where he met many of the writers Alex would have known; and, after briefly working in films in Budapest and Vienna, he even made his own youthful pilgrimage to Paris. Here he met Vincent Korda, who encouraged him to paint, but by now De Toth was determined to be a film-maker.

Back in Budapest, the writer Ferenc Molnár wrote him a letter of introduction to Alex, the 'king of the hustlers', with whom he had worked during the First World War, and De Toth set off for London. Here his familiarity with so many of Alex's formative experiences helped to inoculate him against Alex's charm, and his forthright reminiscences of the Korda brothers offer an invaluable dissident's account.

He arrived at Denham to find a group of Hungarians and other refugees from Europe who had fallen on hard times waiting like supplicants outside Alex's office. Alex, who seemed to assume that De Toth had come for charity too, asked him how much money he needed, and De Toth vehemently made it clear that he had not come for alms. A rather frosty meeting ensued. Alex, who had long been used to adoration, was unsettled by De Toth's coolness, and, although he gave him a job, made sure that he was kept out of his way, passing him on to Vincent and Zoltán.

'He doesn't like you, he doesn't dislike you,' Zoltán explained. 'He doesn't know where to put you. You were the first "drift-in" Hungarian who refused to take money from him. That bugged him. He likes to buy people to exercise power over them. You refused him that chance.'[5]

Alex was 'frighteningly intuitive', De Toth thought, but marooned by his own colossal conceit. When he 'spoke to people he didn't see them. He saw himself next to them in a mirror.'[6] De Toth was amazed by the lengths that Alex could go to in order to impress, but felt that the scale of his ambitions trapped him. The deals became more important than the films. In his constantly shifting world it was impossible to take stock, impossible to state any belief with certainty or even to feel much satisfaction from genuine achievements. For everything was negotiable.

By contrast, Zoltán was 'an open book with very large print on its pages, all in black and white'.[7] And Vincent, who De Toth clearly felt should have remained in Paris to be the considerable painter he would surely have become, was a stoic: 'He was aware Alex had set him on the wrong track, but he never complained, he blamed himself and suffered in silence. A martyr with a wry sense of humour.'[8]

II

The gilded chaos of Denham reached its peak with *Knight without Armour*, which went into production in early September 1936, just as Alex was putting the finishing touches to *Rembrandt*. A romantic drama about a Russian countess who falls in love with a British secret agent, it starred Marlene Dietrich at the very height of her fame and Robert Donat, whose own reputation was growing fast but, as he would uncomfortably discover, still lagged far behind Dietrich's.

Alex originally decided to do the film because he had been having such trouble getting Donat to make up his mind about his next subject after *The Ghost Goes West*. Madeleine Carroll, with whom Donat had appeared in Hitchcock's *The Thirty-nine Steps*, had been reading the James Hilton bestseller between takes, and persuaded Donat that it would make a great film with excellent parts for both of them. Donat bought the rights and passed them on to Alex. When Madeleine Carroll turned out to be unavailable, it occurred to Alex that the project would make the perfect vehicle for Marlene Dietrich, whom he had signed up in Hollywood the previous autumn. But as she was the super-star of her age, her presence changed the whole nature of the venture, her salary of £100,000 representing half the original budget estimate. Alex built up her role of a Russian princess, which had been unimportant in the novel, while at the same time he whittled down the salary of £30,000 that he had agreed with Donat, although it seemed a mere snip by comparison. 'He begged me as a great favour to waive part of my salary and accept a small weekly salary and a lump sum when the film was released,' wrote Donat to his parents. 'He is in dire distress and I have no compunction but to accept. His two Wells' pictures cost the earth and his new studios are very expensive.'[9]

Dietrich's arrival in London was greeted by a fanfare from the world's press, whom the following day she grandly entertained to tea in her suite at Claridge's. Donat had been invited along too, but in light of the Dietrich-mania could easily have been mistaken for her valet. A circular to the United Artists sales force reported:

> Dietrich's reception in England on her arrival there for Korda's picture was one of the biggest ever to be given an American film star. The press of the world watches her every move. If you have noticed the syndicated photographs of Dietrich coming to London and from Salzburg, you will see that the presence of this star in any spot – and particularly in a film – is the equivalent of front-page news.[10]

At Denham they prepared for her arrival by knocking together two dressing-rooms so that she could have a sitting-room as well.

It was perhaps unsurprising that Donat should have had a massive nervous reaction to all this hullabaloo. After a few days of filming, he collapsed with a severe attack of asthma and went into a nursing home. Marlene Dietrich rang him up several times to wish him a speedy recovery – 'Play your part; you must not die' – but her concern seemed only to prolong his absence. The director, Jacques Feyder, tried to shoot around Donat as much as possible, but soon Alex talked of having Laurence Olivier take his place.

It took a cynic in the form of the Hollywood gossip columnist Louella Parsons to suggest what must have really been going on:

> This pesky illness didn't show signs of getting better until he had been completely assured that Marlene's royal retinue didn't mean a less auspicious role for him. The attack of temperament, pardon me, this siege of asthma, lifted promptly when a new script was submitted to Donat who has, apparently, recovered health with a sense of humour.[11]

But the fact that Donat really did suffer from chronic asthma made the true state of his health unusually difficult to gauge. David Cunynghame, who had long experience of showbusiness illnesses, noted with a certain nuance, 'He certainly is to a certain extent a sick man.'[12]

On his first day back, Donat arrived to find the sound stage in darkness. Then suddenly all the lights came on, and Marlene Dietrich, standing before the crew, toasted him with champagne: 'Welcome back – Knight Without Asthma!' If this wasn't undermining enough, she soon trumped it by announcing to an evening paper that she would rather act a love scene with Charles Laughton than with any other actor in the world.[13]

Donat wrote to his parents:

> Basil Rathbone warned us all that she would be sweetness itself for a few weeks, enough to get talked about and raved about in the press. Then she would begin to be ruthlessly selfish. And so it proved to be! ... Her greediest, nastiest trick is to rehearse 'cold' – that is, not to give any hint of how she will play the

scene. Meanwhile she and her secretary watch carefully what I am going to do. Then she goes to her dressing-room on some pretext and is absent for about half an hour. When she comes back she has worked a mass of tricks into her performance – most of them stolen ideas of mine.[14]

The one crumb of comfort for Donat was that he did not suffer alone. In theory, Jacques Feyder was answerable only to Alex, but in practice he found that he had to defer to Dietrich in everything. 'As she only made "Marlene Dietrich" films,' he recalled, 'she did everything she could to ensure that the film remained a Marlene Dietrich film.' He discovered that she possessed a formidable technical knowledge with which to achieve this. 'You would hear her giving orders to the electricians: "Add two more lamps on the right, raise the spotlight on my back a little." '[15] The biggest differences of opinion occurred over her costumes, which paid no regard to the script. Feyder might suggest that her character ought to dress more modestly, but she insisted on wearing only perfectly pressed *haute couture* outfits. 'If the situation made it seem too far-fetched, she simply asked for a change to be made in the script.'[16] Through a mixture of seductiveness, charm and patient diplomacy, she always eventually got her way.

Towards the end of shooting it was Feyder's turn to be ill. Norman Spencer was a gofer on the production. 'I was very impressed because Korda came down and took over directing for a couple of weeks until he was well. I thought to myself, not many bosses of studios can come down and just take over directing.'[17]

But it was as much a sign of desperation. As Donat commented, Alex had been 'constantly nagging because of the expense',[18] which all the delays and personality clashes had enormously increased. Alex had always been drawn to outstanding individual talent, whether in a director, writer or star, but the trouble with such people was that they were as likely to go their own way as yours. As Alex's ambitions soared, his day-to-day life had become more and more a matter of taming wild horses.

//

One of the wildest was Robert Flaherty. In 1934 the 'Father of documentary' had made *Man of Aran*, which chronicled the daily life of inhabitants on a remote island off the west coast of Ireland. Financed by Gaumont-British, it had been known at the studio as 'Balcon's Folly', but garnered huge international acclaim if minimal box-office revenue. In the wake of its success, Flaherty sought to find finance for an idea that he and his wife Frances had originally had five years previously when they were living in Hollywood. 'Wherever we took our camera, from one primitive scene to another,' Frances recalled,

> we used the native people as our characters and took our material from the stuff of their lives. We found what good actors native children can be, and how appealing they unfailingly are to an audience. So we had this idea; why, if we wrote a film-story around extraordinary adventures that a native boy might have in his native environment, wouldn't it be possible to 'star' that boy himself in the film?
>
> We set about to write a story that might film. This was not a very congenial practice for us. We usually worked from the barest of outlines, preferring to 'find' the story in our material. However, experience had taught us that to gain backing for a picture, something had to be offered besides my husband's enthusiasm for places and peoples – something on paper.[19]

The story they developed concerned the relationship between a young Indian mahout and his elephant. They approached Alex, whom Flaherty had known in Hollywood. The release of Julian Huxley's short, *The Private Life of the Gannet*, in late December 1934 would have given them the hope that he would be receptive, and sure enough Alex expressed instant enthusiasm for the idea.

It reminded him of one of Kipling's *Jungle Book* stories, he said, 'Toomai of the Elephants'. Here was an opportunity to make not just a *succès d'estime* like *Man of Aran* that no one would go to see, but a film of genuine commercial appeal. Flaherty, fed up with being poor, was delighted. The resemblance of his idea to the Kipling story seemed like a wonderful omen. How clever of Alex to notice it!

The rights to the Kipling story were bought and Flaherty set to work on a script with Lajos Biro. Alex probably felt pleased with himself to have persuaded Flaherty to accept such a written framework. It had never happened before. But as soon as Flaherty got to India in March 1935, he attuned himself more and more to the atmosphere about him. Just as *Knight without Armour* changed to accommodate the Dietrich image, Kipling gradually yielded to Flaherty. The script served as little more than the sketchiest of guidelines for a documentary account of the boy's life day-to-day. Flaherty, who had a vast new world to explore, would quite happily have stayed out in India for ever. 'For months I heard absolutely nothing,' Alex recalled many years later, 'but still we had optimism, but ... you know, when you spend money for eight, nine months and no film comes back, you start to get worried.'[20] It was perhaps typical of Alex's casual attitude to money that he had not become worried a lot earlier.

By March 1936, after all Flaherty had seen and heard, Kipling's story had become little more than a token flavouring in a very different film. Frances Flaherty kept a diary of the production. Her entry for that month began:

> We have been writing our story, rewriting it. For three weeks we have done nothing else. It has been a hard task – has torn our combined brains to tatters and drained them white – such an effort – really terrific. But we are pleased with the result. The mould is finally cast; now to give it life.[21]

But 4,000 miles away, back in London, Alex had decided that now was the time to intervene. From the Prudential there came increasingly concerned mutterings about his extravagance – perhaps they already had an inkling of the losses that were soon to be announced – and one of the most flagrant examples of that extravagance was the film crew that had been over a year in India with nothing yet to show for it. So Alex asked Zoltán to find out what was going on and then, after an adverse report, sent an American director, Monta Bell, out to India.

According to Flaherty's cameraman, Osmond Borradaile, Bell had interested Alex in a book called *Siamese White*, about a ghost elephant. 'He had convinced Alex that the incorporation of this story would breathe new life into our film.'[22] So Bell arrived in India with instructions to film the appropriate scenes. It is a particularly bizarre story because nothing about Bell's previous career suggests that he was equipped for such a mission – he was perhaps most famous for directing *The Torrent*, Garbo's first film in Hollywood. Borradaile recalled:

> Bell didn't like the jungle and wanted to return to the bright lights as soon as possible! But he didn't get away before Flaherty received and read a copy of *Siamese White*, which turned out to be a story of a man named White, who lived in Siam – a bit embarrassing because an elephant had actually been white-washed to play the ghost. All the footage shot on this blunder – and a good chunk it was – went into the ash-can.[23]

The episode has all the hallmarks of a Korda stratagem. The ghost elephant was almost certainly a ruse to justify Bell's presence. Once out in India, he was in a position to confirm Zoltán's report. Alex preferred to maintain the illusion of faith until there really was no alternative.

The arrival of Zoltán in India was the sign that this moment had finally come. He viewed the footage, now many hours long, but found it hard to discern anything that resembled a coherent narrative. In June 1936 the film crew returned to England. Alex viewed a rough cut of the footage and ordered a salvage mission. 'The absence of a story was noticeable,' observed John Collier, the writer who was given the task of supplying one. 'It was suggested that a very simple story should be devised, such as could be shot (in the studio and on the lot) in about 5,000 feet of screen-time and that this should be grafted into an equal amount of Bob's material.'[24]

It wasn't entirely fair to Flaherty to speak of 'the absence of a story'; it was more that there wasn't enough of a story: Flaherty regarded the Kipling outline as secondary to capturing the atmosphere and way of life of the India in which he had found himself.

The three main characters in Kipling's original story were the elephant boy, a white hunter called Petersen Sahib and the elephant. In India, perhaps the luckiest discovery had been that of a young mahout to play the part of the boy. After Alex had gone to such lengths to hide Merle Oberon's Indian origin, it was some irony that by making the most of this child's background he should create one of his biggest stars. Osmond Borradaile found Sabu Dastigir in the stables of the Maharajah of Mysore, which he had visited to see some of the elephants that would be taking part in the film. 'He told me that his father had been a mahout who had died in the service of the Maharajah,' remembered Borradaile, 'and that he had come to the stables to collect his father's pension in the form of food for the family.'[25] The man Flaherty chose to play Petersen Sahib was a plantation owner called Captain Fremlin. Back in London, it was decided that, unlike Sabu, he didn't have 'star quality', and that he should be replayed in the studio by the actor Walter Hudd.

It's easy to conclude from the scale of Alex's interventions that Flaherty's *Elephant Boy* had somehow completely failed to meet his expectations. But he ought to have known exactly what to expect. *Man of Aran* was a pictorially beautiful film, which depended far more on poetic observation than on narrative. The 'actors' were drawn from the islanders Flaherty was making the film about. Essentially a director of silent films, he had never in his life shot conventional dramatic scenes. The dialogue in *Man of Aran* – such as it was – arose out of the circumstances found on location, and was used not to advance the narrative or to explain a character, but in the way of 'sound effects' to enhance the realism of the scene. *Elephant Boy* – had Flaherty finished the film – would have been the same.

When Flaherty set out for India in February 1935, Alex could afford to be indulgent. But a year later, when London Films faced financial ruin, the urgent necessity was to maximize whatever commercial potential the film possessed. The narrative, which had been lightly sketched, was made overt, and the personality of Sabu, who stood out from Flaherty's footage, was built up. Flaherty had given the boy very few lines to say. Wanting to capture his innate charm, he had allowed him as much as possible to be himself. But now close shots, filmed at Denham, in which Sabu had extra lines, were interpolated into the original Indian footage. It was not enough for him just to ride along on his elephant, he had to talk about the experience in terms that would make the alien seem cosily familiar. There was even a prologue, in which Sabu, against the pearly-grey of a studio backdrop, sets the scene. 'And here's the beginning of our story . . .'

The new direction that *Elephant Boy* took at Denham was so contrary to Flaherty's whole method that there was really nothing he could usefully contribute. Zoltán took over and embarked upon a hurried effort to create India in England. A bamboo forest sprang up along the banks of the River Colne, elephants were hired from zoos, and London's cafés were combed for dark-skinned actors. The new white hunter scenes were then shot at night so that the makeshift scenery should appear more convincing.

Everything was done to make what had started out as a spontaneous, improvised film seem instead classic and literary. The very first image is of a closed book embossed with the picture of an elephant, which then opens to reveal the credits on its pages. It was the sort of reassurance Alex felt the audience needed: they were not about to watch a dull documentary, but an adventure story. Robert Flaherty had been safely contained.

Alex had the right of final approval, so Flaherty had little choice but to acquiesce. He stayed with the production, his chief occupation being to provide members of the cast with drams of whisky on the frosty autumn nights down by the Colne. It must have been heart-breaking for him to watch his film become something else. If he had been free to finish it, it might have made a wonderful Flaherty documentary. Instead, it was an awkward mish-mash – a pedestrian adaptation of Kipling with marvellous travelogue footage and a brilliant new personality for the screen – the elephant boy, Sabu.

Many of Flaherty's admirers were puzzled by why he didn't disown the film; indeed he even helped in its promotion. The answer probably lies in his contract with London Films. He was on a percentage: '2½ per cent on the first £130,000 of producers' gross revenue; 5 per cent on the next £20,000, and thereafter 7½ per cent.'[26] Loud complaints about how London Films had butchered his masterpiece wouldn't have helped him to reach those escalators. After years of struggling to make films which were universally acclaimed but went largely unseen, here was an opportunity to make some money at last – a nest egg to put by for his old age, if not towards his next venture, although that wouldn't be for years.

Alex does not come out of the *Elephant Boy* saga very well. Preoccupied as usual by too many other things, he failed properly to monitor the production's progress. The result was that Flaherty, who had been encouraged to think that he could do what he liked, finally ended up with no freedom whatsoever. The best that can be said of Alex is that he became a hostage to fortune: once it was clear that London Films was in trouble he had to do whatever he could to make *Elephant Boy* a commercial success – although it was too late even for that. The box-office receipts of £100,000 exceeded the takings of all Flaherty's other films put together, but it had cost £150,000 to make.[27] In contrast, *Man of Aran* had cost a mere £20,000: 'Balcon's Folly' paled into insignificance compared to Alex's.

Flaherty's return to England just as Alex began to direct *Rembrandt* would have provided a timely reminder of the conflict between commerce and art. The thwarting of Flaherty's artistic vision might well have lent some melancholy inspiration for Alex's. The intensity of *Rembrandt* owes much to the circumstances of its making. Alex, the director-mogul, was peculiarly well placed to identify with both Rembrandt and the burghers of Amsterdam. This schizoid element made life at London Films very unpredictable. What Alex gave with the hand of an artist, he could quickly take away with the hand of the businessman.

//

About the only predictable thing in those early days of Denham was that every week there would be an executive meeting. But if the meetings served to minute the growing chaos, they seemed little able to control it. Flaherty going his own way in India, Donat's asthma, Marlene Dietrich's ego – all these things were beyond the reach of conventional business management.

'The Comptroller submitted for consideration a detailed estimated cost of production of *Knight without Armour*,' read the minutes of the executive meeting for 18 September 1936, 'showing that the picture would cost £187,335.'[28] Two months later, on 10 November, the executive meeting reported that the estimated expenditure had risen to £216,543, and the actual cost would end up being well over £300,000.

At the same meeting Alex reported that across the board expenditure had exceeded forecasts and there were insufficient funds to complete the year's programme. He didn't raise the question of further funds. He must have known that it would have been no use. The Joint Secretary of the Prudential, Ernest Lever, expressed his dismay that yet another forecast had proved so inaccurate, and, following a discussion, the meeting resolved that after *I, Claudius* – which had been about to go on the floor for many months now – all production should be suspended until July 1937 when the position would be reviewed. The meeting also decided that attempts should be made to sell the potentially extremely expensive *Lawrence of Arabia* project to another company. 'It was, however, agreed that Mr Korda should formulate plans for the preparation of about four stories in order that these might be properly prepared and budgeted by the end of June, affording the Company the opportunity of producing one or more under favourable conditions during the second part of 1937.'[29] It's hard to imagine that this crumb of comfort could have raised anyone's spirits. For when was the last time that a Korda production had been properly prepared or budgeted?

Outwardly, with the sound stages full and gigantic sets on the lot, everything seemed splendid. But Alex's empire was already beginning to unravel. Indeed, even before Denham had opened, Elisabeth Bergner and Paul Czinner concluded their own separate deal to produce films directly for United Artists, and this set a precedent that others would soon follow. The former head of the legendary UFA studios, Erich Pommer, had worked with Alex as an associate producer since the beginning of the year, but in December 1936, during negotiations to renew his contract, he told Alex that he intended to set up a production company with Charles Laughton. Together they had approached United Artists, who were eager to give them a distribution contract for twelve films.

On 18 December, Alex cabled the owner-members of United Artists:

Pommer treated with me up to the last second regarding his future contract and his decision to go away with Laughton came to me in the middle of our discussions as a perfect surprise. It is obvious if I want to keep this organization intact, which is the chief interest of United Artists, we must avoid the impression that any one of the executive staff can go away taking one of my stars and have a free entry into United Artists. I really feel that in this case I have been let down badly by both these gentlemen, both of whom have been rendered great services by myself. Especially Pommer, who has been given chance he never had since leaving Germany.[30]

But the very precariousness of London Film Productions, which it was impossible for Alex to conceal completely, made United Artists all the more anxious to encourage other sources of supply. Of particular concern was the recommendation of a Parliamentary Committee that the quota for British films should be raised to 50 per cent when the Films Act came up for renewal in 1938. Murray Silverstone set out the case for approving the Laughton–Pommer contract in a cable. Metro-Goldwyn-Mayer, he explained, were embarking on a British production schedule for world release, and were keen to finance Laughton–Pommer films. 'If Metro gets quality British pictures they will for first time be able to supply exhibitors which together with their own important line-up will make them greatest force here.'[31] Reluctantly Alex had to accept the situation and patch up his differences with Pommer and Laughton. The alternative was not only to lose them to a competitor but also to forfeit important revenue that their new company could provide as renters of space in a studio which it suddenly seemed Alex would be using very little himself.

//

The intrigues of Pommer and Laughton were rather minor compared to those of Merle Oberon. She spent most of 1936 in Hollywood working for Samuel Goldwyn, who now shared her contract with Alex. In early November she returned reluctantly to England to star in *I, Claudius* opposite Charles Laughton. Alex had originally wanted her to return in early September, but as usual the starting date of the film kept on being put back and back. Merle wasn't surprised to discover on her arrival that the script had yet to be finished. 'There is still no sign of starting *I, Claudius*,' she wrote to Goldwyn after several more weeks had gone by.

> I really rather wish they wouldn't – I somehow feel it won't be an overwhelming success . . . I wish you'd make Alex hurry up and do something – I hate hanging about – I've travelled so much since I returned for want of something better to do! Paris – St Moritz – Northumberland and now Wales – I shall have the railway lined on my face soon – if Alex doesn't work me.
>
> I miss California and your Studio – Oh dear! Wish you'd drag me back – but for heaven's sake don't tell anyone I said so. I'd be called disloyal or something.[32]

Between the lines though it may have been, the message was very clear. Alex was washed up, and surely Goldwyn must be able to pull some strings to get Merle back to Hollywood. It would take a little longer for the world to know it, but just six months after the great studio at Denham had opened, the dream of a thriving film industry in Britain had come to an end. From the end of 1936 onwards the Prudential would regard London Films as a liability from which they had to extract themselves in as orderly a fashion as possible.

14. HANGING ON

Alex desperately needed some turn of fortune, but everything suggested that his ambitious film version of Robert Graves's novel *I, Claudius* would be the usual shambles. Three writers, Carl Zuckmeyer, Lajos Biro and Lester Cohen, laboured on the script, which was taking far longer than anyone had anticipated. 'The *Claudius* scenario is a great joke,' commented Graves in a letter to a friend; 'its permutations in and out of German, Hungarian and English as various big-shots take turns at it would make you laugh.'[1] The whole business, he wisely concluded, was one that you could not afford to take seriously. 'Films are insane: if they occasionally drop gold on our hats as we pass, that's all right.'

I, Claudius was to have been the last film Alex directed before devoting himself exclusively to being a producer. But in November 1936 he announced that he had forthwith given up film directing. He had reached his decision, he told the *Sunday Dispatch*'s film critic, Connery Chappell, 'because he thinks he is too old at 43 to direct films'.[2] However, the decision, made at the very time he was struggling to put the much delayed *I, Claudius* into production, was much more a reflection of the troubled state of his relationship with Charles Laughton. It had taken the threat of legal action to persuade the temperamental star to appear in the film and, in the circumstances, Alex did not relish yet another battle with him on set.

The choice of Josef Von Sternberg as Laughton's new director might have seemed like an attempt to punish the actor. Sternberg had a reputation as a tough man with little tolerance, as Alex would have known. 'When I asked him why he did not wish to direct this film himself,' Sternberg recalled in his memoirs, 'he gave me gruesome details of the difficulties he had endured in directing Laughton, interlarding his recital with effusive flattery of my ability to direct the devil himself.'[3]

Sternberg approached film-making rather as a general would a battle. The actors and the technicians were deployed here and there with their strict orders. As he strutted about the set in his riding boots and breeches and with a bandanna bound about his head, he would seek to efface all egos that rivalled his own. This approach had worked in Hollywood with Marlene Dietrich, because it was Sternberg who had turned her into a star in the first place, and established the lines along which her personality would subsequently develop. But Laughton was already a big star, and possessed an intuitive cast of mind that Sternberg did not understand. He lacked the necessary patience and empathy to puzzle out the nuances of human emotion that Laughton sought to capture and could offer his star no constructive advice, only bewilderment that he should want to make a straightforward matter complicated.

Before filming began, Laughton visited Sternberg in his office and asked him how he should play the part. Sternberg simply replied that he was perfect as he was. For Sternberg, movie-making was a question of personalities not actors, and Laughton must have left the room feeling rather hurt that his new director should have considered his craft of so little account.

Sternberg found rehearsals with Laughton exhausting, but filming would be far worse.

> Beginning with the first limp, he dragged a different foot each time, alternating according to his mood, and sometimes attempted to drag them both . . . Promptly at nine he would enter a stage which had been prepared for the day's work, look everything over, and then declare that he would not be able to play his part there, as he had prepared himself to interpret a sequence for which no stage as yet had been made ready.[4]

Sternberg's response to such behaviour was to treat Laughton as a creature to be outwitted rather than understood.

When he finally consented to act in a space designated by him, and lights and machinery were adjusted accordingly, he would startle everyone, though not me . . . by insistence on another space where, as he put it, the aura was more favorable to his emanations. We neglected nothing to capture him, and would quickly rearrange the necessary machinery to establish a new ambush.[5]

Sternberg's ridiculing tone itself explains why he had so much trouble. Laughton was not the sort of actor who could be hunted into a performance. 'It was not a nightmare, it was a daymare,' commented Sternberg. 'There was a rumour that the capers indulged in by Claudius were part of a deliberate plan to wreck Alexander Korda, but I cannot give credence to this, as this was too perfect a performance.'[6]

When I, Claudius began filming in February 1937, Alex was making fresh objections to United Artists' plans to support a separate Laughton–Pommer production company. So there was certainly an incentive for Laughton to carry these increasingly bitter negotiations on to the studio floor. But his behaviour was less an act of sabotage than a determination, in the face of his abandonment, to be all the more himself. 'Charles felt more and more martyred and set out for the studio every day as if he had been called to the rack,' observed Elsa Lanchester.[7] 'Repeatedly he stated that he could only play where he sensed a sympathetic current,' commented Sternberg.[8] But at that time there was precious little sympathy to be had from either Sternberg or Alex.

Laughton's co-star, Merle Oberon, was scarcely less miserable. While she kicked her heels in London waiting for I, Claudius to begin, with one starting date after another slipping by, she longed to be back in Hollywood, where they made proper movies. But Samuel Goldwyn had failed to take the hint that a rescue should be arranged. When at last she saw a script in January 1937, it only made her feel worse. She cabled Goldwyn to express her despair. The film would have neither box-office nor entertainment value, she told him. Even more upsetting was her part. While to many people who knew her she might have seemed ideal to play Claudius's scheming wife, she thought the role completely at odds with the more positive screen image she wanted to build up for herself:

> Messalina nothing. No acting opportunities. Heavy old fashioned vamp. Secondary Laughton. Feel miserable. Think Claudius would undo everything you have done. Do not want do picture. Need your friendship, advice badly. Would be confidential. Awaiting reply. Not spoken Korda yet.[9]

If she had hoped Sam would fix things for her, she was disappointed. He suggested that she speak to Alex herself. 'Tell him exactly how you feel. You must appreciate I cannot interfere.'[10] Alex responded to Merle's complaints by having the script revised yet again, but once the production finally began the great battle of wills between Laughton and Sternberg must have made her feel inescapably 'secondary'.

The production stumbled on into mid-March. Then there came an even worse day than usual. Claudius was supposed to be kicked into Messalina's chamber and, as he lay there sprawled on the floor, to raise his head and stutter, 'This is not how I would have chosen to appear before you.' Lunch came and went and still Laughton could not give a satisfactory performance of this apparently simple scene. Sternberg summoned Alex. He sat and watched for a while, and then, as Sternberg recalled, went over to Laughton and explained the scene as if to a child.

> Korda waited, and what went through his mind is not known to me. Claudius time after time came through the door, hit the floor with a thud, raised his head to expose a face that had no relation to anything except the normal attitude of someone asking where the post office is, and muttered, 'Just exactly what is it that I am to do?' At five o'clock we stopped and dismissed the stage.[11]

That day, 16 March, marked the end of *I, Claudius*. In the evening Merle was involved in a car accident and taken to the Middlesex Hospital with concussion and bruises. Alex made half-hearted attempts to replace her with another actress but finally abandoned the production, a decision that suited everybody except the insurers. The joke going around Denham Studios was that Alex must have been driving the car.

The surviving evidence suggests that Merle wasn't that badly hurt. 'I was shocked to hear of your accident but am delighted to know it wasn't serious,' Goldwyn cabled on the day of the accident. 'Please cable us exactly how you feel and know we all love you here.'[12] Merle's secretary replied on her behalf to say that she was making a good recovery. But two weeks later, on April Fool's Day, Merle cabled Goldwyn herself. While there was 'no disfigurement', she felt a 'little nervy after concussion'. After a few more days in hospital, she went to stay with her friend Lady Moryth Benson in the country to recuperate. It's impossible to know for certain, but a *maladie diplomatique* seems likely. It would not have been the first time.

The pity is that the surviving footage of *I, Claudius* reveals one of the great Charles Laughton performances. With hindsight, the agony of self-doubt he endured during the production was an index of how completely he had managed to get under the tormented emperor's skin. Such was the thin line between genius and madness, triumph and disaster.

//

In spite of the spectacular collapse of *I, Claudius*, Alex was making a real effort in 1937 to turn over a new leaf. A sign of his readiness to draw a line under the wasteful film-making of the past was his decision to pay off H. G. Wells rather than put into production two more Wells stories, *The New Faust* and *Food of the Gods*. He also embarked upon an across-the-board cost-cutting campaign, making a point of leading by example.

He waived his producer's entitlement to a fee of £5,000 per picture and a 5 per cent share of the gross receipts until such time as London Films made a profit. He gave the Prudential an option to acquire his equity in London Films for a nominal payment and surrendered 50 per cent of his right to the profit on his share in United Artists. To encourage economies he voluntarily accepted a 20 per cent cut in his salary and persuaded the other executives of London Film Productions to do the same. To the extent that he had been responsible for the previous losses, he was now doing his best to atone for them.

A slump that had taken over the British film industry as a whole forced the Prudential to lift their temporary ban on production. When Denham Studios opened the previous year, film companies had been flocking to take up the available space, but now there were so few tenants that it began to make economic sense for London Films to expand its own programme of films to keep the studios busy. But the Prudential were still wary of advancing any money for production themselves. So Alex looked elsewhere.

Since he was a part-owner of United Artists, it seemed to him only fair that United Artists should provide him with financial support in a time of crisis. Murray Silverstone suggested that if he could plan a series of less ambitious pictures of proven box-office value, then he might be able to get an advance. But his request in January 1937 for a $500,000 loan did not go down well. Mary Pickford sent a memorandum to the United Artists management expressing her opposition. It was 'setting a dangerous precedent', she argued, which, if granted, would give every other stockholder producer the right to make the same demand. 'Personally, I closed Pickford–Lasky and went out of business rather than make such a request to my fellow stockholders. Nor did I, during my year and a half of financial difficulties, seek one favor from United Artists, although it might have meant my remaining in business.'[13] She was no more sympathetic to a suggestion that Alex should be given past dividends in cash instead of having them go against the purchase of his stock as had been originally agreed. 'I believe we will have to take a very firm hand with Mr Korda,' she observed, 'and insist upon his going through with his contract.'

On 2 February, Alex's fellow stockholders resolved to postpone a decision on Alex's loan request until the financial affairs of London Films had been investigated. It did not help the harmony of future negotiations that the man chosen for this task was F. M. Guedalla, United Artists' lawyer in London and a man Alex regarded as his arch-enemy. As well as working for United Artists, Guedalla represented several of Alex's contract stars, including Charles Laughton and Robert Donat, and Alex believed that he poisoned them against him.

In a long cable, dated 4 February, Guedalla detailed the sorry tale of losses, extravagance and inefficiency, and criticized Alex for his 'swollen head' and failure to take advice, but concluded that finally United Artists should, in their own interests, do what they could to help him out of his crisis.[14] A few days later the stockholders sent a cable agreeing in principle to a loan, but hedged the offer with numerous conditions. 'I must say if I tried to borrow on a gold watch from a second-rate pawn shop the terms would be arranged in a better spirit,' commented Alex to Goldwyn. 'You all seem to forget that on my shoulders rests the burden of the greater part of United Artists' future in this country.'[15]

Yet Alex would complain bitterly when a few weeks later United Artists attempted to lighten that burden by giving distribution contracts to other British producers. 'Recent happenings convince me that it is contrary to vital interests of my company to be distributed in future by United Artists,' he wrote in a letter that was read out at a special meeting of the stockholders on 11 March 1937.[16]

> When our basic agreement was made I was led to believe by other partners, subsequently by Dr Giannini also, that my company's and my own position in the British market would be recognized and that United Artists would regard us as the mainstay of their British interests.

He complained about the decision to distribute other British pictures, and also argued that the principle of stockholders having equal rights and duties did not apply in practice as the production burden was 'absolutely unequally divided'. On these grounds he asked for the dissolution of his contract. The meeting passed a resolution denying that United Artists had committed any breach and insisting that he honour the agreement.

The only ally Alex had among the United Artists stockholders was Sam Goldwyn. But in important issues they were routinely outvoted. The situation reflected a fundamental divide between the United Artists stockholders. As active producers, Alex and

Goldwyn were most dependent on the success of their own pictures; but Mary Pickford, Douglas Fairbanks Sr and Charlie Chaplin had ceased active production, and benefited most from the distribution of other people's pictures. While Alex and Goldwyn wanted lower distribution terms and feared that too many pictures would compromise the effective exploitation of their films, their non-producing partners wanted United Artists to take on as much product as it could handle at as high a distribution fee as possible.

Alex's dissatisfaction with United Artists went back to his earliest days as a stockholder. 'It seems that the worst theatres are retained for British pictures and you would dump our pictures in houses which will play both good and bad pictures,' he cabled to United Artists' sales director, Arthur Kelly, on 16 November 1935.[17] When more complaints followed, Kelly passed on Alex's anger to his salesmen in a circular letter dated 8 January 1936:

> London Films enjoy the reputation of being the greatest producers of pictures in Great Britain, and have acquired this reputation by their earnest effort to make outstanding pictures regardless of the cost. Every production that has come from London Films has cost them as much, and in some cases more than has been invested by its American associates in negative, but the returns in the Domestic market on their pictures have been totally inadequate and has brought around a very serious condition of affairs because the London Films are not securing a return on their investment that they hoped would come to them by virtue of the big financial risk they have taken.
>
> We in the Domestic Department have not made the contribution we should. There is a tremendously wide difference between the Contracts Taken and the play-off on London Films as against the pictures of our American producers. From now on I must inform you that this condition has got to be remedied. All alibis of salesmen that the exhibitor will not contract in advance for London Films productions but will book them as and when they come along, will not be tolerated. . . .
>
> I have heard that there is a tremendous amount of resistance on the part of the exhibitors against what is called a

'foreign' film, but then United Artists is supposed to have the finest salesmen in the motion picture industry and I have enough confidence in them to feel that if they make up their minds they can break down this resistance.[18]

But they didn't. A year and a half later, Alex was still struggling, the grosses of his pictures falling far short of what was needed to break even. It was in these circumstances that in the spring of 1937 he banded together with Goldwyn in a bid to buy the company. At the time it seemed an extraordinarily confident and audacious move, although it was more a case of 'not waving but drowning'. Gaining control of United Artists was the most obvious way to keep afloat. It would make it possible to alter the distribution fees in favour of the active producers and also to lift restrictions in Alex's contract that prevented him from producing films for other companies.

In May 1937 Alex travelled to Hollywood. On 22 May, he asked the board of United Artists for a personal loan of $75,000, which they granted, holding his share in United Artists as security. They also agreed that for a period of one year the distribution fee on Korda films released in England but not in America would be at actual cost. They were doing their best to help out a fellow stockholder who was clearly in trouble, but appreciated that leniency at this time was also a key to facilitating the exit from United Artists that the three non-producing stockholders desired. On 24 May, Mary Pickford, Douglas Fairbanks and Charlie Chaplin granted Goldwyn and Alex an option to purchase their stock for $2 million each. 'Now all they have to do is raise the money and pay it to us,' commented Clarence Ericksen, Douglas Fairbanks's business manager, 'and let's all hold the thought that they will be able to do so.'[19]

A Byzantine series of negotiations followed, as Goldwyn and Alex attempted to chisel the price down or to persuade Pickford, Fairbanks and Chaplin to accept part-payment in stock. Pickford and Fairbanks were amenable, but Chaplin insisted, with the inflexibility of a Shylock, on being paid the complete sum in cash.

The Prudential did what it could to help the two producers. In November Ernest Lever accompanied Alex to New York to negotiate on behalf of a number of British financiers. On 14 November it was announced that the purchase had been concluded. Goldwyn returned triumphantly to the West Coast, and Alex made plans to sail back to Europe. But Fairbanks and Pickford were furious to discover that part of the deal involved United Artists giving Alex and Goldwyn a loan of $4.5 million. The proposal was 'outrageous', commented Fairbanks, who believed that it would probably be *ultra vires* for a stockholder of United Artists to agree to such terms. So the deal was off again. Fairbanks refused to renew his option when it expired at the end of the year and advised Charlie and Mary to refuse too. 'We three must protect ourselves and rehabilitate United,' Fairbanks declared in 'Three Musketeers' fashion.[20]

For a few days Alex could have basked in the belief that the Prudential had come to his rescue again. Instead, just three weeks later, he found himself back in Hollywood begging for further concessions that would allow the company's survival. The failure of United Artists to secure an adequate return on his pictures in America, he told a meeting of the stockholders on Wednesday, 8 October, had caused London Film Productions to lose $2 million instead of making a profit of $2 million and as a result the company was in imminent danger of being thrown into liquidation.

'There was considerable discussion,' the minutes of the meeting reported, 'in which it was pointed out to Mr Korda that the English-made pictures universally did not sell well in the United States, that they did not enjoy a profitable vogue, and it was suggested that the matter would be looked into by the officers of the corporation.'[21]

There was another meeting on Friday morning, at which Alex presented a formal letter. In view of the likelihood of London Film Productions going into liquidation, he requested either to be released from his distribution contract with United Artists, or to be allowed to produce several films per year for outside interests in addition to those that he was obliged to produce for United Artists. The latter arrangement, he said, would enable him to get the finances which might avoid the necessity of London Films liquidating.

A special meeting was convened on Tuesday, 27 December to consider his request. Pickford, Fairbanks and Chaplin all agreed that his contract should be amended to allow him to produce films for distribution by other companies for a limited period of five years. But Goldwyn, Alex's erstwhile ally, refused such concessions unless he had the same changes in his contract.

The result was stalemate. The year ended with the United Artists' stockholders unable to grant any concessions because of Goldwyn's dissent and with the threat of liquidation for London Films as close as ever. Alex stayed out in Hollywood, brooding over his inability to make any headway. Temperamentally ill-suited to cope with such inactivity, he announced in the New Year his intention to sue Pickford, Chaplin and Fairbanks for misrepresentation. He argued that he had entered into his stock-holder contract with United Artists only on the understanding that they would produce films for United Artists on a regular basis, which they had failed to do. These claims were unsupported by the facts and were not pursued, but they were a sign of his desperation.

//

The irony was that in the course of 1937 Alex had done much to make London Films a viable company. After the colossal costs of films like *Things to Come* and *Knight without Armour*, he had presided over a production programme of modestly budgeted features which seemed set to show an overall profit. There was *The Squeaker*, based on a story by Edgar Wallace, whose material came perhaps as close as it was possible to ensuring success at the box-office; *The Return of the Scarlet Pimpernel*, with a bargain basement Barry K. Barnes stepping into the shoes of Leslie Howard as the Pimpernel; *Paradise for Two*, a Jack Hulbert musical; even *Twenty-one Days*, disrupted though it was by the great Olivier/Leigh romance and Alex's star-grooming – all these films managed to keep their costs down to the right side of £100,000. If there was nothing that quite matched the spectacle of the previous year's production, Alex could point to a bold new venture in embarking upon a programme of Technicolor features. Three went into production in the course of the year: A. E. W. Mason's adventure story *The Drum*, and two romantic comedies – *The Divorce of Lady X*, which was a remake of the 1932 film *Counsel's Opinion*, and *Over the Moon*.

The latter two starred Merle Oberon, whose mood had improved enormously since the débâcle of *I, Claudius*. Alex was at last making a real effort to take her wishes seriously. *The Divorce of Lady X* was 'the real McCoy' because, as Merle put it to Goldwyn, 'the girl has a chance to look ravishing with divine clothes'.[22] After shooting had finished on *Lady X*, she stepped straight into another light comedy role in *Over the Moon*. Furthermore, in July 1937, soon after *Lady X* had gone into production, Alex had agreed to pay the novelist Francis Hackett to write a life of Anne Boleyn, the part that Merle had longed to play in a full-length feature ever since her cameo in *The Private Life of Henry VIII*.

Versed as she was in Hollywood efficiency, Merle's correspondence with Goldwyn offers a useful barometer of London Films' increased professionalism. 'I've been working like a beaver,' she wrote in late 1937. 'I saw *The Divorce of Lady X* the other day and it's quite good. The color – although I haven't seen it all in color yet – is excellent.' And *Over the Moon*, which she was currently working on, was so far 'awfully good' and she was convinced that it would turn out to be an 'excellent comedy'.[23] She was particularly impressed by René Hubert, who had designed her costumes.

> My clothes have never been quite like they are in these two films. I know when you see the films you will be very surprised at my dresses. I know how interested you are in clothes and how much you know about them. That is why I write to tell you about René Hubert – in case by any chance you should want him to dress me any time – he really is brilliant and very economical.

The letter marked a landmark in the Oberon–Goldwyn correspondence. After years of whingeing about London Films' general ineptitude and disorganization, now for the very first time Merle was suggesting that it had something it could teach Hollywood.

However, this didn't mean it could pay its bills. As the Prudential had imposed a strict embargo on spending any more money on production, an important part of London Films' smooth running in 1937 involved fending off creditors, especially in the latter half of the year. In October, for example, Dr Herbert Kalmus, the head of Technicolor, was dismayed to find that a cheque for £7,500 had bounced just as London Films was about to begin its third colour production, *Over the Moon*. His board of directors would give him 'no authority whatsoever to permit defaults of this sort',[24] he declared to Kay Harrison, who now ran Technicolor in England. But as all London Films' cheques were bouncing at this time, Harrison's attempts to secure immediate payment proved futile. 'I feel some diffidence in making any suggestion, but if Dr Kalmus can persuade his colleagues to allow you to hold the cheque a little longer,' wrote London Films' finance director C. H. Brand, 'such forbearance would be very helpful.'[25]

Alex's great triumph in 1937 was to continue production long after the Prudential had turned off the tap. Although there were several very good reasons to feel close to despair, somehow he managed to maintain an outward appearance of normality. If he had spent much of the previous year digging a very deep hole for himself, now he displayed a remarkable agility of mind and resourcefulness in addressing a critical situation.

The Drum was an example of how he could when necessary produce a spectacular film with economy and lightning speed. Early in 1937 he asked the novelist A. E. W. Mason to write an original film story with an India setting for Sabu. By the end of April Mason had delivered a story of 20,000 words. Lajos Biro and Mason then worked on a script, while a camera unit was despatched to India to film shots of spectacular settings. Its departure was slightly delayed because in these very early days of Technicolor there was just a handful of suitable Technicolor cameras in Britain, all of which were booked for the Coronation of George VI. The colour film stock had never been used in such climate conditions before, so the trip was as much a pioneering venture as the *Sanders* expedition to Africa had been two years previously. The studio sequences began to be filmed at Denham on 23 June, and the exterior scenes involving actors were filmed during August in the Welsh hills near Harlech.

The opening location shots of the North-West Frontier mountains must have been breathtaking in 1938 when colour was still a novelty, and, under Zoltán Korda's direction, Wales and India were merged seamlessly in an adventure of genuine spectacle. The story itself was very simple: Sabu plays a young prince who summons a relief force to the aid of a British garrison threatened by his wicked uncle. But as no opportunity was lost to photograph large gatherings of the faithful at prayer, armies marching in or out of dusty forts, or the competing pageantry of the Indian tribes and the British military, it somehow seemed a much bigger film than it really was. Its final cost would be £136,000, which was modest for a spectacular Technicolor film, and it would make a healthy profit with receipts on its first run of well over £200,000. Like Britain itself would come to do in later years, Alex was punching above his weight.

But if Alex had lost none of his appetite for spectacle, 1937 none the less marked an intellectual retrenchment. Unpredictable box-office risks like *Things to Come* or even *Rembrandt* were put aside in favour of projects that had clear popular appeal. Not that he would admit that there had been any such change of direction. In an interview in July 1937 he declared that the cheaper films were 'not a sign of decay but of growth'. In spite of the talk of crisis it was business as usual. 'I have built up a company which is active, thriving, and still growing. And all the developments at Denham which appear to have given cause for alarm, and for "I-told-you-so-ing", are only normal steps directed to realizing the plans on which it has been built up.'[26]

Sursum corda!

15. FREE!

'Free after two thousand years! Two thousand years ago, King Solomon, master of the Djinns, imprisoned me within that bottle. For me this is the first moment of my new freedom.'

– The Thief of Baghdad

Alex arrived back in England on Wednesday, 19 January 1938 after a stormy Atlantic crossing. His two-month trip to the United States had been a failure. He had neither won control of United Artists nor secured more favourable terms in his distribution contract. But in the ritual homecoming interviews he glossed over his troubles so convincingly that the newspaper headlines announced not the collapse of the United Artists deal, but his intention to spend £1,800,000 on fifteen films. He couldn't go into details, he said, but he had been pressed by several American companies to produce for them. The first film would probably be *The Four Feathers*, starring Robert Donat; then there would be a film about the Russian ballet; and an Irving Berlin musical which he hoped Ernst Lubitsch would direct. Regaled with all these wonderful plans, many of the reporters completely forgot to ask Alex why he had gone to Hollywood in the first place. When the subject did come up, through a careful choice of words Alex managed to turn even this to his credit. As he told the *Daily Mail*, he 'refused to complete the deal' – *refused*, not failed to do so.[1] Economic circumstances had changed so much since the option was first obtained that he and Goldwyn came to the conclusion that the purchase price was no longer fair.

It was true that several American companies had discussed the possibility of Alex making films for them. But he was not free to pursue these negotiations so long as he was bound by his United Artists contract. The fifteen films and the £1,800,000 were therefore impressive-sounding but empty figures. Only one comment he made to the newspapers on his return had the ring of sincerity: 'In Hollywood no one talks of failure. Everyone talks of success.'[2]

But in private even Alex had to consider the consequences of failure. In the week following his return, he wrote a twenty-page memorandum, which analysed the various options available to secure a future for London Films and to relieve the Prudential of the burden of supporting it. Paramount, Twentieth Century-Fox and MGM had all offered to buy a stake in London Films, but any intervention from an American company at the present time, Alex argued, would be 'to save a sinking ship', and a much better deal could be achieved if first 'our own house is put in order'.[3] This was a euphemism for borrowing more money from the Prudential, an idea that its directors had long ago ceased to find appealing.

In March, Ernest Lever expressed to Mary Pickford his hopes that United Artists would take a constructive attitude to London Films' difficulties. The only immediate practical solution, he explained, was for the company to collaborate with other production companies in return for financial support:

Attractive offers of this kind have already been made to 'London Films' and in my view it is greatly to the advantage of United Artists to approve of such an arrangement . . .

On the other hand, if there is any unwillingness on the part of the other shareholders of United Artists to deal with the matter on these common-sense lines, the only alternative to the 'Prudential', as principal creditor of 'London Films', is to put the Company into liquidation and to make arrangements for the occupation of the studios with some entirely fresh group.

I personally should be very reluctant if we were driven to this course as I much prefer to maintain the present relationships. The matter is, however, very urgent and unless a decision is taken quickly I shall have no option but to take the drastic course.[4]

The response of the United Artists stockholders was to authorize Sam Goldwyn and Douglas Fairbanks Sr to set off on a fact-finding mission to England. The discussions that ensued in the first half of April 1938 led to both a complete reorganization of United Artists and more lenient distribution terms for its producers, which both Alex and the Prudential had long been arguing for. But it was not enough to change the Prudential's conviction that London Films' future lay in an amalgamation with another company.

Alex himself had outlined their preferred solution when in his long memorandum he discussed the possibility of amalgamating London Films with Pinewood Studios, General Film Distributors and the Odeon Circuit:

> An association with the Pinewood Group (Rank and Lord Portal) has been under discussion for many months. Innumerable conversations have taken place, but it seems that the advantages of any such combination are on the other side rather than on our side.
>
> The Pinewood studios are situated a few miles from Denham. They make pictures which are chiefly distributed by an organisation called General Film Distributors. The pictures they produce are mediocre. They have no properly functioning organisation and their distribution organisation is also not at par with first-class ones, although if given high-class product it might shape itself into a first-class distribution company.
>
> For us an amalgamation with this group would only be advisable in the following instance; that in exchange for our taking over their studios and organising them along with our own, they should take the risky part of financing the mutual future output of the production companies.

Alex, who could not hide his distaste for this option, would have been dismayed to discover how seriously the Prudential took the idea. It had for them the appeal of being an entirely British solution. Their one reservation was that it would be better if under the new arrangement London Film Productions didn't have to produce any films of its own at all. But they were advised by their lawyers that such a cessation of production would make London Films and Alex liable in damages for breaking their contract with United Artists. 'In our view the damages would be substantial,' the lawyers commented, 'and would be measured by the loss of profit to the Distributor by reason of the contract not being carried out.'[5]

A little reluctantly, therefore, they worked out a modification. London Film Productions, which would cease to produce films itself, would run Denham Studios and be amalgamated with the Pinewood Group. But Alex would be set up in a new production company with just enough finance to meet the minimum obligations of the United Artists distribution contract.

At the beginning of August 1938 Percy Crump wrote a memorandum explaining the proposals, underlining the words 'private and confidential' three times in blue crayon. He emphasized some points that were essential to a proper understanding of the situation:

> The fact that we have lost a great deal of money through our association with K. must be faced. We cannot now start from scratch ... K's engaging personality and charm of manner must be resisted. His financial sense is non-existent and his promises (even when they are sincere) worthless. In other words, he is impossible to work with, and whatever is done we must be prepared to lose his services if he will not submit to our decisions. K. is a very dominant man and also very dangerous to converse with owing to (among other things) his powers of persuasion. For some time past he has been treated far too leniently bearing in mind our knowledge of him.[6]

In November Ernest Lever circulated within the Prudential the final blueprint for the reorganization. It amounted to a kind of amicable divorce. Alex would lose control of London Film Productions, but receive a generous settlement with which to form a new company. The Prudential would continue to have a substantial investment in the separated studio company, but would be in a much better position to realize their investment if they so wished. Above all, they would be free of any responsibility to find further finance. Lever ended his report with this conclusion:

> I submit that whatever loss, if any, ultimately emerges from the operation of my plan it will in any case be less than that which would result from immediate liquidation, and in addition adverse publicity, with its probable harm to the 'Prudential' business generally, will be minimised if not entirely avoided.[7]

But the following month London Films' annual report led to just the sort of adverse publicity that Lever had feared. 'Korda's £3,000,000 Film Company Makes £756 Profit!' ran the headline in the *Daily Express*. 'The most surprising news,' reported the article, 'is that the company will soon hold only ten £1 shares out of 750,000 in the company controlling Denham Studios.'[8] More embarrassing details followed.

In the circumstances Alex had little choice but to accept the Prudential's reorganization. In December 1938 he arrived in Hollywood, where he persuaded his United Artists partners to approve the formation of a new film company to be called Alexander Korda Film Productions. On 16 January 1939 a meeting of the stockholders resolved that the films produced by this new company 'should be accepted by United Artists Corporation for all purposes as if they were pictures produced by London Film Productions'.[9] The only dissenter was Sam Goldwyn, who argued that the resolution amounted to a technical violation of his own contract with United Artists, which he had long wanted to be free of.

On 20 March 1939 the birth of Alexander Korda Film Productions was made public. A London Films press release announced:[10]

> As a further step in the reorganization of the Denham Studios and London Films' production groups, a new film company has been formed for the production of the individual films of Mr Alexander Korda. The new company will continue the tradition set by London Film Productions in producing only pictures for the world market. The films of the new company

will be presented by London Film Productions and distributed throughout the world by United Artists, of which Mr Korda is one of the owner members.

Everything was phrased so as to suggest a continuity. But in practice London Film Productions had ceased to have any active role. It possessed the title to all its old productions but, in accordance with Lever's masterplan, Denham had been amalgamated with Rank's Pinewood Studios, 'leaving the truncated London Films Company gradually to liquidate'.

Debt, as both the Prudential and Alex knew, was a fluctuating, insubstantial thing, which so long as it didn't land, offered the hope of a reduction and even being transformed into a benefit. But now it had landed, and no one could conceal that the Prudential had paid a heavy price for its association. In the Prudential archives there exists a graph which charts London Films' 'loan indebtedness'. It outlines the situation during the crucial period over which London Film Productions was broken up. The inked line rises from a figure of £1,170,000 in February 1938 to a peak of £1,330,000 in September 1938 before inclining slowly down to £1,260,000 by November 1939. But it was a tiny note underneath that revealed the full cost incurred in supporting Alex:

An amount of £1,495,000 which was formerly loan indebtedness of London Films has now been converted into Share Capital and Debenture of D&P Studios Ltd, Notes of Korda Productions Ltd (£345,000), Preference Shares of Korda Productions Ltd (100,000). This amount is not included in the above graph.[11]

//

The wrangling over the future of Alex and his company coincided with one of his biggest productions, *The Four Feathers*, and it was perhaps a sign of the intensity of boardroom discussions that Alex delegated the day-to-day production decisions to an associate producer, Irving Asher. *The Four Feathers*, which had already been made twice before, was the archetypal British Empire story. Harry Faversham comes from a family with a strong military tradition, but believes himself to be unsuited to a military career. On the eve of his regiment's departure for the Sudan, he resigns his commission, and receives three white feathers from his former comrades, and a fourth from his fiancée. He sets off for the Sudan determined to prove his bravery, and so earn the right to return the four feathers. The film had been one of those projects that kept on being put back and back. Alex had wanted Robert Donat to star, but the actor wasn't happy with the script and over a period of a year rejected rewrite after rewrite. In April 1938, fed up with Donat's intransigence, Alex released him from his contract and gave the leading part to John Clements instead. Shooting of the interior sequences took place at Denham between July and September 1938. Then in October Zoltán Korda went out to the Sudan with a large unit to film on location. The principal actors, Ralph Richardson and John Clements, went along too. David Cunynghame's diary gives some sense of the scale of the picture. On 6 November Zoltán 'rehearsed the burning of the Zareba camp using 103 Fuzzie Wuzzies, 375 Shendi Horse dressed as Dervishes, 25 Shendi Horse dressed as Sudanese'. When he filmed the Battle of Omduran a few days later, there were 1,734 natives.

The crew returned to England in time for Christmas. There were a few shots to be completed in the studio, but otherwise there was nothing to do but to wait for Alex to view the footage and to pass judgement.

Aware that *The Four Feathers* would be the first production of his new company, Alexander Korda Film Productions, Alex was more determined than ever to fashion it into the perfect box-office attraction. After running a rough cut of the picture at the beginning of February, he asked for two weeks of added scenes and retakes.

The usual bitter arguments followed. On the third day of retakes, 17 February 1939, Cunynghame recorded Zoltán working 'distressingly slowly because of his disgust at having to make particular scenes'. There's no specific mention of what these scenes were, but some of the bad feeling may have been caused by the different attitudes of the two brothers to imperial conquest. While Alex shared his friend Churchill's view of the Empire as one of Britain's great achievements, Zoltán's sympathies lay with the native peoples who had to endure British rule whether they wanted it or not. His own experience of Alex's paternalistic dictatorship at London Films would have given him a peculiar insight into how they must have felt.*

On 3 April Alex held a preview of the film at the Majestic Cinema in Wembley and, although the reception was favourable, he cut it by about ten minutes as a result of the comments. The film received excellent reviews after a première at the Leicester Square Odeon on 17 April, but still Alex cut it by another fifteen minutes 'in response to requests from America'.[12] It was a film that he could not afford to have fail. Eventually, even in spite of having a general release in Britain that coincided with the closure of cinemas for a fortnight at the beginning of the war, it would become one of Alex's most successful films, with box-office receipts of over £300,000.

//

Away from the studio, 1938 was the year in which a romance with Merle Oberon finally blossomed – news that seemed to fill the Prudential with as much alarm as Alex's production plans. 'He has on several occasions obtained loans from London Films of about £3,000 each which, so far as I know, are still outstanding,' observed Percy Crump in August 1938. 'One of these loans was made just about the time he presented M.O. with a piece of jewellery estimated to cost the same amount.'[13]

In September the couple were spotted yachting in Mexican waters, but, as Louella Parsons pointed out in her column, they were well chaperoned by friends. 'I don't think there is any doubt in the world that Merle and Alex are fond of each other, and perhaps later may have an announcement to make, but each insists now there are no matrimonial plans.'[14]

After over a year away, Merle was back in Hollywood playing in another Goldwyn picture, opposite Gary Cooper in *The*

---

* One of the black extras who had worked on *Sanders of the River* was the future Prime Minister of Kenya, Jomo Kenyatta, then a student at the London School of Economics. He and Zoltán would remain lifelong friends.

Cowboy and the Lady. After that, in mid-November, she was due to begin work on *Wuthering Heights*. In a notable departure from her previous attitude, she begged Goldwyn to allow her to return to England between pictures.

By December, when both Merle and Alex were in Hollywood, Miss Parsons was able to give her readers some more conclusive news. Merle 'has told her closest friends that she is in love with him and Alex has made no secret of his admiration for the beautiful English actress'.[15] It seemed now less a question of if than when.

Alex and Merle provided Hollywood's big romance that Christmas and were photographed together in public several times. On one occasion he visited Merle on the set of *Wuthering Heights*. She was shooting the scene in which Cathy marries Linton, who was played by David Niven. As it was common knowledge in Hollywood that Merle and Niven had once been going out together, a Goldwyn publicist put out a tongue-in-cheek story about Alexander Korda being present at their marriage. It was just a harmless jape, but Alex was furious.

'Of all the idiotic tasteless tricks this is certainly the record in indecent and low publicity,' he cabled Goldwyn.[16] 'It would be too good if I could believe that you had no hand in it . . . I regard it even graver because we had differences in business and certainly to hit back this way is the sign of a man of no character and of no taste.' Usually, he would have taken such an incident in his stride. The failure to do so in this case was a sign both of how deeply he had been smitten and also of a vulnerability. He was nearly twenty years older than Merle, and knew of her affairs with not just David Niven but also several other men much younger than himself. He might also have reflected that the last time Merle had considered marriage, it was to Joseph Schenck, at the time fat and sixty years old but also one of the most powerful men in Hollywood. In the past Merle had always put her career first. The only small solace to draw was that as one of Hollywood's most bankable stars she now had less reason to use him. It was a near-even match, and, whatever the sedentary, exercise-avoiding Alex may have lacked for an outdoor girl whose favourite habitat was the beach, none the less she was genuinely fond of him, and appreciative of his wisdom, humour and taste. It was impossible not to admire his achievements and, to the extent that Merle too was completely dedicated to her craft, she valued his example as an inspiration.

Alex returned to England early in February 1939. Merle was due to join him there two months later after attending a special preview performance of *Wuthering Heights* in the presence of America's First Lady, Eleanor Roosevelt. Was she going to marry Alexander Korda, a reporter asked when she stopped off in Chicago on the return journey. 'Yes or no?' 'I won't say yes and I won't say no,' she replied.[17] Alex met her at Le Havre when her ship, the *Normandie*, arrived on 6 April. A brief holiday in the South of France followed. They stayed at the Hôtel du Cap at Antibes. Among the other guests there were Jack and Joseph Kennedy, Marlene Dietrich and Josef Von Sternberg. Everyone assumed that Alex and Merle were sleeping together, but they occupied separate suites, both being by nature secretive and mindful of outward propriety.

The two were seen together again in public in London at the première of *The Four Feathers* on 17 April. The large, glittering bracelet on Merle's arm must have caused some qualms in Holborn Bar, but still a polite 'No comment' awaited all inquiries concerning their marriage plans. Teasing the press was a game they both enjoyed enormously.

It was certainly easier to play than the marriage itself would be. Almost from the outset there was a note of disappointment. 'I was a little shocked by the ceremony,' said Merle after their wedding in Antibes on 3 June 1939.

> It was brief; so abrupt. We were married by a justice of the peace – but I thought there would be a little more to it. It didn't amount to much more than saying 'Do you want to marry this woman? Do you want to marry this man? All right – you're married.'[18]

But Alex's present to Merle of a necklace that had once been worn by Marie Antoinette would presumably have made some amends.

On their return home to England three days later, Merle,

who did not want to live in Alex's house in Avenue Road, went house-hunting. Eventually they found a large house in Denham, but any hopes Merle might have had of enjoying the first few months of her married life in peace evaporated when Alex persuaded his brothers and their families to move into the house too. It was also a shock for someone who went early to bed, did not smoke and had a small appetite to adjust to Alex's insomniac life-style with its heavy dependence on rich food and cigars.

Feeling trapped by her surroundings, Merle longed to return to work. Alex promised to star her in a film version of *Manon Lescaut*, although it seems doubtful that he was any more serious about this than he had been earlier about *Anne Boleyn*. Goldwyn for his part dangled the prospect of her appearing with Gary Cooper in *Hans Christian Andersen*, if she could be back in Hollywood by September. Merle begged him to wait until after *Manon Lescaut*, which Alex told her it would be impossible to finish before the end of September. But in the event, much to Merle's annoyance, neither *Manon Lescaut* nor *The Constant Nymph*, another star vehicle Alex had purchased for her that summer, got off the ground. Already the marriage was under strain.

Alex had gained a wife, but lost a studio. As he prepared his new company's first production, *The Thief of Baghdad*, he must have found it embarrassing to turn up for work in the place that had once served as the symbol of his film empire now that it was no longer his. Most dethroned kings can hide their shame in exile, but Alex still had his office in the Old House by the river, and he still had to walk among his staff – most of whom were now no longer his staff. But at least, now that he had no huge studio to run, he could concentrate on making films again.

The first of many directors to work on *The Thief of Baghdad* was Marc Allegret, but he struggled to produce a satisfactory script and resigned at the end of February 1939. Alex then gave the assignment to Ludwig Berger, a German director who had made a name for his film versions of musical productions. He had recently had a great success with a film made in Paris called *Les Trois Waltzes*. Berger, who had a doctorate in musicology from Heidelberg, had his own distinct way of making films. He believed that the entire look and action should be dictated by the music, which contrary to usual practice would be composed before filming had begun.

Alex's decision to choose Berger stemmed from his own conviction that music should play a prime role in *The Thief of Baghdad*. In January 1939, many months before the production itself began, he had hired the composer Mischa Spoliansky 'to write, compose, adapt and arrange such themes, songs, compositions and arrangements as may be required'.[19] But after the success of *The Four Feathers* opening in April, when several critics singled out Miklós Rózsa's score for praise, Alex asked Rózsa if he would like to compose the music for *The Thief of Baghdad* instead. Rózsa's Sudanese and Arabic themes in *The Four Feathers* had amounted to an excellent rehearsal for an oriental fantasy, and Alex wasn't going to let the small matter of a signed contract with Spoliansky get in the way.

But now Berger insisted that the Viennese composer Oscar Strauss, with whom he had worked closely on *Les Trois Waltzes*, should write the score. As music was of such importance to Berger's method, Alex had to accept this choice of a key collaborator if he still wanted Berger to be the director. So Strauss was engaged. 'Naturally this came as a shock,' Rózsa recalled – like Spoliansky before him, he too had had a signed contract. But Alex told him that he was still on the production team and that he should have faith that everything would turn out right in the end.[20] It would just be a matter of a little simple engineering.

The manoeuvres that followed were an example of Alex's flair for manipulation. Strauss's pre-production music began to arrive from Vichy, where he was taking a cure. Both Muir Mathieson, Alex's musical director, and Rózsa thought it 'turn-of-the-century Viennese candy-floss',[21] which would ruin the film. Alex summoned them to his office for a meeting with Berger, at which they voiced their objections. He told them that in all artistic matters Berger's decision was to be final, but once Berger had left the room he told Rózsa to go ahead and write his own music. He then arranged for him to have an office next door to Berger's.

'Keep playing your music until he comes in and listens to it,' he said. 'Don't say I told you to do it, just say you wrote it off your own bat and let him hear it.'[22]

Berger's confidence in Strauss had already been shaken by the meeting in Alex's office. So when he overheard Rózsa's melodies from next door, the hint must have been pretty clear. Finally he knocked on Rózsa's door as Alex had predicted he would, and invited the composer to play some more pieces. Genuinely impressed, he then went to see Alex and told him that he preferred Rózsa's music. So Berger's decision *was* final, but he had been firmly pushed into it by Alex.

Berger began filming on Friday 9 June. Straightaway he put his special technique into operation. The actors would play the scene to an audio playback, moving in synchronization with the music. But when he attempted to shoot the scene in which Abu the thief first appears, the result was chaos. 'Sabu', recalled Rózsa, 'was expected to move like a puppet in a puppet theatre, the actors like dancers in a pantomime, but to appear at the same time to be acting quite spontaneously and naturally. They just couldn't get it right, and after a week's work we had practically nothing to show.'[23]

Alex intervened, insisting that the scene be shot again without music, which would be added afterwards in the conventional way. The only sequences to use Berger's highly artificial method of pre-composed music were scenes which in themselves involved artifice – the Flying Horse galloping across the skies, the Silver Maiden dancing with her six arms.

Even without the pre-recorded music, Berger's vision of a minimalist, stylized Arabian Nights fantasy conflicted with Alex's more lavish concept of a Technicolor extravaganza. But Alex was unable to sack the director without having to pay out an enormous sum in compensation. So instead he watched him closely, stepping in whenever a scene did not meet with his approval.

Fundamentally at odds with Berger's approach, Alex came to rely more and more heavily on Michael Powell, who had been employed as director of a 'B' unit. In view of Powell's subsequent reputation as one of Britain's great film directors, it would be tempting to suggest that he was the key creative figure, but David

Cunynghame's diaries make it clear that all the way through Alex was the dominating force, just as prepared to overrule Powell as he was Berger.

'So much better than real people,' says the Sultan of Basra when he shows off to the Grand Vizier his miniature puppets who dance without strings. It was with a rather similar attitude that Alex allowed a whole troupe of puppet directors to take their places behind the camera. On 10 July a third unit began to photograph the flying horse sequences on a special ramp erected in West Hyde, under the supervision of a special effects director, Lawrence Butler. Then, shortly afterwards, a fourth unit was formed to work with the American director William Cameron Menzies, who directed trick photography sequences of the djinni and the flying carpet. On 18 August, the fifty-ninth day of shooting, Berger would be finally 'faded out', in Cunynghame's words, to be replaced by the American director Tim Whelan, who had just finished directing the film *Q Planes* which Alex had produced for distribution by Columbia. And so, juggling all these efforts, Alex, in the words of John Justin, Sabu's co-star in *The Thief of Baghdad*, 'controlled the film totally and, effectively, directed it'.[24]

//

The contrast between what Berger had intended and what Alex subsequently imposed provided an excellent example of the grandiose Korda style, as John Justin recalled:

> A scene under Berger's direction involved June [Duprez], Sabu and me, a donkey, a bale of straw and a short flight of wet steps. When Alex re-did this scene, it filled the whole of the biggest stage at Denham and included a dozen camels, mules, horses, three elephants, 400 extras, tons of fruit and vegetables.[25]

The scene showed the Princess arriving at her father's palace. But for Alex it was never enough simply to arrive in a place, particularly if you were a beautiful princess. So ten trumpeters fanfare the approach of her procession. Then twenty galloping horsemen clear the crowds in the market square, trampling down the stalls of the traders. Five archers appear and unleash arrows at the stragglers. 'It is death to look upon the Sultan's daughter,' a panic-stricken passer-by hurriedly explains, diving behind a door as an arrow thuds into the wood. The blind Prince Ahmad, dispossessed of his kingdom, and his young friend the thief Abu quickly take cover on a low roof, and from their hiding-place watch the large procession. In the vanguard the Princess's musicians play a marching tune. Behind them follows a group of Nubian standard-bearers, and then, escorted by their handlers, the Princess's animals which include several birds and a caged leopard. The Princess herself is borne aloft on a white-painted elephant, flanked on either side by ladies-in-waiting who fan her with peacock-feathers. The result might easily have been far-fetched in another's hands, but Alex raised such extravagance to a high level of art, the rich detail facilitating the fantasy. Lush and intoxicating, the images pulled the audience into the *Arabian Nights* dream.

After such an arrival it seemed entirely natural that Ahmad should fall in love with the Princess at first sight and then with Abu's help seek to engineer a meeting. Hiding in a tree above her garden pool, Ahmed is mistaken by the Princess for a djinn. When the Princess ruffles the water, to her great distress the Djinn disappears. Ahmed then drops out of the tree and stands before the Princess in person.

'Who are you?' asks the Princess.

'Your slave.'

'Where have you come from?'

'From the other side of time, to find you.'

'How long have you been searching?'

'Since time began.'

'Now that you've found me how long will you stay?'

'Until the end of time. For me there can be no more beauty in the world but yours.'

'For me there can be no more pleasure in the world than to please you.'

Then they kiss.

From first question to kiss the scene takes exactly forty-eight seconds. The two have never been formerly introduced before, but we know that they will love each other for ever.

Alex's achievement was to create a world in which such expression seemed entirely plausible. But this Technicolor fairytale was very expensive. Among the carefully catalogued budget figures that the Prudential kept of London Films' productions, none is to be found for *The Thief of Baghdad* since it was made for Alex's new company, but United Artists estimated the final cost to be nearly $2 million or £400,000, which would have made it easily Alex's most expensive production up until then. As John Justin commented, 'If it had been the mess it looked like being, then Korda would have been finished.'[26]

Of all Alex's heroes, the Thief of Baghdad – the boy Abu – comes closest to epitomizing the way he would have liked to have thought of himself. 'Abu, the little thief,' wrote Alex,

> steals to relieve the hunger of others and to promote romance in the universe. He laughs at the world as he does his marvelous tricks of magic. And who among us would not give a great deal to be with him when he finds the magic bottle that imprisons that slave of all slaves, the jinni? At heart we are all Abus, and we yearn to perform his kind of legerdemain – the kind that gives happiness to mankind. *The Thief of Baghdad* is the closest we may ever come to realizing that ideal. Salaam![27]

16. THE SERVICE

As war approached, Alex raced to finish *The Thief of Baghdad*, filming on Sundays including even the Sunday of 3 September on which war was declared. The last full shooting day was Saturday, 4 November. Then, after many weeks of special effects work, a rough cut was ready for Alex to view on 29 December. He made his usual list of retakes and added scenes, which would eventually be filmed in America. The general consensus was that *The Thief of Baghdad* was a fine film, but Alex no longer seemed to be very interested. The war presented him with a much bigger adventure, which was the climax to a struggle he had been secretly engaged in for some time. Alex was so adept at concealing the truth, so full of tricks and stratagems and reasons behind reasons, that it was only natural that even being a film producer should have been a front for something else.

//

In the early months of 1937, as *I, Claudius* wended its way to disaster, a young graduate called Andrew King was at Denham being given an intensive course in the film business. It was a career that he could not possibly have anticipated when he came down from Cambridge the previous year.

Unsure of what he wanted to do, he had left his name with the University Appointments Board, specifying an interest in travel. Some weeks later, he received a letter from a mysterious organization called 'The Albany Syndicate', offering him an interview in London. In a one-room office, furnished with just two chairs, a desk and telephone, he met a Mr Hayward, a man of about sixty with a hawk nose, dark-rimmed glasses, a small moustache and piercing eyes.

'We had a chat,' King recalled. 'He said, "I understand you've just been to Germany and Austria. Now tell me about them. What were your impressions?" I said, "Well, sir, I can only say this, I am absolutely certain that there *is* going to be a war between Nazi Germany and Britain. I can't see how it is going to be avoided."'

This comment seemed to impress Mr Hayward. But by the end of the interview, King still had no idea what job he might be expected to do.

'Well, as a matter of fact, this is something which requires a bit of discretion at this moment,' Hayward replied. 'I hope I can trust you. There are a group of people in the film world who are more and more worried about how our films aren't getting enough market, and particularly in Europe.'

Six weeks later King was summoned to another interview. He turned up at the office to find the door locked and so waited outside. After a few minutes a large, rather lanky figure came walking towards him. The man introduced himself as Mr Crane. Hayward hadn't been able to come, he explained, and had sent him in his place.

Crane took King off to the Berkeley Grill. 'During the lunch I kept saying, "Well, can you give a little bit more detail about this job in the film business?" And he kept on side-stepping. But eventually I realized that he was adopting a confidential way of speech, and just before he said it, I said to myself, "He's going to ask me to join the Secret Service," and he did!'

The organization King was about to join was actually even more secret than the Secret Service. Its origins went back to 1930, when Robert Vansittart, a far-sighted and unusually independent Permanent Under-Secretary at the Foreign Office, formed what became known as 'Vansittart's Private Detective Agency' to gather information on the rise of Fascism in Germany. The Secret Intelligence Service itself, which had been neglected by successive governments, was then poorly placed to perform such a task. The bulwark of this new agency would be businessmen who had contacts in Germany, but Vansittart turned to a member of the Secret Intelligence Service to organize and recruit for it.

Colonel Claude Dansey was the head of the SIS station in Rome. As a veteran of campaigns against the Matabele, the Boers and the Mad Mullah, he was the sort of character who might easily have featured in one of Alex's British Empire epics. He joined the Secret Intelligence Service during the First World War, pursued a business career in the 1920s, making a wide range of contacts, and then resumed his work for the Service in 1929.

In 1935 SIS was penetrated by the German Abwehr, and Vansittart's Private Detective Agency assumed a new importance as the head of SIS, Admiral Quex Sinclair, commissioned Dansey to operate a separate intelligence service that would operate in parallel but independently of SIS. This secret service, which grew out of Vansittart's Private Detective Agency, was called Z Organization.

The mysterious Mr Hayward, who had interviewed Andrew King, was none other than Claude Dansey himself – Colonel Z. And Mr Crane was Commander Kenneth Cohen, Dansey's deputy – Z2. The new organization took offices on the eighth floor of Bush House, which were rented under the name of C. E. Moore.

Andrew King, who began work there in October 1936, was given the name Z18 and a salary of £450 a year tax-free. For the first few weeks there was very little to do. Dansey explained that he was trying to organize cover for King to work in films in Europe, but that the situation was not quite ripe yet. 'Of course all that time,' King recalled, 'he was talking to Korda.'

King had the impression that Dansey and Alex were very close friends and that they had known each other for a long time. The very nature of their association means that there is no hard evidence as to when the two men first met, but it seems likely that it would have been in late 1931 when Alex was establishing himself as a producer in England. At that time Vansittart and Dansey would have been actively building up their network of contacts and on the look-out for anyone with useful Continental connections. Alex's contempt for Nazism, his intimate knowledge of Austria and Germany, as well as his continuing business association with those countries, must have made him seem an extremely promising prospect. Both men would have realized that the kind of international film company Alex was setting up, with offices all over Europe, would provide perfect cover for the activities of their agents.

Manipulative and secretive and with a taste for intrigue, Alex was born to be a spy. So many of his films from *The Prince and the Pauper* onwards suggest a yearning for such a double life. He was really the perfect colleague for Dansey, by affinity attuned to the spymaster's elusive, conspiratorial nature. Both men preferred, in Somerset Maugham's words, 'devious ways to straight'. So it's difficult to imagine that Dansey and Vansittart would have had to work very hard to enlist his support, but in any case they were able to offer irresistible terms that included access to some of Britain's most influential people. Alex was in effect joining the most secret but powerful club in the world, which was able at key moments to offer invaluable behind-the-scenes support. In 1932 Vansittart and Dansey, through the Secret Intelligence Service, helped him to obtain his stake in London Film Productions. It is likely too that they had an instrumental role in persuading the Prudential to back London Film Productions in 1934, as Dansey's circle of business associates included the two pivotal figures in the negotiation, Montagu Marks and Sir Connop Guthrie. The international expansion of London Films that the Prudential's money facilitated would certainly have helped to strengthen their secret network.

One of the weightiest members of the club was Winston Churchill, whom Dansey had first got to know as long ago as the Boer War, when they both served in the same regiment, the South African Light Horse. As Churchill was not only out of political favour in the early 1930s but also in somewhat straitened circumstances, Dansey steered him in the direction of Alex, who was happy to provide him with gainful employment.

The 'All for one and one for all' nature of Dansey's network would have encouraged Alex's generally cavalier approach towards money. It was easier to disregard the strict rules of profit and loss when you felt that the continuing existence of your company was of national importance, and that in any grave circumstance you could rely on powerful friends to come to your aid.

Dansey arranged with Alex that London Film Productions would provide cover for his agents in Europe, and in early 1937 Z18 was sent off to Denham on a training course. King recalled an enjoyable few weeks. He saw several celebrities – including a disconsolate Charles Laughton eating his lunch in the studio restaurant still dressed in his Claudius costume – and he made friends with a South African cutter in the editing department, Henry Cornelius, who would years later become famous as the director of the comedies *Passport to Pimlico* and *Genevieve*. Whenever anyone asked him what he was doing, he told them that he was going to work in Foreign Sales. No one seemed to be suspicious.

After his training was over, King went to have an interview with Alex, who had organized cover for him in Vienna. The company that distributed his films there was already fully staffed, so Alex suggested that he operate independently as his talent scout.

> He said, 'You must keep in touch with Cunynghame, and of course if you find budding film stars that's wonderful, but otherwise you can concentrate on things like looking at film scenarios that ambitious young men want to submit for your attention and that sort of thing.' That sort of thing! And that was that.[1]

King arrived in Vienna in the summer of 1937. He made contact with various people that Dansey had named and also found the time to send a few scenarios back to David Cunynghame. By February 1938 he was certain that the Germans were about to march in, warned Dansey, and he slipped out of the country. 'I thought, if the Nazis are coming I really don't want them to find *me*.' Two weeks later the *Anschluss* occurred.

Alex's chief role in the two organizations was to provide cover, and several other Z members trained at Denham. But when it was appropriate, he would play a more active part. The refugees André De Toth had noticed waiting outside his office were an example. Alex actively encouraged contacts who had fled

Nazism in Central Europe to turn to him for help. He would then assess their value as sources of useful information and pass the most promising candidates on to the Z organization.

It's possible that in an even more mysterious venture shortly before the war Alex sent a film crew, at Dansey's request, to North Africa to photograph the features of a region that British intelligence believed would become an important battlefield. The costume designer Marcel Vertès claimed to have worked on the fictitious film, *King Pausanius*, that served as a cover. No trace of this venture can be found in Cunynghame's diaries, where one would have expected to find a mention, but the notion itself is entirely plausible. Years later, after the war, a fellow member of the Secret Service club, Graham Greene, recalled Alex confiding to him during a holiday they spent together aboard Alex's yacht that he had obtained 'a currency allowance of some size from British Intelligence' because they were going to photograph the length of the Yugoslav coastline.[2]

It's a tantalizing exercise for the lack of evidence, but with hindsight it's possible to suspect the hidden involvement of British intelligence at just about every stage in Alex's career in Britain. Had Dansey, for example, in some way nursed along Alex's deal with Ludovico and Giuseppe Toeplitz? He had been head of the SIS station in Rome until 1935, and must have regarded the Toeplitzes, with their high-level connections among the Italian Fascists, as extremely promising sources of information. Then there was Alex's documentary about flight, *Conquest of the Air*, which he began to make just as Germany was beginning to build up its air force. In 1934 he would send a couple of researchers to Germany to attend an air pageant and to interview the air ace Ernst Udet, who would become a leading figure in the newly strengthened Luftwaffe. Vansittart's Private Detective Agency, one imagines, would have been eager to have some involvement.

After the war Alex treated King to a private lunch and offered him a career in the film business. King chose to remain a full-time member of the Secret Intelligence Service – with which the Z organization had amalgamated at the outbreak of hostilities in 1939 – but several other agents took up Alex's offer, including King's friend John Codrington, who was Z3 in Dansey's organization and also a veteran of the London Films training course. Dansey himself joined the board of Alex's newly acquired company, British Lion, in 1946, and although he died the following year, Alex's connections with intelligence continued.

The Second World War serves as a kind of unofficial watershed in what former members of British Intelligence are prepared to reveal about their activities. So it's difficult to state with any certainty what assistance Alex provided from 1945 onwards, but as Greene's anecdote suggests, he was happy to help in whatever way he could. Perhaps no other pursuit better summed Alex up. While he often dismissed film-making as a rather trivial and tedious activity, the Service – with its bluffs and counter-bluffs – offered endless potential for keeping him amused. It must also have appealed to his self-importance. He was a cynic, but an idealist, whose ultimate fulfilment depended upon belonging to some noble cause. In the Service he could indulge his taste for intrigue and his 'devious ways', yet still imagine that he acted with integrity.

//

As Alex struggled in the summer and autumn of 1939 to finish *The Thief of Baghdad*, his sources of information on the dangerous turn of current affairs would have been impeccable. He kept in touch not only with Dansey but also with Sir Robert Vansittart, who lived close by in Denham Place. A lyricist of considerable ability, the diplomat spent much of his spare time writing songs for *The Thief of Baghdad* and working on the script. At the end of 1937 Vansittart had been replaced as the Permanent Under-Secretary at the Foreign Office by the incoming minister, Anthony Eden, and now had the grand but empty title of Chief Diplomatic Adviser to the Foreign Office, a position without influence. With his reputation as an outspoken opponent of Nazi Germany, he had been deliberately sidelined. If Sir Robert could find time to write songs, the French newspaper *Figaro* commented over-optimistically in August, then there could be no immediate danger of war.

In fact, Vansittart and Dansey confided to Alex their belief that war was coming that autumn. And, together with Churchill, who on 1 September 1939 regained office as First Lord of the Admiralty, they discussed how Alex might best contribute.

Michael Powell recalled Alex summoning his principal employees to a meeting a week before the outbreak of war. He explained that he had promised Churchill to make a big anti-Nazi film on the day war was declared and that in return the Government would promote the film industry as an essential war weapon. 'All he asked of us was that we would go with heart, mind and soul into making his new picture, and work with whomever we were assigned to.'[3]

On the Sunday morning of 3 September, after the air-raid warning that followed Chamberlain's announcement that Britain was at war, Powell found himself in a large concrete coal bunker at Denham with the cast and crew of *The Thief of Baghdad*. Their extravagant costumes, he felt, made the occasion somehow seem all the more menacing. Alex, he remembered, was smoking one of his cigars as usual. With Merle Oberon holding on to his arm and crying next to him, 'He took a deep breath and sent a perfect smoke ring into the air.'[4]

17. FOR KING AND COUNTRY

With the start of the war Merle realized that *Manon Lescaut* would not be made. She felt bored and lonely at the house in Denham and longed to get back to Hollywood. Alex had wanted her to stay with him in England, but she refused, and just three weeks after the declaration of war she set sail for America aboard the *New Amsterdam*. In Hollywood she did what she could to scotch the rumours that she and Alex were getting divorced after only four months of marriage. 'I couldn't possibly make my home here,' she told Louella Parsons, 'as Alex couldn't leave England and I wouldn't leave him. I am here now because Alex and our friends in the Government think it best for me to work instead of doing nothing till they find some use for me in England.'

The lengths Merle went to to tell the world and herself that she was still in love with Alex had a touching aspect. She made a point of wearing in public the jewellery that he had given her. When a reporter asked her about three intricately designed diamond roses that she wore in her lapel, she explained that Alex had bought them for her. 'As he was leaving the shop, he saw an elaborate diamond tiara on display in a showcase. In the centre of it were three diamond roses. He called the salesman and told him to take out the roses and have them made into clips. So here they are. And aren't they glorious?'[1]

It was wonderful to have a husband who had such taste and imagination, she said. So few men knew how to buy gifts that women really like. 'When she speaks of Korda,' the reporter observed, 'she usually says "my husband", in a proud, fond way. But sometimes she says "Mr Korda" – and just as proudly.' The tone was of a sort of respectful love, of someone desperately trying to convince herself that she was in love.

Merle felt guilty for having left England so quickly and she wanted to love Alex, but it had to be on her own terms. She had to be in California. In spite of the talk that she would return to England, she soon put down roots in Hollywood, buying an English-style manor on the Copa del Oro Road in Bel Air as well as a beach house. In November she began work on the aptly named *Till We Meet Again*.

//

The big anti-Nazi film that Alex had promised Churchill was begun some days before war was even declared. *The Lion Has Wings* was a propaganda documentary designed both to show the evils of Nazism and to demonstrate the ability of the RAF to defend Britain. Vansittart and Churchill were outsiders in the British establishment of the 1930s not only because they thought that every effort should be made to stop Hitler, but also because they liked the movies. When Alex began work on *The Lion Has Wings* it was a freelance effort which had received no Government sanction. The officials within the Ministry of Information whom he approached for support were rather sniffy about their dealings with him. 'The film fraternity generally are most unreliable and tricky,' commented Mr G. E. G. Forbes, the man at the Ministry chiefly responsible for the negotiations.[2] He hurried to get an agreement set down in writing because he believed such a document essential to control the actions of a producer 'whose brilliant artistic abilities and sincere desire to serve this country are combined with the artistic temperament to an extent which might cause embarrassment'.[3]

The first embarrassment would not be long in coming. On 30 August United Artists' head office in New York received a request from Alex that they guarantee a bank loan to cover the production costs of *The Lion Has Wings*. There would be great kudos in financing the first British propaganda film, he argued. Bending the truth, he told them that the Ministry of Information had asked him to make the film, although it had been he who had approached the Ministry first.

The New York office cabled back its acceptance on condition that the Ministry of Information recognized United Artists as the worldwide distributor. In his enthusiasm to be of service Alex omitted to mention this important detail to the Ministry, who had insisted on a British distributor. A month later, while Alex was negotiating such a deal, United Artists sent a cable reminding him of their position. 'Our contract with you provides that all pictures produced by you must be distributed through our corporation and its subsidiaries and the contract does not permit you to produce pictures for other distribution.'[4]

Alex cabled back: 'Hardly credible, but do not think you are yet informed that we are at war in Europe . . . Film in question is straight propaganda made on official request and authorities have last word about distribution.'[5] Yet it was United Artists he had asked to help finance the film in the first place. It was just one more example of Alex maintaining two contradictory positions until they collided. The situation was finally resolved by persuading the Ministry of Information to allow United Artists to be the distributor.

As far as the Foreign Office were concerned, the biggest embarrassment was that the film should have received the support of the Ministry at all. The policy of the British Government was that there should be no open propaganda in the United States. The then Foreign Secretary, Lord Halifax, observed:

> The fact is that at the moment the Americans, in their intense fear of being inveigled into war, have started a regular witch-hunt for propaganda . . . I am only too conscious of the danger of embarking at the present moment, when public opinion in the United States is so solidly behind the Allies, on anything which could be misinterpreted as a subtle attempt to influence United States opinion in our favour.[6]

The Lion Has Wings wasn't even subtle.

In his discussions with the Ministry of Information, Alex had raised the possibility of producing not just one film but a series under the general title of 'Britain Prepared'. Alex was certainly inspired by a wish to serve his adopted country, but he also wanted to anticipate the way the wind might blow. He

undoubtedly hoped that the Government would invite him to
direct the war effort of the British film industry. Indeed, as long
ago as 1935, when he had become an owner-member of United
Artists, he had sought a written exemption from his contract in
the case of Government service.* There was every possibility that
commercial film production in Britain might cease, so it was a
good time for Alex to prove his value to the Government.

Alex had spun so much publicity about *The Lion Has Wings*
that many people thought he was already the head of the Ministry's Films Division. The real head of the Films Division, Sir
Joseph Ball, was furious to learn that the famous documentarist,
John Grierson, had sent an open cable not to him but to Alex,
seeking his approval for a plan to spread propaganda in the
United States. In a note to the Foreign Office, Ball observed that
Grierson had once been head of the GPO Film Unit, which had
recently been seconded to the Ministry, but this relationship was
most unlikely to be renewed. 'The GPO's experience of him in
that connexion gives no reason to regard him as possessing the
degree of discretion required for the proposed work.'[7] Ball went
on to complain of an even worse indiscretion Grierson had
committed in sending a second open cable to Alex from Hollywood requesting 'carte blanche and the allocation of a fund to
enable him to "get something organized" – the "something"
being clearly indicated by the text of the cablegram as propaganda in one form or another'.†

The spectacle of Alex, the king of British features, and Grierson, the 'Father of Documentary', both hustling for influence at

---

* From a letter agreement between Alexander Korda and United Artists, 19
September 1935 (London Film Productions Archive): 'In case the Authorities,
solely in the public interest and for the encouragement, development and
promotion of the British Film industry, should invite Mr Korda to take part in
the reorganization of the British Film Industry, or a very substantial portion
thereof, Mr Korda shall have the right to undertake this commission.'
† 'I liked Korda very much personally,' Grierson would comment in an
interview many years later, 'but he was the sort of person I would have
discussed the whole world with but never worked with.' (See Elizabeth Sussex,
The Rise and Fall of British Documentary (University of California Press,
1975), p. 120.)

the beginning of the war has a predictable symmetry. Alex in those first few weeks was scarcely less indiscreet than Grierson. When Merle Oberon arrived in Hollywood in mid-October 1939, she went to considerable lengths to spread the message, presumably at Alex's bidding, that whatever might be happening in England Alex would be in the thick of it. 'My husband, you know, is by far the greatest figure connected with the English films,' she told the *Chicago Herald-American*.[8] 'We don't know, yet, what the war is going to do to the English film industry . . . For the time being my husband is producing pictures for the Government.'

On 2 November, in a story which was probably encouraged by Alex himself, the *Evening Standard* reported that he was about to hawk 'his new propaganda film' around the United States and that American moguls were only waiting to receive the go-ahead from the Ministry of Information to unleash their own propaganda efforts in support of Britain. The Foreign Office read the piece with consternation. 'If this news gets around in America nothing will more successfully kill the film, ruin Korda's reputation, and generally defeat every purpose which the film may have been designed to promote,' observed an official.[9] Alex himself, who was *en route* for New York, was instructed by cable to call in on a Foreign Office representative as soon as he arrived to be briefed on the issues at stake.

The necessity to muzzle him as swiftly as possible became even more apparent when it was discovered a few days later that he had requested the Ministry of Information to pay for a special publicity agent in America. On 13 November the Foreign Office sent an urgent cable in cypher to their representative in New York:

> This proposal is quite unacceptable and you should inform Mr Korda that His Majesty's Government cannot countenance anything which might give the impression that his efforts to secure distribution of the film have been undertaken on their behalf or have their support.[10]

Exasperated by Alex's ignorance of Government policy and the Ministry of Information's failure to seek proper consultation, the Foreign Office rebuked the Ministry of Information for their handling of the situation, reminding them that the Government had undertaken not to spread propaganda in the United States. 'This film, *The Lion Has Wings*, seems to be the first definite breach in this guarantee to the Americans, and I think it will be extremely difficult to defend if it gets challenged.'[11]

When Alex met the Foreign Office's representative in New York – a Mr Angus Fletcher, based at the British Library of Information – on 13 November, he confided to him that *The Lion Has Wings* was a piece of crude propaganda, which was what he thought had been called for. He was very surprised to learn that this was not the case at all. Rather than attempt to brazen it out or to minimize the gravity of the situation, as many of the officials at the Ministry of Information had attempted to do, he instantly appreciated the Foreign Office position and gave assurances that he would do everything he could to rectify the damage.

Suddenly no one seemed more anxious about the effect *The Lion Has Wings* might have in America than Alex. He had to set off at once for California, but before he did so he arranged for Fletcher to see the film at a private showing, asking that Fletcher let him know what he thought of it as soon as possible.

Fletcher later summarized his comments for the Foreign Office. Much of the propaganda, especially in the first third of the film, he had told Alex,

> was quite unnecessary in this country, where opinion had already made up its mind that Hitler was wrong and, by and large, that we were right, and that as it stood that part of the film could only strike an American audience as a rather obvious attempt to win its sympathies. I would therefore have preferred that the film should take for granted many of the points which it so laboriously made.

Alex then confided that he feared the film might cause a lot of trouble and asked whether Fletcher thought it could be redeemed for American audiences if the first part were remade in Hollywood. 'I replied that this was not a matter on which I was competent to express an opinion; obviously, it all depended on how it was remade. My own idea had been rather that it should be edited, and this I suppose would mean shortening.'[12]

It's difficult to know quite how sincere Alex was about remaking the film. His professions of grave concern are perhaps better regarded as an example of an astute sense of psychology. He had been forced into an about-turn, but his show of contrition and apparent eagerness to do whatever he could to make amends won the respect of the otherwise deeply put-out Foreign Office officials. 'Mr Korda seems to be behaving quite sensibly,' one of them observed.[13] In the end Alex didn't re-edit the picture, but prefaced the American release with the explanation that *The Lion Has Wings* was a British-made propaganda picture showing the defence organization of the Royal Air Force and that it was being shown in the United States for its interest as one of the first such films to come from the warring countries.

Alex adopted a tone of apologetic regret for his actions, safe in the knowledge that he had the perfect mole in the Foreign Office to put in a compensating good word for him. Fletcher attended the special screening of *The Lion Has Wings* with a colleague, Mr Gorer, who wrote a detailed report of the film. Fletcher then sent a copy of this report to the Foreign Office in London, where it worked its way through the echelons. 'This film was obviously produced in a great hurry for home consumption,' Gorer had written.

> From the technical point of view it is remarkable that any full-length film could have been produced in less than two months; but all through the film shows signs of hurry. Technically it is extremely indifferent and uneven, with dull cutting, mixed photography and complete lack of any internal rhythm . . .
>
> My belief is that for an American audience, for whom the various symbols have not such a poignant meaning, the chief impression would be simply of boredom. But apart from that, it seems to me likely that it would be adversely interpreted as blatant pro-British propaganda, which indeed it is. The American audience is now extremely aware of overt propaganda and contra-suggestible to it. Anything which they can label propaganda is immediately regarded with suspicion and distaste . . .[14]

In spite of the observations of Gorer and Fletcher, the Foreign Office applied no pressure to have the film re-edited. The general consensus was that the damage which had already been done would only be compounded by further official involvement. So by the time the report reached the Chief Diplomatic Adviser to the Foreign Office, it had become an academic matter. Sir Robert Vansittart observed on 17 December:

> The film had faults, but, having regard to the remarkably short time in which it was produced, it seemed to me a creditable effort on the whole. Mr Gorer is really too pernickety a critic. He would not only look a gift-horse in the mouth, but pull its teeth out one by one to be quite sure of them. The type is conscientious and not uncommon. But let us please remember that we have only made one film of this kind in 4 months of war – and it happens to be this one![15]

Sir Robert gave no hint that he had played a part in instigating the film in the first place, even though it was well known to his colleagues that he had worked for Alex. He did, however, make it known that he would soon be seeing his friend, who had just returned from America, and that he would discuss with him future plans for film production.

The man Anthony Eden had steered into a backwater as an 'almost fanatical crusader' must have been exasperated by the mealy-mouthed attitude of his Foreign Office colleagues. Their efforts to be tactful to the Americans amounted to a denial of the obvious. For all its failings *The Lion Has Wings* had at least stated with vigour the case that Vansittart had been making for years: Hitler was a problem not just for Britain but for the world. But Vansittart had long since become accustomed to the indifference with which his counsels were received. He himself would comment of the post of Chief Diplomatic Adviser, 'It was, as everyone knows, a polite device to get rid of me to please the Germans.'[16] He had only stayed on at Churchill's urging: if he couldn't influence Government policy it was none the less important for the anti-appeasers to know what that policy was. He would resign once Churchill had become Prime Minister, on 10 May 1940.

Michael Korda would write of *The Lion Has Wings* that 'Alex had cashed in his life insurance policies to finance it, and completed it in less than two months without any assistance from the Government.' This is the story that Alex no doubt happily told people afterwards, when it was important politically that such a blatant propaganda film should be regarded as 'a gesture of free enterprise'. But the truth was that he had received much more assistance from the Government than it cared to admit, the principal source of finance being not Alex's life insurance policies but the British Treasury.[17]

//

When Alex returned from America on 27 December 1939, David Cunynghame found him 'in an apparently depressed condition regarding his personal production prospects in England'.[18] He seemed to have little idea of what he would do next, but Cunynghame expected that Winston Churchill would be one of the men he would consult before reaching any decision. Over the next three weeks he had dinner with Robert Vansittart several times. On at least one of these occasions, 13 January 1940, Claude Dansey was also present. No record exists of their conversation, but it is not difficult to imagine the sort of things that might have been said.

Early in the previous year, when Alex announced the formation of his new company, Alexander Korda Film Productions, he had spoken of his plans to make films in Hollywood. Stressing that this was not because he intended completely to abandon production in England, he explained: 'If I make a film there I shall do so because I believe it will have a better chance in America and that there are better facilities for certain types of picture.'[19] The beginning of the war could only have made this seem an even more attractive option. The lavish scale of a Korda production was not something that a country at war could easily accommodate. In England there might be an opportunity to take on the role that many people thought he already had as director of the country's wartime film policy, but the furore over *The Lion Has Wings* would have given him a taste of the endless scope that existed within official echelons to ensnare his freedom of action.

At their various dinners Alex would have outlined these possibilities, and Dansey in turn, almost certainly in concert with Vansittart and Churchill, would have nudged him towards the Hollywood option as the best way of serving not only his own but also Britain's interests. A vital objective was to sway American public opinion behind the war. Recent experience had revealed the dangers of open propaganda, but with his Hollywood connections Alex was perfectly placed to play an invaluable behind-the-scenes role.

In the summer of 1940 a confidential Ministry of Information report set the guidelines for a campaign of persuasion to bring America into the war. The policy was defined as one of 'No propaganda'. Britain should confine itself to presenting a truthful picture of what it was fighting for, 'leaving it to the American Government and people to make up their own minds regarding the facts of the case, and regarding the action if any which they should take, instead of trying by any and every device to force particular policies upon them'.[20] Implicit in this approach was the belief that the United States and its citizens would resent any form of moral pressure from abroad. The report went on to rank films in the order of their propaganda importance. The most valuable British films were those that were 'automatically assured of American distribution by reason of their employment of producers, directors and stars with names which are "box-office" in the United States'.[21] But much more valuable to the war effort were pro-British American films made in America. Alex's chief role in the next two years would be to get Hollywood to talk America into the war.

In the course of 1940, as Alex prepared for the switch to the West Coast, his film-making activities in Britain gradually wound down. In February there went into production at Denham one last feature film called *Old Bill and Son*, based on a famous cartoon strip about a veteran too old for active service who follows his son to France. As usual there were several scenario changes in the course of the production, although in this case

Alex, who could not have anticipated that the Germans would dodge the Maginot Line and swiftly bring about the collapse of France, was completely blameless. The last shooting day was 10 June.

There were also several abortive plans for various propaganda shorts. The most notable was a royal film featuring the Queen, which was to be shot in Technicolor. But it was called off at the beginning of May after the proposed director, 'Puffin' Asquith, was charged with being drunk and disorderly. A repressed homosexual and the son of the First World War Prime Minister Herbert Asquith, Puffin was an angelic but rather nervous figure who would spend much of the 1940s under the influence of drink. (On one occasion soon after the war, when he and his regular screenwriting partner Terence Rattigan were having lunch with Alex, his head dropped into the soup. 'Even that he does with so much grace,' said Alex.)[22]

On 24 May Alex confided to David Cunynghame that he intended to close down the company in Britain as soon as possible. On 19 June he set off by flying-boat for Lisbon on the first leg of his trip to Hollywood. Vincent followed with his wife and child a few days later.

'I wonder will I ever see them again,' wrote Cunynghame on 16 July after saying farewell to the few remaining employees of Alexander Korda Film Productions. The following day he reported to an RAF base in Grantham.

While the rest of the Korda family had decamped to America, Peter, who was physically unfit for the armed forces, stayed on in London in the Avenue Road house and worked for the British Volunteer Ambulance Corps. When the house was bombed in the Blitz, he moved to a flat in Curzon Street. At Alex's request, David Cunynghame would look him up whenever he was on leave in London to make sure that he was all right.

//

In California Alex took up residence with Merle in her large mansion in Bel Air and assumed his natural position at the head of the British film colony, which included such prominent figures as Sir Cedric Hardwicke, Alfred Hitchcock and Herbert Wilcox.

As Britain's position in the war worsened, these Britons – so conspicuously absent from their country in its time of need – became increasingly the targets of censure, even though the British Government had advised them that they could best contribute to the war effort by staying in Hollywood. The most virulent of the critics was Michael Balcon, now the production chief of Ealing Studios. In May 1941 he wrote an open letter to Bill Mooring, the Hollywood correspondent of the British magazine *Picturegoer and Film Weekly*, challenging him on the comments in his articles about the 'gallant and wonderful work' that the British colony were doing on behalf of democracy. While they could enjoy the sun and luxury of California, their former colleagues back in Britain were risking their lives in bomb-damaged studios to chronicle the country's struggle. 'These gentlemen left this country for America after the Munich crisis,' Balcon wrote.

> They are badly needed here by an industry which fed them in happier times and which now lacks their talents. And what is this fine work that you hint at . . . that these gentlemen are doing 'to save democracy'?
>
> Am I to presume that Mr Herbert Wilcox's production, *No, No, Nanette* is a part of this vital contribution to our war effort? Or is Victor Saville's film *Bitter Sweet* intended to spread the gospel of Britain's might?[23]

Such sarcasm would have been all the more irritating to Alex because he could not answer back. Although he used his considerable influence in Hollywood to facilitate Britain's propaganda policy, the efficacy of this role depended on his silence. He might have drawn some private amusement from the resemblance the situation bore to one of his most successful films. In public Sir Percy Blakeney plays the part of a dandy, but really he is the Scarlet Pimpernel. Shuttling back and forth between Hollywood and London just as often as the Pimpernel crossed the Channel, Alex exposed himself to considerable personal danger, but the true purpose of these trips was not something that he could confide to the *Picturegoer*.

One such trip occurred just before the Fall of France. A few weeks previously Alex had worked out with United Artists a tentative production programme of four films to follow the completion of *The Thief of Baghdad*: *Sinner*, with Merle Oberon; *Gone to Earth*, with Vivien Leigh; *Jungle Boy*, with Sabu; and *Lady in the Dark*, with Merle Oberon and Melvyn Douglas. But with Britain now under threat from invasion and Winston Churchill recently installed as Prime Minister, there was a sudden change of plan.

After a roundabout wartime journey that took him via Tangier, Alex arrived in London on 17 May 1940 'in good form personally and as fatalistic as anybody regarding the war'.[24] On 29 May, just two days after the surrender of Belgium, he met the new Minister of Information, Duff Cooper, regarding a 'proposed "American" propaganda film'. Cunynghame's quotes around the word 'American' were significant: as the Ministry of Information report on British propaganda policy makes clear, the envisaged film, *Lady Hamiliton* – or *That Hamilton Woman* as it was called in the United States – would be all the more valuable to the British war effort if it were perceived as a Hollywood film.

Alex had been toying with the idea of making a film about Nelson ever since Robert Donat persuaded him to buy the rights to J. L. Hodson's biography in 1936. Donat eventually decided that he didn't want to do the film and the project returned to the back burner until in September 1938 Alex made a tentative announcement that he hoped Merle Oberon would star as Lady Hamilton.

All mention of the idea was dropped again soon afterwards, but now the conjunction of circumstances revived the project. With England suddenly facing an aggressive power just across the Channel, the story of Nelson saving England from invasion offered an obvious and suitably uplifting historical parallel, which could be used to exploit the new mood of sympathy in the United States. Vivien Leigh, who was conveniently under contract to Alex, and Laurence Olivier made for perfect casting as the two lovers, since they were both at the height of their Hollywood stardom and, like their characters in the film, had themselves been engaged in a highly public affair.*

---

* They would get married in the course of the production.

After his meeting with Alex, Duff Cooper sent this cable to an Olivier anxious to return home from Hollywood: 'Think better where you are. Korda going there.'[25] The film was presented to the actor as being the best way in which he could contribute to the war effort. In London Alex persuaded R. C. Sherriff to come out to California to write the script, telling him that he had the support of the British Government.

Back in America, Alex cloaked his true intentions with the announcement that his next production would be a Technicolor epic about Cortez's conquest of Mexico. Merle Oberon, he told the press, would portray Marina, the beautiful Indian girl who was Cortez's guide and interpreter. It would have been difficult to imagine a subject more far removed from Britain and its Empire, which had long provided the background for so many of Alex's films. Anyone taking the announcement at face value might have thought that he had abandoned his adopted country as a lost cause. In a marked departure from his usual practice, he continued to avoid any mention of *That Hamilton Woman* until it was in production.

In Hollywood Sherriff was teamed with the Austrian director and screenwriter Walter Reisch, who had worked for Alex in England in the 1930s and had now built up a reputation at MGM as a writer of strong roles for female stars. They had to write an outline as quickly as possible so that the parts could be cast and the sets designed, but hardly any dialogue had been written when Alex began to shoot the picture in September 1940. 'From then on it was a desperate race to keep up,' Sherriff recalled. 'It was like writing a serial story with only a week between your pen and the next instalment to be published.'[26] Occasionally he and Reisch would be sent away by Alex to rewrite a scene and they would have to stay up all night to produce the new pages on time. 'We were haunted by the fear that the production would catch up on us, that one day we might not be able to turn out enough for them to carry on with.'[27]

As filming progressed, the censors of the Motion Picture Producers' Association were also sent instalments of the script. Joe Breen, the director of the Production Code Administration, gave a provisional response in a letter dated 16 September. The political significance of the film drew no comment. For the purposes of the Production Code, *That Hamilton Woman* was 'a story of adultery' which needed to have 'compensating moral values' to be acceptable. From the outline that Alex had previously suggested in conversation, Breen had felt that such values could be easily injected into the last half of the story, but now a month later he confessed to Alex his disappointment at the latest instalment, which seemed to lack the three conditions of moral correctness that he had earlier summarized. In such adultery stories it was necessary that (a) the adultery was established as wrong; (b) the adultery should not be condoned, justified or made to appear 'right and acceptable'; and that (c) the adulterous parties be punished.

> It seems to us that the present treatment of your story falls short of the Code requirements because (a) it does not definitely establish the adultery to be wrong, and (b) the adulterous situation *is* condoned, justified, and to a certain degree at least, made to appear right and acceptable. Whether or not there is to be any punishment for the adulterous parties, as required by (c), we will, of course, not know until we receive the balance of the script.[28]

The result was more late nights for R. C. Sherriff and Walter Reisch as they sought to address these criticisms. Their solution was to introduce a scene in which Nelson's father, who had conveniently been a parson in real life, condemns his son's affair with Lady Hamilton and begs him not to see her any more.

Breen welcomed the scene, but suggested the scriptwriters 'punch up' the parson's speech to make it an even more definite condemnation. He even provided some dialogue as an example of the sort of thing Sherriff and Reisch might consider:

> This alliance of yours cannot help but end in disaster and I beg of you to break it up. Don't be fooled by any seeming happiness which you may think you are now enjoying . . . You can't defy the laws of God without being made to pay the price. Unless you catch yourself now, both of you will surely end up in the gutter.[29]

The 'very positive condemnation and prediction of disaster which will follow as a result of their sin', Breen observed, 'is very, very, very important', and he underlined the words 'as a result of their sin'. In the final film the Production Code's scheme of things duly prevailed. Lady Hamilton does end up in the gutter, Nelson presumably having paid for his adultery at Trafalgar.

'The Nelson film is nearly over,' Vivien Leigh would comment on 4 November. 'We have *rushed* thro' it because apparently after Thursday there is no more money! – Alex's usual predicament.'[30] But the real reason, which naturally Alex kept quiet about, was to maximize the film's propaganda value by releasing it as early as possible. The world première took place at the Four Star Theater, Hollywood, on 19 March 1941.

Barely six months had passed since the first day of shooting. The production had been set up and completed so quickly that, contrary to the usual practice, United Artists had had no time to pre-sell it. Two days after the première, Arthur Kelly, a vice-president of the company, urged his salesmen 'to bring in quick returns on this magnificent work'.[31] The critics had described Vivien Leigh's performance as 'superb', he told them, and *That Hamilton Woman* was the first important picture that Leigh had made since starring in *Gone with the Wind*, the biggest box-office picture the industry had ever known.

Therefore in THAT HAMILTON WOMAN –

> You have a woman of the moment;
> You have a timely picture;
> You have a great screen lover;
> You have a great producer;
> You have a great production;
> You have great photography;
> You have a brilliant cast;
> You have action;
> You have bigness;

In fact, you have all the essentials that go to make up what you are looking for – a smash box-office picture![32]

The pressbook for *That Hamilton Woman* conveyed the copious opportunities for propaganda that the film offered. Among the publicity tips was a recommendation to interview 'the local British Consul or any other British notable connected with the government ... for comments on Lady Hamilton as one of the world's renowned beauties and a representative of the role that British womanhood has played in shaping the events of that country'. Another paragraph suggested a 'program of special songs':

> Especially timely right now is a musical radio feature based on British naval and other traditional songs, which you can stage as a one-shot feature on your local station leading into a natural plug for *That Hamilton Woman* which contains much orchestral and choral music suggesting the English tradition.[33]

But Alex's great feat was to have made a film firmly in the American tradition. *That Hamilton Woman* has all the style and grandeur of a vintage MGM costume drama – the splendid, fairytale extravagance that the British cinema has rarely understood and certainly never been able to afford. When Emma learns that Nelson is waiting for her on the balcony to say goodbye, she doesn't just step out on to a balcony, but sweeps across the cavernous space of her vast bedroom and the equally vast landing. The marble-clad distance outstrips any sensible measure of reality to capture the flight of her emotions. In production terms, Vivien Leigh's farewell dash was the equivalent of the 300 camels in *The Four Feathers* or the ten trumpeters who fanfare the arrival of the Princess in *The Thief of Baghdad*. Alex knew how to lull a mass audience into a state of receptive well-being. 'Propaganda can be a bitter medicine,' Alex told Laurence Olivier when he asked him to play Nelson. 'It needs a sugar-coating – and *Lady Hamilton* is a very thick sugar-coating indeed.'[34]

Beneath the sugar-coating lay the plea for active participation that the British Government had deemed too risky to make openly. In the opening scene itself Nelson's second-in-command, Captain Hardy, speaks angrily of those countries that are 'neutral against England' and 'so scared of Bonaparte they daren't lift a finger for the people brave enough to fight him'. The message was pretty clear: England expected every American to do his duty.

//

Alex's enormous value to the British propaganda effort lay in his wide range of Hollywood contacts and his ability to pass in the town as a native. When the British film executive Arthur Jarratt arrived there in early 1941 with a brief from the Ministry of Information to 'meet the important people in America',[35] Alex gave a dinner in his honour. The guests included L. B. Mayer, Harry and Jack Warner, Darryl Zanuck and Harry Cohn. The only notable absentee was Walt Disney, who had to attend the opening night of *Fantasia*. If Jarratt found that the Hollywood moguls were on the whole predisposed to help in any way they could, it was largely because Alex had paved the way. He spoke the Hollywood idiom well enough to know what would go down well, and, besides encouraging the Hollywood propaganda effort, actively promoted British films that would appeal to an American audience. He would use his influence, for example, to secure the US release of Powell and Pressburger's *One of Our Aircraft Is Missing* and Noël Coward's *In Which We Serve*.

Alex's close contacts with the Ministry of Information increased once Churchill's appointee Brendan Bracken became the minister there in July 1941. If Bracken, as Churchill's close friend and political ally, was a key member of the wartime 'Kitchen Cabinet', Alex was one of the figures in the scullery ready to run errands and make himself helpful in any way he could. As the secrecy of this connection was vital, Alex communicated with Bracken via encrypted cable. Alex would send any message he might have for encoding by letter to the British Information Service in New York, and the British Information Service would then in turn forward to him the cabled replies by letter. On 5 August 1941, for example, he contacted Bracken concerning *Target for Tonight*, the Ministry's first big feature documentary:

> Understand film is of exceptional quality. I think one could do more with this picture than ordinary American distribution, which is for these documentary pictures not extensive enough,

by weaving a story around it. I would be happy to do it and take care of its distribution if you think this is useful. If picture is formed as proper commercial vehicle one could have ten to twelve thousand theatres play it. Will you please advise me if you want me to work on this idea, in which case I would need not only cut finished picture but also all material shot to it.[36]

Alex may not have been working behind enemy lines, but the importance of bringing America into the war made him one of Britain's most valuable agents.

The necessity for extreme discretion was underlined by an attack on the film industry by one of America's leading isolationists, Senator Gerald Nye. In a radio broadcast on 1 August 1941 he asked rhetorically, 'Who is pushing and hauling at America to plunge us into this war?' and then he singled out the movie companies.

At least twenty pictures have been produced in the last year – all designed to drug the reason of the American people, set aflame their emotions, turn their hatreds into a blaze, fill them with fear that Hitler will come over here and capture them, that he will steal their trade, that America must go into this war – to rouse them to a war hysteria.[37]

That Hamilton Woman was one of eight films that Nye mentioned by name.

While in Blitzed England Michael Balcon may have felt that the British actors and directors in Hollywood had abandoned their country, as far as Senator Nye was concerned they were the 'British Army of Occupation', and the leaders of Hollywood's foreign committee were 'almost all heavy contributors to the numerous committees of all sorts organized, under the guise of relief to Britain, Greece, or Russia, to propagandize us into war'. If he had chosen to name individuals, Alex – who happened to be vice-president of the Royal Air Force Benevolent Society – would have been high up on the list.

Hollywood looked on nervously as on 9 September 1941 the subcommittee of the Senate Committee on Interstate Commerce began hearings to investigate war propaganda calculated to bring the United States into the European war. *That Hamilton Woman* was on a list of seventeen films drawn up by the isolationists to prove that Hollywood supported intervention. Members of the film industry were subpoenaed to appear before the committee, where they could be cross-examined on not only the subject of the inquiry but also their business conduct and political associations.

On 11 September Alex was asked to prepare a statement about *That Hamilton Woman* for Wendell Willkie, the Republican presidential candidate who had run against Roosevelt the previous year and had been engaged by the motion picture industry as their advocate at the congressional hearings. In a long letter Alex set out to demonstrate, with effortless dissimulation, that the film had no propaganda intention whatsoever. Nelson's political speeches, he argued, simply reflected the historical reality of the Napoleonic Wars.

The most controversial speech in the film for its contemporary ring was Nelson's address to the Admiralty concerning the Peace of Amiens:

> Napoleon can never be master of the world until he has smashed us up – and believe me, gentlemen, he means to be master of the world. You cannot make peace with dictators. You have to destroy them. Wipe them out! Gentlemen, I implore you – speak to the Prime Minister before it is too late. Do not ratify this peace!

The speech, Alex argued, was composed from passages in Nelson's letters, conversation and interviews. He quoted at length from 'the most authoritative book on the subject', which, conveniently for his case, happened to be written by one Captain A. T. Mahan of the United States Navy.

> As you will see from these quotations, the speech Nelson makes in the film about 'making peace with Dictators' is absolutely truthful in spirit to the historical facts. In speaking of Napoleon, he used the word 'Despot' and we have substituted this with the more modern word 'Dictator'. For instance, we would not use 'thees' and 'thous' in a picture, as they would fall rather heavily on the public's ear and would be too cumbersome for the public to follow. In another film of mine,

The Private Life of Henry VIII, I used modern language all through the film. This is not my innovation by any means, as Bernard Shaw wrote his *Caesar and Cleopatra* in absolutely modern dialogue thirty years ago.

The fact that the film shows a great similarity between the Napoleonic era and the present day is only natural. Anybody making a film about Nelson could not help but dramatize this similarity. In the same way if one was making a picture about even more distant times, let us say, the Fall of Athens, one could not but reproduce the famous Philippica of Demosthenes to show that undefended aggression and its consequences will always be the same.[38]

If there were any members of the Senate Committee familiar with the *Philippica* of Demosthenes, they would have found the reference entirely apposite and hard to challenge. In his deposition Alex displayed an erudition way beyond that expected of a film producer – or for that matter a senator – and also took advantage of an encyclopaedic knowledge of his own profession. Wendell Willkie wanted to know how the Nelson story had come to be chosen. It was, Alex explained, a love story 'well known in history as well as in romantic fiction':

As a matter of fact, it was produced once as a silent picture by First National Corporation, starring Corinne Griffith, titled *Divine Lady*. The picture was then hailed as great entertainment and was a financial success.

As a matter of interest, we might mention that a picture was produced also in Germany in silent days and was called *Lady Hamilton*, starring Conrad Veidt as Nelson, and Liane Haid as Lady Hamilton.

Still previous to that in the very early days of cinematography, Lady Hamilton's story was produced as a two-reeler picture. So it is obvious that this great romantic love story was always in the minds of film producers who had suitable actors and actresses to play the two chief roles.[39]

Alex also drew Wendell Willkie's attention to a letter that his New York office had received two weeks previously from the United States Naval Academy at Annapolis, Maryland:

My dear Sir:

We showed *That Hamilton Woman* to the Regiment of Midshipmen last week-end. The film is so admirable both as a documentary record of the life of Nelson and as a picturization of history and of the background the era represented that it stands out as a significant achievement. While the film is still current I am writing to ask what steps we should take to obtain a copy for the permanent possession of the United States Naval Academy. I feel sure that you can give us the best advice.

Very sincerely yours,

Allen B. Cook

Assistant Motion Picture Officer for Booking [40]

There is no evidence to suggest that this letter was other than genuine, but such was Alex's talent for trickery you can't help imagining that he fixed it somehow. Whether it was enlisting the aid of the Naval Academy or 'the great American Naval historian' Captain Mahan, Alex succeeded in making *That Hamilton Woman* somehow seem part and parcel of the American Way.

One of the guests Alex entertained in his Bel Air home that summer was the British intelligence agent Harford Montgomery Hyde. He had been sent by his boss William Stephenson to discuss how Alex might best be able to use his connections to help British Security Co-Ordination, a secret espionage organization that Stephenson had set up in America the previous year at the direct request of Churchill. Alex's West Coast office – at 1040 North Las Palmas Avenue – had already been operating for some time as a cover for British intelligence agents, much as London Films' branches around Europe had done before the war. So it is unlikely that Alex would have been much surprised when he was subpoenaed to give evidence on 12 December to a Senate investigation into the activities of 'foreign agents', nor would he have been much disturbed. He had enough ruses and stratagems at his command to keep any number of Senate committees tied up for years. It is possible even that when the Japanese rendered his appearance unnecessary by bombing Pearl Harbor on 7 December, he rather regretted the end of an amusing game, which, like that of being a secret agent, was a welcome diversion from the routine business of making movies.

//

While Alex affected a casual detachment from the wartime fortunes of his adopted country, back in England the redoubtable Michael Balcon committed the entire resources of Ealing Studios to the war effort, carrying on in spite of the Blitz and the blackout and all the shortages. No other British producer could match his public commitment to the national cause, but his films failed to appeal to an American audience and therefore, according to the Ministry of Information's own estimate, were of little propaganda importance.

If anything, Balcon's forthright but dangerously blinkered outlook often made him a liability. In June 1941 Ealing Studios signed a distribution contract with United Artists. The agreement obliged United Artists to distribute Ealing films that were suitable for the American market, but to Balcon's intense annoyance none ever seemed to be.

The final straw was Alex's acquisition for United Artists of *One of Our Aircraft Is Missing* and *In Which We Serve*. In a cable Balcon instructed his American representative to complain to the head of United Artists' Foreign Department: 'If despite our repeated representations American franchise or stockholders allowed purchase of competitive films to our detriment whilst our films still without exploitation or revenue, he must face fact that we shall take steps forthwith to protect our interests.'[41] It was 'nothing short of scandalous', declared Balcon, that 'competitive traders' could obtain large advances while Ealing had received nothing. But those competitive traders, as Alex recognized, had produced films of real propaganda value in the United States, which would have been undermined if Balcon's wishes had been respected.

Once America had come into the war, Alex's most important mission for Britain had been achieved. In June 1942 he was awarded a knighthood. Other recipients included the airplane manufacturer Frederick Handley-Page and the inventor of radar, Robert Watson-Watt. While the announcement must have baffled many of the film-makers who had stayed in Britain, not least Balcon, it was greeted mostly with amusement by the British colony in Hollywood – Korda should remake *Knight without Armour*, suggested Alfred Hitchcock.

It was the Americans who took it most seriously. One of the most sincere tributes came from David Selznick, who with the sharp insight of which he was often capable came closest to capturing the award's importance:

> The stature it has given to the whole business, and the dignity it has given to the profession of producing, is doubly significant first, because it comes in the midst of war, from a people and a Government that for years have been in a life and death struggle; second, because it comes from Winston Churchill – for, as I suppose you know, only the Prime Minister can recommend such honors to the Kings; and third, because this is no peace-time knighthood of the type dished out to business men and politicians, but a war-time recognition that has simultaneously been given only to a few airplane manufacturers and one or two other men whose important contributions to the struggle for victory is universally recognized.
>
> It is unimportant whether the recipient is Alexander Korda or Joe Doakes – the point is it is recognition of the motion picture business, and of the motion picture-producing profession. However, everyone in the business should feel deeply indebted to Korda because his efforts, which have been conducted quietly and without fanfare or publicity, have won this honor which should be accepted as an honor to us all.[42]

18. A KNIGHT IN HOLLYWOOD

Once America came into the war, Alex stayed on in Hollywood with increasing reluctance. He would almost certainly have come back to England for good if an appropriate role could have been found for him. Just three days after Pearl Harbor, he asked Claude Dansey to get a passage for him on the northern air route. He arrived back in Britain on 19 February 1942 after a bone-rattling bomber flight from Newfoundland to Prestwick, near Glasgow. The passengers, who sat on parachutes in an unheated bomb bay, had to wear life-jackets and oxygen masks. Alex, who had failed to adjust his mask correctly, nodded off and slowly began to turn blue. Luckily, the Navy captain sitting next to him, Tom Hussey, noticed in time to save him from suffocating.* David Cunynghame, who would greet Alex upon his arrival at Claridge's, noted his exuberance 'after a somewhat Arctic Bomber flight of 8½ hours'.[1] Probably, it was just joy that he was still alive.

In London Alex had dinner with his son Peter, as well as David Cunynghame and his wife Pamela, and talked of his hopes of getting a Government job. But the following day Cunynghame learned from Dansey that the chances of such a thing were very small, and by the time Alex met Churchill a few weeks later he was probably resigned to the widespread attitude in official circles that he was still much more useful in America than in England. The Prime Minister, Alex would later tell a New York newspaper, had been sitting up in bed with his food on a tray. During their long meeting he would stare at the window from time to time.

---

* After the war, Hussey worked for Alex as his personal assistant.

244

Then suddenly he threw off the bedclothes, got up and marched over to it. 'Dammit,' he declared, 'because of this fog I can't send a single plane out to bomb the Hun.'[2]

With a similar sense of frustration Alex settled down once again in Hollywood. After he had finished *That Hamilton Woman*, he sought to keep out of politics and to blend in with the background as much as possible. His next film, *Lydia*, directed by Julien Duvivier, stood out for the Americanness of its story, told in flashback, in which Merle Oberon plays an elderly Boston lady who meets four old flames and recalls her past romances. Two more big Hollywood productions followed: Ernst Lubitsch's *To Be or Not to Be*, a production which Alex took over from fellow United Artists producer Walter Wanger; and *Jungle Book*, with Sabu. There were no expensive location trips to India this time. In the midst of the war, the film was of necessity done on the sound stages and back lot of General Service Studios in Hollywood.

//

Based in California, Alex was able to play a more prominent part in the affairs of United Artists. In September 1941 he achieved something of a coup for the company by negotiating a deal for David Selznick to become a stockholder producer. Having won the Academy Award for 'Best Film' in successive years with *Gone with the Wind* and *Rebecca*, Selznick was regarded as the movie-producing genius who would engineer a revolution in United Artists' fortunes. He soon got into his stride with a formidably long memorandum that began, 'I think we have got to do something, and immediately, to bring order out of the chaos which presently characterizes consideration by United Artists of the countless deals which are being presented to it for its consideration.'[3] But amidst the entangled syntax there was a great deal of common sense, and Alex – somewhat in the manner of a guardian uncle – circulated an approving memorandum in reply. 'Just one more thing,' ran the last paragraph. 'I want to remark how very happy I am that David is coming along with such fine, constructive and intelligent proposals.'[4]

But nothing could prevent a natural rivalry soon taking hold.

Selznick's credits had included such films as *David Copperfield*, *A Tale of Two Cities* and *Anna Karenina*. Both men prided themselves on their adaptations of the literary classics, and often found themselves pursuing the same property. When in December 1941 Alex announced his intention of producing a film version of *War and Peace*, Selznick quickly let him know that he had registered his interest on this subject with the Motion Picture Producers' Association two years previously and had no intention of waiving his rights.

Highly suspicious, and combative to the last degree, Selznick hated to think that anyone could enjoy the slightest advantage over him. He was furious when he learned that Alex had received a percentage for negotiating distribution deals for *In Which We Serve* and *One of Our Aircraft Is Missing*. 'If there are any commissions to be made,' he warned the United Artists management, 'I expect to cut in on them, or at least have my company cut in on them, either directly or through its ownership in United Artists.'[5] He was also 'surprised and frightened' to hear that Alex's laboratory in England was responsible for producing United Artists prints: 'I think this warrants a little investigation as to price, quality, terms, etc.' Such zealousness placed a considerable strain on cordial relations. Friendship was impossible with a man who counted everything.

The rivalry was at its most intense over the group of British film-makers who came to prominence during the war. Emotionally, Alex felt that only he had the right to deal with them, an attitude which Selznick certainly did not respect. He had already signed up Alfred Hitchcock to make *Rebecca* and notched up a considerable success. So he was naturally interested when in October 1940 Carol Reed's Hitchcock-like *Night Train to Munich** was released to excellent reviews in America. Reed's previous film, *The Stars Look Down*, had also garnered considerable praise. In the summer of 1941, Selznick invited Reed to work for him. His approach was favourably received, and although no final deal had been concluded, he pretended that one

---

* The US title was *Night Train*.

had. The subject came up when he met the United Artists stockholders in early September 1941. Reporting on the occasion to his close colleague Daniel O'Shea, he commented:

> Chaplin told as a tale of my 'astuteness' how he had seen one of the best pictures he had ever seen in his life the other night, *The Stars Look Down*, and had immediately gotten busy to sign up Carol Reed, only to discover that we had him. Korda's hair stood right up on end and he asked me if it was true. I told him it was. I suggest we had better move very fast before Mr Korda moves in on us, because I know of his great interest in Reed.
>
> I think we ought to get something in writing with Reed just as soon as possible.[6]

But Alex must have moved faster than even Selznick had anticipated. For soon afterwards, Reed pulled out of the deal, explaining that he had decided to stay on in Britain to make propaganda pictures. 'Do you think by any chance any interest on Korda's part in Reed may have been what caused the sudden change on Reed's part?' Selznick asked O'Shea in a memorandum marked 'Confidential'.[7]

Determined not to be caught out a second time, Selznick asked his London representative, Jenia Reissar, to keep him in close touch with what was happening in the British studios. When Alex made his spring 1942 visit to England, he met the leading film-makers and reported back on their general desire to receive distribution in America through United Artists. 'I agree thoroughly that it would be advisable to try to work something out with this group,' Selznick commented in a memorandum dated 7 May 1942 circulated among the United Artists stockholders, 'and in fact have had negotiations with each of them pending for some time.'[8]

It was a challenge to which Alex had to respond. 'If Mr Selznick reserves the right to deal with these producers individually, I must also reserve the same rights for myself,' he warned.

> Although these producers mentioned to me that they have had offers from Mr Selznick on various occasions, they definitely impressed me with the fact that they do not wish to work for

anyone, but want to retain their independence. In my opinion, that would be the only basis of dealing with them.

Alex also questioned Selznick's assumption that the English producers would be willing to allow United Artists to have the final word on the stories they chose. 'They definitely would refuse to accept such approval, but I am sure that they could be influenced to welcome our advice and guidance.'[9] Alex's new-found respect for the independence of film-makers was less genuine than a reflection of the fact that, in spite of his bluff, he was in too weak a financial state, and too uncertain of his future, to do any deal himself.

The exchange of memoranda spurred Selznick on in his attempt to round up the English film-makers. In June 1942, Daniel O'Shea sent a long letter to Jenia Reissar outlining Selznick's attitude to the negotiations she was to conduct on his behalf. Far the most attractive prospect, he stressed, would be a deal with either Noël Coward or Carol Reed.

Selznick was 'willing to give complete freedom to Noël Coward or Carol Reed under almost any circumstances',[10] but this declaration was so hemmed in with provisos as to be almost meaningless. If the film was not to be of a known property, Selznick would have to approve an original outline first. He would also want an American to be present during the production to ensure that there were no expressions incomprehensible to Americans, and the right to make some scenes in two ways where no compromise could be reached that fitted both markets.

How to make English movies that appealed to Americans – this was a problem that Alex had been grappling with for a decade. Selznick, having used English talent to win the 'Best Film' Oscar two years running, was convinced he had the answer. The trouble with English movies was that they were too English. The key thing was to eliminate any expressions or accents that an American audience might not understand. It was a process that he routinely used with foreign actors in his own movies. When Ingrid Bergman starred in *Intermezzo*, an American was on set at all times to advise her when her accent became hard to understand. Even after the films had been made, foreign actors would be redubbed if necessary. 'An outstanding case of this was *Rebecca*,' Daniel O'Shea explained to Reissar.

> We found through our preview cards, which are very elaborate in form, and unlike those used by any other studio, that Olivier was not understandable through a large part of the picture. We kept re-dubbing and kept previewing until this criticism was eliminated entirely, even though it meant Olivier had to do hundreds of lines with a less British accent.[11]

O'Shea was so convinced by the effectiveness of the Selznick approach that his letter took on a crusading tone. Selznick could 'do a great service to the entire British film industry', because if his method was adopted it would greatly increase the market for British films in America. The subtext of such a message was that the British film-makers no longer needed Alex.

Selznick was particularly anxious to court Two Cities, the company with which Alex had negotiated the American distribution deal for *In Which We Serve*. It seemed best placed to gather Britain's leading film-makers under its umbrella, and Reissar was instructed to inform its flamboyant chief executive, Filippo Del Giudice, that Selznick could offer a much better deal than anything that Two Cities could hope for from Alex.

Selznick's acquisition of stock in United Artists signalled an aggressive campaign to eclipse Alex's influence within the company. Alex's perpetual financial worries seemed to offer the perfect opportunity. Neither *That Hamilton Woman* nor *Lydia* had performed strongly enough to go into profit, leaving Alex still dependent for future production on cobbling together whatever loan arrangements he could. In January 1942, when both Daniel O'Shea and Alex were in New York, Selznick decided to reveal his hand, suggesting to O'Shea in a cable that he should raise with Alex the idea of buying him out. 'Plant with him that this might be a good time for him to get a big gob of money which he would have free of taxes.'[12]

Alex on this occasion politely declined the 'gob', but Selznick stepped up the pressure. A week later he complained to the

United Artists' management about its recent practice of making available large advances for production. 'There will be a strong temptation on the part of the management to use this money quickly,' he warned.

> There would be at least an equally strong temptation on the part of all owners, my company included, to dip into this money for production purposes. As soon as one owner dipped in, the others would want to dip in to the same extent, and the first thing we knew, the very existence of the company would be dependent upon whether or not the pictures in which this money was invested paid out.[13]

Alex was clearly intended to be the prime target of such criticism. Not only were his pictures struggling to pay out, but United Artists had reluctantly gone to the lengths of setting up a separate company to produce *To Be or Not to Be* because Alex had been unable to find the finances for it alone. It had also advanced him $300,000 to enable him to make *Jungle Book*.

In stockholder disputes the management of United Artists tended to side with those owners who most vigorously defended the purpose for which the company had been set up. It was supposed to be a distributor, not the source of production finance that recent circumstances had caused it to become. Since in 1942 it was an increasingly ailing distributor which was having great difficulty in securing enough product, Selznick's arguments carried enormous weight.

As a producer whom United Artists had gone to great lengths to support, Alex suddenly looked very isolated. Of his three fellow stockholders, Selznick had the financial strength to support his own productions, while Mary Pickford and Charlie Chaplin made too few pictures to need United Artists funds.

After Alex had set off in February 1942 on his bomber ride to England, David Selznick met with Pickford and Chaplin. Soon afterwards, on 16 March, Ed Raftery, then President of United Artists, sent this cable to Alex at Claridge's:

> After thoroughly considering company's present precarious financial status, and after frankly facing increasingly frightening outlook for our future as well as the further threats to our

very existence of world and industry conditions, the other owners are in agreement that company simply in no position to consider gambling further through investments or advances to assist production by Mary, Charlie and yourself even if money was available for this purpose, which at this moment is most improbable ... As a first step Mary and Charlie have agreed to waive all company financial assistance for their productions but provided you do likewise.[14]

It was an absurd, discriminatory document because of the lack of Pickford and Chaplin product, and Alex must have suspected that Selznick, seeking effective control of United Artists, was the prime instigator.

A month later, in April, Selznick considered pressing for the strict enforcement of the terms of an agreement United Artists had made in October 1941 to hand over to Alex his shares in the company. This stock had been held as security until such date as Alex had paid the balance of the original purchase price – a date which kept on being put back and back – but in return for a promissory note they were given to him absolutely. Now, in a memorandum marked 'confidential', O'Shea passed on to Selznick the legal advice that it was possible 'to cause a foreclosure of the pledge of Korda's stock' as Alex had fallen behind with the payments required under the new agreement.[15]

Alex was hanging from a cliff by his fingers. It seemed to require only the firm application of Selznick's boot to force him to relinquish his grip. But the ever-shifting alliances among the United Artists stockholders came to his rescue. O'Shea commented:

As a practical matter, unless all of the owners except Korda are in agreement as to the procedure, it seems to me unlikely that the Board of Directors will take action against Korda. I suspect that Chaplin would rather fancy himself in the benign and benevolent role of the indulgent creditor, particularly if he feels you are determined to see a foreclosure and as soon as he knows that you are being blamed for it.[16]

In the weeks that followed the situation changed dramatically in Alex's favour. In May, with the deals for *In Which We Serve*

and *One of Our Aircraft Is Missing*, he secured some badly
needed product for United Artists. Then on 10 June his knighthood was announced. Suddenly Alex seemed an asset again. A
month later, the United Artists board had second thoughts about
its decision not to provide production finance. 'It all comes back
to the proposition that in order to get product at this time we
may have to assist in financing it,' commented Ed Raftery.[17]

But this temporary respite could not remedy the essential
precariousness of Alex's finances, nor the disadvantage of belonging to a company whose owners were at perpetual loggerheads.
The authority that he continued to hold depended chiefly upon
the sway he held over British film-makers; but this would ebb
once those film-makers ceased to perceive him as the best gateway
to the American market. Without an effective power base, he
would find it increasingly difficult to fend off the aggressive
competition of such rivals as Selznick. Meanwhile, in Britain
other film moguls, like Arthur Rank and Filippo Del Giudice,
were springing up to fill the vacuum that he had left behind. The
announcement of the knighthood in June marked a watershed,
setting Alex to thinking how he might best arrange his future.
When some weeks later Sidney Bernstein was in Hollywood on
behalf of the Ministry of Information, he found Alex gripped by
indecision, pondering several scenarios simultaneously. 'Korda in
Hollywood was rather like this,' he reported back to London
in an amused 'personal note':

> Dear Sidney
>   Please advise me.
> Shall I work in Hollywood?
> Shall I work in England?
> I am tired of films.
> Shall I work with Louis B. Mayer?
> He wants me to be a Vice President of MGM.
> Shall I work for Political Warfare in England?
> I am still tired of films.
> If I work for MGM will the British industry
>   say I have sold out to an American company?
> Shall I make 'War and Peace' in England?
> Shall I make 'War and Peace' in America?

Shall I make 'War and Peace' for Metro in Hollywood?
Shall I make 'War and Peace' for Columbia in England?
Shall I make 'War and Peace'?
I want to go back to England.
It's your duty (meaning me) to stay in the US
    and have rank of Colonel.
People don't like me in England.
People do like me in England.[18]

Alex was certainly in a quandary during the summer of 1942, but his display for Bernstein was as much the cultivated vagueness of someone who hesitated to reveal his true mind. He would unquestionably have preferred to return to England, but not if he couldn't have a role there that suited his sense of his own importance.

Soon after he arrived in England in late August 1942, he received a proposal from Arthur Rank that he should coordinate the Rank Organisation's £2 million-a-year picture programme. It seemed ideal, and on Sunday, 13 September Alex celebrated the offer by treating his guests to champagne and a dinner of oysters, roast partridge and ice-cream. '100% pre-war,' observed David Cunynghame, 'it certainly helps to keep one going.' Alex's future seemed settled. Just over a week later, accompanied by Merle, he went to Buckingham Palace, where on 22 September he received his knighthood. The following day, 23 September, Merle set off on the long trip back to Hollywood, where she was due to appear in a film. When she arrived in New York, she announced that she would be closing her house in Bel Air, as she and Alex intended to live in England for the remainder of the war.

But Alex's dreams of a splendid new start soon began to crumble. At Rank, he had hoped to preside over the output of a film combine that had grown rapidly in recent years to rival the size of a Hollywood studio, but by mid-October the proposed agreement had been scaled down to just a three-picture deal.

It's not hard to imagine why Rank got cold feet. The Prudential, who shared with the Rank Organisation the ownership of Denham and Pinewood Studios, would almost certainly have raised strong objections to Alex managing a large programme of films in light of his past extravagance. The film-makers themselves, who were enjoying an unparalleled degree of creative freedom under the Rank Organisation, had even less reason to look forward to Alex's return.

Thwarted in this direction, Alex discussed with Brendan Bracken the possibility of his taking over as director of the Films Division of the Ministry of Information. The trouble was that the incumbent, Jack Beddington, was doing an excellent job, which he showed no sign of wanting to give up. So although Alex felt – with some justification in the light of all he had done – that Britain owed him a big job, it couldn't be so easily created. On 18 October, Cunynghame noted in his diary, 'AK is very much hoping that Brendan Bracken will give him a job at the M o I – I doubt it. If nothing materializes in this direction AK returns to America.'

On 27 October, Alex set off for America by the northern air route via Prestwick and Newfoundland, but got stuck at Prestwick. Three days later, he tried the southern air route via Bristol and Brazil, but got stuck at Bristol. Finally, on 4 November, he left for New York aboard the *Queen Mary*, which had to fight off a U-boat attack in the mid-Atlantic. This journey captured the nature of his life as a wartime film producer. It was impossible to plot a direct line anywhere. If he was to come back to England permanently, he had to accept that it would probably be by a slow, unpredictable path and that at any moment his plans might be blown out of the water. The only firm arrangement he had was the three-picture deal with Rank, which was scheduled to begin with a large Technicolor version of *War and Peace* at Denham in the spring of 1943. He had to hope that some bigger and more prestigious deal would suddenly present itself.

//

In November 1942 Alex made over to United Artists the receipts of *The Thief of Baghdad*, *That Hamilton Woman*, *Lydia* and *Jungle Book* in settlement of a debt of over $600,000. As part of the same settlement he was released from the obligation to distribute through United Artists. There were rumours that he might stay in Hollywood to produce films for Twentieth Century-Fox, but whatever he may have suggested in the process of jockeying for influence, a return to England was just about his only certain goal.

A few weeks later the ideal opportunity seemed to present itself. In early January 1943 MGM proposed that Alex should make films for the company in London. They would provide 100 per cent finance and give Alex a 25 per cent share of the profit.[19] It was a fantastic deal if only Alex could come to terms with the fact that he would be sacrificing his independence – something he hadn't done since making Quota pictures for Paramount ten years previously.

In the movie mogul league, Louis B. Mayer was the King of Kings. As someone had once commented of Alex, he was a man you worked for, not with. When Michael Balcon had briefly been head of production at MGM-British before the war, he had found it a humiliating, scarring experience. He remembered Louis B. Mayer as 'a short, stout man enthroned in an enormous, lavishly over-furnished office, ruling his empire with a mixture of ruthlessness and sentimentality'.[20] He knew that his days with MGM were numbered when Mayer flew into a rage and threw open an office window. 'For a moment . . . I thought his choler had risen so high that he wanted a breath of air, but no – it was so that an entire company which was filming outdoor scenes in the garden below should have the benefit of hearing him give me the ticking off of a lifetime.'[21]

There were several reasons why Alex hoped for a better relationship. His stature in Hollywood, after all, was immeasurably greater than Balcon's. Not only did he possess a knighthood and a quarter share in United Artists, but he had a track record of making movies that Americans went to see. It is true that they tended to be more expensive than most American studios wanted to pay, but MGM was the biggest studio of them all. It could afford the premium, probably regarding Sir Alex as a fitting adornment to its prestige.

But Bernstein's amused note suggests that Alex must have entered the new arrangement with some reluctance. Whatever the reality of the situation, the idea that he might defer to anyone was a nonsense, and his determination not to do so led to yet another sham. MGM's official announcement in March 1943 described the deal as 'the most important merger in the history of British–American film production'. In a press conference held at MGM studios, Alex echoed this carefully chosen formula. 'It is my belief,' he declared, 'that great benefit to both the American and the British film industries will result from this merger of our activities.'[22] But 'activities', along with a handful of story properties and artists' contracts, were all that Alex had to give to this partnership. To call it a merger was to stretch the truth very far indeed.

It wouldn't even have been true in the days when Alex had been in charge of London Film Productions with its studio and a staff that numbered thousands. Coincidentally, a deal with MGM had been one of the options that the Prudential had considered back in 1938 when London Films was facing liquidation. Then Alex had summed up the advantage of such a deal as 'an unlimited help, both administrative and artistic', but the disadvantage was that 'we would become more or less a branch of an American organization'. It was a fair summing-up of the situation five years later, except that, shorn of London Film Productions, Alex barely even amounted to a twig.

19. PERFECT STRANGERS

It's hard to pinpoint the exact moment that Alex returned from America. His visits to England had been so frequent and lengthy that in a sense he had never really left. His residence at Claridge's, where he would routinely stay, became so permanent that it was more accurate to assume that a departure marked not the end of a visit to England but the beginning of one to America. When in late 1943 he bought a large house in Belgrave Square, he had already been in England for some time, planning his new MGM outpost. The exclusive address was less a reflection of Alex's extravagance than that of Louis B. Mayer, who had been adamant that MGM should have the grandest premises in London – Apsley House at Hyde Park Corner, which had once belonged to the Duke of Wellington and was familiarly known as No. 1 London, had been considered.

The return to England marked a permanent shift in the larger dynamic of the Korda family. While Vincent returned to England in early 1943, Zoltán stayed on in Hollywood to direct *Sahara*, starring Humphrey Bogart, for Columbia. Its success enabled him to break away and build his own independent reputation as a director, free of Alex's long shadow. Zoltán settled down in Hollywood with his family and, although he would work with his brother once again in the 1950s, he would do so only on a film of his own choosing, *Cry the Beloved Country*, from Alan Paton's anti-Apartheid novel, a subject that contrasted markedly with the Imperial epics which Alex had him direct in the course of the 1930s.

Vincent, however, continued to tag along with whatever Alex mapped out for him. In doing so he would gain a reputation as one of the cinema's great art directors, but, according to his friend André De Toth, came to feel a deep sense of personal failure for not having lived up to his painter's vocation. When Vincent was working in Hollywood, he hired an apartment as a painter's studio, where he would sneak away to paint as often as he could. On one occasion De Toth was summoned to the apartment by Vincent's landlady to find his friend sitting slumped on the floor in despair amidst his paintings. 'Every canvas was slashed, and the frames were busted.' Wondering what sort of pain could have driven an easy-going man to such violence, De Toth reached the bitter conclusion that 'he was destroyed by his own brother who robbed him and let him live drained and empty'. But Vincent, as loyal as ever, defended Alex: 'He tried to do for me what he thought was the best . . . I could've stayed in Cagnes-de-Mer, he didn't force me to go to Marseille'. If painting was truly his vocation, then he had only to resist Alex's blandishments and, as Zoltán had done, go his own way.[1]*

//

Alex's new Belgravia office offered a telling contrast to the dingy offices of Wardour Street, where the rest of the British film industry was based. Vast and stately, the five-storey house, which had once belonged to Lady Harcourt, was Alex's Emerald City, 'a fit palace for a film king to dream ambitious plans', in the words of the reporter who visited Alex soon after he had moved in.[2] But behind his description of Alex's lavish new surroundings could be detected a tone of faint mockery at the pretension, for everyone knew that the new power in the land was Arthur Rank: his organization controlled the two biggest studios in the country, owned several production companies, a film distributor and two cinema chains; each year it was responsible for more than half the feature films made in Britain. In 1943, if you worked in films, Arthur Rank was impossible to avoid and Alex, who had wanted to show off his new house, would not have welcomed the reminder when the reporter used the occasion to ask him what he thought of Rank's plans to capture the world market. 'When I

---

* For an example of Vincent's painting, visit the website Fine Arts in Hungary.

came to this country I was a nobody. My first film had a world market,' he replied testily.

Alex, who after the previous year's negotiations with Rank probably felt some resentment that he was not personally in command of this empire, was determined to regain his position as Britain's unrivalled film king. He might have thought that he was well placed to do so with the aid of MGM's millions, but in wartime Britain he quickly found that there were plenty of obstacles to hinder his freedom of action. Money alone was not enough.

The British cinema, which Alex had done so much to nurture, had come of age and was now no longer dependent on him. The wartime privations had brought into being a new egalitarian spirit which was at odds with Alex's essentially feudal method of doing business. It was no longer enough to whisper a few words into the ear of another chieftain and to expect him to have his army turn out. There were board meetings to be held, union officials to be consulted.

Even working in Denham, the great studio Alex had built, was no longer a straightforward matter. Most of Britain's studios had been requisitioned by the Government and so space was at a premium. When Arthur Rank told the management board of Denham Studios that he wanted Alex to have space to make *War and Peace* in the spring of 1943, they accommodated this wish, but agreed that otherwise no departure should be made from the practice of 'treating all tenants on an equal footing' and that Alex should be asked to sign a standard studio agreement just like anyone else.[3] In the event Alex's production plans were postponed, but he duly received a copy of the standard studio agreement when he made another request for space the following summer.

Rather than stoop beneath his dignity to fill in the form, Alex discussed his requirements directly with Arthur Rank, who again agreed to put them before the board in person. In a separate conversation, another director of the studio company, Richard Norton, outlined to Alex the general difficulties that the war had placed on space, labour and equipment. Alex replied, 'Tell your Board that I have influence with Government Departments and that all difficulties would disappear, and the Board should bear this in mind when considering space for me.'[4] But such utterances were regarded as arrogance and had the reverse effect to that intended. When Norton duly repeated Alex's comments in the board meeting, Rank, who had no knowledge of Alex's secret service connections, retorted that he felt Alex's contacts with Government Departments were no better than theirs, and that it would be 'wiser for the company to continue to make its own arrangements . . . for the benefit of all tenants alike'.

Alex found the situation intolerable. Denham, he believed, was rightfully his and with MGM's money he intended to win it back. After further wrangles over his requirements, he suggested to Rank that he should be allowed to participate in the management of the studio, as he visualized that after the war all Rank's producers would go to Pinewood, while he, Alex, would remain in Denham. When Rank turned down this proposal, Alex made a fantastic offer. In exchange for the establishment of a joint committee to run the studio, he would arrange for world distribution of Rank's films through MGM. It's unlikely that Alex had troubled to ask Louis B. Mayer first, but Rank took the proposal very seriously. It 'was a very attractive offer,' he told a meeting of the directors on 22 July 1943, 'which in the interest of the British Film Industry he felt he should accept as such an opportunity had never occurred before.'[5]

But the offer was greeted with scepticism by those who had had previous dealings with Alex. Richard Norton asked why the proposed committee was necessary since the studios were already very well run, 'unless this was the thin edge of the wedge to obtain control'.[6] He agreed that it would be fine to make such a concession in return for the world distribution of British pictures, but he doubted that Alex was in a position to give such a guarantee. Cyril Ray, who was the Prudential's nominee on the board, stated that 'in view of the Prudential's past experience his directors were apprehensive of Sir Alexander Korda going to Denham',[7] but that he too was inclined to give the proposed committee a trial run if in return Alex really was able to secure world distribution for British films. The meeting passed a resolution to form such a committee, but 'if it did not function then Sir

Alexander Korda would have to revert to the present system and be treated as an ordinary tenant'.[8]

To no one's surprise Alex's promise turned out to be an empty one and he remained an ordinary tenant. Gradually, he came to accept the fact that his hopes of regaining Denham were a dream, that in the great studio which he had once owned he was now regarded less as a saviour of the British film industry than an inconvenience.

Shortly before he took up his lease for space at Denham, Alex asked if the office he had once occupied in the Old House by the river could be made available to him. The request had to go before a meeting of the board, at which the managing director Spencer Reis explained that there could be difficulties as it would mean displacing other production companies. It was not the way Alex was used to being treated.

The times had certainly changed. Not even the backing of the mighty MGM could challenge the sway of the new king of the movies in Britain, J. Arthur Rank. Unable to wrest back control of Denham, Alex began to inspect other studios, but nearly all of them had been requisitioned by the Government to be used as storage depots or factories for war production. Although he had been working to set up his first film for MGM, the situation encouraged him to go slow on any more ambitious production plans – as did conversations with Brendan Bracken and Claude Dansey about the future progress of the war. In the autumn of 1943, the Russians were pushing back the Germans on the Eastern Front, and the conflict had turned decisively in the Allies' favour. Bracken, somewhat indiscreetly, told Alex that Germany was expected to make one last aerial assault on London with radio-controlled bombs before surrendering at Christmas. It confirmed Alex's view that it would be best to take it easy for a while and to await the imminent end of the war.

//

In the circumstances, Alex must have regarded his début film for MGM, *Perfect Strangers*, as light practice to keep his hand in. He intended that it would star Vivien Leigh and Robert Donat. Since each had been 'discovered' by him and each had won an

Academy Award in an MGM film, it served as a perfect opening to the joint venture.

A pair of contracts, one with Alex, one with David Selznick, governed Vivien Leigh's film career: Alex had the right to use her in one film a year, as opposed to Selznick's two. But as Leigh had refused to leave England for the remainder of the war, Alex, negotiating on behalf of MGM, hoped to acquire Selznick's ration as well as his own. However, these plans were disrupted by the wartime shortage of studio space, Alex finding it difficult, as schedules were postponed, to be precise about when he would actually use her. He had booked a stage at Denham for the end of October 1943, but the starting date was postponed for a month when Carol Reed's film *The Way Ahead* went over schedule.

'You must realize that working conditions here are not like in happy Hollywood six thousand miles away from war,' he tried to explain to Selznick at the end of November 1943.

> As here there is only one studio and only six stages are available for almost the whole film industry everyone's delay obviously delays everyone else. At the present moment my starting date in the studio is the first week of January but it would be too rash to think that this is definite. I might be delayed a further two weeks ... I am afraid the cold realities of the war still do not penetrate Hollywood's balmy air.[9]

But Alex himself had difficulty adjusting to wartime realities. Although he finally took up the tenancy of Denham Studios on 24 January 1944 and the director Wesley Ruggles had arrived from America, there was still no workable script. Rather than concentrate on producing one, he suddenly announced in February that he was off to America for a few weeks. His marriage with Merle was under strain and he wanted to get back to Hollywood to patch it up.

MGM, who had installed Ben Goetz as their representative in London, were furious. They were paying not only for an empty studio, but also Robert Donat's salary at £2,000 per week. To make matters worse, Vivien Leigh was now no longer available because of all the delays and had been replaced by the then comparatively unknown Deborah Kerr.

On 3 March, when Alex had been away for some weeks, David Cunynghame, who had recently returned to work for Alex full time after a spell in the Air Ministry, noted: 'Today was one on which one's faith in Alex is overly taxed. Ben Goetz "let out a mouthful" about the way in which things were going.'

When Alex got back to England on 21 March, there were just thirty-four pages of script cobbled together by the writers Anthony Pelissier, Gerald Kersh and Miles Mallinson. 'Not a busy day at the office,' commented Cunynghame on 6 April, 'as it is daily becoming more apparent that nothing will be done on production until Alex has finished work on the script of *Perfect Strangers*.' Meanwhile, Wesley Ruggles, one of MGM's most highly paid directors, passed his time shooting atmosphere shots and filming wardrobe and make-up tests for Donat and Kerr.

The first shooting day was Monday, 24 April, but hardly anything was done because Donat had an attack of asthma and went into a sanatorium. When he returned to work on 5 May, he argued over the direction of the film with Wesley Ruggles, who then refused to turn up at the studio for three days running. Alex sacked him on Saturday, 13 May and made his début as the new director of *Perfect Strangers* two days later, but the script was still unfinished and the production limped along in a haphazard fashion. 'Never have I been so unhappy,' wrote Donat after sixteen weeks of filming. 'It is Korda. He is unhappy too – for personal reasons – and he is bored and impatient with his own picture . . . No script to go on – just a mass of blarney from AK. Our first complete script arrived five days ago.'[10]

Glynis Johns, who had a supporting role in the film, recalled that Alex directed the film with 'a lot of style and a lot of grace and a great wit', but that 'he was a little brittle at times. It wasn't normally this way.' She recalled that on one occasion 'he suddenly looked down at me, and said, "Oh, you're the same height as Merle." I thought it was an odd remark, but then I realized afterwards that the break-up was going on.[11]

When Alex wasn't directing or labouring over the script, he spent much of his time writing long personal letters to Merle. In their crumbling relationship lay much of the inspiration for the unnumbered pages of script which in dribs and drabs made their way to the actors in the course of the production. *Perfect Strangers* tells the story of a timid clerk and his wife – Robert and Cathy Wilson – who are separated from each other at the beginning of the war and have their lives transformed by military service. In their new surroundings, they each gain worldliness and confidence while imagining that their partner has stayed the same. When they meet again after three years, each resolves to tell the other that their marriage must end as they have become 'perfect strangers'. But after a night of quarrelling, they adjust to the way their characters have changed and pledge themselves to each other anew.

Alex was far from being a timid clerk, but he would have found it all too easy to identify with the couple's predicament. He had long been separated from his own wife, who had changed her mind about coming to England with him and stayed behind in Hollywood to continue her career as a film star. All through the year 1944 when *Perfect Strangers* was being made, Alex could have read in the newspapers the rumours of how he and Merle were drifting apart.

In the film Cathy Wilson falls for a naval architect while serving as a Wren in Scotland. After an evening out with him, she tells her friend Dizzie, 'It's a wonderful sensation to dance with the right man,' and confides that she had never danced with her husband. Since the physically indolent Alex was not the kind to take readily to the floor, fun-loving Merle might have expressed much the same sentiment to the handsome Hollywood cameraman Lucien Ballard, with whom she began to go out in late 1943. They had met while making *The Lodger* for Twentieth Century-Fox. Just three years older than herself, Ballard was the lover that Merle, now a woman of considerable independent means, preferred to the father figure that the much older Alex tended to play.

Nor was it the first time that Merle had strayed. In late 1941 she had an affair with the RAF fighter pilot Richard Hillary, who had come to broadcast in the United States under the auspices of the Ministry of Information and would soon afterwards become famous with the publication of his book, *The Last Enemy*. Hillary returned to London at the end of 1941, but they would meet again the following autumn when Merle came to England on the occasion of Alex's knighthood. The affair 'was not heavy and major', Hillary would tell his biographer, Lovat Dickson, 'but it was lighthearted, cheerful'.[12]

Alex had no choice but to accustom himself to Merle's dalliances, which were well known and must have caused him enormous pain. David Korda remembers seeing them together in the house in Bel Air. 'As a boy, I suppose one isn't really much aware of these things, but I sort of had the feeling that he did adore her.' He recalled an anecdote his father Zoltán told about a visit Alex made to a famous Hollywood restaurant called the Brown Derby. 'Supposedly, Alex left the table and went to have a pee, and two men were standing next to him, and one said, "Oh, you know who's screwing Merle now." And Alex heard this and fainted. She gave him a pretty terrible time.'[13]

Merle was the one person who could make Alex drop his shield of cool detachment. André De Toth recalled a meeting with him that must have taken place during Alex's rushed visit to Los Angeles in early 1944. De Toth was by this time a successful Hollywood director. Alex asked him to read a script for a film called *Dark Waters* in which Merle was about to appear and then took him out to lunch:

> He said, 'What do you think?' I said, 'It's the biggest piece of shit I have ever seen.' He said, 'That's what I think.' It was the first time he ever agreed with me. He said, 'Look, I can't let her down.' Tears coming out, real tears coming out of his eyes . . . 'Merle is committed to this. We are divorced,* but I love her. Please help me help her.'

De Toth, who was fond of Merle, agreed to direct the picture. Soon afterwards Alex said he was feeling ill and left the lunch early. 'For a fleeting second he stood naked in front of me, in front of himself. The realization of it must have hit him hard.'[14]

In *Perfect Strangers* Cathy Wilson tells her husband, 'I'm not

---

* Contrary to De Toth's recollection, at this stage Merle and Alex were still married, although Merle had made it absolutely clear that she wanted a divorce.

a meek child wife,' and she's angry to be patronized when she attempts to explain how she has grown apart from him. 'I was actually afraid of hurting your feelings,' she continues. 'Your feelings – as if you had any that weren't exclusively concerned with your own swollen, overbearing, impossible ego.' The comments don't quite fit the meek clerk of the film, or even the confident member of the armed forces that he becomes, but are the sort that might easily have passed between Sir Alexander and Lady Korda on the few occasions that they spent any length of time together. Many years later Merle would comment of their relationship: 'I remember saying to him once how much I loved him. And he said, "Oh yes, just like a father." But I think he resented that.' Yet in practice it was the only kind of love that she wanted from Alex, and the only kind that he knew how to give.[15]

In light of the parallels, the happy ending in which Cathy and Robert are reconciled seems like wishful thinking. Alex finished filming *Perfect Strangers* in early October 1944 and set off for Hollywood two months later for his own matrimonial reunion. But a few days before his arrival, Merle chose to make her rift with him public. 'Merle believes that the two years of constant separation from her husband is to blame for their parting,' reported Louella Parsons. 'I know that Merle has been in constant communication with him over the telephone, hoping to straighten out her tangled matrimonial affairs, but apparently that's out of the question.'[16]

The sudden publicity was Merle's way of making it plain to Alex that any attempt to make her change her mind was futile. This time there would be no MGM ending. Alex stayed in Hollywood for two months, not in their Bel Air home but the Beverly Hills Hotel. In the New Year, as if the break-up of his marriage had not been enough to make him feel old, he collapsed during a dinner at Romanoff's.

On 4 June 1945, almost exactly six years after she had married Alex in France, Merle divorced him in Mexico. In a suit that Alex did not contest she cited incompatibility as the grounds. Three weeks later she was married by proxy to Lucien Ballard, while they were both in Hollywood working together on the film *As It Was Before*. 'We were unable to get away from the studio,' she explained, 'so my attorney arranged the proxy marriage to conform with Mexican law.' [17]

It reflected the huge importance she attached to her career that she should have been too busy even to attend her own wedding. Three years later she would announce her intention to divorce her cameraman husband in a telegram to the Hollywood columnist Hedda Hopper – this was Hollywood etiquette, which Merle observed scrupulously. It was to her public that Merle would always prove the most constant.

Her next affair, with the young Italian Count Cini, went some way to securing her reputation as Hollywood's dark-eyed *femme fatale*. After visiting her in Cannes, where she was on holiday, Cini took off for Venice in his private airplane. Merle waved goodbye to him with a handkerchief and the plane circled to make a low-level salute. Hitting a tree, it crashed to the ground, killing the count instantly.

Undeterred, Alex, who had never ceased to love Merle, was among the first to travel to the Riviera to offer his sympathy. But although they remained close, there would not be the resumption of married life that Alex had hoped for. Merle was fond of Alex, in awe of him, but the thirty-year-old Count Cini had been just one more example of the consistent preference that she had displayed over the years for men with playboy souls. The sophisticated Alex was an indoor creature, whose habitat was more the salon than the beach or the ski slopes. He may have been too much in love with her to see the truth clearly, but he had already captured the essence of his attitude towards her in *That Hamilton Woman*. The art connoisseur Sir William Hamilton worships his young wife for her beauty as he would one of his statues – although they had the added advantage that they did not run off with sailors. Merle, for her part – like Lady Hamilton – had too much independence of spirit to settle for the passive life of the bejewelled society hostess.

Of her marriage to Alex, André De Toth would comment, 'I knew two Merle Oberons, one while they were married, and one when they divorced. And you had a feeling that somebody had just let a bird fly out of a cage. Merle suddenly became much more free and easy.'[18]

The actress Joan Fontaine recalled dining with Alex soon after his divorce from Merle:

> Over an excellent glass of Château-Lafite he warned me, 'No matter what, Joan, aim for the impossible. If you accomplish all your ambitions, there is nothing left.' Puzzled, I asked the silver-haired producer what he meant. Holding his glass up to the light, he sighed. 'I was a poor boy in Hungary when I conceived my dream ... I wanted to belong to the most important nation, to become rich, respected, marry the most beautiful woman, be world-famous.' He sipped thoughtfully from his goblet. 'I've done all those things. I became a British subject, I founded my own film company, I owned a yacht, Winston Churchill is my close friend, I married Merle, I was knighted.' Alex sadly contemplated the dark-red drop at the bottom of his wine-glass. 'Now ... now I've no more dreams left.'[19]

While another man in Alex's position might have warned the actress of the folly of worldly ambition, it was a mark of Alex's incurable discontent to suggest that she could never be ambitious enough. 'Having been condemned by nature and fortune to an active and restless life...' The words of Swift from *Gulliver's Travels* with which he had identified as a young, 'accursedly restless' director in Hollywood would remain true to the very end.

Perfect Strangers did not finally open until the end of August 1945, nearly a year after Alex had finished making it. By this time Merle Oberon had been married to her new husband for some months, and her relations with Alex had ceased to be of topical interest. So it was unlikely that the newspapers would draw any embarrassing comparisons. Instead, they concentrated on the fact that this was the first première of a Korda film for nearly three years and, as the first offering of the new MGM-London Films, it was an Event. 'Korda is news again,' commented the *Observer*. 'A Korda film is once more something that cannot be ignored. You may like it; you may dislike it; but you cannot just dismiss it.'[20]

Elspeth Grant, writing in the *Daily Sketch*, was one of those who disliked it. 'Shiploads of Wrens at the press showing laughed in a hearty, sailorly fashion,' she commented. 'But as Sir Alexander Korda's first film for the company the picture is not worthy of the occasion, or the stars, or the time spent on it.'[21]

The aftermath of the war was a strange time in which reviewers frequently made their criticisms according to standards of utilitarian and social value that they applied not only to the films they watched but also to the circumstances in which they were made. Alex, with his extravagant working methods and his failure to respect the necessary regimentation of wartime, was bound to be the object of extreme disapproval.

//

When Alex finally finished filming *Perfect Strangers*, he had no other production ready to take its place at Denham, and he had to release the stage for the remaining six months of his contract. The trade press criticized him fiercely for the disruption he had caused to other producers when studio space was so short.

But the difficulties of wartime production had convinced Alex from very early on that he needed a studio of his own. As he clearly wasn't going to be allowed to have Denham back, on 14 April 1944 he bought, on behalf of MGM, the Amalgamated Studio in Elstree from the Prudential for £225,000. Currently being used by the Government as a storage depot, it would not be derequisitioned until the end of the war. So Alex decided that, rather than take part in the unseemly business of haggling for studio space, after the completion of *Perfect Strangers* he would postpone his production programme until the return of peace. Meanwhile he would concentrate on building up the Korda-MGM organization.

On the same day, 14 April, he bought back London Film Productions from the Prudential. It had in effect been a dormant company ever since the Prudential had taken it out of Alex's hands in 1939 – the previous activities of film production and studio management having been divided between the newly created companies Alexander Korda Film Productions and D&P Studios. The only remaining assets were the films it had made, which past experience seemed to suggest were not to be regarded as of any great worth. So the Prudential, which had always intended to liquidate the company as soon as was conveniently possible, accepted Alex's bid of £100,000. 'The amount which Korda has offered is considered to be materially in excess of the value of the assets now remaining in the company,' observed the internal report recommending this decision.[22]

This was probably true so long as Alex's old films remained in the hands of an insurance company that knew nothing about the film business, but just a week after the sale David Cunynghame was figuring 'that with careful management Alex may get about £300,000 out of them'.[23] In fact, he would get many times that sum.

The year 1944 may have been a very bad one for Alex's romantic prospects, but it hugely improved his financial standing. On that *dies mirabilis*, 14 April, he also reached a long-delayed settlement with United Artists. Ever since the beginning of 1942 he had been receiving regular offers from David Selznick for his stock. In July 1943 he gave Selznick an option to purchase the shares for $650,000. But once negotiations had begun, encouraged by United Artists' increasingly bullish talk about its future, Alex fell back on his Churchillian tactic of *mise en demeure*.

Four months later, on 29 November 1943, he accepted an offer of $930,000 from United Artists itself. But foolishly, the chief negotiator, Teddie Carr – who would have done better, like Alex, to have taken his time – approached Rank just two days later to inquire about the basis on which he might wish to acquire a holding in the company now that Alex had sold his.

The following day Alex told Carr that he had been disturbed to hear rumours that Rank might be buying his shares and he delayed signing the formal agreement. 'Am not particularly concerned about this,' Carr cabled to the New York office, 'as feel sure my verbal agreement on which we shook hands . . . constitutes binding deal.'[24] But Alex backed out none the less, citing some technicality as his excuse.

His hope was that he might be able to sell his shares directly to Rank for a better price. When the United Artists owners expressed their reservations about having another English stockholder, he wrote to the president of the company arguing the wisdom of accepting Rank into the fold.

> I cannot see any reason why owners refuse to have him as financially and personally he has the highest possible standing. I see the point that partners do not want two English partners but I am perfectly willing to work out a deal myself with Rank here regarding my stock so that there would be only one partner remaining in England.[25]

United Artists, who by this time were heartily sick of dealing with British stockholders, agreed instead to buy back Alex's stock for $1,025,000. Alex's opportunism had netted him $95,000.

//

Just before the end of the war, Alex wrote the introduction to a lavish brochure announcing the future programme of MGM-London Films. He went to considerable lengths to suggest that in spite of having made just one film since his return to England, he had not been idle. 'Our producers and writers have prepared and completed screenplays which are now ready for production,' he declared.

> We have also acquired new studios at Elstree, the most modern in the United Kingdom, and intend equipping them so that they will be the most up-to-date in the world. Immediately these studios are released from their wartime occupation and as soon as the equipment is available, we will embark on our production programme at an annual expenditure of several millions of pounds, giving employment to thousands. As these pictures are assured of worldwide distribution they will make a great contribution to the essential post-war export trade of Great Britain.[26]

A dazzling array of names followed. Among the nearly twenty writers who had signed exclusive contracts with Alex were Robert Graves, Graham Greene, H. E. Bates, Evelyn Waugh and Arthur Koestler. Fourteen screenplays were ready for production, including *War and Peace*, *The Pickwick Papers* and Arnold Bennett's

The Old Wives' Tale. Vivien Leigh was going to appear in a film version of Enid Bagnold's *Lottie Dundass*. Carol Reed was going to direct Nevil Shute's *Pastoral*. R. C. Sherriff was going to produce a screen version of Rudyard Kipling's *Habitation Enforced*. And so on.

To onlookers Alex's announcements often seemed like impossible dreaming, but usually he could count on a handful of productions eventually being made. It was a question of chance and circumstance – the right star or director being available for the right film at the right time. At the outset he could sincerely believe that all had the chance of being made even if he expected a few to fall by the wayside. In this case, however, he would not make one of the future pictures announced for the MGM-London Films programme. The first film, *Perfect Strangers*, would also be the last.

In late October 1945, after a meeting with Louis B. Mayer in Hollywood, Alex announced his resignation as head of MGM in Britain due to 'prolonged ill-health'. The real reason was his extravagance and his general indifference to MGM's fortunes, which he made little effort to conceal. *Perfect Strangers* had cost $2 million to make, a colossal sum for an intimate wartime drama, and Alex was being just as profligate with MGM's money in gathering together an extremely expensive but not obviously useful collection of writers, directors and stars.

It's difficult to imagine that Louis B. Mayer could have dredged up much enthusiasm for the future screenplays that, say, Koestler might write, or appreciate how a British musical called *Heart of Gold* could make a positive contribution to the MGM balance sheet. Of the fourteen future productions Alex had announced only a handful would have appealed to Mayer, yet MGM had to bankroll the substantial pre-production costs.

Mayer had wanted Ben Goetz to keep an eye on the London outpost, but Goetz was no more able to say no to Alex than to Mayer himself. He watched helpless as Alex spent over a year dabbling at *Perfect Strangers* like an amateur watercolourist returning to his canvas whenever he had a spare moment. When Alex took the *Perfect Strangers* unit up to Scotland to film on location in August 1944, Goetz looked on as Alex rejected one apparently perfect setting after another. 'He behaved just as he has on half of the new sets on the picture,' observed David Cunynghame. 'He was exasperating and Goetz confided in me that he could not make head or tail of the whole business and marvelled how I stood up to it.'[27]

On the rare occasions when Goetz did stand up to Alex, the result was usually a blazing row. One of the worst occurred in September 1944 over the critic James Agate, whom Alex had put on the MGM payroll several months before. 'I wish that Alex was on stronger ground,' commented Cunynghame, 'as Goetz was merely being critical about the value James Agate was giving to the company – quite a reasonable matter for investigation.'[28] Matters reached a head in March 1945 when MGM discovered that Alex had bought the rights to Winston Churchill's unpublished *History of the English Speaking Peoples* for £50,000 and charged it to their account. It was hard to imagine what sort of film could ever emerge from such a deal. Called to task by MGM's lawyer in London, Sidney Wright, Alex switched the sum to Alexander Korda Film Productions, but threatened to resign unless MGM backed his judgement in future.

From the very outset, Alex had regarded MGM principally as a convenient stopgap while he made his mind about what he really wanted to do. As long as the war was on, he still hoped that the Government might give him an official job. A familiar presence at Belgrave Square was Claude Dansey, who every now and then asked for Alex's help in providing cover for various secret missions. In June 1944, Vincent's departure to work on a documentary film in Rome, which had recently been liberated, was one such ventures. In November 1944 Alex discussed with Brendan Bracken the possibility of making propaganda films about the Beveridge Report and the importance of Britain continuing the war against Japan with renewed urgency. 'The propositions seem to me somewhat futile,' commented Cunynghame, 'as there are no scripts or indications as to who is to pay for the films.'[29] But Alex was drawn to such ventures as being of more consequence than anything he might do for MGM.

The liberation of France encouraged the rather sniffy attitude he had towards low-brow American film executives. At the end of March 1945, he went over to Paris for the first time since before the war. He spent his evenings talking with old friends such as Marcel Pagnol and Marcel Achard. In a city temporarily without taxis he would find himself walking back to his hotel in the small hours through empty streets. These exhilarating few days offered a form of rejuvenation, a break from the cocooned life he led in London as the pasha of British films. On 2 April he was present when Charles de Gaulle presented the Croix de Libération to Paris at the Hôtel de Ville. There was the buzz of a country he loved coming alive. The visit strengthened his sense of a European identity and his desire to contribute to the renewal of a European film culture.

Alex occupied a unique position in the film world, both pulled between and seeking to reconcile the conflicting traditions of Hollywood and Continental cinema. A few weeks after his Paris trip, Cunynghame reported him as 'quite rational although somewhat erratic. We are now setting out to launch a large cinema for French films in London!'[30] Every time Alex's heart sank at the thought of *Lassie Come Home*, he could cheer himself up with *Les Enfants du Paradis* or *La Belle et la Bête* or *Rome, Open City*, just a few of the classics of Continental cinema that he would introduce to the English-speaking world.

The only thing that might perhaps have made a difference to Alex's lackadaisical attitude to MGM would have been if he had had his own studio. Needing to be in control, he had the same distaste for renting space that some people have for sharing a bathroom. So when the war ended, there was the brief hope that he might spark into life. In June he obtained MGM's authority to pay the Ministry of Works £75,000 for immediate possession of the studios that he had bought the previous year. Cunynghame noted that he was 'very excited'.[31] But in the same month Alex had to postpone what would have been his first post-war production, Enid Bagnold's *Lottie Dundass*, since the proposed star, Vivien Leigh, had fallen seriously ill. Soon afterwards Eddie Mannix, the vice-president of MGM, arrived in town. Cunynghame noted 19 June to be 'a somewhat mysterious day', which Mannix spent closeted away alone with Alex, over whom he seemed to exert 'a surprising influence'. No details of that meeting were recorded, but as the following day Alex seemed 'very troubled in making up his mind what to do with regard to MGM', we can speculate that Mannix had presented an ultimatum that he must toe the line. Exactly three months later, when he was in Hollywood, he gave Louis B. Mayer his answer. On 19 October, he telephoned the London office with the news that 'as MGM was so uncompromising he was leaving the company'.[32] It was a divorce that probably both sides would have felt was long overdue.

20. FORWARD INTO THE FUTURE

'Forward into the future, alone and unafraid. The past is dead. The future is yours, and nothing's going to stop you.'

— Perfect Strangers

After the announcement of his resignation from MGM Alex let it be known that he wasn't just ill, he was bored. 'He told me he just isn't interested in pictures,' wrote the columnist Louella Parsons.[1] It was partly true – Alex had been complaining about the tedium of film-making ever since his return to England. But he wasn't tired of the wielding of influence and the pulling of strings. It was in his blood.

On his way back from Hollywood he stopped off in New York where, together with Vincent, he met Sidney Bernstein in the St Regis Hotel. Bernstein had ambitious plans to produce and distribute films with Alfred Hitchcock and Ingrid Bergman. He had formed a company called Transatlantic Pictures and intended to build his own British studio.

He discussed his plans with Alex, who revealed that on his return to England he was going to open negotiations for the purchase of Sound City Studios at Shepperton, and suggested that, rather than build his own studio, Bernstein might like to join him in this venture. Bernstein in turn confided that he had begun negotiations to buy the film distributor British Lion from a director of the company, Harry Judge, who had a controlling interest, and he invited Alex to participate.

Both men left the meeting with a different understanding of what had taken place. Bernstein thought that a definite agreement had been reached: he would purchase a distribution company and sell Alex a half-share; in turn, Alex would purchase a studio and sell him a half-share. Alex, on the other hand, would later maintain that their discussions were merely vague and inconclusive talks about future projects in which they might or might not cooperate.

As the conclusions of their conversations were never set down on paper, it's impossible to be certain over what, if anything, had been settled. One can only comment that Alex's whole approach to business was based on vagueness – as Bernstein, who only three years earlier had been so amused by his indecision over whether to stay in Hollywood or return to England, ought to have known.

What is certain is that as soon as Alex got back to London in November 1945, he got in touch with Harry Judge and the other major shareholder in British Lion, and acquired the company for himself. When Bernstein asked for half the shares, Alex refused, just as he refused to sell a half-share in Sound City Studios, which he acquired shortly afterwards.

The wrangling between Alex and Bernstein came to a head in May 1946 when the British Lion Film Corporation announced a public share issue to raise capital of £1 million. On 18 May Bernstein sent Alex a letter threatening court action unless he stopped the share issue and transferred to him half the shares in both British Lion and the Shepperton studios. In the same letter he insinuated that Alex had bribed the British Lion shareholders to reach a deal with payments of £5,000, and accused him of improperly financing the purchase by causing British Lion subsequently to pay London Films £160,000 for the rights to reissue its old films.

Alex responded to this ultimatum with a curt reply. 'I have received your letter of May 18th. I regard it as insolent, and offensive to myself and others.'[2] But he said nothing about calling off the share issue or meeting Bernstein's other demands, so Bernstein initiated court proceedings.

The transaction to reissue Alex's old films was 'not entered into bona fide', stated the writ that Bernstein's lawyers put before the court a few weeks later, but was brought about by the defendant Korda solely to provide part of the purchase money for the purchase of the said shares. In the result the assets of British Lion have been diminished and the Ordinary Shares of British Lion have been reduced in value.[3]

The lawyers argued over the case for years. It was eventually settled out of court, but whatever the legal outcome might have been, it was one more example of the fact that if Alex could achieve an advantage by stealth, he would do so.

In this very ungentlemanly way Alex swiftly set up the beginnings of another film empire. The announcement of the public share issue was if anything an even more audacious move than his abuse of Bernstein's trust. Twelve years previously, when the Prudential had suggested such a course as a way of raising capital for London Film Productions, Alex had argued against it until there was a clear idea of the company's profit-earning potential. The Prudential went on to lose over £2 million keeping London Films afloat. So it was extraordinary that Alex should now seek to raise capital by the issue of British Lion shares.

That he was able to do so without any public outcry owed much to the anxiety of the Prudential to avoid embarrassment. Rather than liquidate London Film Productions, which it had the power to do at any point from 1936 onwards, the Prudential had preferred to hide the scale of the financial disaster, keeping the company in existence until Alex bought back the remaining assets in 1944. The result was that the true state of London Films' insolvency had never been publicly revealed. Just in case any bad memories were jogged, Alex tactfully declined to go on to the board of directors named in the share prospectus.

In 1946 the British film industry was riding an enormous wave of confidence. Cinema attendances were the highest they had ever been, many British films had won enormous critical acclaim, and there seemed to be every hope at last of establishing a consistent presence in the American market. The industry's biggest problems were structural. The Rank Organisation exerted a near-monopoly over the industry, and the Government was anxious to encourage competitors. British Lion's bid for finance was carefully couched to exploit these circumstances.

'The future policy of the Directors', stated the prospectus, 'will be to make available to independent producers complete facilities, including production finance, for the production of films and subsequently to arrange for their distribution.'[4]

From the break-up of MGM-London Films, Alex had salvaged production agreements with the producer Ted Black and Britain's leading film director Carol Reed, and he quickly built on this nucleus. His first signing in February 1946 had a 'bread-and-butter' appeal, which would have reassured potential investors that he really did intend to turn British Lion into a profitable concern. While a decade before he had sought to dazzle the film world with such exotic names as René Clair, Jacques Feyder or Marlene Dietrich, now he offered them Herbert Wilcox and Anna Neagle. Together over the last few years the producer and his film star wife had been responsible for some of the most success-ful but bland films ever made in Britain. In exchange for shares in British Lion, Wilcox agreed to make six films over four years, at least three of which would star Neagle. It was about as close as you could come to prudence in the film world.

Once the British Lion share issue had successfully taken place, Alex became more adventurous. At the end of May he contrib-uted over $30,000 to the finance of Orson Welles's stage musical *Around the World*, which was based on Jules Verne's novel *Around the World in Eighty Days*. The payment was effectively an inducement for a film deal that followed three months later. For a fee of $75,000 per picture Welles agreed to appear in three films as 'artist and/or director and/or producer'.[5]

Step by step, Alex was attempting to put together a vertical combine after the model of the Rank Organisation. The missing piece in this jigsaw was a chain of cinemas – although it was not for want of trying. At the beginning of January 1946 Alex had tried to persuade his former United Artists partners Goldwyn and Selznick to join him in the purchase of a showcase cinema. 'There is no other possibility of having any other theatre at all in the West End,' he pointed out, 'and for first run one is today entirely dependent on the Rank combine who own all the first-run cinemas.'[6]

But both producers knew Alex well enough to suspect a catch.

When Selznick asked his representative in London, Jenia Reissar, to investigate, she reported back that the cinema Alex had in mind had originally been a theatre, but was a 'dismal failure'. Before the war it was used only for trade shows and had the reputation of being unlucky. Although Alex had described it as 'just behind Leicester Square', in fact it was some minutes' walk away in a 'rather slummy Italian district called Soho'.[7] Soon afterwards Goldwyn and Selznick jointly declined Alex's offer. In March 1946, once he had purchased the British Lion shares, Alex suggested to Sidney Bernstein that he should merge his Granada cinemas with British Lion. It was the only basis on which Alex might have consented to Bernstein receiving a share in the company that he had originally negotiated for, but Bernstein refused and the descent into litigation quickly followed. Alex eventually acquired a West End cinema in October 1946, the Rialto in Coventry Street. It would open on Friday, 29 November with the successful première of *Les Enfants du Paradis*.

In June 1946, Alex moved into new offices at 146 Piccadilly opposite Hyde Park Corner, and while the newly purchased studios at Shepperton were being re-equipped, he concentrated on putting together a programme of films which would begin production in the new year. With an eye as ever to securing distribution in the American market, most of the projects he announced were built around a big box-office star – Paulette Goddard, to appear in *The True Story of Carmen*, David Niven in *Bonnie Prince Charlie* and Cary Grant in a film which was not specified. Orson Welles was to produce, direct and appear in a Technicolor production of Oscar Wilde's *Salome*, while Alex himself would direct *An Ideal Husband*. Meanwhile, Damon Runyon was signed to write an original film story, in which Alex hoped that Bing Crosby would appear.

These plans were affected by the usual process of attrition. Damon Runyon took the first instalment of his $100,000 fee and then promptly died. *The True Story of Carmen* was dropped because Columbia had rival plans to make the story with Rita Hayworth, and *Salome* foundered over Welles's objections to the star that Alex proposed, Eileen Herlie.

Alex had been tempted also to abandon Ted Black's production of *Bonnie Prince Charlie*: 'I rather fancy that he has cold feet about the script and the whole project,' commented David Cunynghame.[8] But in the end Alex went ahead much against his better judgement, and this ill-fated film, which began location shooting on 8 August 1946, opened the new production programme of the reconstituted London Films.

Alexander Korda was back, more powerful than ever before, making films again but also presiding over the fortunes of a large studio and distribution company. At this point it's worth reminding ourselves of the comments that Ernest Lever had made just before the Prudential stepped in to deprive Alex of Denham Studios nearly ten years previously: 'It is unfortunately true that on account of his temperament and his opportunism in financial matters Mr Korda is a dangerous element in any business, but more particularly if he is in a position of control.'[9]

The entries that Cunynghame confided to his diary during the following weeks traced the development of what the Prudential had identified as a nightmare scenario. On 12 August: 'Alex is more despotic than ever. He has put Vincent in complete charge of the studios.' On 2 September: '[Alex] and Vincent are running the studio in such an autocratic manner that no member of the board is conversant with what they are attempting to do.' In theory, Alex was answerable to the board of a public company; in practice, the members of that board, cowed, charmed or bamboozled, invariably behaved as if it were the other way round. In June 1946, Alex whisked the newly appointed chairman of British Lion, Hugh Quennell, off to Monte Carlo to celebrate the success of the recent share issue. Over the weekend, according to Cunynghame's diary, Quennell 'managed to lose £1,200 which the company will presumably pay'.[10] There was no one quite like Alex to ensnare you with bonhomie and to lead you into temptation.

//

In March 1947, the first big Technicolor film to go on the floor at the newly refurbished Shepperton Studios was not *Bonnie Prince Charlie*, which had to wait for David Niven to become available in May, but Alex's own production of *An Ideal Husband*, brought forward after the difficulties over *Salome*.

With their sophisticated dialogue and sedate pace, Wilde's plays were not obvious subjects for big-budget international films, and Alex's apparent readiness to make two in the same season betrayed a personal enthusiasm.

The 'ideal husband' of the play is a respected politician, Sir Robert Chiltern. He and his wife hold a reception at which the flower of London society is gathered. But the evening is marred by the arrival of the amoral Lady Cheveley, an acquaintance from the past who has for many years been living in Vienna. Lady Cheveley explains to Sir Robert that she has come to enlist his support for an Argentine canal scheme that Sir Robert was intending to denounce in the House. Unless he gives the scheme his endorsement, she will make public her knowledge that many years ago as a young man he sold a Cabinet secret, an act of deceit upon which his subsequent career and fortune rest. Rather than compromise his principles a second time, Sir Robert speaks out against the scheme in spite of Lady Cheveley's threat. He is saved from ruin when his friend Lord Goring discovers a bracelet that Lady Cheveley has stolen and uses it to blackmail the blackmailer.

With a thin and rather creaking plot, *An Ideal Husband* was not Wilde's best play – as several critics would point out when the film was released – but it was the one that meant the most to Alex. Wilde's depiction of the rich and powerful held up a mirror to a world in which Alex himself had won a place. He understood the pursuit of success and the temptations to which men of ambition could succumb.

'Wealth has given me enormous power,' Sir Robert tells his friend Lord Goring. 'It gave me at the very outset of my life freedom, and freedom is everything. You have never been poor, and never known what ambition is.' These words would have struck a chord with Alex, who had chosen a similar path. He might also have seen something of his own life in Sir Robert's description of his mentor Baron Arnheim, 'a man of a most subtle and refined intellect, a man of culture, charm and distinction':

I remember so well how, with a strange smile on his pale, curved lips, he led me through his wonderful picture gallery, showed me his tapestries, his enamels, his jewels, his carved ivories, made me wonder at the strange loveliness of the luxury in which he lived; and then told me that luxury was nothing but a background, a painted scene in a play, and that power, power over other men, power over the world, was the one thing worth having, the one supreme pleasure worth knowing, the one joy one never tired of.

Baron Arnheim lived in Park Lane just a short walk from where Alex had his penthouse in Claridge's, and they were near neighbours as much in their lifestyles as their addresses. Courting politicians, showing off the expensive paintings on his walls, treating his guests to the finest delicacies even in the midst of austerity – Alex enjoyed all the trappings of power and had not hesitated to make the necessary compromises of principle in their pursuit.

Lady Cheveley calls her request to Sir Robert to lie to the House 'a commonplace stock market swindle'. Over the years Alex had pulled off plenty of swindles of his own. But none the less he was still a man of genuine if tarnished ideals, who – as Sir Robert had done – would have found in the incorruptible Lord Goring an attractive example of practical morality. Goring's belief that on occasion you had to embrace trickery to live a good life was a paradoxical precept to which Alex could aspire. Here was a London society version of Abu, the little thief, who, in Alex's words, 'steals to relieve the hunger of others and to promote romance in the universe'.

//

'When will you realize that I am not an honest man!' Alex once asked when his attention was drawn to some undertaking he had broken. Hugh Stewart, who recalled this anecdote, was one of two 'associate producers' to work on *An Ideal Husband*. Every day during the making of the film he used to accompany Alex to the studio in his chauffeur-driven car. They would talk about the day's work, but also about a lot of other things. One day Alex asked Stewart if he had any ideas of his own for a film. Stewart told him of a story about a Welsh valley that is flooded to provide water for an English town. It was not a film that he wanted to make, said Alex. But shortly afterwards he commissioned Emlyn Williams to write an original treatment based on exactly this idea, and it was made into *The Last Days of Dolwyn*, starring Edith Evans and the young Richard Burton. Alex, for whom dissimulation had become virtually a default mode, did not bother to make an apology or give an explanation, and Stewart realized that it was pointless to tackle him on the subject. If you were Alex's employee, you would benefit from his considerable generosity and kindness, but it was always on his terms.

'Associate producer' was an important-sounding credit which in other film companies did often signify considerable independent authority, but in practice Stewart found that his role was to pass on Alex's wishes to people Alex did not have time to deal with himself. The title was a confidence trick, another example of Alex making something seem more important than it really was. Alex was far too imprecise ever to state the exact roles of his associate producers, but seemed to envisage that Stewart, who had previously been an editor, should oversee the cutting-rooms, while Phil Brandon, in the manner of a first assistant, should be in charge on the floor.

The presence of Stewart and Brandon enabled Alex to cover more ground and maintained a sense of continuity during his frequent absences. The biggest distraction for Alex was when in May 1947 Julien Duvivier began to direct *Anna Karenina*, starring Vivien Leigh as Anna, on an adjacent stage. Having been engrossed with the direction of *An Ideal Husband*, only at the very last moment did Alex discover that there were major difficulties with Jean Anouilh's script of *Karenina*. So every spare moment he had between takes of *An Ideal Husband* he would devote to revising *Anna Karenina*.

'Look at the lamb,' commented Constance Collier, who was playing Lady Markby, 'he's not with us at all. He's not directing this film – he's directing Tolstoy. Look at him reading *Anna Karenina* between shots.'[11]

Cecil Beaton, who had designed the costumes for both films, recalled how after a take on *An Ideal Husband* Alex summoned a stenographer and sat down under an arc light to dictate. 'When the result of this dictation appeared a few hours later it was a revelation. In spite of the conditions in which he had been working, he had written an absolutely brilliant analysis of Tolstoy's book. He pointed out where the Anouilh–Duvivier script had gone wrong, and why and where it must be rewritten.'[12]

The notes, Beaton wrote in his diary, were then given to a 'hack-writer who has just completed a bad picture'.* When Vivien Leigh challenged the choice of writer, Alex explained, 'If I give the job to Rodney Ackland, or a good writer, he'd produce *his* version of *Anna*. I want my outline to be copied faithfully.'[13]

During the making of *Anna Karenina* Cecil Beaton happened to be in the middle of a love affair with Greta Garbo, who had played Anna in the classic MGM version of twelve years previously. In long letters he kept her posted on progress, an exercise that required considerable tact as she had not starred in anything for years and must naturally have felt some jealousy. 'I think *Anna* will be a good film,' he wrote on 22 June. 'It is well directed. The leading lady is not Anna – she is not you – but she is sympathetic and has great character and style.'[14] As he watched the wind-machines fling imitation snow at Vivien Leigh – a mixture of perspex, salt and cement – he wondered whether Garbo had suffered such a 'squalid gruelling' on her studio platforms.[15]

//

Employed as a translator and technical adviser on the film was Baroness Moura Budberg. A sort of real-life counterpart to the Russian Countess that Marlene Dietrich had played in *Knight without Armour*, she was one of the larger-than-life figures to which Alex was irresistibly drawn. Born Maria Ignatyevna Zakrevsky in Kharkhov in 1892, she was the daughter of Count Ignat Zakrevsky. In 1911 she married a Russian diplomat who was killed by his own peasants in 1918, and then a Baron Budberg

---

* The 'hack-writer' was Guy Morgan, a former film critic of the *Daily Express*, and the 'bad picture' a police thriller called *Night Beat*. 'Strangely enough,' commented Morgan, 'it was the only picture in that year among the Korda productions that showed a substantial profit'.

whom she later divorced. She subsequently became the mistress of first the British secret agent Sir Robert Bruce Lockhart, then the writer Maxim Gorky, and, after coming to England in 1933, H. G. Wells. After the latter had died in her arms in August 1946, the Baroness inherited a small legacy, and Alex, who had known her since the 1930s, in turn inherited her. In her mid-fifties, she was no longer young enough to be anyone's mistress, but she became an indispensable part of Alex's social circle, a source of wit and gossip, and someone who was as formidably well read as he was. A party game the two used to play was to take a classic novel and question each other on its most minor characters.

Baroness Budberg made it her business to attend as many parties as she could and keep Alex up to date with the social and literary scene. She often used to give rather amateur *soirées* of her own in her Kensington flat. 'There'd be one or two literary people like C. P. Snow,' recalled the producer Norman Spencer, 'and there'd be a bottle of gin, and orange juice on the table. There'd be some desultory conversation, and then after about an hour Moura would say, "Well, sorry you have to go." . . . She had a kind of grandeur about her, of the old world.'[16]

After the production of *Anna Karenina* came to a close, Alex took Moura Budberg on as his scenario adviser. In an industry which depended upon a predominantly young audience, it was not a forward-looking appointment, and was typical of Alex's own attachment to the pre-war world.

//

In the filming of both *Anna Karenina* and *An Ideal Husband*, Alex as usual liked to do everything. 'The upshot of course,' commented Hugh Stewart, 'was that a lot of things didn't get done.'[17] Hopelessly overwhelmed with a myriad of problems competing for his attention, Alex often failed to tackle any single problem with the necessary rigour. Cecil Beaton was 'full of admiration for his quickness, perception, subtlety and flair',[18] but felt that he undermined himself by falling back too readily on the glib remark. When the actress Martita Hunt, who had been called in to coach Michael Wilding, complained that he was 'too common' for the part of Lord Goring, Alex retorted that it didn't matter because the people who saw the film would be common. 'An easy comeback is a mistake,' observed Beaton.

> By degrees I began to realize how readily Korda excuses himself when he is in the wrong. His intention was to make the highest quality film. When I complained about a library set being particularly phoney and vulgar he shrugged: 'Well, the Chilterns are *nouveaux riches*.' That is not what Wilde intended them to be. That is not why we went to Paris for the hats, and to Wildenstein to hire Louis Quatorze tapestries.[19]

But Alex lived in a world that required the continual juggling of competing demands. It was no easier to be an international movie producer than it was to be an ideal husband. The Technicolor glamour required to lure the 'common people' into the picture palaces inevitably entailed compromise. Beaton himself was called upon to interpolate lines into the script from other Wilde plays to justify the American accent of Paulette Goddard who played Lady Cheveley.

Alex's need for control led him to take on endless unnecessary tasks. Just as *An Ideal Husband* was about to go onto the floor, for example, there had been labour problems at Shepperton. It was Alex who rushed over to the studio to try to solve them. Three weeks later there was a make-up strike. Again it was Alex who stepped in to settle it. David Cunynghame turned up at the studio to find him 'so overwhelmed by the make-up strike that he could not think of anything else'.[20] Meanwhile, the actors and technicians were left on the *Ideal Husband* set killing yet more time. 'Poor lamb,' Constance Collier might have remarked, 'hasn't he got anything better to do?'

//

No sooner had Alex completed *An Ideal Husband* than he turned his attention to *Bonnie Prince Charlie*. He was unhappy with the sets and the script, as well as the director Robert Stevenson, whom he sacked in September 1947. Alex persuaded Anthony Kimmins to take over the direction, while he himself laboured on salvaging the script. The original producer of the film, Ted Black, was effectively sidelined. Hugh Stewart, who was asked to help coordinate the efforts of various scriptwriters, recalled that Alex was delighted with the fresh start. But as everyone was now dancing to his tune, which he never seemed to be able to find time to explain properly or even to be sure of himself, it wasn't surprising that the individual efforts lacked conviction.

Alex's staff had to resign themselves to his continual meddling, never knowing when he might unstitch some arrangement they had negotiated or enter into some other commitment without consulting them first. His habitual feeling that something could have been done better than it had been was often the occasion for irrational outbursts of anger. Cunynghame remarked upon one particularly tiring day which ended with Alex fulminating over the management of the Rialto Cinema – about which, however, 'he professed complete ignorance'.[21]

//

In June 1947 production on *An Ideal Husband* was suspended for two weeks while Alex went to New York to negotiate a deal with Twentieth Century-Fox to distribute his productions in America. The four-year agreement, announced on 1 July, made provision for fourteen films. 'This is the most important releasing contract Twentieth Century-Fox has ever made,' commented Fox's president, Spyros P. Skouras. 'It will do much to strengthen good will between the two great English-speaking nations.'[22] But barely a month later the British Chancellor, Hugh Dalton, seemingly unconcerned about relations between the two great English-speaking nations, imposed a 75 per cent duty on imports of foreign films. The American film industry retaliated with an embargo on its exports of films to Britain, but Fox still went ahead with the agreement, although it might have been better if it hadn't. For the good will that Skouras had spoken of at the time of the agreement was non-existent, and, dissatisfied with the box-office returns, Alex pulled out of the agreement after less than a year, seriously damaging his reputation for knowing the American market.

When *An Ideal Husband* opened at the Carlton on 13 November 1947, Alex must have wondered if he even knew the English market. 'The less said about the première the better,' commented

David Cunynghame. 'There was hardly any applause at the end of the picture.'[23] The following day Alex sulked over the several mediocre reviews while Vincent panicked. 'I cannot imagine what caused him to choose this Oscar Wilde compound of epigram and melodrama,' wrote Richard Winnington in the *News Chronicle*, 'or, having chosen it, what should have compelled him to be so literal and stagey in its transcription.'[24] Nearly all the reviews echoed Winnington's bafflement at the choice of subject.

The reviews for *Anna Karenina*, which opened two months later, on 23 January 1948, were even worse. 'So much talent, taste, toll, and trouble have gone into the making of *Anna Karenina* that it is a pity to have to record that it turns out to be a magnificent, beautiful bore,' wrote Fred Majdalany, the critic of the *Daily Mail*.[25] 'Big, pretty, dull,' agreed the headline of the *News Chronicle* review.[26] This time the consensus was that Alex had chosen not the wrong subject but the wrong star. 'In the end the film must depend entirely on the personality of the actress playing Anna,' commented Majdalany in a perceptive review. 'Vivien Leigh's combination of animated porcelain and civilized spitfire, while admirable for Scarlett O'Hara, does not fill out to the mature, all-womanly, universal character of Anna.'[27] Some reviewers made the inevitable comparison. 'I never, alas! saw Garbo's Karenina,' wrote Margaret Lane in the *Evening Standard*, 'but *she* had that quality which breaks the heart, and this is a theme that more than any other requires it.'[28]

A few weeks later, perhaps emboldened by the reports of the London opening, Garbo attended with Cecil Beaton a private screening of *her* version of the film at the MGM studios in Culver City. 'That's very well done,' she would interject every now and then. She was pleased to find that in spite of the passage of time the film bore up so well, although she had an unreasoning dislike of her voice, which Beaton however found 'deep and beautiful', containing 'so many varying lights and shades – such tenderness and such strength'. He was touched to have seen the film in her presence, and thought that many of the sentiments expressed might have been Garbo's own. 'Her performance was very moving and so full of warmth and understanding and possessing everything that her successor lacks.'[29] Looking at Alex's *Anna Karenina* today, it's hard to dispute Beaton's verdict. In one of the lapses of judgement to which Alex now seemed more and more prone, Vivien Leigh had been badly miscast.

London Film Productions could hardly have had a more miserable start to a new year. *An Ideal Husband* and *Anna Karenina* looked like being two expensive failures,* while *Bonnie Prince Charlie* was still mired in Shepperton Studios, eating up money. With each passing day it seemed only more likely that it would be yet another flop, but no one knew quite how to end it. At one time Alex might have been tempted to leave it on the shelf, but with its budget soaring well over £500,000, it had become too costly an embarrassment to hide.

//

Immersed in his reborn empire, Alex had no more time than he had ever had for his son Peter, who as usual had been left with an allowance to sort himself out. In *Charmed Lives* Michael Korda would tell a much repeated anecdote of how Alex had once given his son a five-pound note with the words. 'Don't spend it; waste it.' But in Peter's case such an attitude was just another confidence trick, an attempt to make up for what Alex was not prepared to give him. Peter didn't need to be told to waste money. He'd been trained to do this from the earliest age. He was the child who had everything. So, in the absence of any hands-on guidance, Peter predictably became the quintessential young man about town, dining out with beautiful women, driving fast cars and crashing them. On 6 August 1945 he was involved in a serious motor accident and badly fractured his skull.

Occasionally he would work for London Film Productions in the scenario department, but he must have found it hard to escape the shadow of his father, and it was understandable that he should have wished to strike out in his own direction. In early 1947, he applied for a patent for a device that would arrest the momentum of airplanes landing on the decks of aircraft carriers. When the

---

* Costing approximately £430,000 to make, Alex's *Anna* had by 1950 grossed just £230,000.

Navy showed no interest in developing the invention, he became a journalist in the air industry.

In March 1948 he married and settled down with his wife in the country, where they would raise four children. His life may not have been remarkable for any great achievements, but he managed to achieve the domestic stability that had so completely eluded his father.

'Alex was so lonely in his suite at Claridge's,' recalled the actress Christine Norden, 'that he spent most of his leisure hours in my Portman Square penthouse.' Alex had signed Norden for MGM-London Films in 1945. Her name was his invention. 'You are cool, like crystal,' he declared, 'and those cheekbones look Nordic. We'll call you Christine Norden.' Soon after Alex's divorce from Merle Oberon, they began going out together. Born Molly Thornton in 1924, she was the daughter of a Sunderland bus driver whom three Hungarian friends of Alex – the composer Nicholas Brodszky, film producer Alexander Paal and photographer Stephen Hajnal – had spotted in a queue outside the Royal Cinema in Edgware Road.* The three explained that they were in the film business, persuaded her to agree to be photographed in Hyde Park the next day, and then sent the pictures to Alex.

Molly, as she was known, had in fact already been in showbusiness as a singer since she was twelve. During the war, as leading lady of ENSA's *Column One*, she was the first performer to step ashore on the beaches of Normandy after D-Day, appearing in shows put on in makeshift theatres often close to the front line. A few weeks earlier she had married the bandleader Norman Cole, but they separated immediately after Molly gave birth to a son Michael in March 1945.

With long golden hair, high cheekbones and green eyes, she had the sort of 'bombshell' looks that instantly turned heads, and the arrival of her baby son did not keep her out of showbusiness for long. By the time Alex saw the pictures of her in early August 1945, she already had an appointment for a screen test with the Rank Organisation.

---

* By one of those pleasing coincidences the film that happened to be playing was Alex's *That Hamilton Woman*.

In her unpublished memoirs, Norden recalled Paal taking her to meet Alex at Claridge's. 'I was introduced to a very tall, imposing-looking man, with a shock of white hair and the softest, most seductive Hungarian accent,' she recalled later. 'He had a way of asking questions without being rude, almost like a doctor's bedside manner. We made an appointment to meet at his office at Metro-Goldwyn-Mayer at eleven the following morning . . . As I left the penthouse suite, he kissed my hand as only a Hungarian can. It was courtly and romantic.'[30]

After a successful screen test, Molly Thornton, now renamed Christine Norden, was introduced to the world in a blaze of publicity. In the best Fifi D'Orsay tradition Alex's publicists set about reworking her past. She was now not the daughter of a Sunderland bus driver but of a Norwegian sea captain. Before she had even appeared in a film, she was set up in a luxury penthouse in Portman Square, signing autographs and opening shops in front of huge crowds.

Christine's arrival in Alex's life occurred when he was at his most emotionally vulnerable. The divorce from Merle and her subsequent marriage to Lucien Ballard had occurred only a few weeks earlier. He was still deeply in love with Merle, although he strove, as usual, with as much bravado as he could muster, to make the best of the situation.

Soon after Christine's screen test, Merle received a telephone call from him. 'You don't need to worry about me any more,' Merle later remembered him saying. 'I've just met the girl I plan to make my new star . . . and the next Lady Korda.'[31]

More amused by than in awe of Alex, Christine was happy to play along. 'Every time I saw "Sir Korda" in his office,' she recalled, "giving me fatherly – and sometimes not so fatherly – advice, I would sit there looking as much like an angel as possible. Then, from an ivory box on the desk, I would take one of his large Havana cigars, bite the end off and puff away.'[32] She saw no point in postponing the obvious and, according to her memoirs, became Alex's mistress in 1946.

Christine was romantic, playful, intelligent, but also down to earth with the sort of independence of spirit that Alex had previously admired in Merle and Maria. While Christine treasured the relationship for all the things that Alex could teach her, Alex found as much comfort in what they already had in common. Her combination of homeliness and glamour appealed to someone whose own peasant roots lay intact beneath the outer shell of his city sophistication. An anecdote by the film director Guy Hamilton serves well to illustrate this dual nature. He recalled being summoned to lunch at Alex's penthouse in Claridge's for a pep talk before he made his first film. In the dining room were three silver salvers with domed lids. Alex whisked off the lids to reveal a pair of salamis – 'They come from Vienna Budapest. Pass your plate, dear boy' – and a pile of poached eggs. That was lunch. 'Help yourself,' said Alex, as he began chopping up the salamis.[33] It was an example of a talent for mixing the grand with the simple that Christine shared.

In 1947 Christine made her screen début as the nightclub singer Jacqueline Delaney in the thriller *Night Beat*. 'I sang, danced, got drunk, seduced men, murdered my lover and then committed suicide,' she recalled. 'When they said they were introducing me, they meant it!' The film's success at a time when the world had yet to hear of Marilyn Monroe or Diana Dors made her, in the words of the *Daily Worker*, 'Britain's number one oomph girl'.

A 'prestige cameo' in *An Ideal Husband* followed.

As Mrs Marchmont, Christine Norden was by a long way the most miscast actress in the film. With her blonde hair and angular features she seemed to belong more to the Russian steppes than a London society drawing-room. Cecil Beaton had made some attempt to soften the impact by having her wear a mouse-coloured wig. But when Alex saw it, he protested: 'Cecil, dear boy, in Victorian times, they still fucked, you know, just the same as we do today. There were blondes, then, there are blondes now, there will always be blondes. Get rid of that wig!'[34]

In his eagerness to promote her, Alex was unconcerned about whose feathers he might ruffle. In the opening sequence of *An Ideal Husband* the characters in the story drive their carriages around Hyde Park Corner in the order their names appear on the screen. To the displeasure of many in the cast, Christine appeared after the star of the film Paulette Goddard, but before Diana

Wynyard, Michael Wilding, Glynis Johns, Hugh Williams, Sir C. Aubrey Smith and Constance Collier. The fact that another actress in a small part, Harriet Johns, was in the carriage with her did little to lessen what seemed like an obvious snub. At the première Constance Collier was heard to remark, 'Cochran used to have Young Ladies instead of chorus girls. Korda has whores with claws.'[35]

But Christine was by nature happy-go-lucky and not scheming in the way Constance Collier's remark suggested.* Admiration, amusement and a taste for a glamorous life governed her relationship with Alex far more than ambition. He in turn showered film roles on her like jewels. They were not judiciously chosen because from the outset his attitude to her was as much personal as professional. When she began to receive offers from Hollywood, Alex refused to release her from her contract. 'No my little goddess, you are not going,' he told her. 'You know I lost Merle that way. I am not going to lose you too. I could not bear that.'[36]

But Christine was a free spirit not to be imprisoned in a cage. Alex had no choice but to accept that she would take other lovers too. In 1947, her first husband, Norman Cole, petitioned for divorce, citing as the cause one of these lovers, the musician Hamish Menzies. He also successfully claimed custody of their son Michael on the grounds that Christine was an unfit mother. She would not see Michael again until he was twenty.

Alex pulled the necessary strings to keep the story out of the papers and took comfort from Christine's promise that she would marry him when the divorce came through. But Christine had already fallen in love with Jack Clayton, a production manager she had met on the set of *An Ideal Husband*. The two were married at Marylebone Register Office on 13 December 1947.

'I'll have that man blacklisted in every studio in the world,' shouted Alex.

---

* Christine's talent for the scathing remark would have won her few friends among the acting profession. When at the last moment Alex put her into the film *Mine Own Executioner*, she took to calling Dulcie Gray, her far more experienced co-star, Gracie Dull.

'If you put my husband out of work, I might have to sell my memoirs,' replied Christine, who had been privy to some of Alex's less above-board transactions.[37] Clayton kept his job and eventually became one of Britain's most acclaimed directors.

It was an *Ideal Husband* situation, the sort of thing that Lady Cheveley might have done. There were some aspects of life, Alex was discovering, in which being powerful counted for very little. Here he was a cuckold again. Whether it was Maria throwing soup plates in his face, Merle indulging in serial infidelities or, even worse, his mistress marrying one of his underlings, Alex's bitter experience was time after time one of public authority and personal humiliation.

'It broke his heart when Christine married Jack Clayton,' Merle later commented. 'He never quite got over it. Lovers he could tolerate, but not a husband taken in preference to himself.'[38]

Christine's very capriciousness might have offered some hope that sooner or later, like the wind, she would turn again. And indeed, within months her relationship with Clayton had foundered and she had returned to Alex. But it must have been obvious that she fell as far short of an ideal wife as he did of an ideal husband.

'I loved Alex with all my heart,' Christine wrote in her memoirs, 'but I was not *in love* with him. I made him laugh. He loved to look at me, to have me around. He taught me about food, art, all the things I'd never dreamed about. He bought me jewels I had no appreciation of. They meant nothing to me. Money meant nothing to me. I was all the time searching for something I could not find.'[39]

Alex was funny, clever, wise, but Christine was far too much of a realist ever to regard him as a credible lifetime partner. 'He was, after all, 31 years older than me – ten years older than my own father.' This gulf between their ages tormented him. 'He told me of a dream he had very often,' wrote Christine. 'I was dancing for him on a very lonely beach in white chiffon. We were both laughing and singing Hungarian songs. I would drift further and further away from him, until I seemed to be dancing on the ocean, out out out until I finally danced out of sight. He would wake up in a cold sweat of terror. I know this was true. I lay next to him many times when he had this dream. This dream became a prophecy.'[40]

Sadly, in the years that followed, as British Lion became more and more mixed in financial difficulties, Alex would suffer plenty of other nightmares beside.

21. NEVER PAY CASH

Soon after the end of the war, the Rank Organisation came to the conclusion that the independent producers it had so lavishly financed were a luxury it could no longer afford. Severe restrictions began to be placed both on their budgets and their choice of subject matter, so that one by one the producers broke away and allied themselves with the British Lion group, which had been established with the express purpose of supporting independent production. Notable arrivals in the course of 1947 included Powell and Pressburger, and the production team of Anatole De Grunwald, Anthony Asquith and Terence Rattigan, and in early 1948 Alex began negotiations with Frank Launder and Sidney Gilliatt.

But it was clear that the £1 million which had been raised through the public share issue would not be enough to finance British Lion's increasingly ambitious production plans, and Alex began to lobby for Government help. Just a few days after the disappointing première of *An Ideal Husband* in November 1947, Alex was already working on figures for Sir Wilfrid Eady, the Permanent Secretary at the Treasury, who would become a sort of Government godfather in Alex's attempts to secure public finance.

On 12 February 1948, with Eady's advice, British Lion applied to the Finance Corporation of Industry (FCI) for an advance of a further £1 million. As it was the Government's stated policy to encourage British film production, the President of the Board of Trade, Harold Wilson, was asked to support the application. On 25 February, he wrote to Lord Bruce, the chairman of the FCI:

We regard British film production today as an important dollar saver and a potential dollar earner and we are anxious to see all the resources of the industry in the way of studios and manpower being used to the fullest possible extent. This is even more the case at the present time when the Americans have ceased to send their films to this market, and it is by no means certain when or to what extent those imports may be resumed.[1]

The following day, a memorandum was circulated within the Board of Trade encapsulating the Government's attitude to the film industry:

The problem is essentially one of finding finance for an industry, which, although peculiar, must be made worthy of having finance for it. If it is ever allowed to get about that the Government are prepared to put up money for films or are even thinking of putting up money themselves we shall never be able to get the atmosphere which will put our film industry on a sound financial basis. However – short of an all-round subsidy – serious objections on grounds of public policy would lie against any suggestion that the Government should themselves directly finance an industry of such enormous entertainment and propaganda potential.

But it must be recognized that the film industry is not one which normal financial channels look upon with favour. Its habits are peculiar, most of the people engaged in it are rogues of one kind or another, and a good deal of money has been lost by unwise investment in it, or by the uncontrolled behaviour of producers. The problem therefore seems to be to find an existing organization (if there is one) or if not, to set up a new one which can venture into this new field with sufficient authority and determination to enable them to make a success of it.[2]

The Board of Trade imagined a bank which would commit itself to providing consistent support for British film producers. Its hopes that the FCI might take on such a role were dashed when the FCI eventually turned down British Lion's application for finance. It was hardly surprising as several of FCI's shareholders were insurance companies that had in the 1930s lost money through just the sort of 'unwise investment' in the film industry that the memorandum had mentioned.

So the Board of Trade considered a modified scheme. Independent producers would be coralled into one organization, which could vet the viability of individual projects with the expertise that the financial institutions lacked. This one organization, representing the interests of the most reputable producers, it hoped, would then prove to be a more attractive candidate for finance.

In the following weeks, meetings with Board of Trade and Treasury officials became a regular feature of Alex's diary, as he lobbied hard to become part of the Government's plans. The charm offensive included inviting the leading personalities in the film industry to a dinner at which the President of the Board of Trade was guest of honour. The late Jill Craigie, who was then a young documentary film-maker, attended it. 'I arrived at the dinner to find myself sitting next to Laurence Olivier on one side, I think it was Carol Reed the other side ... and Korda at the dinner turned to Harold and said, "You see, I've got the British film industry – here it is." '[3]

Alex may have been by some way the British cinema's rogue-in-chief, but in this case the Government was less the dupe of Alex than his co-conspirators, for it saw in British Lion a convenient means of rationalizing a business that it wanted to support and yet keep at arm's length.

In April 1948 a Board of Trade memorandum formulated the new policy:

It is the declared policy of HMG to encourage the maximum production of British films, both as an essential national asset and as a certain dollar saver and potential dollar earner.

This expansion will involve the provision of additional working capital for the industry, particularly for the independent producers.

HMG see grave political objections to the employment of Government capital in an industry which can be so easily used for propaganda purposes, and they are anxious if possible to avoid this.

The necessary financial support can be given to independent producers either through a new institution set up for that

purpose or through an existing firm re-organized and strengthened for the purpose as necessary.

The objections to a new institution are:-

(a) It will take a long time to set up, and the need for
assistance to independent producers is urgent.

(b) It will be very difficult to secure the right sort of technical
advice. The men who are competent to administer this
kind of financial assistance are very few in number, and
are all actively engaged in the industry.

HMG believe that an efficient instrument for their purpose
can be formed from an existing company, British Lion Film
Corporation Ltd. This Company already finances a number of
the best independent producers. It is a reputable firm with a
good record and its Managing Director, Sir Arthur Jarratt, is
probably the most competent adviser in this field to be found
in the film industry today.

To enable this Company to play the part contemplated
for it, it would require a substantial addition of capital. It
is recognized that the Board would probably need to be
re-organized and strengthened, and that special arrangements
might be necessary to ensure that Sir Alexander Korda's
dominating position in the Company as a shareholder could
not be used to obtain for him exceptional treatment as a
producer. It is clearly understood that the object is to provide
adequate working capital under proper safeguards for the film
production industry, although the 'chosen instrument' is an
individual firm.[4]

Alex, for whom power and influence had always been more important than money alone, was only too pleased to be an 'instrument
of Government policy', and at the invitation of the Board of Trade
he outlined in a long memorandum the role that British Lion might
play. Its detailed and cogently argued paragraphs might have
rolled off the pen of a top Whitehall mandarin. Alex's combination
of intellect and authority left many people with the impression
that somehow he had missed his true calling. Churchill, who had
benefited from Alex's extravagance as much as anyone, once said
that Alex would have made a great prime minister if Rockefeller
had been his chancellor. His reasoned arguments were advanced
with such a lofty detachment that it was hard not to be lulled into

thinking that he cared not one jot for his own interests but had only the greater good of the nation at heart.

'The great weakness of the independent producer,' Alex explained, 'is his very independence.'

> While the producer who makes a film for the big combines and for the American companies is certain to have his product exhibited whether it is good or bad, the independent stands entirely on his own and unless he produces a smash hit, he is liable to great financial loss. Even if his film is out of the ordinary, he has very little chance of proving his film's worth, as the distributors and the exhibitors, who are his primary clients (and not the public), are very conservative people, who very rarely believe in something new or bold. The weakness of the independent producer is that he has no continuity of production. For instance, he makes a film, then he has an idea for another. Before even starting the film he has to pedal his idea to the distributor, he has to bend this idea to the primary patron's taste, often to such a degree that the original idea is almost unrecognizable, but without first getting distribution he cannot get the necessary money. Therefore the independent producer is ultimately governed in the selection of his subject by the distributor of the film.[5]

The Government's previous policy of establishing a film bank, he suggested, would not have been an effective solution because such a corporation would only loan money but not address all the other problems of film production. He then modestly put forward the alternative proposal that he already knew the Government was minded to pursue. It was made without any particular insistence, but just seemed to flow as the logical consequence of his previous observations. British Lion was barely mentioned, but it didn't really need to be. It was just taken for granted as the inevitable conclusion.

> The grouping of those independent producers, whose past performances make them reliable film-makers, into one enterprise which not only would help to finance but also to distribute their films and would also furnish them with studios and production facilities, is the only way I see which, on a commercial basis, could ensure their future existence.

Grouped together, their weakness as individual traders would disappear. The group would deal with every aspect of their commercial and financial activities. While one single picture, however good, is of little worth in the film industry where hundreds of films are constantly on the market, the output of fifteen to twenty films a year by a group of producers represents a force which every exhibitor has to take into account, for an important part of this business would depend on the Distributor selling the films of this group. As in show business it is inevitable that there will be some failures, and as the chief aim of every production company is to protect its weaker films, if the group stands together for the distribution of its films, the weaker can have some measure of protection from the stronger.[6]

The President of the Board of Trade, who must have spent much more of his time worrying about Britain's shipbuilders and car factories, merely questioned a minor clause and scrawled in red ink on top of the memorandum, 'It seems OK to me.'

From this moment the power of HM Government was behind Alex. On 14 June 1948 British Lion approached the FCI a second time. The opening lines of the application gave the impression of a company less anxious to seek financial aid for its own purposes than to advance a national cause:

The Government has recently stated that it wishes to see instituted a method of financing independent film production which will not only provide the necessary finance but will also ensure the economic use of the money . . . The President of the Board of Trade has informed this company (British Lion Film Corporation Limited) that he considers that the Company's purposes and methods of operation make it a suitable instrument for this policy.[7]

One might almost have thought that British Lion had been requisitioned. It was an irony that while Alex was never able to play an official role when his political ally Churchill was Prime Minister, he tumbled effortlessly into one under the new Socialist Government.

As the understanding with the Government was that British

Lion would consider finance not just for the independent producers already associated with the company but also any reputable
producer that might subsequently come along, the request for
capital was now £2 million – double the original figure. It was
needed, the letter of application concluded, 'to enable the Company to maintain its existing scale of operations and at the same
time to provide for cautious but progressive expansion in accordance with the policy of the Government'.

But the Government's added weight made little difference. The
FCI, no more enthusiastic than it had been before, reiterated its
previous objection: however much British Lion's request for aid
might be hedged around with Government guarantees and safeguards, film finance was still speculators' finance.

After the negotiations had broken down at the end of June
1948, Alex got in touch with the First Secretary at the Board of
Trade, Rupert Somervell. '[He] poured out his troubles to me at
great length,' wrote Somervell.

> It becomes clear, however, from what he told me that if British
> Lion do not within a very short time receive additional finance
> they will be unable as a matter of common prudence to
> continue with the programme they have in view, with the
> result that the Government's whole policy for expanding film
> production will be completely upset.[8]

It was perhaps unwise to take Alex's pleas completely at face
value, but the Board of Trade did so out of its own desperation
to patch a deal together. It spent the next weeks attempting to
attract other City backers to finance British Lion in conjunction
with FCI, but nothing could budge the FCI from its fundamental
objection to investing in film production. So reluctantly the
Government stepped in, announcing its intention to provide
financial assistance to the film industry through a 'National Film
Finance Company'. And before this new fund had even been
established, its organizing committee was requested by the Treasury and the Board of Trade to consider the terms on which it
might 'as a matter of urgency, make a substantial loan to British-
Lion'.[9] Such direct assistance was the outcome the Board of
Trade had most wanted to avoid, but, having only recently raised

the quota for British production to 45 per cent, it had little choice if it were to preserve its credibility.

Reading through the Board of Trade files today, one can only marvel at the practised ease with which officials disregarded inconvenient truths that might have hindered their chosen policy. Their readiness to allow Alex to continue to play a pre-eminent role at British Lion was an example. 'I should personally be disinclined to press for some alteration of his relations with British Lion at this moment,' commented Sir Wilfrid Eady.

> In the first place if he is bought out somebody has to find that money . . . In the second place there is, I think, some advantage in having somebody like Korda 'knocking about the office'. As I understand the position he is only a shareholder and has no control or undue power over the policy of the Corporation in respect of production propositions that are put to them, and does not interfere with any production which British Lion are financing.[10]*

The executives of British Lion, and even more so the 'independent' producers who associated themselves with the company, would have found such an assertion laughable. There may have been no written rule codifying such interference, but it inevitably took place through the sheer force of Alex's personality.

//

The prospect of becoming a custodian of public money did nothing to deter Alex's taste for extravagance. At the beginning of August 1948 he and David Cunynghame went on a business trip to Rome. They were dissatisfied with the distributor of their films in Italy, and wanted to interview possible alternatives. On their way down, they stopped off in Antibes for a few days. Vincent, 'dressed super-artistically', was there to welcome them. After a meal at a hotel called Le Bon Auberge, they went at

---

* Alex did his best to soothe any concerns with a characteristically magnanimous offer: 'As the studios are now well organized and British Lion is successfully established, I would be willing to retire from the position I have occupied up to now, and would take my place as one of the independent producers.'

Alex's insistence to the casino in Cannes, where they stayed until three in the morning. Alex lost £125, Vincent £5, and David Cunynghame didn't gamble at all.

The following day, Alex was back at the casino, this time with Orson Welles. Cunynghame, who wanted to get an early night, wasn't there to record the losses, but if they were at all in keeping with Alex's general fortunes in the late 1940s they would have been considerable. The next day they continued on their way to Rome, where they stayed at the Excelsior Hotel.

Among the other guests there were Binnie Barnes, and Merle Oberon with her husband, Lucien Ballard. On 6 August, this gathering was enlivened by a tremendous crash in the small hours and the sound of splintering glass. 'Merle's husband caught her in someone else's bedroom – fortunately not Alex!' Cunynghame wrote in his diary. 'Anyhow, hell broke loose and during the day Alex did what he could to help Merle.'

Merle's tryst had been with Giorgio Cini, whose family owned the Excelsior. In the evening Cini would make a hasty departure with Merle after first having had Ballard thrown out of the hotel. But this action seemed only to give Ballard's jealousy an even more dangerous edge, since he then followed them to the Grand Hotel in Venice with a gun. Here the two lovers narrowly averted calamity by climbing down a balcony and escaping on Cini's yacht. After seeking Alex's advice a second time, Merle sent Ballard this telegram: 'Don't Do It. I didn't.'[11]

Sorting out Merle's romantic problems must have been extremely painful for Alex. He was still in love with her himself, and would probably have been very pleased to welcome her in his bedroom at the Excelsior if only she could have made her way there discreetly. Instead, once again he found himself playing the reluctant role of father. After Merle's hurried departure, Alex was left to have a gloomy meal with Cunynghame and London Films' representative in Rome, Peter Moore. Doubtless, among other things, they discussed their failure to find a new distributor. Unlucky in love, unlucky in business. This seemed to be Alex's lot nowadays.

The only bright spot in an otherwise unproductive trip was an invitation to Myrna Loy's birthday party. Alex had directed her in one of her first films, *The Squall*, when he was working in Hollywood during the 1920s.

He joked with her about her role as a 'geepsy' temptress. 'Oh well,' she said, 'that was a long time ago, and I was only a child actress.'

'Yes,' replied Alex, 'and I was only a child director.'[12]

Loy had spent the past few weeks shooting a film, *That Dangerous Age*, for Alex on the island of Capri. Her costumes, which had been made for her by the Fontana sisters in Rome, 'were heavenly', she later recalled, 'the most elegant clothes I've ever worn in a picture. That was Alex Korda, always the best at any cost.'[13] Alex had also arranged for her to stay in the Villa Crespi, with its majestic view over Capri's rocky coastline. When later she arrived in London for the studio filming at Shepperton, Alex suggested that she and her husband, Gene Markey, take a suite at Claridge's. 'At those prices!' commented Myrna Loy in her memoirs, but 'I have a feeling *he* paid.'[14]

//

From now on, however, it would be the British taxpayer who paid. Alex's first cheque from the British Government, for £1,200,000, arrived on 15 October 1948. At once he had to repay his bankers £800,000. Two weeks later came the première of *Bonnie Prince Charlie*, which the papers had taken to calling a £1 million epic rather more persistently than Alex might have cared for. Previously he had always been able to rely on the release of a film that would boost his fortunes at a critical time. *Henry VIII* had put him on the map; *The Scarlet Pimpernel* had made up for the failure of *Don Juan*; and *The Four Feathers* had been the solid commercial success he needed to launch Alexander Korda Film Productions. But now it seemed to be the other way around. Premières came to be dreaded as harbingers of yet more box-office disaster. *Bonnie Prince Charlie* was so bad that the critical response was itself a news item. 'Almost without exception,' reported the *Weekly Scotsman*, 'the morning papers either yawned or laughed at the film. By Sunday the London Press were pretty unanimous that "Korda's Prince Charlie is nobody's darling".'[15] Rattled by the reviews, Alex took out a two-page advertisement to defend the film. 'Some of the London critics have written about it not with a pen but with a hatchet,' he commented. But it was a desperate gesture, as pointless as Canute seeking to turn back the waves – especially since deep down he agreed. During the production he had come to despair of the project and could not even bring himself to watch the completed film. Alex was bad-tempered and despondent for days afterwards. 'I do not wonder that he is nervous with one flop on his hands after another,' commented Cunynghame.[16]

The very public failure of *Bonnie Prince Charlie* served to increase the vigilance of both the Government and the banks. Regular meetings took place during the last part of the year as the National Film Finance Corporation sought to place stringent conditions on British Lion for further loans from the Government. In December one of British Lion's chief bankers, the National Provincial, refused to make further advances. Cunynghame attributed the decision to the bank's 'lack of confidence in being able to give up sufficient time to watch Alex',[17] who was now becoming so worried that he was even talking of moving out of Claridge's and selling his Rolls.

The crisis forced him to consent to a more independent British Lion board. 'It was considered advisable that Sir Alexander Korda's nominees should retire . . . and an independent Chairman be elected,' commented H. C. Drayton, who replaced Hugh Quennell as chairman of British Lion in December 1948.[18] Alex's two other retiring nominees were David Cunynghame and Harold Boxall. 'The new setup starts a new chapter in Alex's career,' observed Cunynghame. 'I wish I felt more confident of the outcome, but I do not believe that Alex has sufficiently learnt his lesson of having to work properly with the chairman of a public company. All the same, he appears to treat the appointment as a life-saver.'[19]

It was. In the course of the following year the NFFC loans, which began to flow again after the boardroom change, reached a total of £3 million. Without this assistance, the new chairman reported at the annual general meeting in November 1949, the company would have been in receivership. For the financial year ending 31 March 1949 alone a production loss of £1,388,797 was brought into account. All except two of British Lion's productions for that year had made losses.

But at least Alex could console himself that it wasn't his money. One of the independent producers to seek support from British Lion in 1949 was Bill Macquitty, who had just produced Jill Craigie's film *Blue Scar* with family money. After the Rank Organization had refused to distribute it, Macquitty and Jill Craigie arranged a meeting with Alex and the President of the Board of Trade. The film was run in Alex's private viewing theatre and Macquitty recalled the conversation that took place with Alex, who helped to arrange the vital distribution deal.

'How much did it cost?' asked Alex.

'Forty-five thousand.'

'How did you make it for so little?'

'I paid cash for everything.'

'Great mistake,' Alex replied. 'Never pay cash.'[20]

Alex arrived in London in August 1931 to direct films for Paramount-British,
setting up his own company, London Film Productions, in February 1932.
This photograph was taken in December 1933, soon after the successful
London, Paris and New York premieres of *The Private Life of Henry VIII*.

The Korda family are entertained in Paris by Alex's old boss,
Robert Kane, head of Paramount-France. Taken in the mid-1930s,
this is one of the last photographs to show Alex and Maria together.

Alex arrives at the premiere of *The Private Life of Don Juan* on
5 September 1934 with bright new star and future wife Merle Oberon.

Five years after leaving Hollywood without a job, Alex made a triumphant return in September 1935. After successful negotiations to become a joint owner in United Artists, he posed for the cameras with his new partners, Hollywood legends Douglas Fairbanks Sr, Mary Pickford, Charlie Chaplin and Samuel Goldwyn. Also in the picture are United Artists executives Murray Silverstone and Dr. A. H. Gianini.

When Alex's new film studio opened at Denham, Buckinghamshire in May 1936, it was the biggest and most modern in Europe. But less than three years later, beset by increasing financial troubles, he would be forced to relinquish control. He regarded its loss as his 'greatest failure'.

Above. The Denham canteen during the production of *I, Claudius* in early 1937. Mary Pickford chats to Charles Laughton whose epic struggles with his character brought the production to a virtual standstill. Alex looks as if he would prefer to throttle him.

Left. Soon after the outbreak of war, Alex moved to Hollywood, where he played a vital if necessarily covert role in Britain's propaganda effort to bring America into the war. One of his major contributions to the campaign was *That Hamilton Woman*, filmed in six weeks, in the autumn of 1940.

Alex leaves the Palace with Lady Korda after receiving his knighthood,
23 September 1942.

Young hopeful Molly Thornton puts her head on the line. Her screen test for MGM-London Films is conducted by Georges Périnal, Alex's favourite cameraman.

As Christine Norden, Molly would become Alex's mistress and Britain's first postwar sex goddess. Recently, she achieved immortality when a crater on Venus was named after her. Here she is joined on bed by Alex, four *Life* journalists and her dog Pie.

Above. Alex enjoys a few moments' respite on the set of *An Ideal Husband* (1947). It was the last film for which he took a credit as director. It was an activity which he found tedious and, in spite of his considerable talent, often compared to going down a mine.

Right. Alex, Vivien Leigh and Laurence Olivier at the opening of *Anna Karenina*, 21 January 1948. Sadly, the next day's reviews would wipe off their smiles.

Alex and his young bride-to-be Alexa Boycun pose for the photographers on the occasion of their engagement in Antibes on 3 June 1953. They married five days later. The 36-year age gap did not bode well, but in a telegram that gallantly flung optimism before experience Laurence Olivier and Vivien Leigh wrote: 'We drink to your loves in love's own elixir and we joy in the joy of Alex and Alexa.'

Faithful always. Vincent stands by his brother in a typically rumpled suit. An art director of genius, he was an indispensable part of the Korda film empire.

22. AULD LANG SYNE

'Should old acquaintance be forgot...'

In the spring of 1948 Alex proposed co-production deals to each of his old partners in United Artists, Sam Goldwyn and David Selznick. In return for a substantial investment at the production stage, the Americans would receive the Western Hemisphere rights of the films that London Film Productions made for them. The attraction for Alex of such an agreement was that it protected him against the vagaries of American distribution, which rarely seemed to work in his favour. But the disadvantage was that his partners would naturally want to have a say in what they were buying, and Alex ought to have remembered from his United Artists days that they would fight hard.

The co-production Alex proposed to Goldwyn was a remake of *The Scarlet Pimpernel*, one of his great early successes. Alex had been wanting to return to the scene of this particular triumph since he first began to put together production plans for his newly acquired British Lion group in 1946. He had persuaded Powell and Pressburger in 1947 to make it their first film for British Lion, but the project was postponed because of the unavailability of Rex Harrison.* Now the project was resuscitated again, but, in a compromise on what would have been perfect casting, the starring role was given to David Niven, who was under contract to Goldwyn.

As Niven had only just got back to Hollywood after the fiasco

---

* The director–writer team went on to make *The Small Back Room* instead.

of *Bonnie Prince Charlie*, the prospect of another assignment for London Films filled him with deep gloom. Rumours of his reluctance to come to England reached Alex, who cabled Goldwyn for confirmation that Niven would cooperate. The star finally resigned himself to the return trip, but – determined to cushion himself against the hardship of life in austerity Britain – insisted that Goldwyn should make a number of demands on his behalf. He was to have his own house within 20 miles of the studio, with a housekeeper, servants and a gardener. If this did not prove congenial, he wanted to have the option of moving into a suite at Claridge's, with a special account 'to take care of the excessive tipping that is necessary for normal living'.[1] He was also insistent that he should receive weekly, a $100 food parcel from the United States, and monthly, a case of Scotch and a case of gin.

Goldwyn was quick to express to Alex a number of his own concerns. On 8 July 1948 he sent a cable about the diction of British actors: 'I hope *The Scarlet Pimpernel* will avoid the mistakes of some previous British pictures, which made the English more English than they really needed to be.' Then on 27 July he cabled his alarmed reaction to Powell and Pressburger's script, which he felt lacked the 'melodrama, action and warmth' of the Leslie Howard original.

The following day, in a long letter, he warned Alex that it would be 'completely suicidal' to begin production on the basis of the script as it stood. By putting the Pimpernel's exploits into a political framework, Powell and Pressburger had made the mistake of 'trying to combine the realisms of today with the heroics of the past'. The result was a slow, complicated story that was difficult to follow. He urged that the writers should avoid such 'elaborate fanciness' and instead return to the lines of the original Leslie Howard script. 'There is no sense in changing just for the sake of change. This should be as nearly as possible a remake of *The Scarlet Pimpernel*.'[2]

Alex assured Goldwyn that he agreed with all his criticisms, but the script was only a first draft which Powell and Pressburger would improve enormously. To allay concerns even further, he accepted Goldwyn's offer to send a script consultant,

Max Wilkinson, who would help Powell and Pressburger to rework the script.

Two weeks later Alex reported back on progress, lacing his cable with everything that Goldwyn could possibly want to hear:

> Through the very useful visit of your Mr Wilkinson, Powell Pressburger have now constructed the whole story, which I am convinced will please you very much. Myself enthusiastic about it. It is full of fun and excitement. No historical speeches or allusions. The relations between Pimpernel and wife human and touching. I am sure now we will have a great picture.[3]

But Goldwyn was still nervous and suggested that Powell and Pressburger should come to Hollywood for a script conference. Alex found this obvious lack of confidence deeply irritating. He was not used to others telling him how to produce a film, but he also had complete faith in Powell and Pressburger, who had just achieved an enormous success with the recent release in London of *The Red Shoes*. It was impossible for Powell and Pressburger to travel to Hollywood, he explained to Goldwyn, because the writer–director team were about to embark on location shooting in France. Instead, he offered to send the rough-cut sequences of the film as it was made. But he added the comment: 'I feel you ought to have as much faith as when the contract was signed. Our contract clearly states: a) that the final approval of the script rests solely with me and b) that the picture will be produced by myself.'[4]

Goldwyn then switched his concerns to the leading lady. He urged Alex to cast Susan Hayward, or if this was not possible, some other actress who had some box-office value in the United States. Alex's choice of Margaret Leighton, who had then appeared in two as yet unreleased films, *Bonnie Prince Charlie* and *The Winslow Boy*, filled Goldwyn with alarm. Nor was he any happier when at Michael Powell's urging Alex suggested the French actress Michèle Morgan instead – Lady Blakeney had been French in the original book. Goldwyn wrote to Alex at the end of August:

> Girls like Margaret Leighton and Michèle Morgan are practically useless in the box-office competition every picture has to meet these days. If you find it impossible to go for Hayward, I

urge that you find someone who will do the picture justice both on the screen and at the box-office.[5]

Alex, who lacked the dollars to pay for Susan Hayward or for that matter any of the other Hollywood stars that Goldwyn suggested, stuck to his preferred choice of Margaret Leighton. But by this time Goldwyn had had the opportunity to see her in *The Winslow Boy*. 'She is completely unsuited for the part,' he cabled on 20 October, 'is unknown here and will never be a star in this country. Using her can mean box-office disaster and I trust you will abandon this idea and use an important actress who will add to the picture.'

David Niven, who was now in England and resented the fact that this hitherto unknown actress had been billed as his co-star in the forthcoming *Bonnie Prince Charlie*, egged Goldwyn on. Leighton's appearance as Lady Blakeney, he objected, would breach Goldwyn's assurances to him that he would play opposite only major women stars. But once again Alex had the right of final approval. 'Powell, Pressburger and myself absolutely convinced that Margaret Leighton is first-class choice to play Lady Blakeney and she is doing so,' he cabled Goldwyn on 21 October.

Years later Michael Powell would write that he had not wanted Margaret Leighton to play Lady Blakeney at all. He thought she looked like a 'cross-eyed horse' and he hinted that she was an example of the sort of boudoir casting that had led Alex to give the part of Mrs Marchmont in *An Ideal Husband* to Christine Norden:

> Why the hell did Alex, apart from the obvious reason, want her to play the fascinating, volatile, fashionable, and perfidious Lady Blakeney? I was still young enough – I *am* still young enough – to think that the good of the film comes first. Alex waved away my furious objections with the glowing tip of a Corona: 'You will enjoy working with her, Mickey dear. She is very *spirituelle*.'[6]

A week after Alex's cable, *Bonnie Prince Charlie* opened in London. Copies of the press coverage were passed on to Goldwyn by his publicity director Lynn Farnol with the note, '*Bonnie Prince Charlie* is a pretty dismal bust.'[7] In light of his concerns over the script of *The Scarlet Pimpernel*, Goldwyn would have taken particular note of the comments of the *Daily Express* reviewer, Stephen Watts: 'I suppose Korda, as the boss of the enterprise, must bear the blame ... Most uncharacteristically, he has allowed a shapeless script, devoid of pattern or climax, to meander across the screen.'[8] Determined that *The Scarlet Pimpernel* should not suffer a similar fate, Goldwyn now sent detailed script notes to Powell and Pressburger via Max Wilkinson.

'We were so crushed by Goldwyn's attitude toward us, and toward our version of the film, and by Alex's helplessness or unwillingness to help us, that we gave way all along the line,'[9] recalled Michael Powell. But if this is true, these concessions were made with no visible sign of protest or reluctance at the time. On the contrary, Powell, who could be every bit as duplicitous as Alex, went out of his way to suggest an attitude of constructive cooperation and unwaning enthusiasm for the task in hand, possibly because Goldwyn had dangled before him the possibility of directing a forthcoming production of *Hans Christian Andersen*. 'Please assure Goldwyn that his recommendations have impressed us and that we are not in disagreement with any one of them,' he wrote to Wilkinson. 'Also you can quote me that *Pimpernel* will be Niven's greatest personal success.'[10]

Goldwyn replied to Powell directly:

Believe me, my criticism of script motivated only by desire to have great picture. My confidence in you and Pressburger as artistic craftsmen best exemplified by our Andersen suggestion, but best of us cannot overlook necessity nowadays for warmth for emotion for drama as well as for surface beauty. You assure me now picture will have all these qualities.[11]

Alex had plenty of encouraging words of his own, writing to Goldwyn on 2 December:

The film is going ahead wonderfully well and the rushes to date promise a tremendous film. Without any doubt Powell and Pressburger are doing the best job of their lives and the material we have is really of extraordinary beauty and I am sure that the picture will be all we wish.

Goldwyn could not resist a barbed reply. 'I have known for some time that they have a great sense of beauty, but I have always felt that they could do more for the story element than they have done in the past.' He went on:

I am particularly pleased that you are so enthusiastic, but to be very frank with you, Alex – which is the only way I know to be – there are times when you do not pay as much attention to stories as you should. I understand that you got very angry at the critics for their reviews of *Bonnie Prince Charlie*, but some people who have seen the picture have made the same comments to me.[12]

In March 1949, after seeing a rough cut of the film, Alex sent a characteristically glowing report to Goldwyn: 'You know I don't like exaggerations' – that must have brought a smile to Goldwyn's lips – 'but in my opinion this is one of most beautiful, one of greatest and grandest films I have ever seen. Its size and beauty are really stupendous.'[13] But he said nothing about the story.

In June Powell and Pressburger travelled out to Hollywood themselves to view the film with Goldwyn. They would probably have been too swollen-headed with recent successes to have had any idea of what lay in store for them. But Alex, after his own run of bad luck, might almost have expected Goldwyn's bitterly disappointed reaction when he rang him from Rome on 23 June:

– Alex, I saw the picture and I think it is the worst picture I have ever seen in my life, and I have just told Pressburger and Powell just that. It is simply beyond me how anybody can go out and do a job like that. There is no audience in the world will understand the picture.

– I can't understand that because I have shown it to about two hundred people, and they all think it is wonderful.

– Well, I had fifty people who are honest people and say what they think, and they thought it was elusive as a story.

A record of this conversation exists because Goldwyn was careful to note it down in case of future legal action.[14] Two weeks later his representative, James Mulvey, was in London to seek a termination of the agreement. The film was 'unmerchantable', he argued, and not what Goldwyn had contracted for. Alex for his part contended that it was a good picture which was fully in keeping with the terms of the production agreement – although he admitted that it might not have been as good for the American market as Goldwyn had hoped. He offered to order retakes, but refused to cancel the agreement. In that case, said Mulvey, Goldwyn would proceed with litigation.

There was clearly going to be no easy way out, but, to his credit, Alex was still able to make a joke of it. In Hollywood, he told Mulvey, Goldwyn had told Powell and Pressburger that the picture was so bad that he would give £100,000 to get out of the deal.

Powell's account of the meeting with Goldwyn in Hollywood was that he and Pressburger had arrived late and were 'shattered' by Goldwyn's rudeness in starting the film without them. After it was over, Goldwyn left the theatre without a word, leaving his wife, Frances, to speak to them. 'My husband says he is going to talk to Alex. The transport office will contact you in the morning to arrange your flight back to London. I hope you have a safe journey. Goodnight.'[15]

Hurt that Goldwyn so disliked the film, it was perhaps natural that in his memoirs Powell should resort to the cliché of the ill-mannered and philistine mogul. But the surviving correspondence suggests that from the outset, Goldwyn treated Powell and Pressburger with considerable courtesy and respect for their talent. He was naturally determined that they should in turn respect what he needed out of the partnership. He expressed his wish for a strong narrative not with any undue tyranny, but out of the sincere belief that it was in the best interests of all concerned. In the various communications with Powell and Pressburger, Max Wilkinson went to lengths to explain his employer's viewpoint.

> It is his observation based on years of experience that here, as well as in England, the *story* is more important today than

ever before – more important than any spectacle, however
brilliantly brought off, or cast. This, in a nut shell, is why he
has expressed his anxiety as he has. He knows you will direct
the picture beautifully, but he has wanted to make certain that
the *human* values are in the script.[16]

It was probably a mistake to have expected Powell and Pressburger – especially in the wake of their success with *The Red Shoes*
– to toe the line, but Goldwyn's insistence on a clear story was
hardly unreasonable.

Watching *The Elusive Pimpernel* (as the remake was titled)
today, one is left with the conclusion that of all the key figures
involved in its making, Goldwyn was by far the most wronged
party. Alex should not have tried to persuade Powell and Pressburger to make a story that did not really suit them, just as
they should not have accepted the assignment in the first place.
The size and beauty of the film may have been, as Alex put
it, 'stupendous', but such visual brilliance could not hide Powell
and Pressburger's unease with an old story that they would have
preferred to escape; it served as a means of transporting Powell's
camera from one splendid setting to another, but otherwise
pushed firmly into the background. Casting was another weakness. Margaret Leighton may have made a poor Lady Blakeney,
but David Niven was even worse as the Pimpernel. A part that
required him to play not only the Pimpernel and his alias Sir
Percy Blakeney but also the Pimpernel's various disguises exposed
his weaknesses badly. Used to emanating a single star persona,
he struggled to achieve a distinct delineation between several
different roles. Neither a swashbuckler nor really an actor, Niven
was as unsuited to play the Pimpernel as Vivien Leigh had been
to play Anna Karenina.

The dispute would eventually be settled by Goldwyn agreeing
to retakes after all. 'How much did they cost?' a reporter asked
Alex at a news conference. 'Two per cent of the cost of the
picture,' he replied. 'How much did the picture cost?' 'One
hundred per cent.'[17]

//

Alex, who once expressed a wish to learn ancient Greek in his retirement and liked classical allusions, might have compared his attempts to cooperate with his old partners to Scylla and Charybdis. For when he wasn't being chided by Sam Goldwyn, he was being savaged by David Selznick. In the case of the latter, the cliché of the philistine mogul fell far short of what was needed to convey the terrible truth.

In May 1948, during the same New York trip in which he concluded his agreement to produce *The Elusive Pimpernel* for Goldwyn, Alex negotiated a much bigger deal with Selznick. London Films would produce *Tess of the D'Urbervilles*, directed by Carol Reed, with Jennifer Jones; *A Tale of Two Cities*, directed by Powell and Pressburger, with Gregory Peck; *An Outcast of the Islands*, directed by Carol Reed, with Robert Mitchum; and *The Third Man*, directed by Carol Reed, with Joseph Cotten and Alida Valli. In return for exclusive Western Hemisphere rights the Selznick Releasing Organization would provide a large share of the production cost and the Hollywood stars without charge.

But Selznick soon began to find the degree of Alex's cooperation disquieting. His uncharacteristic scrupulousness in observing every term of the contract suggested that the agreement mattered more to him than Selznick had thought. Selznick's suspicions were further fuelled by rumours that Hollywood might soon be boycotting British cinemas again, making any pictures Alex produced with American stars all the more valuable. Selznick regarded the situation as an opportunity to force Alex to retrade the deal:

> I am sure that he will surrender to an extraordinary extent rather than run the risk of losing any of these pictures, which become many more times as important as they were before the new threat of boycott of English theatres by the large American companies. We should use this advantage to the full.[18]

The agreement was eventually whittled down to the two Carol Reed pictures, *The Third Man* and *Tess of the D'Urbervilles*, but Reed was reluctant to make *Tess*, and in October 1948 Alex persuaded Selznick to substitute *Gone to Earth*, based on the novel by Mary Webb, instead. Alex had discussed the project with Selznick as long ago as January 1940. Then they had imagined it as a vehicle for Vivien Leigh; now it seemed perfect for Selznick's latest discovery and soon-to-be bride, Jennifer Jones.

//

Alex's post-war record had been one of costly and often ill-judged failure, but against the run of play *The Third Man* revealed him at his very best. The previous year he had suggested that Carol Reed should make a film from a Graham Greene short story called 'The Basement Room', about a young boy in a large Belgravia house who lies to the police in order to protect a servant from being implicated in a murder. The resulting film, *The Fallen Idol*, was a small masterpiece, which deserves to be much better remembered today. When Greene and Reed approached Alex with the germ of the story that would become *The Third Man*, Alex was anxious to encourage a fertile partnership, but as usual, in stipulating that the film should be set in Vienna, had a number of other motives. The location shooting was a convenient way to use up foreign currency that he was unable to remit home under post-war restrictions, but also provided cover for his intelligence friends. As one of the flashpoints in a new and rapidly developing confrontation between East and West, Vienna was a popular destination for spies, and London Films was perfectly set up to organize their efficient deployment. Alex's representative in Austria, Elizabeth Montagu, had worked for the American intelligence agency OSS during the war, and at 146 Piccadilly, in charge respectively of the publicity and the travel departments, were two former members of the British Secret Intelligence Service, Ingram Fraser and John Codrington.

Whatever the ulterior motives for filming *The Third Man* in Vienna, the strong personal rapport that existed between Carol Reed, Graham Greene and Alex augured a remarkable film. All three shared a penchant for sardonic, bitter-sweet observation which in the forlorn and occupied city of 1948 Vienna found a perfect subject. The meeting of minds was such that Alex was determined that Reed should have the freedom to make the film in the way he thought best and he used his considerable guile to fend off the interventions of his co-producer David Selznick, who was equally determined that Reed should make the film in the way he, Selznick, thought best.

Selznick's persistent and overbearing demands on virtually every aspect of the production would have made a nervous wreck of a lesser man. But Alex fielded them with a habitual display of obliging consideration which was calculated to mollify without seriously yielding ground. Treading a delicate path between diplomacy and decisive action, Alex sent Graham Greene and Carol Reed out to California for two weeks of script conferences with Selznick, yet quickly fended Selznick off when he began to complain that Reed and Greene were not following the suggestions they had agreed with him. He refused to send Reed back to America for further conferences and when the director began to film on location in Vienna forbade Selznick's representative from visiting him there. As the unanswered memoranda from Selznick piled up, Alex brushed aside the complaints from Selznick's London office: 'Mr Reed is in the middle of a very hard and responsible job, working day and night. Therefore he cannot be expected, and I am sure Mr Selznick does not expect him, to sit down and write copious answers on copious notes.'

On every matter from casting to costumes Alex made clear his determination to defer to Reed's good judgement. Convinced that Orson Welles would be box-office poison as Harry Lime, Selznick bombarded Alex with the names of alternative stars that included Noël Coward, Cary Grant, Dana Andrews, Robert Mitchum, and even David Niven – on the grounds that it would be killing two birds with one stone as Niven was already working for Alex on *The Elusive Pimpernel*. 'Had long talk with Carol about Lime,' Alex cabled Selznick:

> He thinks that Orson could give a tremendous performance in this part. Picture greatly depends on Lime being extraordinary in attraction and superior in intellect. Carol convinced he could have tremendous performance out of Orson, who enthusiastic [about] playing role. While I do not profess knowing as much as Mr Gallup about box-office values, cannot believe him being a detriment. Please give thought to Carol's firm conviction, which I fully share.

When Selznick complained that Valli was not wearing glamorous enough clothes, again Alex resolutely backed his director:

> Carol Reed feels very strongly, and I fully agree with him, that to put a glamorized Valli in the Viennese atmosphere will kill the whole realism of story. We do not feel that silks and frills make a woman more attractive than simple clothes especially if the atmosphere demands nothing else. We are convinced that Valli in a macintosh and beret can be as attractive and charming as many stars wearing fashion creations.

Alex's deft handling was an example of the brilliant cosmopolitan fixer at work. In Hollywood the moguls looked on him as the only producer in Britain who understood their values, but he was also equally at home in the capitals of Europe. His network of contacts meant that there was always someone on either side of the Atlantic that he could call upon to lend vital assistance. For the location shooting in Vienna, Alex turned to Karl Hartl, who had thirty years previously been his assistant when he was himself making films in Vienna for Count Sascha Kolowrat. Now, as head of the Count's old company, Hartl provided Reed and his crew with production facilities at Sievering Studios on the outskirts of Vienna. When a writer was required to write American dialogue for Joseph Cotten, Selznick was quick to suggest every big name from Norman Mailer to Paul Gallico, but Alex quietly engaged the New York playwright Jerome Chodorov, who had worked in England with the American director Willie Wyler during the war and knew Carol Reed from that time. Currency restrictions meant that there was no straightforward way of finding the dollars for Chodorov's $15,000 fee, but Alex arranged for him to be paid in old books and silver. There was a touch of Harry Lime in Alex – he was the sort of man who 'could fix anything'.

//

The price of the freedom that Alex had managed to steal for Carol Reed on *The Third Man* was heavy and persistent intervention by Selznick in the production of *Gone to Earth*, which Powell and Pressburger were due to commence in the spring of

1949. The fact that the star of the film was Selznick's wife-to-be Jennifer Jones only made a dangerous situation even more volatile. Powell and Pressburger had already crossed Selznick by threatening not to make the film unless he accepted their choice of cameraman.* On 20 April 1949, Selznick made his irritation plain in a memorandum to his lawyer, Milton Kramer:

> While I think that this team is perhaps the most gifted in the world in the field of the physical appearance of a film, and are not likely to be satisfied with less than a top cameraman, I do not know the man's work. I think it likely that I will approve it, but I also think it important that this team be stepped on.

The memorandum set down a long list of Selznick's rights that Kramer was to spell out to Alex, extending to every conceivable aspect of the production. Before filming began, his consent had to be obtained for not only the cameraman, but also the costume designer, the make-up artists, the hairdresser and even the stand-in. He had approval of the final script but also of the principal members of the cast, observing to Kramer:

> I have already approved one of the two principal men, David Farrar, but as to the other man, I want to make very clear that I want to know who it is. I don't want suddenly to find Jennifer playing opposite some fairy or at least some actor who looks like a fairy, such as Powell and Pressburger cast in *Red Shoes*.†

Selznick was a notorious megalomaniac, but the endless conditions were partly a sign of his lack of confidence in handling Alex. He feared that if he did not restrain him with a net of legal restrictions, he would wriggle free and somehow turn everything to his advantage. 'Dealing with Korda is still a career,' he warned Kramer.

---

* Christopher Challis.
† It's difficult to know for certain which fairy Selznick was thinking of. There was the principal star Anton Walbrook, but also the ballet dancers Anton Dolin and Leonid Massine.

You will still find him affable and charming, extraordinarily sharp and intelligent, and making more sense in his discussions than any of the less charming, less gifted, less imaginative and less intelligent but more dependable and consistent leaders of the American film industry. I still question whether the two of us, even operating together, are a match for him in any trading. But at least let us have a try at it.[19]

A week later, on 25 April 1949, Selznick met Alex in Hollywood. He was pleased to be able to tell him that while he felt the script still needed some work it was the basis for a 'superb and distinguished picture'.[20] They agreed that Selznick would discuss the required script revisions with Powell and Pressburger in person when in a few weeks' time he would be in Europe on his honeymoon with Jennifer Jones. Alex, who had thoughtfully found a villa for the couple in San Remo, was due to visit them himself, but Selznick, fearful of the influence he might have, postponed the arrival of Powell and Pressburger until after his departure.

The script conference eventually took place in mid-June at the Grand Hotel Dolder in Zurich. Also present was Powell and Pressburger's production designer, Hein Heckroth. On 16 June 1949, Selznick wrote to tell Alex that he was delighted with the result, more convinced than ever that Powell and Pressburger would produce one of the best films in many years. He had found them open-minded and cooperative. There was a complete meeting of minds and excellent progress had been made. He even declared his determination to prove to Alex once and for all that the rumours about his being difficult were just not true. 'When I am dealing with able and talented people, such as Powell and Pressburger and Heckroth, there are no difficulties. I know that you feel as I do – it is only with ungifted people that one has any difficulties in this business.'[21]

But a week later Powell and Pressburger were in Hollywood to show *The Elusive Pimpernel* to Sam Goldwyn. The shock waves of that encounter jolted Selznick out of his brief complacency, and he proceeded to make life just about as difficult for the pair as he possibly could. Arriving in London on 18 July, in the same week as Powell and Pressburger began shooting *Gone* to *Earth* on location in Shropshire, he sent them fourteen closely typed pages of script notes, with the reminder that any deviation from his wishes would be a breach of contract. He also sent a copy to Alex, warning him how important it was that Powell and Pressburger should take his suggestions seriously. 'Of course, in the final analysis they will have to listen to me, because I won't approve the script until it is right.'[22] Not only had he usurped Alex's role as producer but he behaved as if he were the director of the picture as well.

He followed up on the script notes by demanding a series of on-location script conferences. Powell attended them with feigned good humour, but a barely civil Pressburger made little attempt to disguise the fact that he found them a waste of time. Selznick complained to Alex of his intransigence, calling him 'a pompous, stubborn man'.[23] Further evidence that the bonhomie of the Zurich meeting was completely dead came in his complaints concerning the hours that Jennifer Jones was expected to work. Annoyed to find his weekends with his wife disrupted by filming, he threatened to forbid her from working any longer than the hours specified in her contract.

On 19 August he had the chance at the Venice Film Festival finally to see *The Elusive Pimpernel* for himself. 'While I couldn't understand what Goldwyn meant when he said he couldn't understand it,' he commented, 'I now understand perfectly because there was no one alive who could understand it except Powell and Pressburger.'[24]

The Elusive Pimpernel naturally became a rod with which to beat Powell and Pressburger even harder. At Selznick's insistence Alex reluctantly summoned the pair to a meeting at which he reminded them that they had a contractual obligation to film a script that had Selznick's approval. Further lengthy conferences followed, at which Powell and Pressburger struck a pose of reluctant compliance. On 6 October, Powell wrote to Selznick to assure him that he and Pressburger were doing their best to amend the script according to his wishes. 'If you are right,' he concluded, 'it will be worth it. But I hope you will remember the words of Kim: "I will change my faith and my bedding but *thou* must pay for it." '[25]

Selznick, however, thought that Alex should pay for it. He resented the fact that Alex had been away on holiday for all of September when he had been locked in some of his most protracted meetings with Powell and Pressburger. Alex, he reasoned, was enjoying the services of a top-class producer for nothing.

A more forthright man might long before have told Selznick that he was being outrageous, that his meddling in *Gone to Earth* was prejudicing the success of the film, but Alex, who was rarely content to settle for the plain truth if he could manipulate a situation to his advantage, humoured Selznick instead. He was doing a grand job. How lucky Powell and Pressburger were to have him on the scene. His hope was that he might be able to pursuade Selznick to give him a share of the Western Hemisphere rights for *The Third Man*. Selznick had seen the film for the first time at the end of August and had pronounced it 'superb'. It was clear now that the film was likely to make a fortune in America, but Alex was not entitled to a penny of those earnings, unless he could persuade Selznick to change his mind. Powell and Pressburger, who had to bear the brunt of Selznick's unwanted interventions, were pawns in a larger game.

Over the weeks that followed Alex begged Selznick for an agreement that better reflected the commercial potential of *The Third Man*. But Selznick would not budge. 'I am bored to death with his crocodile tears about how bad a deal he made,' he declared.[26] Incapable of seeing a situation from any other viewpoint than his own, he even took Alex's increasing irritation as a personal affront. 'I am appalled and disappointed by his antagonistic attitude,' he complained, 'especially in view of my extraordinary unpaid efforts at neglect of my entire business to practically produce *Gone to Earth*.'[27]

What rubbed salt into the wound was the way Selznick swaggered around as if he were chiefly responsible for *The Third Man*. In America he planned to release it as 'A Selznick Picture'. Incensed, Alex sent him the following cable:

Don't you think it is a mistake to put your American trademark on our films? While I don't dispute your right to do so I feel that it is really misleading the public into thinking that these pictures are produced in Hollywood by your company. Don't you think that a truer statement of fact would be more useful and less open to criticism?

Selznick had his London representative Jenia Reissar write to Alex on his behalf. She explained that to use the London Films trademark on the picture would require a financial sacrifice that Selznick was not prepared to make. Since Alex's recent releases in America, *An Ideal Husband*, *Anna Karenina* and *Mine Own Executioner*, had all been flops, exhibitors were now inclined to look with suspicion on new Korda films. The rather tactless letter did, however, offer the material concession that Selznick was willing, 'out of a gesture of friendship', to advertise the film as 'A Selznick Release' instead of 'A Selznick Picture', but the offer served only to increase Alex's fury.

Replying not to Reissar but directly to Selznick, he wrote, 'I have seldom read a stupider or ruder letter. It is full of fishwifely insinuations for which I do not blame Miss Reissar, as I am certain that the insinuations and rudeness come to her on the telephone or in one of your voluminous cables to be transmitted to me.' He rejected 'with contempt' the argument that his name prejudiced the success of the film and considered his friendship with Selznick to be 'spoilt'.

In the weeks that followed Selznick's lawyers made the necessary concessions to heal the rift. The film would be advertised as a Selznick 'release', not 'picture', and Alex would have a personal credit and the right to have his name on the advertising. But Alex now refused to hand over the negative of *The Third Man*, alleging that the Selznick Releasing Organization had been responsible for other breaches of contract, although he did not specify what they were.

But everyone knew what the real game was. As Selznick put it in a letter to Carol Reed, 'Korda himself admitted that his actions were confessedly designed to acquire a drastic change in his contracts with me and to force me to pay him huge sums from American releases for which he had not bargained at the outset.'

Alex's 'maneuvers' made Selznick only more determined that Powell and Pressburger should fulfil their obligations to him in the tiniest detail. But when on 21 November 1949 he arrived at Shepperton Studios to discuss with them the retakes and additional scenes he wanted, they advised him that they had been told by Alex not to participate in such discussions. Selznick retaliated by ordering Jennifer Jones not to report for work on the film. Alex then told Powell and Pressburger to finish the film as best they could without her.

The differences between the two producers eventually led to the inevitable showdown in court. Hoping to recover the world rights of both *The Third Man* and *Gone to Earth*, Alex applied for rescission of his contract with Selznick, and in May 1950 the dispute went before an arbitrator in a New York court. As far as *Gone to Earth* was concerned, the arbitrator took the view that the unpredictable nature of the creative process was not something that the contract had allowed for. Selznick may have been 'over-fussy', but it was clear that, regarding the version to be shown in America, 'the picture was to be tailor-made to his measurements, and if he thought the shoulders were not quite right, there is no doubt of the fact that the tailor had to make them right'.[28]

Many of the troubles that Alex encountered in his business dealings stemmed from the fact that his instincts were those of an artist, not a tailor. He was inclined to regard a contract not as a black-and-white document with precise meaning but as susceptible, in the manner of a work of art, to endless nuances. In an arbitration hearing the more legalistic Selznick was perhaps bound to have the edge. The transcripts of the case make rather sad reading. For they make clear how Selznick's behaviour must have made any creative process quite impossible, yet at the same time how this was an irrelevant issue in what was finally a commercial transaction. It was the sort of situation that Alex had depicted in a scene in *Rembrandt* a decade and a half previously: the artist paints the officers of the civic guard, who are then so disappointed with the result that they demand a two-florin rebate for each officer lost in the shadows.

London Films were ordered to film the extra scenes for *Gone* *to Earth* that Selznick had requested.* But much more costly to Alex was a separate ruling that the lucrative Western Hemisphere rights of *The Third Man* belonged to the Selznick Releasing Organization for a period of ten years.

It was a bitter outcome for Alex, especially as Selznick had so clearly been the destructive force in the partnership. Some months later, after the various details of the judgment had been implemented, a journalist questioned Alex about his relations with Selznick. 'Everything is all settled,' Alex replied. 'I no longer know Mr Selznick!'[29]

After the mauling that Powell and Pressburger had suffered during the production of *Gone to Earth*, it was hardly surprising that exhibitors turned out to be disappointed with the final result. The ABC chain turned it down for general release, and London Films had trouble finding a first-run West End cinema in which to open the film. 'The picture may be lucky in finding a resting place at the Rialto,' commented David Cunynghame gloomily.[30]

The Rialto, which Alex had bought as a showcase, was turning out to be more of a celluloid graveyard. There the British première of *Gone to Earth* took place on Friday, 22 September 1950. The notices were poor and David Cunynghame recalled the occasion as 'the most stone-cold première' he had ever attended. 'If Powell and Pressburger were not such a nastily arrogant couple one would feel sorry for them over *Gone to Earth*.'[31] He would soon have a second occasion to feel sorry for the pair when *The Elusive Pimpernel* followed *Gone to Earth* into the Rialto at the beginning of November. 'It was not quite so bad as yesterday's very harsh critics wrote – but nearly so.'[32]

//

Alex's highly publicized production difficulties only served to foster the internal strife within British Lion. Arthur Jarratt, head of distribution, had long questioned Alex's policy of big-budget production, and the appointment at the end of 1948 of an independent chairman in place of Hugh Quennell emboldened

---

* Selznick eventually chose to have the scenes filmed by Rouben Mamoulian under his supervision in Hollywood.

him to speak out with increasing forthrightness. Political support for Alex's leadership was also ebbing away. British Lion, commented Harold Wilson in a Parliamentary debate on 14 December 1949, 'was struggling against the incubus of a succession of highly picturesque, but not on the whole remunerative productions'.[33] It was a considerable understatement.

When Alex bought into British Lion, he had hoped to acquire a greater say over the pictures he made and how they were distributed. But the failure of those pictures, and the necessity of once again begging for financial support, had in practice led to a surrender of control. With his tendency towards the grandiose, he had lost touch with the public mood. In a more egalitarian post-war world he was beginning to seem like an anachronism. Writing of his amazement that the Archers had allowed Alex to talk them into making *Gone to Earth*, Michael Powell would comment: 'Once more, as with *The Scarlet Pimpernel*, [Alex] was looking back to his past, before the war, when he had created Denham Studios and made wonderful films for an audience that no longer existed.'[34]

During Alex's absence in America and the years of comparative inactivity that followed, a new generation of film-makers had emerged in Britain, who under the impetus of the war increasingly sought to make films that reflected the society around them. The documentary film movement, the independent producers who worked first for Two Cities and then under the benign, non-interventionist rule of Arthur Rank, the nucleus of young film-makers at Ealing Studios under Alberto Cavalcanti and Michael Balcon – these were the sources of progress for the British cinema during the 1940s. Alex, by contrast, remained wedded to the literary adaptation and a vision of Britain that only occasionally ventured into the twentieth century. It was emblematic that his first big production had been *An Ideal Husband*, with its nostalgic introduction harping back to the 'gay Nineties'. This Britain of society *soirées*, gentlemen's clubs and over-panelled libraries was the one to which Alex belonged emotionally. The country at large, however, as his friend Winston Churchill had discovered in the 1945 election, was keen to move on.

23. ELSEWHERE

By temperament Alex was prone to sudden enthusiasms and varying moods. He could switch quickly between deep depression and high-spirited confidence. But if his temper was often unpredictable, he had always seemed fully capable of addressing London Films' many troubles. Indeed he almost needed the troubles to keep his agile mind occupied. It was on the rare occasions when there were none that he would have what his brother Vincent described as his 'tongo-pongo' days – hatching schemes and inventing things for himself to do.

Alex may have been an autocrat, but he was able to instil a huge sense of camaraderie among those over whom he ruled. As he made his early forays into film production, it would not have been too far-fetched to compare London Films' swashbuckling progress to that of the Pimpernel and his band of loyal followers, who placed their total faith in their leader's fabled ability to get out of any tight corner. In the early days of British Lion's difficulties, it was the same. Alex could always be depended upon to steel his comrades' nerves and conjure up a solution from somewhere. 'Times are worrying and I am very glad that Alex is due back,' David Cunynghame confided to his diary in February 1948 when Alex was away on some business trip. But as crisis followed crisis, it soon became clear that even Alex had his limit.

Like some shadow version of King Midas, everything Alex did seemed to turn to dross. In the 1930s he had had to cope with financial difficulties every bit as severe as he experienced twenty years later. But the critics had consistently hailed him as the most bold and inventive producer around, and a series of successes at the box-office from *Henry VIII* to *The Four Feathers* spoke for themselves. Now his films – almost uniformly – flopped and received bad notices, and his effectiveness as a producer was being increasingly questioned. Even the rare triumphs had some sting in the tail – there could scarcely have been a greater one than *The Third Man*, but his failed efforts to secure a share of the American receipts just seemed like further proof that his luck had turned. The death of his mentor Lajos Biro in September 1948 would have been a particularly bad blow. There was no one now in whom he could confide.

The troubles on all sides overwhelmed Alex. He found it hard to shake off his gloomy moods, which he no longer bothered to conceal. Emlyn Williams recalled the words of encouragement with which he was sent off to direct *The Last Days of Dolwyn*:

> I leave it all to you, my dear Emmaleen, you know what you want, I will give you all the expert technicians I can, and please come to me in doubt and trouble for I have been through the whole bloody mill. It will be a nice film though of course I know and you know that there won't be a damned penny in it, but it's worth doing, before the whole business gets in a worse state than it is already – oh, films are finished, I'm an old man, I'm finished. Kaputt. Good luck.[1]

With actors, writers and directors Alex managed to maintain a dignified demeanour – fatalistic and charmingly *distrait*. But those who worked with him every day became the victims of his frustration. There would be uncontrollable outbursts of temper in which he would dress down even the most senior members of staff for imaginary failings or for faults that were as much his own. He struggled even to observe the common courtesies. In the past, for example, when he had set off on his many trips abroad, he would always make a point of saying goodbye to his colleagues. Now he just slipped off without a word.

At the beginning of 1949 the new, independent chairman of British Lion, Harold Drayton, who had been appointed at the insistence of the National Film Finance Corporation, announced a massive economy drive. Alex made superficial attempts to comply, but the resulting investigations into London Films' finances only made him more secretive. Easily rattled, tired and exhausted, he had even broken out into a nervous rash. Bouts of frenzied, desperate activity to tackle one problem or another would alternate with quieter moods that David Cunynghame described as 'a sort of calmness derived of despair'.[2]

Alex's unlucky streak, which had begun with the opening of *Anna Karenina* in 1948, would reach its height with a bitter 'winter of discontent' in the early months of 1950. In January Drayton made it clear that London Films would not be allowed to make more than six films over the next two years. Not that Alex had any stories ready to put into production anyway, since for many weeks he had been embroiled in his two disputes with David Selznick.

His general dissatisfaction with everything and everyone had begun to express itself in a cynicism and mistrust of his colleagues which unfortunately, in the general breakdown of morale, often proved to be justified. In mid-January 1950 Alex accused the head of the company's Rome office, Peter Moore, of embezzlement, summoning him to London to explain himself. When Moore was allowed to return to Rome without any charges being brought, it was less due to Alex's conviction of his innocence than to his sense that here was a man he could use.

In the midst of this collapse of confidence, Cunynghame, who had worked with Alex and his brothers longer than anyone – even since before there was a London Films – became very depressed himself. His loyalty, which seemed only to make him a more ready victim for Alex's ill-temper, had never been more severely tested. He could see that Alex had now become a divisive force, as much working against the interests of British Lion as promoting them. 'It is a sign of his loss of leadership that no one cares a damn,' he wrote on 22 February. 'The studio morale is about nil and prospects likewise.'

A few weeks later, on 13 March 1950, Cunynghame made perhaps the saddest entry in a journal that chronicled the fortunes of Britain's greatest film producer over a quarter of a century:

> I have no illusion whatsoever that if it suits Sir Alexander
> Korda I will most readily be made his scapegoat, but for
> my own British-born conscience I want to be sure of my
> position. I learn daily how very scurrilous are Alexander
> Korda, Vincent Korda and Zoltán Korda – so called. I still do
> not know their baptismal names, but I wish that I had never
> met any of them.

This was the verdict of a man who eight years previously had
described Alex's knighthood as 'a tardy and insufficient honour,
but possibly a forerunner of something more commensurate to
what he has done for the country'.[3] When a few weeks later a
harsh letter was received from the National Film Finance Corporation,
he merely commented, 'I am amazed that Korda's way of
operating has been tolerated so long.'[4]

Cunynghame had long since paid for his 'British-born conscience' by being shut out of Alex's confidences, but he feared
that in his desperation Alex had now stepped beyond the bounds
of legality. 'I only wish that I had more confidence in his integrity
and sense of responsibility,' he noted on 16 May 1950. 'However,
my advice is sought about nothing and I am kept as little
informed as possible, which is not difficult for Korda with such
creatures as Aussenberg around him.'

Julius Aussenberg was a Czech, whom Alex had known since
his days in Berlin during the 1920s. In charge of overseas
distribution, he was a popular figure in the Piccadilly office.
David Russell, who was in charge of London Films' overseas
publicity, remembered him as a good-humoured, convivial character whose idea of a good evening was to eat goose dripping on
bread washed down with champagne and plenty of anecdotes.
'After the First World War it was the lawyers who wrecked the
world,' Aussenberg used to say, 'now it is the accountants.'[5]

Together with Alex he did what he could to remedy this state
of affairs. Cunynghame got an inkling of their scheme when the
German distributor of Alex's films, a Herr Fritzche, came to
London in May 1950, and he was forbidden by Alex to discuss
business matters with Fritzche alone. Instead, he was to tell
Fritzche that any matters concerning German distribution were
entirely Aussenberg's responsibility. 'It all looked to me too much

as if Korda feared an indiscretion on Fritzche's part if he was left alone with me,' observed Cunynghame. 'The more I see of the present trend of events the more I suspect Korda of feathering his nest abroad.'[6]

Confirmation that such suspicions were justified comes from Robin Lowe. The son of the film star John Loder, he had recently married the daughter of one of London Films' principal backers, Sir Charles Hambro. In 1948 Alex gave Lowe a job working as a dialogue coach to the Austrian and German actors on *The Third Man*, and soon afterwards Lowe became an assistant to Aussenberg.

Every six months or so Aussenberg used to visit London Films' German offices. On one occasion, much to his surprise, Lowe was asked if they could go in his car. When they arrived at their hotel in Germany, Aussenberg asked him to leave the ignition key with the porter:

> He said he wanted to leave some luggage in and get it out later. The next day we drove to Zurich and stopped outside a bank, and he opened the boot, and there were wads of notes in the boot which he duly took into the bank. Now had I not been totally naïve I would have said, 'Well, I'd like ten per cent of that.' Unbelievable. I mean, I could have gone to gaol.[7]

Similar arrangements were likely to have been in place in other countries. When an 'unsavoury and undesirable' distributor visited from Madrid, Cunynghame imagined that Alex was 'well in on the carve-up'.[8] And on a trip with Alex to the Paris office, he was unsettled to overhear a whispered conversation about sub-rosa payments to Alex and Vincent. Even the till in Piccadilly was no longer safe. 'Not a happy day,' wrote Cunynghame on 14 June 1950, after discovering that Alex had given £150 to the person responsible for looking after the foreign cash payments and taken £350 for himself.

Two days after this raid on the foreign cash payments, Alex spent a day in Zurich, presumably to see his bankers. As he attended to such apparently misgotten increases in his private fortune, perhaps he had occasion to ponder the example of Sir Robert Chiltern. Wilde's 'ideal husband' had obtained his wealth

and power through the theft of a Cabinet secret, but had proceeded to build an irreproachable life, subsequently remaining a
man of principle even under the most severe of tests. If Alex had
ever thought that he could aspire to such a model, now it must
have seemed a fairy-tale.

Yet outwardly he was as successful and influential as ever. His
nephew Michael Korda, then a young man, would write of how
he looked upon Alex with envy, would have liked to have been
Alex if he could. The South of France became an increasingly
regular refuge. Long drawn to the sea, Alex bought a yacht,
which with wistful irony he named the *Elsewhere*.

In her memoirs Christine Norden remembered how Alex had
come to choose the name. ' "I'm going to build us a yacht," he
said. "We will both go over the ocean together, so that you will
never disappear from my life." I said, "Alex, don't be silly, what
would the studio say when they can't find me? What would you
say to all your business associates?" He smiled and said, "We
would say, my darling, we are, "Elsewhere".'[9]

After a brief inaugural trip across the English Channel in July
1949, *Elsewhere* took up station in Antibes. At first Alex stayed
close to shore, safely tethered in one Riviera resort or another.
But he soon began to venture further and further afield. In the
summer of 1951, there was a long cruise of the Aegean and the
Bosphorus. It was perhaps the perfect relaxation for a man of
Alex's restless temperament. On a yacht you can be still, yet
constantly on the move. It was the equivalent of Churchill's brick
walls.

'He liked to play an old sailor in a T-shirt and a battered
yachting cap with a white stubble on his chin,' recalled Graham
Greene, one of Alex's most welcome guests.[10] There was an
unspoken pact to change the subject if anyone on board talked
about films. 'He could talk about pictures, the poetry of Baudelaire, the theatre – anything but films.'[11] On the few occasions
when the conversation did trespass on this territory, it was usually
marked by a note of disillusionment. 'When my friends and I
were young in Hungary,' he once said to Greene, 'we all dreamed
of being poets. And what did we become? We became politicians
and advertisement men and film producers.'[12]

The crumbling edifice of his film empire had become a burden that he preferred not to think about, and he fled south as often as he could, in the words of the despairing Cunynghame, 'a cheap imitation of Nero who fiddled whilst Rome burnt'.[13] Whether at sea on his yacht, or in the South of France, or even in his office at Piccadilly, these days Alex seemed to be elsewhere most of the time. In late 1950 there were two films in production, Carol Reed's *Outcast of the Islands* and Zoltán's *Cry the Beloved Country*. The Alexander Korda of old would have followed these films closely, there would have been furious rows with Zoltán, but now he was content to stand back.

There were also increasing signs of ill-health. At the beginning of 1951, after his personal physician, Dr Csato, diagnosed glandular fever, he was away from the office for many weeks, but even after his return, his staff were struck by his lassitude and suspected that his condition was far worse than they had been told. As Alex had confided to Emlyn Williams, he had indeed become an old man.

//

Ever the optimist, Alex might have consoled himself with the thought that things could only get better. And very slowly they did. In the summer of 1950 he met an old friend from his days at Paramount in France. Ilya Lopert had worked in the editing department at Joinville Studios and now ran his own distribution company. Based in New York, he had established a network of cinemas in most of the key American cities. With backing from the New York financier Robert W. Dowling, president of the City Investing Corporation, he signed in December 1950 a distribution agreement with British Lion and London Films that had 'the express purpose of ensuring the proper showing and distribution of British and American films of exceptional artistic merit throughout the US'.[14] The post-war expansion of arthouse cinemas across the United States had created a new market for British films that had previously been regarded as too obscure or sophisticated for mainstream American tastes.

The first film to be distributed under the new agreement, Powell and Pressburger's *Tales of Hoffmann*, amounted more to a statement of intent than a money-maker in itself. On 1 April 1951 there was a charity presentation of the film at the Metropolitan in New York. After the performance Michael Powell ran into Murray Silverstone, who twenty years previously, when he was head of United Artists in England, had helped to establish Alex as Britain's leading producer. 'Mickey,' he said, 'I wish it were possible to make films like that . . .'[15] Two weeks later the film had its première at the Carlton Cinema in London. There was no 'spontaneous outbreak of applause', reported Cunynghame, but 'the picture was regarded as an unusual and courageous experiment, which it is'.[16] In the years to come the partnership worked well. The Americans Lopert and Dowling were 'most intelligent', offering constructive advice as to how films might be tailored to appeal to the American market, but never attempting the sort of gross interference that Selznick had practised.

There was some embarrassment in April 1951 when the chairman of the National Film Finance Corporation, Lord Reith, reported to Parliament that it was unlikely that British Lion would be able to repay its loan of £3 million by the scheduled date of October, but otherwise the financial crisis of the previous three years was over. At the annual general meeting that year the chairman Harold Drayton declared that there was every reason to expect that the company would now begin to show a profit. He praised Alex for the part he had played in securing the Lopert deal, but pointedly stressed that the chief cause of the recovery was due to the fact that British Lion was 'now producing films at an average cost considerably lower than those produced prior to March 1949, without any sacrifice of quality'.

Quick to accept the *fait accompli*, Alex set out in November 1951 to show that he could make a film as cheaply as anyone. *Home at Seven* – which Alex always called *Seven at Home* – was based on a successful West End play by R. C. Sherriff, about a man who fears that he has committed robbery and murder during a bout of amnesia. It was the first of a series of small-scale 'planned' films, which were intended to use fewer sets and to facilitate a short shooting schedule through intensive rehearsals. Alex 'has done an incredibly fine job of shooting the film in

fourteen days including three days retakes', commented Cunynghame. 'He has certainly set the pace for the others.'[17] Considering
himself far too grand for such an activity, Alex gave the director's
credit to the star Ralph Richardson, but he was delighted with
the result and back to his old affable self. Two weeks later, on 17
December 1951, he began to rehearse his next 'planned' film,
which had the appropriately festive title, *The Holly and the Ivy*.
'Morale in the House of Korda is high,' noted Cunynghame,[18]
although it would be dented when on 19 December Alex was
admitted to hospital for several weeks' observation. The doctors
thought that he might have shingles, Alex told his colleagues at
146 Piccadilly, but really it was his heart that concerned them.

For the film-makers at British Lion, the slowing-down of Alex
had a rather positive side. Too weary to pursue any of his own
stratagems, he turned into a mentor genuinely concerned to give
the most constructive and disinterested advice he could. During
his forty years of film-making he had encountered just about
every situation it was possible to face and had invaluable experience to pass on. While a little earlier Powell and Pressburger had
found themselves hopelessly tied up by Alex's scheming, David
Lean, in 1951, joined British Lion late enough to benefit from
this more detached approach. When he and his associate producer
Norman Spencer discussed the idea of making a film about the
Sound Barrier, they found Alex 'marvellously receptive'. Later
there were difficulties with Terence Rattigan's script, but Alex,
recalled Spencer, made the perceptive comment that nudged the
entire project along the right path.

> We all sat in his office and Alex said, 'You know, I think,
> Terry, you've written a story about a big aircraft designer and
> his son ... If you change that son into a daughter ...' And
> Rattigan's face lit up. It changed the whole slant of the story.
> Originally it was father against son. Here it became father
> against daughter, which enabled the son to become the son-in-
> law ... It opened up all sorts of doors.

//

British Lion's return to stability allowed Alex to indulge in a
variety of dabbling. The early 1950s were a wonderful time for

all manner of gadgets from the small to the very, very large. On the one hand, there was television. While other film producers shied away from a perceived rival, Alex embraced it as an obvious partner that provided a perfect market for the smaller films he was beginning to make. With his usual élan, Alex bounded far ahead of the field. While rival media moguls had just begun to plod into commercial television, Alex, who had applied for a television wave-length in June 1952, soon announced that he was abandoning it as too old-fashioned, explaining:

> I still believe there should be an alternative programme to the BBC, but not by having programmes sponsored by commercial firms. The public should be able to dial for what it wants and pay 6d. or 1s. for each programme. This is subscription TV – not sponsored TV. Subscription TV is as advanced as the jet airplane – and it is because I believe we should get into the jet age right away that I have left the old commercial idea.[19]

On the other hand, the films that were to continue to attract audiences to the cinema in the television age would have to get bigger and more spectacular. Alex would be the first British producer to make films in Twentieth Century-Fox's new wide-screen format, Cinemascope, and, returning from a trip to America in early 1952, he described his discovery of the even bigger Cinerama in a converted tennis court. First, an ordinary 'flat' film was projected on to the middle of a giant semi-circular screen. 'Then,' said Alex,

> the whole screen seemed to burst and the complete semi-circle was filled with three-dimensional action in colour. The effect was really amazing. No spectacles to wear and no practical objection to overcome. It is as big a thing as the coming of the talkies. Whoever puts it on first will stampede the business, just as Warner Brothers did nearly thirty years ago.[20]

Alex would live up to his comments about the jet age when on 9 October 1952 he flew in the world's first jet airliner. To publicize the French première of *The Sound Barrier*, London Films arranged a special flight from London to Paris of the first Comet to be delivered into commercial service. Cutting the journey time between the two cities to forty minutes, the occasion received the sort of press coverage that today would probably require a manned flight to Mars. Millions of Parisians came out on to the streets as the Comet swooped down low over the city. It hurtled down the length of the Champs-Elysées, turned tightly above the Eiffel Tower, dipping one wing tip so that it almost touched the top, and then landed at Orly airport a few minutes later.

Among the passengers were David Lean, Ann Todd and Norman Spencer, as well as several test pilots. 'When we went to get on the plane,' recalled Spencer,

[Alex] said to me, 'Norman, you and the other pilots, you sit at the back, you're young fellows . . . You've all got your lives in front of you.' He had a sort of naive theory that it was safer at the back. 'I'll sit in the front, you sit at the back.' His concern was rather touching.

A particularly good omen was Winston Churchill's victory in the General Election of October 1951. It represented a return to an order that Alex understood. Since the early 1930s the fortunes of the two men had been strangely entwined – not that Alex the film producer ever seemed to benefit. Over the years he had spent vast sums of money on Churchill, discussed all sorts of deals, but nothing substantial ever emerged. His latest idea that Churchill should narrate a film autobiography was the subject of several meetings during 1951, but was quietly dropped in the run-up to the General Election.

Alex's enthusiasm for clinching bad deals with Churchill reflected an almost schoolboy-like devotion. After hearing Churchill give a radio speech in 1947, he wrote to him: 'It was wonderful to hear your voice again. Myself and my friend who listened with me, were touched to tears remembering your war-time speeches and all that they meant to us and to the world. You have given a new hope to the country – the hope to have you again, and soon, at the helm.'[21] The words were gushing but genuine. Churchill was perhaps the only man alive he could look up to. Whenever the latest volume of Churchill's history of the Second World War was published, Alex would send his personal copy to Churchill for his inscription. He was touched when in the third volume, *The Grand Alliance*, Churchill praised *That Hamilton Woman*. Thanking him for his kindness, Alex wrote: 'In my craft, where we produce only for the day, it is indeed a very great honour, of which I am very proud.'[22] The relationship was marked by warmth and mutual regard, yet also by a formality. Churchill, who was twenty years older than Alex, was a father figure to a man who more usually had to bear the burden of performing that role for other people.

Whenever there was an important première, Churchill would of course be invited. And every year Alex would remember his birthday with the gift of a few crates of champagne or pots of caviar. One year he even sent brandy and quails' eggs by messenger to where Churchill was holidaying in the South of France. There was no calculation behind these gifts; they were sincere gestures of appreciation for a man he admired and sought to emulate.

Occasionally Alex's devotion could cause him to venture beyond the bounds of propriety. When in September 1951 Churchill appeared in a short film on behalf of the RAF Benevolent Fund, Alex offered to arrange its distribution in the big cinema chains. He did what he could to engineer its release during the October General Election campaign, and had to be warned by Churchill's advisers that such an overt use of a charitable appeal for political propaganda could easily backfire.

//

But there were too many skeletons in Alex's cupboard to allow him to feel content for long. The one that rattled most loudly in the early 1950s was his first wife, Maria. She had still not come to terms with their divorce, often referred to Alex as 'my husband', and styled herself Lady Maria Beatrice Korda. She lived in Italy on a very generous settlement, but had no intention of remaining quietly in her gilded cage. There was an ever-present danger of her swooping into London, and she did everything she could to keep herself in the forefront of Alex's mind. Norman Spencer recalled being in his office one day when a secretary brought in a letter on a silver salver:

Alex gave one look and he sighed. 'This is a letter from my first wife.' He opened a drawer in his desk, and there were four or five letters unopened. He put it on top of them, and he said, 'This one says she still loves me. This one says I'm a sonnovabitch. This one says she still loves me. This one says I'm a sonnovabitch.' Closing the drawer, he added: 'I don't open them, I know what's in them.'[23]

Suffering from religious mania, Maria believed that Alex's godlessness had caused the rift between them. But she still hoped that the prodigal might return, and even had an idea for how he might make repentance. The distribution of Alex's films in Italy, she reasoned, earned him a substantial revenue that currency regulations prevented him from taking out of the country. He should use this money to help her film a Life of Christ. But Alex wouldn't listen to her or answer her letters. So she wrote to the one person who she knew enjoyed his unquestioning obedience.

The new Prime Minister had been in Downing Street barely a week when a letter from Maria plopped on to his mat. 'With great joy I read today in the paper that you are coming to Rome,' she wrote. 'This gave me a secret hope that perhaps you will be able to receive me for a couple of minutes, when I could beg you to talk with Mr Korda so that I shall be able to realize my greatest dream, to make the Life of Christ.'[24]

She explained that she would like to have Churchill's daughter Sarah play the Virgin Mary, while Stewart Granger would be Christ, 'as he possesses that grave severity and dignity and looks honest and frank, handsome and tall just as Christ looked'. She herself would play Mary Magdalen, and Orson Welles – who had recently appeared in a similar role in *The Third Man* – would play Judas.

'I have such confidence in you, Mr Churchill, that I feel sure that you will be able to help me spread the light of Christ.' All he had to do was to tell her husband to make the film. 'For once he can use his money in a religious way.'

No record exists of what reply, if any, Churchill sent her, but a few weeks later Maria sent him a Christmas card with an even more outlandish request: 'My dream would be fulfilled if you could honour with your presence in Lourdes the pilgrimage of four thousand soldiers wounded from the Korean battlefield.'[25] She enclosed a book she had written called *The Miracle of the Soldier of Lourdes*, which she dedicated to Churchill. Her plan was to transport the soldiers across the Atlantic on a specially chartered boat from New York. Even if no miraculous cure took place, she felt sure that the trip would refresh them. A few days later she sent a letter and a bunch of flowers to Churchill aboard the *Queen Mary* as he set off on an official visit to the United States. She explained that she had contacted the State and Defense departments in Washington concerning transport for the soldiers, but received no constructive help. 'So, dear Mr Churchill, I thought as you go [to] Washington anyhow, perhaps you could say one or two kind words to the authorities about this beautiful pilgrimage.'[26]

This time she received a civil servant's reply: 'The Prime Minister has asked me to thank you for the flowers which you sent to him on board the *Queen Mary* and for your message of good wishes.'

Put out not to hear from Churchill himself, she wrote to him again asking him to confirm that he had received her letter and her book. She also enclosed a preface that she had written in his name, seeking his permission to include it in the book. It took the form of a speech that she hoped that Churchill would deliver at the Shrine of Our Lady at Lourdes. It's worth quoting at some length – not just as an amusing Churchill spoof but because it is an example of the passion and flair for drama with which once Maria had inspired the young Sándor Korda. Here, thinly disguised as Churchill, was the spirit of the woman whom Alex had once directed as Delilah:

> I address my speech to you, American soldiers, wounded in the Korean battlefield, but this is also a speech to all soldiers who have for centuries past been sacrificed down the long years from time beginning, when from early times the first men were sacrificed on the battlefield to preserve the peace and security of their wives and children waiting at home.
>
> So this meeting today in Lourdes is the silent urgent call to the great soldiers of the past to help us and to heal us.

To all who were the protectors of the soldiers and all who were soldiers and saints:-

Michael the Archangel

Joan of Arc

Ignatius Loyala

Wellington

Nelson

Napoleon

They were all great soldiers. They will gather here around us and help to heal the wounded and sick soldiers of Korea through the Miracle wrought by the Shrine of Our Lady of Lourdes.

Accompanying the spirits of the past will surely be those gallant few heroes of the Battle of Britain.

'Never have so many owed so much to so few.'[27]

Maria's efforts were repaid with another cold letter from a civil servant. Mr Churchill did not want his name to be associated with the speech. He hoped that she would excuse and understand him. Maria wrote back at once:

I am really ashamed to bother you so much and to take advantage of your kind nature, because you really are the most human person I have ever met, but I feel that this is the last great chance of my life.

Alex never gave me a chance in my life, he shut the door between me and my dreamland which is ART. My husband prohibited me from the greatest love I ever had. I was never permitted to be an artist, I was doomed all my life to be a kept woman, a rich man's fancy. *Just a beautiful nothing.*

It seems to me that you are fated to open the door to me, to my ART.

Please I beg of you humbly withhold your decision with regard to the permission for the preface until you have read the book.[28]

A few days later, without waiting for a reply, she sent Churchill another letter to explain that she had had second thoughts:

Before giving the printers the preface which I wanted to be signed by you, I read it again. How wonderful and wise you are!

A politician does not talk in this language, no matter how religious he may feel inside. It is really more of a woman's talk, a woman's speech. I will publish it under my name.

But how greatly you would help me, if with your own style you would say just a couple of words as an introduction to my book.[29]

At this point, Churchill's personal secretary told the Prime Minister about Maria's letters, but continued to field them on his behalf. Sir Alexander Korda's ex-wife, he explained, was 'well known as abnormally eccentric'.

Furious at being fobbed off by the secretary's letters, Maria was determined to extract a personal reply from Churchill himself. So on 14 March 1952 she wrote to him:

I don't believe that you ever received my book, and as you are very busy, this letter that you sent me was just the decision of your secretary. If your secretary should again refuse me, not you Mr Churchill because I don't believe anything but good of you, then I will force my husband Sir Alexander Korda to bring me to you. It would be unbelievable that you could brush me off with three lines after all this trouble and work I have had with my book this winter. I don't believe you could do things like that.

. . .

Remember what Our Lord said: 'Knock and it shall be opened.' I am certainly knocking, in fact almost kicking your door down.[30]

At last Maria received a letter from Churchill himself: 'Thank you for your letter of March 14. I am sorry that I can neither see you nor help you in the way you suggest.' These are the only words that the carbon copy in the Churchill archive records, but Maria's reply suggests that he probably added a few lines to the typewritten message in his own hand:

Many thanks for your letter dated 24th of March. As I read the letter I could not feel any sadness of your refusal. I am so honoured, that you wrote me personally, in a most gentle and generous way.

I am sure that the refusal is connected with some political

reason. Otherwise wherever you can do a favour, you are the man who does it, you always did. You were always such a great friend of my family, and *you gave us so much for so little*. I am very devoted to you. And I always shall be. I will follow your activity with great devotion. And I wish you all the luck and success in the world . . . It makes me really happy to see such a great man handwrite, no matter what he writes for me. The only thing, that makes me sad, is that I cannot write you any more. There is no excuse any more, to write you. It made me very happy, to correspond with you . . . And so it is, Mr Churchill, I say good-bye to you![31]

It was enough that she had received a human response, which was perhaps all she had been looking for from the beginning.

Maria was clearly impossible, and dismissed by most people as a crackpot. But behind the hounding letters and crazy schemes lay the loneliness of an intelligent but neglected woman. Finally, she elicits sympathy and even admiration. Of the three women Alex would marry, she was certainly the most formidable, and, for all the embarrassment she may have caused, the most true.

When Alex opened the drawer full of her letters, he didn't reveal what *he* thought of Maria. But the fact that he had kept them suggests that he still had some regard for her. She came from elsewhere – the time before his disillusionment, the time when, as he confided to Graham Greene, he still dreamed of being a poet.

24. A HOME AT LAST

'Your Grace is sad tonight.'
'What can we do to cheer Your Grace?'
'What could you do to cheer my loneliness?'
'Your Grace is lonely?'
'Ah, that is the penalty of greatness, sire.'
'Greatness. I would exchange it all to be my lowest groom who sleeps above the stable with a wife who loves him.'

– The Private Life of Henry VIII

Maria was finding it every bit as difficult to accept her divorce as Catherine of Aragon had 400 years previously, but one way Alex could drive the point home was to marry again. It was about the only sensible reason that anyone could come up with for his betrothal in June 1953 to the twenty-five-year-old Alexa Boycun, thirty-five years Alex's junior. The daughter of Ukrainians who had settled in Canada, she had come to London to learn singing, but, as Michael Korda put it, 'basically she was one of those attractive young women about town who appear at parties and are expected to make themselves agreeable to the guests'.[1] Moura Budberg, who, as a well-known salon habitué and a former mistress to two of the twentieth century's great writers, had some expertise in these matters, played the match-maker.

It was a task she took upon herself after Christine Norden, Alex's helplessly off-and-on mistress, had finally bowed out of his life. Christine's last adieu had been characteristically romantic and rash. She had fallen in love with a penniless sergeant in the United States Air Force called Mitchell Dodge and, abandoning her film career in England, followed him back to America.

On the night before her departure, in August 1952, she received a letter from Alex begging her to marry him. It really tore my heart', she recalled years later, 'but I would have been marrying Alex for all the wrong reasons.'[2]

After such a débâcle, it was perhaps too much to expect that Moura could find a girl who would marry Alex for the right reasons, but none the less her choice did suggest some attempt to learn from previous mistakes. So Alexa had neither fair hair like Maria and Christine nor dark hair like Merle, but auburn. Even more important, as the newspapers were pointedly told, she had no ambition to appear in films, nor, it seemed, any other sort of ambition beyond the strictly social. She was a simple girl, whose father worked as a gardener, a simple girl who would be content to be a home-maker. That, at least, was the theory. But no amount of wishful thinking could disguise the enormous age difference. For Christine thirty years had seemed too much, now it was nearer forty. Alexa may have tried to convince herself that she was in love with Alex, but it was hardly surprising if most of the time she just felt bored and trapped.

Moura Budberg aside, few of Alex's confidants thought that the wedding was a good idea. 'Vincent was gloomy about it,' wrote David Cunynghame, 'as I am during the few moments that I give any thought to this idiocy.'[3]

For some time Alex had been making conscious efforts to get more out of life, and, now that he had lost Christine, probably viewed his betrothal to Alexa in the same spirit with which the previous month he had bought a Canaletto to add to his fast-growing art collection. She would be a trophy bride.

'Some men retire at sixty,' Alex told a journalist at about this time. 'I am fifty-nine. I am clearing my desk so that younger men may clutter it.'[4] The twenty-first anniversary of London Films would only have strengthened his view that it was time to wind down. On 8 May 1953, after a première of *The Story of Gilbert and Sullivan*, he gave a midnight party at the Savoy Theatre to mark this coming of age. The journalist Paul Holt invited him to take stock of his years as a British producer, recording his 'philosophy of living' in the *Daily Herald*:

> BEING POOR: 'I have never regretted it. Poverty brings out the best and the worst in a man. It brought out both in me.'
>
> SUCCESS: 'Like they used to say about the infantry during the war – it is expendable. I have never feared losing it.'
>
> MONEY: 'It promises everything and gives nothing. But you have to have it in order to despise it.'
>
> LONELINESS: 'I am often lonely. I sit and read a book. It does not matter what kind of book, so long as it is not fiction. I only read fiction professionally.'
>
> DEATH: 'I have never been afraid of it. I am one of those very many people in the world who think it will never happen to them.'[5]

But Alex's most telling comment was made in answer to the inquiry concerning how he felt about the film industry itself: 'I am reminded of the Abbé Sieyes who, asked when he had become one of Napoleon's consuls what he did in the Revolution, replied: "I survived."'[6]

One consequence of survival was an increasingly mournful wisdom. Alex may have been just about to take on a new bride, but otherwise his behaviour continued to be that of the old man much more comfortable offering advice to others than receiving it. At the beginning of the year Vivien Leigh had suffered a mental breakdown in Hollywood and that spring she was recuperating with Laurence Olivier at their home in Notley Abbey in Buckinghamshire. On 22 May, to mark Olivier's birthday, Alex sent a crate of Cuvée Coronation champagne with a few reflective words. 'My dearest Larry,' he wrote. 'These sad punctuations of our lives appear with an ever increasing swiftness. "The nimble footed years" – they get nimbler every year. But these are the thoughts of an elder – you have still many years of full life ahead – for the pleasure of the world and for the joy of your friends.'[7]

Did Alex ever express the same kind of sentiments to his young bride? It's impossible to know for certain, but he was not in good health and perhaps there was a tacit understanding that after providing a few years of support and companionship Alexa would be free to start a new life. Whatever, the elder would publicly announce his engagement to her in Antibes, on 3 June 1953, exactly fourteen years to the day after he had married Merle Oberon there. So when he told the press that he and Alexa would be getting married in two or three months' time in Canada, they probably had an inkling that it was far too dull to be true. Photographers and reporters were out in force when the wedding took place five days later in the nearby village of Vence. Among the messages of congratulation was this telegram from Vivien Leigh and Laurence Olivier: ''Tis hard to contrive words sufficiently prolix to express all our wishes for Alexa and Alex. We drink to your loves in love's own elixir and we joy in the joy of Alex and Alexa.'[8]

Alex was so keen to set off on his honeymoon with Alexa that he missed the Queen's Coronation on 2 June. But he was there in spirit. He had the event filmed with Cinerama cameras, made the Rialto Cinema available to royal guests, and lent eight carriages to the procession. There had been a shortage because five years previously Alex had bought fifty from the Royal Household when he was filming *An Ideal Husband*. No one was more adept than him at having his cake and eating it. Alex's 'stupid snobbery', noted Cunynghame, reached a high point 'when he clamoured for a Coronation medal ... oblivious of his much boasted absence from London on Coronation Day'.[9]

With just the occasional flying visit back to London, Alex was away through June, July, August and September. During one of his very brief appearances at 146 Piccadilly, Cunynghame found him 'in a recklessly carefree mood and I thought it almost superfluous to wish him a happy holiday as at the moment he seems to be on holiday most of the time'.

In the autumn the newly-weds moved into an apartment in a large house leased by London Film Productions at 20 Kensington Palace Gardens. Diagonally opposite was the Soviet Embassy, where Alex used to attend several parties. The journalist David Lewin can remember him joking about the furtive figures who from time to time could be seen lingering in the street. 'I'm watching them and they're watching the Russian Embassy.' By this time, so many of Dansey's friends were working for London Films that it doesn't seem far-fetched to suggest that they probably had some hand in the choice of address.* As ever, Alex was glad to help intelligence in any way he could, for example in 1953 allowing covert Government funds in support of the magazine *Encounter* to be channelled through his bank account.

//

Alex had been behaving like a magnificent ostrich for some time. Whilst the fires may no longer have been raging out of control, British Lion was still an ailing company. In 1952 the Government deficit had increased by £400,000, and during a Commons debate on the NFFC loans to British Lion at the end of that year, Alex came under direct criticism. 'Sir Alexander Korda was associated with the lush days of the film industry,' William Shepherd, MP, pointed out, 'and he is not attuned to making films at a cost of £120,000 a time.' It would be better for both British Lion and the country, he suggested, if someone else took over his job. If not, then a full-time chairman should replace Harold Drayton, who, as a director of several other companies, was far too busy to meet the challenge 'of containing Sir Alexander Korda'.[10] The public criticism stung Drayton into even more zealous attempts at cost-cutting, and the British Lion board refused to provide complete financing for any of Alex's films. In October 1953 Alex, who probably felt that his hands were so tied that he might as well go on holiday, told Cunynghame 'that once he had made alternative arrangements he would like to get out of British Lion'.[11] It was a recognition that the cog-wheels of public embarrassment were slowly but relentlessly turning against him. That summer, while Alex cruised the Mediterranean, civil servants had been working hard on a plan for tidying up the Government's rather messy relationship with British Lion.

---

* It must often have been difficult to find anything constructive for them to do. In December 1954 Cunynghame expressed his annoyance at having to find a £400-a-year job for a spy called Ellis: 'It is really a monstrous form of patronage.'

On 20 November 1953 a bill was introduced in the House of Commons to amend the Cinematograph Film Production (Special Loans) Act 1949.* The previous legislation, explained the President of the Board of Trade, had failed to face 'the possibility that a substantial loan might not be susceptible of repayment in due time or within the Corporation's lending powers and terms'.[12] The amendment would permit the National Film Finance Corporation 'to make such arrangements as a prudent creditor might wish to make to collect money or to make a settlement with a debtor'.[13] Not only was specific mention made of British Lion's £3 million debt, but also Alex was subject to further personal attack. A bleak situation was made even worse with the announcement the following month that British Lion had recorded a loss of £150,330 for the financial year 1952/3.

It was really just a matter now of waiting for a well-advertised Sword of Damocles to fall, although Alex did what he could to postpone the inevitable. In the weeks and months that followed he sat through endless meetings not just with Drayton, but with the officials at the Board of Trade as well. A resurgence of his skin rash was an outward sign of the renewed pressure, and he was ill during most of February 1954. In May he embarked on some intensive political lobbying as the decision whether to appoint a receiver for British Lion was referred to a Cabinet Committee, but finally, on Tuesday, 1 June, the Government announced that a receiver would be appointed for British Lion and a new management put in place.

'I don't grow on trees,' Alex famously replied when the receiver, William Lawson, sought his advice on who might best replace him as British Lion's production adviser. It might have seemed a flippant remark since the company's entire share capital had been lost and the total sum of taxpayers' money written off was over £2 million, but Alex knew that films like *The Four Feathers* or *The Thief of Baghdad* could not result from a conventional respect for the rules of profit and loss. 'In films the art – as Mr Dulles said of diplomacy – is to come to the brink of bankruptcy – and stare it in the face.'[14] The Rank Organisation,

---

* The Act that had established the National Film Finance Corporation.

which was steadily reducing its overdraft, would demonstrate the accountant's alternative – 'Carry On' and 'Doctor' films, Norman Wisdom comedies. They made economic sense – just – but hardly stirred the spirit.

As the accountants began to pore over the books of British Lion with renewed zeal, more skeletons in Alex's cupboard began to rattle. In January 1955 auditors discovered improper financial dealings at London Films' Paris office which went back to 1950. In August 1955 auditors reported the suspected misappropriation of over £15,000 by the head of the London Films office in South Africa.

But the cupboard that rattled by far the loudest stood in the Rome office. After Peter Moore had defended himself successfully againt the suspicions of embezzlement in 1950, rather than treat him with increased caution, Alex seemed to place ever greater confidence in him. On Moore's visits to London, the two would often have secretive meetings together. Moore was 'looking more spiv-like than ever,' commented Cunynghame on one of Moore's visits to London in January 1954. 'However, he manages to stay at the Savoy and wines and dines with Korda!'[15]

After the British Lion collapse, it became impossible even for Alex to turn a blind eye to whatever was going on in Rome. In April 1955 he sent Cunynghame and an auditor to Italy 'to see what Peter Moore is up to with our remittances'. The two men arrived in Rome on 19 April to find the office empty. When Peter Moore turned up at 5.30, he 'got quite hysterical'.[16]

While the auditor began to examine the books, Peter Moore caught a plane for Zurich. A few days later, he turned up in London with a letter of resignation and dollar cheques in payment of $50,000 of missing funds. Alex took a suspiciously lenient attitude. 'It would appear from Korda's lack of drive that Peter Moore knows too much and is going to be allowed to get off very lightly,' Cunynghame commented.[17]

//

If financial impropriety was one sign of Alex's cracking empire; the extraordinary thing, really, was that he had lasted as long as he had. When the *Daily Express* journalist David Lewin went to see him on the evening of the receivership announcement, he took along with him a list of the films Alex had made at British Lion with Government money. Alex looked through the list, then handed it back to Lewin with the comment: 'My goodness if I made those films, I deserved to go bankrupt!'[18]

This was not a comment that could have been expected to go down well with British Lion's shareholders, whose investment in the company was rendered worthless. But although there was some criticism of Alex's extravagant ways in the newspapers, there was also a general realization that whoever was in charge of British Lion would have struggled to make it a going concern. The National Film Finance Corporation, through which the Government had given British Lion the £3 million loan, stated in its annual report that it expected in the future to continue making a net loss. The lesson that both Government and business drew was that the film production industry in Britain, regardless of the personalities, was just not a serious business.

Two days after the Commons announcement Alex resorted to his habitual panacea – a fortnight's holiday in the South of France. Back in London, on 29 June he met Robert Dowling, who had flown over from New York for a two-day visit. 'Sir Alex and I are partners now,' said Dowling. 'We shall be putting up the money for his next programme of pictures.' The figure mentioned was $15 million. 'I don't want the ordinary routine films at the rate of ten or twenty a year,' Dowling explained. 'I like a few artistic pictures of special merit.'[19] The following month Alex concluded a deal for the distribution of his films in the United Kingdom with John Woolf, the head of Romulus Films.

Alex might have done better to forsake films completely for the Riviera life that had given him so much satisfaction over the past few years, but 'the showbusiness', as he called it, had become an unbreakable habit. 'Sometimes I think of retiring but then I go to my desk again and know I cannot,' he explained. 'When you have been on the treadmill as long as I have it goes faster and faster and it is not possible to step off.'[20]

Over the following year he put together his last programme of films: Carol Reed's *A Kid for Two Farthings*; David Lean's

Summer Madness; a remake of *The Four Feathers* called *Storm over the Nile*; Laurence Olivier's *Richard III*; a film version of Terence Rattigan's play, *The Deep Blue Sea*, starring Vivien Leigh and Kenneth More; and Anthony Kimmins's *Smiley*. Spared the machinations that had dogged British Lion, Alex was able to concentrate on being a film producer again. With the exception of *The Deep Blue Sea*, all looked like making a healthy profit, but Alex would not live long enough to enjoy their success.

At the end of July 1955 he suffered a heart attack. Alex himself described it as 'minor', but he spent the next three weeks in a nursing home in Queen's Gate, where he needed a bath chair just to get from his bed to the lavatory. When David Cunynghame visited him there on 12 August, he was 'shocked at his appearance', and convinced that Alex was 'a good deal more ill than the family will allow to be known'. On his doctors' advice Alex went down to the South of France for five weeks to recuperate. There, at the prompting of Alexa, who had already persuaded him to sell the *Elsewhere*, he bought a house in Biot, near Cannes, Le Domaine des Orangers, for £52,000.

At Cap d'Ail, he saw Sir Winston Churchill, who was in poor health himself and just a few months previously had resigned as Prime Minister. As the two invalids sat by the sea in the late summer sun, Alex might have remembered that he had written a similar scene a lifetime before. In his short story, 'Sick' ('Betegek'), three invalid friends rest in a sanatorium by the sea. They sit on the terrace in the evenings, glad to have retired from the responsibilities of everyday life. They feel at peace and are resigned to death, but also sense that there might yet be some new experience before them, some great tragedy or joy. 'Tears and laughter, tears and laughter. This is life.'[21]

Alex would have just a little time left for both. In November his doctors made it clear that he had only months to live, and on the 30th, before making one last trip to America, he amended his will. On 13 December there was a royal première of *Richard III*. At the end of the showing the audience stood up and applauded. The press notices the following day were excellent. Alex could scarcely have known a greater triumph in his whole film career.

But over the next few days he behaved as if it had been a failure. 'In spite of record figures continuing for *Richard III* at the Leicester Square Theatre,' observed Cunynghame on 22 December, 'AK was today more melancholy than I have ever known him to be.'

Shortly afterwards, Vincent explained that the cause was Alexa. Unstable and depressed, she had spent much of the previous year in and out of nursing homes. When Alex might have hoped for his young wife to look after him in his sickness, in practice he had had to look after Alexa in hers. To make an already difficult situation even more so, in the past few months Alexa had been having an affair. 'I'm sure that Alex knew about it,' commented David Korda. 'Could not have not known about it.'[22] Yet in one last confidence trick Alex carried on as if he didn't know. Outwardly all seemed to be well with the House of Korda.

It was perhaps the expectation of death that prompted him to agree to a series of interviews with David Lewin for the *Daily Express*. It was, after all, a chance to sum up his life. 'I have never been so happy with anyone as with Alexa,' he told Lewin. 'I never knew a real home life until I married her – and yet I think she would like to leave all this and move with me into two furnished rooms.'[23] Only Alexa, who was sitting by his side, would have appreciated the full measure of the deceptive irony and wishful thinking that the comment contained.

For a week in January 1956 Alex saw David Lewin for the best part of every day. Then one night, over dinner, Alex told Lewin that he would be going into hospital for an examination the following day. Lewin asked if he would be able to visit Alex there.

'Don't you know how to get into hospital?' Alex replied. 'There may be a problem getting in to see me, but you do this. You simply phone the props department at Shepperton, and you ask them for a white coat with a clipboard and a white hat. Then you come and you wear this and they do not stop you. Just ask for Alex Korda and they will show you.'[24]

Lewin never had the chance to try out the trick. The following day, 23 January, he received a telephone call from Alex's butler, Ben Aleck. Alex had died in the early hours of the morning from a massive heart attack.

One person Alex had desperately wanted to see in his last months was Christine Norden. After weeks of searching on Alex's behalf, Carol Reed had in early January found her in New York, where she was starring in cabaret at the Waldorf Astoria Hotel. Alex was very ill, he told her. Deeply upset, Christine agreed to fly back to London as soon as her cabaret run was over.

But it wasn't over soon enough. On the 23rd, Reed rang her from his hotel. He was so drunk that she found it difficult to make out what he was saying. But two words which he repeated over and over again were clear enough: 'Alex died. . . . Alex died . . .'

'I suddenly felt like an orphan, without an identity,' she recalled later. 'I could not grasp or accept that that great life force had been extinguished.'[25]

Vincent, who had been in the South of France for the past week, flew back to London on the same day as his brother's death. When David Cunynghame met him at the airport, he was 'broken-hearted'. The following morning Alex's will was read. The executors were David Cunynghame, Harold Boxall, Vincent and Zoltán Korda. The document shocked me in several ways,' noted Cunynghame, 'mainly because of its limited definition of his wishes.' Vague to the last, Alex's lack of precision would ignite a bitter family dispute that would last for years.

But clause 7 of that will, which required his trustees to 'call in and convert' into money whatever part of his estate had not been specifically disposed of, was clear enough. London Film Productions, in which Alex had a controlling share, would have to be liquidated. It formalized what everyone knew already – that with Alex's death the London Films of old had effectively died too.

Laurence Olivier and Ralph Richardson planned the memorial service which was to be held at St Martin-in-the-Fields on Tuesday, 31 January. They wanted to have a fanfare by William Walton, but on contacting the composer in Italy discovered that it required 150 trumpets. As Alex was no longer around to make this happen, a more modest arrangement was made instead.

On 26 January David Cunynghame called at the chapel in Westbourne Grove to have a last look at the man who had been a dominating presence in his life for twenty-five years. 'I felt strangely unemotional about it – perhaps because he looked so strange to me.' The following day a non-denominational funeral service was held at Golders Green Crematorium for close friends and family. A reporter from the *Daily Sketch* wandered through the carpet of flowers that lay in the Gardens of Remembrance. The 'loveliest wreath of all – Christmas roses, carnations, aconite, freesia and anemones – was signed: "Happy Memories – Winston and Clementine Churchill"'.

The memorial service took place four days later. Olivier delivered the address. He spoke of a wise, kind and clever man, both gentle and strong, a man who had 'managed the difficult and rare mixture of artist and businessman with an extraordinary virtuosity'. He spoke too of a man who 'relished what life had to offer and lived it in a beautiful and enviable style', and of the 'cold newness' that his passing would bring about. 'For – take him for all in all – we shall not look upon his like again . . .'

In the months that followed the executors set about implementing Alex's wish that London Film Productions should be liquidated. Although Cunynghame had long suspected the worst, this process of unravelling Alex's affairs made him only more disillusioned. 'Altogether a disreputable day,' he commented on 21 February. 'One more scandal after another materialized over Korda's affairs.' It was not only Alex's activities that were a cause of dismay, but also the ease with which others had been bought.

'It just shows the difference when the trading is honest,' observed Cunynghame some months later after discovering that London Film Productions had enjoyed a record year. There were other differences too, but much sadder. On 28 June, Cunynghame had attended the première of the last film that Alex had put into production, *Smiley*. He was shocked to find hardly anyone there. The 'half-hearted' party that the director, Anthony Kimmins, gave afterwards was a wake for the end of a glamorous age that Alex's death had brought to a close.

//

Alex's will received probate on 19 May. He had left behind £385,684, a net sum of £158,160 after duties had been paid. 'An insult,' commented Maria. 'It's not even pocket money.'[26] Alex, she maintained, had a 'colossal personal fortune. What happened to all that?' David Cunynghame's diary suggests that Maria had every reason to be suspicious. From 1950 onwards, Alex was travelling regularly to Zurich. Of the first such trip, which Alex made with the accountant-phobic Julius Aussenberg, Cunynghame comments, 'I do not like to think what was the real object of the visit – let alone ask. I certainly think that it related more to Korda's private fortune than film business.' Alex's last trip to Zurich was made on 4 January, just three weeks before his death. Like so much else in Alex's life it may now be impossible to account for, but what sketchy evidence there is suggests that his real fortune – as opposed to the pocket money – may well have been safely tucked away in some numbered Swiss account beyond the reach of his executors in England.

But the chief object of Maria's fury was Alexa. In 1941 Alex had agreed to pay Maria $1,250 for life, but with the proviso that if his total income should drop below $6,000 a month, then his estate would not be liable for more than a quarter of the total monthly income. The income of the estate had now dropped well below this figure, largely because of Alex's decision to put a large part of his fortune into an art collection. His paintings, which were valued at £112,000 for probate, passed to Alexa as 'personal chattels'. Maria took the trustees to court, insisting that the pictures should be sold to raise the income of the estate. When she lost, she appealed unsuccessfully to the Court of Appeal and would have gone all the way to the Lords if permission for a further appeal had been granted. Peter, too, resorted to routine litigation. In March 1958, on the grounds that the executors were mishandling the administration of the estate, he sought an injunction to prevent the liquidation or disposal of assets. His application was unsuccessful. But he was back in the High Court the following February, this time seeking an order that the court should take over the administration of his father's estate. Again he was unsuccessful.

At the same hearing, he complained to the judge that the executors had yet to bury his father's ashes. 'It is the duty of every son to bury his father,' he said. 'It was only today that I discovered he was still unburied. It is an outrage against any standards of decency.' The judge duly made an order for the ashes to be buried.

A week later, on 25 February 1959, Alexander Korda, born in Pusztaturpásztó, Hungary, was buried in Stoke Poges Garden of Remembrance, Buckinghamshire, in a service conducted by a pastor of the Hungarian Reformed Church. As both Alexa and Maria attended the ceremony, it was perhaps too much to hope that he would be allowed to rest in peace just yet. 'Maria started screaming at Alexa that she was a dreadful whore and that she should rot in hell,' remembered David Korda. 'Just terrible, terrible abuse.'[27]

Peter, who knew that his mother would want to speak her mind, wisely chose not to attend and visited the garden the following day. From then on he would visit twice every year to pay his respects. The lasting bitterness of the disputes over Alex's death would be reflected in Peter's choice of a new surname, de Korda, intended not to distance himself from Alex, but on the contrary to declare his closeness – he was the one and only son *of* his father. It was an extreme but understandable gesture, so often had he been shut out of his father's life.

Since then Peter has passed on too, but Alex made too much of an impression on people's lives ever to be completely forgotten. This year, on the anniversary of his death, 23 January, I visited St Martins-in-the-Fields. As I pushed open a door to the vestibule, a blustery wind blew in pale imitation of the driving snow that had made the steps hazardous on the day of his memorial service. Choristers in red cassocks hurried back and forth, too busy to notice the large bouquet of flowers that stood before a side altar with the attached card, 'In Memory of Sir Alexander Korda'. Earlier that day, by one of those pieces of strange timing, I learned that a blue plaque of the sort I had once hoped to find in the village of Alex's birth, Pusztaturpásztó, was soon to be erected at 22 Grosvenor Street, where seventy years previously London Film Productions had had its birth – a welcome public remembrance of Britain's only movie mogul.

Notes

1. THE PUSZTA

1. Michael Korda, *Charmed Lives* (Allen Lane, 1980), p. 34.
2. Ibid., p. 35.
3. Maria Korda, 'The Man Called Alexander Korda', unpublished manuscript, British Library, 1957, ch. 5, p. 3.
4. Paul Tabori, *Alexander Korda* (Oldbourne, 1959), p. 27.
5. Ibid.
6. Interview, *The Golden Years of Alexander Korda* (*Omnibus*, BBC TV, 1968).
7. Tamás Barnabás, 12 November 1983.

2. SÁNDOR OF THE RIVER

1. Michael Korda, *Charmed Lives* (Allen Lane, 1980), p. 44.
2. Alexander Korda, *Kórborlások* (Balla, J., Könyvkereskedö Kiadása, Budapest, 1911), pp. 41–2.
3. Ibid., p. 42.
4. Quoted in Ignác Romsics, *Hungary in the Twentieth Century* (Corvina, 1999), p. 71.
5. Quoted in ibid., p. 72.
6. Michael Korda, *Charmed Lives*, p. 44.
7. André De Toth, *Fragments* (Faber and Faber, 1994), p. 4.
8. Paul Tabori, *Alexander Korda* (Oldbourne, 1959), p. 42.
9. De Toth, *Fragments*, p. 5.
10. Ibid., p. 5.
11. Tabori, *Alexander Korda*, p. 33.
12. Interview with the author, 11 June 1998.

13. Ibid.
14. Ibid.
15. *Radio Times*, 25 December 1953.
16. Michael Korda, *Charmed Lives*, p. 49.
17. Alexander Korda, *Kórborlások*, pp. 41–57.
18. 'The Critic as Artist', pt 2, *Intentions* (1891).
19. Tabori, *Alexander Korda*, p. 34.
20. D. J. Wenden, *The Birth of the Movies* (E. P. Dutton & Co, 1974), p. 28.
21. Ibid., p. 36.
22. Michael Korda, *Charmed Lives*, p. 48.
23. Maria Korda, 'The Man Called Alexander Korda', unpublished manuscript, British Library, 1957, ch. 2, p. 1.
24. Ibid., ch. 2, p. 2.
25. Ibid., ch. 2, p. 1.
26. Ibid.
27. István Nemeskürty, *Word and Image: History of the Hungarian Cinema* (Corvina Press, Budapest, 1968), p. 19.
28. Tabori, *Alexander Korda*, p. 42.
29. Jenö Janovics, 12 April 1936.
30. Quoted in Tabori, *Alexander Korda*, p. 47.
31. Ibid.
32. Ibid., p. 48.
33. *Mozihét*, vol. 3, no. 16.
34. Ibid., vol. 3, no. 40.
35. Ibid., vol. 3, no. 51.
36. *Radio Times*, 25 December 1953.
37. Quoted in Tabori, *Alexander Korda*, p. 53.
38. *Mozihét*, vol. 3, no. 51.
39. Nemeskürty, *Word and Image*, p. 42.
40. *Mozihét*, vol. 4, no. 50.
41. Quoted in Nemeskürty, *Word and Image*, p. 41.
42. Michael Korda, *Charmed Lives*, p. 63.
43. *Mozihét*, vol. 5, no. 14.
44. Michael Korda, *Charmed Lives*, p. 58.
45. Tabori, *Alexander Korda*, p. 60.
46. Michael Korda, *Charmed Lives*, p. 67.
47. Ibid., p. 68.
48. Maria Korda, 'The Man Called Alexander Korda', ch. 4, p. 2.

3. WESTWARD BOUND

1. Michael Korda, *Charmed Lives* (Allen Lane, 1980), p. 72.
2. *Mozihét*, vol. 3, no. 46.
3. *Focus on Film*, March 1978, pp. 35–43.
4. Günter Krenn, 'Der bewegte Mensch – Sascha Kolowrat', in *Elektrische Schatten* (Film Archiv Austria, 1999), p. 38.
5. Stephen Watts, 'Alexander Korda and the International Film', *Cinema Quarterly*, vol. 2, no. 1 (Autumn 1933), p. 13.
6. Karol Kulik, *Alexander Korda: The Man Who Could Work Miracles* (W. H. Allen, 1975), p. 32.
7. Quoted in Paul Tabori, *Alexander Korda* (Oldbourne, 1959), p. 64.
8. Quoted in Joseph Zsuffa, *Béla Balázs: The Man and the Artist* (University of California Press, 1987), p. 106.
9. Maria Korda, 'The Man Called Alexander Korda', unpublished manuscript, British Library, 1957, ch. 5, p. 1.
10. Michael Korda, *Charmed Lives*, p. 77.
11. André De Toth, interview with the author, 7 June 2000.
12. David Korda, interview with the author, 8 June 2000.
13. John Loder, *Hollywood Hussar* (Howard Baker, 1977), p. 71.
14. Ibid., p. 73.
15. Letter from Maria Korda to Winston Churchill, 3 March 1952, Churchill Papers, 2/191 Churchill Archives Centre, Churchill College, Cambridge.
16. Undated and unsourced article on Alexander Korda microfiche, British Film Institute Library.
17. Michael Korda, *Charmed Lives*, p. 78.
18. Kulik, *Alexander Korda*, p. 40.
19. Ibid., p. 44.
20. 'Digest of Maria Korda Contract', 21 February 1927, Warner Brothers Archive, Cinema-Television Library, University of Southern California, Folder 2724B.
21. Heinrich Fraenkel, *Unsterblicher Film* (Kindler Verlag, 1956), pp. 138–9.

4. THE GILDED CAGE

1. *Motion Picture Classic*, vol. 25, no. 3 (May 1927), p. 30.
2. *Variety*, 10 August 1927.
3. Warner Bros Pictures, Inc., 'Comparison of negative costs and gross income on productions released from September 4, 1926 to August 29, 1936', William Schaefer Collection, Warner Brothers Archive, Cinema-Television Library, University of Southern California.
4. Interview in *Classic Images*, no. 228 (June 1994).
5. Cable, 15 June 1927, Warner Brothers Archive, Folder 2726A.
6. 'Comparison of negative costs . . .', Warner Brothers Archive.
7. Both the *Times* and *Daily News* reviews quoted in *Motion Pictures News*, 14 January 1928.
8. *Variety*, 14 December 1927.
9. Paul Tabori, *Alexander Korda* (Oldbourne, 1959), p. 88.
10. Alexander Korda contract, 7 September 1928, Warner Brothers Archive, Folder 2726A.
11. Memorandum from Al Rockett to R. W. Perkins, First National Legal Department, 19 September 1928, Warner Brothers Archive, Folder 1627A.
12. Quoted in Tabori, *Alexander Korda*, p. 86.
13. Ibid., p. 88.
14. Ibid., p. 93.
15. Ibid., p. 96.
16. Ibid., p. 92.
17. Ibid., p. 90.
18. Ibid., p. 92.
19. Ibid., p. 93.
20. *Radio Times*, 25 December 1953.
21. Quoted in Tabori, *Alexander Korda*, p. 96.
22. Ibid., p. 97.
23. Ibid., p. 96.
24. Memorandum from Mr Halper to R. J. Obringer, 19 July 1929, Warner Brothers Archive, Folder 2726A.
25. Interview, 8 June 2000.
26. *Variety*, 15 May 1929.
27. 'Comparison of negative costs . . .', Warner Brothers Archive.
28. Ibid.
29. The *Star*, 9 March 1936.

30. George Grossmith, *G.G.* (Hutchinson, 1933), p. 252.
31. Ibid., p. 254.
32. Ibid.
33. Ibid., p. 243.
34. Tabori, *Alexander Korda*, p. 103.
35. Ibid., p. 105.
36. Ibid., p. 104.
37. The *Star*, 9 March 1936.
38. *Los Angeles Times*, 27 April 1980.
39. Ibid.
40. Tabori, *Alexander Korda*, p. 106.
41. Ibid., p. 96.
42. Peter de Korda, photograph album.
43. Ibid.
44. David Korda, interview with the author, 8 June 2000.
45. *Daily Express*, 29 January 1956.
46. Ibid.
47. Tabori, *Alexander Korda*, pp. 106–7.
48. Karol Kulik, *Alexander Korda: The Man Who Could Work Miracles* (W. H. Allen, 1975), p. 57.
49. Interview with Philip Johnson, the *Star*, 9 March 1936.
50. Maria Korda, 'The Man Called Alexander Korda', unpublished manuscript, British Library, 1957, ch. 6, p. 2.

5. 'SOMEWHERE ON THE MEDITERRANEAN'

1. Osmond Borradaile, 'Life through a Lens: Journals of a Cinematographer', unpublished manuscript, Kevin Brownlow Collection.
2. Marcel Pagnol, *Confidences: Mémoires* (Julliard, 1981), p. 200.
3. Ibid., p. 218.
4. Ibid., p. 221.
5. Ibid., p. 229.
6. Interview with Philip Johnson, the *Star*, 9 March 1936.
7. Ibid., p. 231.
8. Ibid., p. 232.
9. Fresnay and Possot, *Pierre Fresnay* (Editions de la Table Ronde, 1975), p. 42.
10. Pagnol, *Confidences*, p. 232.
11. Ibid., p. 236.

6. 'THE LONDON VENTURE'

1. Paul Tabori, *Alexander Korda* (Oldbourne, 1959), p. 118.
2. Ibid., p. 107.
3. *Sunday Chronicle*, 14 March 1937.
4. Osmond Borradaile, 'Life through a Lens: Journals of a Cinematographer', unpublished manuscript, Kevin Brownlow Collection, ch. 3, p. 10.
5. *Today's Cinema*, 18 January 1932.
6. Maria Korda, 'The Man Called Alexander Korda', unpublished manuscript, British Library, 1957, ch. 7, p. 1.
7. Ibid., ch. 7, p. 1.
8. Letter from Simon Rowson to Alexander Korda, 21 March 1932, London Film Productions Archive, C/006(ii), British Film Institute Special Collection.
9. Loren Kruger (ed.), *Light and Shadows: The Autobiography of Leontine Sagan* (Witwatersrand University Press, 1996), p. 118.
10. Ibid.
11. Anthony Gibbs, *In My Time* (Peter Davies, 1969), p. 72.
12. Kruger, *Light and Shadows*, p. 121.
13. Ibid.
14. Kenneth Barrow, *Mr Chips* (Methuen, 1985), p. 56.
15. Kruger, *Light and Shadows*, p. 74.
16. Emlyn Williams, *Emlyn* (Penguin Books, 1976), p. 284.
17. Kruger, *Light and Shadows*, p. 122.
18. Gibbs, *In My Time*, p. 89.
19. Kruger, *Light and Shadows*, p. 124.
20. Sir David Cunynghame, diary, 12 October 1932.
21. London Film Productions Archive, C/006(i).
22. Letter from Alexander Korda to Paul Czinner, 22 February, ibid., C/006(ii).
23. Letter from Simon Rowson to Alexander Korda, 16 June 1932, ibid.
24. Letter from Alexander Korda to Margaret Kennedy, undated, ibid., C/006(iv).
25. Ibid.
26. Letter from Lajos Biro to Mary Buxton, 28 December 1932, ibid.
27. Letter from Michael Balcon to Captain A.S.N. Dixey, ibid., C/006(ii).
28. Sir David Cunynghame, diary, 30 January 1933.

29. Balance Sheet, 27 July 1933, London Film Productions Archive, Special Collection, British Film Institute Library.

7. SUCCESS

1. Elsa Lanchester, *Herself* (St Martin's Press, 1983), p. 111.
2. Elsa Lanchester, *Charles Laughton and I* (Faber and Faber, 1938), p. 120.
3. Francesco Savio (ed.), *Cinecittà anni trenta* (Bulzoni Editore, 1979), p. 719.
4. Ludovico Toeplitz, *Ciak a chi tocca* (Edizioni Milano Nuova, 1964), p. 135.
5. Ibid., pp. 135–6.
6. Richard Norton, *Silver Spoon* (Hutchinson, 1954), p. 164.
7. Lanchester, *Charles Laughton and I*, p. 120.
8. Karol Kulik, *Alexander Korda: The Man Who Could Work Miracles* (W. H. Allen, 1975), p. 87.
9. Michael Korda, *Charmed Lives* (Allen Lane, 1980), p. 100.
10. Norton, *Silver Spoon*, p. 165.
11. 'Supplemental schedule of contracts', London Film Productions Archive, F11, British Film Institute Special Collection.
12. Interview with Binnie Barnes, in *The Golden Years*, Robert Vas documentary (*Omnibus*, BBC TV, 1968).
13. Lanchester, *Charles Laughton and I*, p. 122.
14. Toeplitz, *Ciak a chi tocca*, p. 140.
15. Osmond Borradaile, 'Life through a Lens: Journals of a Cinematographer', unpublished manuscript, Kevin Brownlow Collection, ch. 3, p. 10.
16. Interview, *Korda: 'I Don't Grow on Trees'*, (*Omnibus*, BBC TV, 1993).
17. *Daily Express*, 24 January 1956.
18. List of London Films' production costs in Prudential Archive, Box 2353.
19. The *Star*, 9 March 1936.
20. Kulik, *Alexander Korda*, p. 101.
21. Memorandum of expenditure, London Film Productions, Prudential Archive, Box 1.
22. Letter to William Philips, 4 September 1933, United Artists Collection, State Historical Society of Wisconsin, US Mss 99AN Series 9B, William Philips Papers, Box 3, File 11.

23. 13 October 1933.
24. 29 October 1933.
25. Korda, *Charmed Lives*, p. 100.
26. Prudential Archive, Box 2352.
27. Extract from BBC radio broadcast, excerpted in Peter Sasdy *Omnibus* documentary (see note 16 above).

8. ALEXANDER THE GREAT

1. Joseph Schenck to William Philips, 11 January 1934, United Artists Collection, State Historical Society of Wisconsin, US Mss 99AN Series 9B, William Philips papers, Box 3, File 9.
2. Ibid.
3. Ludovico Toeplitz, *Ciak a chi tocca* (Edizioni Milano Nuova, 1964), p. 185.
4. Cable from Murray Silverstone, relayed to Joseph Schenck in a letter from William Philips, 27 March 1934, United Artists Collection, State Historical Society of Wisconsin, US Mss 99AN Series 9B, William Philips Papers, Box 3, File 9.
5. Ibid.
6. Osmond Borradaile, 'Life through a Lens: Journals of a Cinematographer', unpublished manuscript, Kevin Brownlow Collection.
7. List of original negative cost and box-office receipts, Prudential Archive, Box 2353.
8. Churchill Papers, Literary 1934, 8/495 Churchill Archives Centre, Churchill College, Cambridge.
9. Eric Otto Siepmann, *Confessions of a Nihilist* (Gollancz, 1955), p. 132.
10. Ibid., p. 133.
11. Raymond Massey, *A Hundred Different Lives: An Autobiography* (Robson Books, 1979), pp. 187–8.
12. Sir David Cunynghame, diary, 27 August 1934.
13. Massey, *A Hundred Different Lives*, p. 188.
14. Sir David Cunynghame, diary, 1 November 1934.
15. Ibid., 3 November 1934.
16. Massey, *A Hundred Different Lives*, p. 187.
17. Interview with the author, 31 March 1998.
18. Ibid.
19. Draft of press annoucement to be released by London Film

Productions on 21 September 1934, Churchill Papers, Literary 1934, 8/495.

20. Note marked 'Given to press 21.9.34', ibid.
21. Toeplitz, *Ciak a chi tocca*, p. 156.
22. Draft for a press release, Churchill Papers, Literary 1934, 8/495.
23. Telegram from Alexander Korda to Winston Churchill, 6 October 1934, ibid.
24. Siepmann, *Confessions of a Nihilist*, p. 136.
25. Letter from Winston Churchill to Alexander Korda, 1 December 1934, Churchill Papers, Literary 1934, 8/495.
26. Alexander Korda to Winston Churchill, 6 December 1934, ibid.
27. Memorandum, 27 December 1934, ibid.
28. Letter from Winston Churchill to Alexander Korda, 14 January 1935, ibid., Literary 1935, 8/514.
29. Eric Siepmann, *Confessions of a Nihilist*, p. 140.
30. Letter from Winston Churchill to Alexander Korda, 28 January 1935, Churchill Papers, Literary 1935, 8/514.
31. Letter from Winston Churchill to Alexander Korda, 31 January 1935, ibid.
32. Letter from Winston Churchill to H. Osbourne, 24 January 1935, ibid.
33. Letter from Winston Churchill to Alexander Korda, 10 June 1935, ibid.
34. Letter from T.E. Lawrence to Charlotte Shaw, 26 January 1935, in *Letters of T.E. Lawrence*, ed. Malcolm Brown (J. M. Dent & Sons, 1988), p. 516.
35. *Daily Express*, January 1956.
36. Ibid.

9. THE FOXY WHISKERED GENTLEMAN

1. Paul Tabori, *Alexander Korda* (Oldbourne, 1959), p. 141.
2. Ibid., p. 142.
3. Ibid., p. 318.
4. 'Report of Mr Montagu Marks to the Camera Committee of Gerrard Industries Limited regarding the Hillman colour process', 19 July 1934, Prudential Archive, Box 2356.
5. Letter from Montagu Marks to P. C. Crump, 19 July 1934, ibid.
6. Letter from Alexander Korda to Montagu Marks, ibid.
7. Undated memorandum, ibid.

8. 'Notes on Sir Connop Guthrie's Scheme', undated, ibid., Box 2354.
9. Letter from P. C. Crump to Alexander Korda, 27 August 1934, ibid., Box 2356.
10. Unsigned memorandum from Sir Connop Guthrie, 'Colourgravure Friday 25th July 1934', ibid.

10. THE PLAYER

1. List of costs and receipts of London Film Productions up to 24 September 1938, Prudential Archive, Box 2353.
2. Ludovico Toeplitz, *Ciak a chi tocca* (Edizioni Milano Nuova, 1964), p. 138.
3. *Los Angeles Examiner*, 9 December 1934.
4. Cable from Samuel Goldwyn to Murray Silverstone, 18 December 1934, Samuel Goldwyn Papers, Margaret Herrick Library, Academy of Motion Picture Arts and Sciences, Beverly Hills.
5. Cable from Alexander Korda, to Samuel Goldwyn, 16 January 1935, ibid.
6. Cable from Merle Oberon to Samuel Goldwyn, 13 February 1935, ibid.
7. Cable from Sidney Franklin to Samuel Goldwyn, 11 March 1935, ibid.
8. Cable from Alexander Korda to Merle Oberon, 5 March 1935, ibid.
9. Cable from Merle Oberon to Alexander Korda, 6 March 1935, ibid.
10. Cable from Douglas Fairbanks Jr to Samuel Goldwyn, 13 July 1935, ibid.
11. Cable from Samuel Goldwyn to Douglas Fairbanks Jr, 13 July 1935, ibid.
12. Cable from Merle Oberon to Douglas Fairbanks Sr, 23 July 1935, ibid.
13. Cable from Alexander Korda to Samuel Goldwyn, 22 July 1935, ibid.
14. Cable from Alexander Korda to Merle Oberon, 14 August 1935, ibid.
15. Sir David Cunynghame, diary, 2 February 1935.
16. Richard Norton, *Silver Spoon* (Hutchinson, 1954), p. 182.

17. H. G. Wells to Arthur Bliss, 17 October 1934, in *The Correspondence of H. G. Wells*, ed. David C. Smith (Pickering & Chato, 1998), vol. 3, p. 543.
18. *Collier's*, 15 February 1936.
19. Ibid.
20. Unidentified and undated newspaper article on Alexander Korda microfiche, British Film Institute Library.
21. Samuel Goldwyn to Merle Oberon, 4 September 1935, Goldwyn Papers.
22. Cable from Alexander Korda to John Myers, undated, ibid.
23. Quoted in *Los Angeles Examiner*, 6 September 1935.
24. *LA Herald & Express*, 6 September 1935.
25. Unidentified newspaper article, 26 September 1935, on Alexander Korda microfiche, British Film Institute Library.
26. Sir David Cunynghame, diary, 29 September 1935.

11. THE BUBBLE BURSTS

1. Cable from Murray Silverstone to United Artists Sales Department, New York, 21 February 1936, United Artists Collection, State Historical Society of Wisconsin, US Mss 99AN, Series 1H, Circular Letters 1936–1943, Box 1, File 3.
2. Cable from Murray Silverstone to Samuel Goldwyn, 21 February 1936, Samuel Goldwyn Papers, Margaret Herrick Library, Academy of Motion Picture Arts and Science, Beverly Hills.
3. John Myers to Samuel Goldwyn, 21 February 1936, ibid.
4. *Things to Come* budget and box-office receipts taken from list of costs and receipts of London Film Productions up to 24 September 1938, Prudential Archive, Box 2353.
5. *Film Weekly*, 29 February 1936.
6. Raymond Massey, *A Hundred Different Lives: An Autobiography* (Robson Books, 1979), p. 192.
7. Letter from H. G. Wells to Constance Coolidge, in *The Correspondence of H. G. Wells*, ed. David C. Smith (Pickering & Chatto, 1998), vol. 4, p. 122.
8. Sir David Cunynghame, diary, 8 July 1935.
9. Michael Korda, *Charmed Lives* (Allen Lane, 1980), p. 105.
10. Letter from H. G. Wells to Constance Coolidge, in *The Correspondence of H. G. Wells*, vol. 4, p. 122.
11. Letter from Alexander Korda to Joint Secretaries of the

Prudential, P. C. Crump and E. H. Lever, 18 May 1936, Prudential Archive, Box 2350.

12. Ibid.
13. Letter from Alexander Korda to P. C. Crump and E. H. Lever, 20 May 1936, ibid.
14. Letter from P. C. Crump and E. H. Lever to Alexander Korda, 4 June 1936, ibid.
15. Minutes of the London Film Productions Executive Committee, 3rd Meeting, 10 June 1936, ibid., Box 2354.
16. Sir David Cunynghame, diary, 19 March 1936.
17. Elsa Lanchester, *Herself* (St Martin's Press, 1983), p. 142.
18. Elsa Lanchester, *Charles Laughton and I* (Faber and Faber, 1938), p. 194.
19. Lanchester, *Herself*, p. 147.
20. Ibid., p. 145.
21. *Spectator*, 20 November 1936.
22. List of costs and receipts of London Film Productions up to 24 September 1938, Prudential Archive, Box 2353.
23. Alexander Korda, 'I was at Home' ('Otthon voltam'), from *Kórborlások* (Balla, J., Budapest, 1911).
24. Ibid.

12. TWENTY-FOUR HOURS A DAY

1. Humbert Wolfe, *Cyrano de Bergerac* (Hutchinson, 1937), p. 13.
2. Ibid., p. 14.
3. Richard Norton, *Silver Spoon* (Hutchinson, 1954), p. 166.
4. Ludovico Toeplitz, *Ciak a chi tocca* (Edizioni Milano Nuova, 1964), p. 158.
5. Quoted by Norman Spencer, interview with the author, 29 September 1998.
6. Norton, *Silver Spoon*, p. 166.
7. Interview with David Korda (Joan's son), 8 June 2000.
8. Toeplitz, *Ciak a chi tocca*, p. 186.
9. Maria Korda, 'The Man Called Alexander Korda', unpublished manuscript, British Library, 1957, ch. 9, p. 2.
10. John Loder, *Hollywood Hussar* (Howard Baker, 1977), p. 105.
11. Quoted in Thomas Kiernan, *Laurence Olivier* (Sidgwick & Jackson, 1982), p. 147.
12. Ibid., p. 148.

13. Sir Anthony Havelock-Allan, interview with the author, 23 March 2001.
14. Hugo Vickers, *Vivien Leigh* (Hamish Hamilton, 1988), p. 49.
15. Sir Anthony Havelock-Allan, interview with the author, 23 March 2001.
16. Kenneth Barrow, *Flora* (Heinemann, 1981), p. 104.
17. Quoted in Vickers, *Vivien Leigh*, p. 76.
18. Ibid., p. 68.
19. Memorandum to David Selznick, 2 February 1937, David Selznick Collection, Harry Ransom Humanities Research Center, University of Texas at Austin, Box 3341, Folder 2.
20. Basil Dean, *Mind's Eye: An Autobiography 1927–1972*, vol. 2 of *Seven Ages* (Hutchinson, 1973), p. 251.
21. Ibid., p. 252.
22. *Evening News*, 12 July 1937.
23. Quoted in Kiernan, *Laurence Olivier*, p. 180.
24. Memorandum from David Selznick to Messrs Wallace, Wright and Richards, 17 February 1938, Selznick Collection, Box 3341, Folder 2.
25. Memorandum, 4 January 1939, ibid.

13. FALLING WITH STYLE

1. Interview with the author, 31 March 1998.
2. Richard Norton, *Silver Spoon* (Hutchinson, 1954), p. 175.
3. Helmut Junge, *Plan for Film Studios* (Focal Press, 1945), p. 22.
4. Ibid., p. 60.
5. André De Toth, *Fragments* (Faber and Faber, 1994), p. 146.
6. Ibid., p. 147.
7. Ibid.
8. Ibid., p. 148.
9. Quoted in Kenneth Barrow, *Mr Chips* (Methuen, 1985), p. 95.
10. Robert Helprin, publicity and advertising for London Film Productions, to G. J. Schaefer, 3 September 1936, United Artists Collection, State Historical Society of Wisconsin, US Mss 99AN, Series 1H, Circular Letters 1936–43, Box 1, File 6.
11. Quoted in ibid., pp. 93–4.
12. Sir David Cunynghame, diary, 9 October 1936.

13. Elsa Lanchester, *Charles Laughton and I* (Faber and Faber, 1938), p. 222.
14. Letter dated 3 January 1937, quoted in Barrow, *Mr Chips*, p. 95.
15. Jacques Feyder and Françoise Rosay, *Le Cinéma, notre métier* (Pierre Cailler, 1946).
16. Ibid.
17. Interview with author, 31 March 1998.
18. Barrow, *Mr Chips*, p. 95.
19. Quoted in Richard Griffith, *The World of Robert Flaherty* (Gollancz, 1953), p. 110.
20. Quoted in Arthur Calder-Marshall, based on research material by Paul Rotha and Basil Wright, *The Innocent Eye: The Life of Robert J. Flaherty* (W. H. Allen, 1963), p. 178.
21. Quoted in Griffith, *The World of Robert Flaherty*, p. 132.
22. Osmond Borradaile, 'Life through a Lens: Journals of a Cinematographer', unpublished manuscript, Kevin Brownlow Collection, ch. 5, pp. 15–16.
23. Quoted in Arthur Calder-Marshall, *The Innocent Eye*, pp. 180–81.
24. Quoted in ibid., p. 183.
25. Borradaile, 'Life through a Lens', ch. 5, p. 9.
26. Memorandum: 'Commissions & percentages from revenues paid by this company as at 14th June 1939', Prudential Archive, Box 2357.
27. List of costs and receipts of London Film Productions up to 24 September 1938, ibid., Box 2353.
28. London Film Productions executive meeting, 18 September 1936, ibid., Box 2354.
29. London Film Productions executive meeting, 19 November 1936, ibid.
30. Cable from Alexander Korda to Dr Giannini and members of United Artists, 18 December 1936, United Artists Collection, US Mss 99AN, Series 5A, Loyd Wright Legal Papers, Box 1, File 9.
31. Cable from Murray Silverstone to Loyd Wright, 19 December 1936, ibid., Box 1, File 8.
32. Undated letter, Samuel Goldwyn Papers, Merle Oberon File 3688, Margaret Herrick Library, Academy of Motion Picture Arts and Sciences, Beverly Hills.

14. HANGING ON

1. Letter to Julie Matthews, 18 January 1937, in *Broken Images: Selected Letters of Robert Graves 1914–1946*, ed. Paul O'Prey (Hutchinson, 1982), p. 275.
2. *Sunday Dispatch*, 4 November 1936.
3. Josef Von Sternberg, *Fun in a Chinese Laundry* (The Macmillan Company, New York, 1965), p. 172.
4. Ibid., pp. 183–4.
5. Ibid., p. 184.
6. Ibid., p. 183.
7. Elsa Lanchester, *Herself* (St Martin's Press, 1983), p. 154.
8. Von Sternberg, *Fun in a Chinese Laundry*, p. 184.
9. Cable from Merle Oberon to Samuel Goldwyn, 8 January 1937, Samuel Goldwyn Papers, Margaret Herrick Library, Academy of Motion Picture Arts and Sciences, Beverly Hills.
10. Cable from Samuel Goldwyn to Merle Oberon, 9 January 1937, ibid.
11. Von Sternberg, *Fun in a Chinese Laundry*, p. 189.
12. Cable from Samuel Goldwyn to Merle Oberon, 16 March 1937, Goldwyn Papers.
13. Memorandum from Mary Pickford, undated, United Artists Collection, State Historical Society of Wisconsin, US Mss 99AN, Series 5A, Loyd Wright Legal Papers, Box 1, File 8.
14. Cable from F. M. Guedalla to Loyd Wright, 4 February 1937, ibid., Series 5B, Dr A. H. Giannini Correspondence, Box 2, File 2.
15. Alexander Korda to Samuel Goldwyn, 10 February 1937, Goldwyn Papers.
16. Cable from Alexander Korda to United Artists stockholders, 10 March 1937, read out at special meeting of the stockholders of United Artists corporation, 11 March 1937, United Artists Collection, US Mss 99AN, Series 2A, O'Brien Legal Files, Box 5, File 5.
17. Cable from Alexander Korda to Arthur Kelly, United Artists Collection, US Mss 99AN, Series 2A, O'Brien Legal Files, Box 5, File 5.
18. Circular Letter, no. 3404, 8 January 1936, ibid., US Mss 99AN, Series 1H, Circular Letters 1936–43, Box 1, File 3.
19. Letter from Clarence Ericksen to Dennis O'Brien, 25 May 1937,

ibid., US Mss 99AN, Series 2A, O'Brien Legal Files, Box 135, File 9.

20. Letter from Douglas Fairbanks Sr to his business manager, Clarence Ericksen, received 1 December 1937, ibid., Series 2A, O'Brien Legal Files, Box 135, File 9.
21. Minutes of annual meeting of stockholders of United Artists, 8 December 1937, ibid., Box 5, File 5.
22. Letter from Merle Oberon to Samuel Goldwyn, undated, Goldwyn Papers.
23. Letter from Merle Oberon to Samuel Goldwyn, undated, ibid.
24. Letter from Dr Herbert Kalmus to Kay Harrison, 13 September 1937, London Film Productions Archive, 'D Files', British Film Institute Special Collection.
25. Letter from C. H. Brand to Kay Harrison, 4 October 1937, ibid.
26. *Film Weekly*, 10 July 1937.

15. FREE!

1. *Daily Mail*, 20 January 1938.
2. Ibid.
3. Prudential Archive, Box 2353.
4. Undated copy of an original letter from Ernest Lever to Mary Pickford, United Artists Collection, State Historical Society of Wisconsin, USS Mss 99AN, Series 2A, O'Brien Legal Files, Box 136, File 5.
5. Joint Opinion, dated 6 May 1938, for London Films and Prudential, prepared by Linklater & Paines, Prudential Archive, Box 2356.
6. Memorandum called 'Films', 2 August 1938, ibid., Box 2353.
7. Memorandum called 'Mr Lever's re-organization scheme', 4 November 1938, ibid., Box 2350.
8. *Daily Express*, 11 December 1938.
9. Minutes of regular meeting of board of directors, 13 February 1939, United Artists Corporation, State Historical Society of Wisconsin, US Mss 99AN, Series 2A, O'Brien Legal Files, Box 4, File 8.
10. Alexander Korda microfiche, British Film Institute Library.
11. Prudential Archive, Box 2354.
12. Sir David Cunynghame, diary, 19 May 1939.

13. Memorandum from P. C. Crump, Joint Secretary, 2 August 1938, Prudential Archive, Box 2353.
14. *Los Angeles Examiner*, 23 September 1938.
15. Ibid., 20 December 1938.
16. Cable from Alexander Korda to Samuel Goldwyn, 26 January 1939, Samuel Goldwyn Papers, Margaret Herrick Library, Academy of Motion Picture Arts and Sciences, Beverly Hills.
17. *Chicago Daily News*, 30 March 1939.
18. *Chicago Herald-American*, 14 October 1939.
19. Contract agreement dated 12 January 1939, London Film Productions Archive, British Film Institute Special Collection, LFP C/114 L(i).
20. *Double Life: The Autobiography of Miklós Rózsa* (Midas Books, 1982), p. 78.
21. Ibid.
22. Ibid., p. 79.
23. Ibid., p. 83.
24. Quoted in Brian McFarlane, ed., *Sixty Voices: Celebrities Recall the Golden Age of British Cinema* (BFI, 1992), p. 144.
25. Ibid., p. 145.
26. Ibid., p. 144.
27. Foreword to *Alexander Korda's The Thief of Bagdad Story Book* (Saalfield Publishing Company, Akron, Ohio, 1940).

16. THE SERVICE

1. Andrew King, interview with the author, 15 March 2001.
2. *The Graham Greene Film Reader: Mornings in the Dark* (Carcanet, 1993), p. 467.
3. Michael Powell, *A Life in Movies: An Autobiography* (Heinemann, 1986), p. 329.
4. Ibid., p. 331.

17. FOR KING AND COUNTRY

1. *Chicago Herald-American*, 14 October 1939.
2. Quoted in memorandum from R. N. Hanscombe to L. Brown, 17 October 1939, Public Record Office, TS 27/474.

3. Note from G. E. G. Forbes of the GPO to the Treasury Solicitor, 6 September 1939, ibid.

4. Cable from United Artists to Alexander Korda and London Film Productions, 27 September 1939, United Artists Collection, State Historical Society of Wisconsin, US Mss 99AN, Series 2A, O'Brien Legal Files, Box 28, File 4.

5. Cable from Alexander Korda to United Artists, 29 September 1939, ibid.

6. Letter from Lord Halifax to Beaverbrook, 16 December 1939, Public Record Office, FO371/22841.

7. Minute sheet, p. 19, Public Record Office, F0371/22840.

8. *Chicago Herald-American*, 14 October 1939.

9. Letter from F. R. Cowell to J. R. Hughes-Roberts, 3 November 1939, Foreign Office Minutes, p. 65, Public Record Office, F0371/22840.

10. Cypher telegram to Mr Haggard (New York), 13 November 1939, ibid., p. 153.

11. Letter from F. R. Cowell to G. E. G. Forbes, 1 December 1939, ibid., p. 157.

12. Letter from Angus Fletcher, British Library of Information, Rockefeller Plaza, 13 November 1939 to News Department, Foreign Office, ibid., p. 113.

13. H. Montgomery, ibid., p. 173.

14. Memorandum from Mr Gorer to Mr Fletcher on the film *The Lion Has Wings*, 13 November 1939, ibid., p. 116.

15. Ibid., p. 110.

16. Letter from Robert Vansittart to Anthony Eden, 10 February 1941, Vansittart Papers, VNST II 1/9, Churchill Archive.

17. Michael Korda, *Charmed Lives* (Allen Lane, 1980), p. 137.

18. David Cunynhame diary, 27 December 1939.

19. London Film Productions press release, 20 March 1939, on Alexander Korda microfiche, British Film Institute Library.

20. Report by American Division of the Ministry of Information, 2 September 1940, Sidney Bernstein Papers, Imperial War Museum Archive.

21. Report by the American Division of the Ministry of Information, ibid.

22. Quoted in R. J. Minney, *Puffin Asquith* (Leslie Frewin Publishers, 1973), p. 121.

23. *Picturegoer and Film Weekly*, 10 May 1941.

24. Sir David Cunynghame, diary, 17 May 1940.

25. Quoted in Anthony Holden, *Olivier* (Weidenfeld & Nicolson, 1988), p. 158.
26. R. C. Sherriff, *No Leading Lady* (Gollancz, 1968), p. 335.
27. Ibid., pp. 335–6.
28. Letter from Joseph Breen to Alexander Korda, 15 October 1940, Motion Picture Producers' Association Production Files, Margaret Herrick Library, Academy of Motion Picture Arts and Sciences, Beverly Hills.
29. Letter from Joseph Breen to Alexander Korda, 30 October 1940, ibid.
30. Quoted in Alan Dent, *Vivien Leigh: A Bouquet* (Hamish Hamilton, 1969), p. 36.
31. Circular Letter, 21 March 1941, United Artists Collection, US Mss 99AN, Series 1H, Circular Letters 1936–43, Box 3, File 6.
32. Ibid.
33. *That Hamilton Woman* pressbook, United Artists Collection, US Mss 99AN, Series 1A, O'Brien Legal Files, Box 186, File 9.
34. Quoted in H. Mark Glancy, *When Hollywood Loved Britain: The Hollywood 'British' Film: 1939–45* (Manchester University Press, 1999), p. 106.
35. Letter from Frank Pick, Director General of the Ministry of Information, to Arthur Jarratt, 24 October 1940, Sidney Bernstein Papers, Imperial War Museum.
36. Alexander Korda to Brendan Bracken, 5 August 1941, relayed to Ministry of Information via cypher cable from British Information Service, ibid.
37. Transcript of radio broadcast printed in the Congressional Record, 4 August 1941, A3975.
38. Letter from Alexander Korda to his lawyer Mendel Silberberg, 13 September 1941, United Artists Collection , US Mss 99AN, Series 1A, O'Brien Legal Files, Box 186, File 6.
39. Ibid.
40. Letter dated 29 August 1941, ibid.
41. Balcon and Baker to Arthur Lee, 2 April 1942, ibid., Box 195, File 6.
42. Letter from David Selznick to W. R. Wilkerson, 11 June 1942, David Selznick Collection, Harry Ransom Humanities Research Center, University of Texas at Austin, Box 307, File 2.

18. A KNIGHT IN HOLLYWOOD

1. Sir David Cunynghame, diary, 19 February 1942.
2. *New York Post*, 28 April 1942.
3. Memorandum from David Selznick to Mary Pickford, Charlie Chaplin and Alexander Korda, 21 October 1941, United Artists Collection, State Historical Society of Wisconsin, US Mss 99AN, Series 5A, Loyd Wright Legal Files, Box 2, File 8.
4. Memorandum from Alexander Korda to stockholders and United Artists management, 27 October 1941, ibid.
5. Memorandum from David Selznick to Gradwell Sears and Ed Raftery, 18 May 1942, United Artists Collection, US Mss 99AN, Series 8B, Gradwell Sears Papers, Box 10, File 8.
6. Memorandum from David Selznick to Daniel O'Shea, 9 September 1941, David Selzick Collection, Harry Ransom Humanities Research Center, University of Texas at Austin, Box 307, File 2.
7. Memorandum dated 23 September 1941, ibid.
8. Memorandum from David Selznick to Ed Raftery, Gradwell Sears and Daniel O'Shea, 7 May 1942, United Artists Collection, US Mss 99AN, Series 8B, Gradwell Sears Papers, Box 10, File 8.
9. Memorandum from Alexander Korda to Ed Raftery, Gradwell Sears and Daniel O'Shea, 8 May 1942, ibid.
10. Memorandum from Daniel O'Shea to Jenia Reissar, 3 June 1942, Selznick Collection, Box 801, File 4.
11. Ibid.
12. Cable from David Selznick to Daniel O'Shea, 21 January 1942, ibid., Box 307, File 2.
13. Memorandum to directors and stockholders, 28 January 1942, United Artists Collection, US Mss 99AN, Series 8B, Gradwell Sears Papers, Box 10, File 8.
14. Cable from Ed Raftery to Alexander Korda, 16 March 1942, ibid., Series 5A, Lloyd Wright Legal Files, Box 3, File 12.
15. Memorandum from Daniel O'Shea to David Selznick, 24 April 1942, Selznick Collection, Box 307, File 2.
16. Ibid.
17. Letter from Ed Raftery to Charlie Chaplin, 13 July 1942, United Artists Collection, US Mss 99AN, Series 5A, Lloyd Wright Legal File, Box 3, Folder 2.

18. Caroline Moorehead, *Sidney Bernstein* (Jonathan Cape, 1984), p. 144.
19. Sir David Cunynghame, diary, 13 January 1943.
20. Michael Balcon, *A Lifetime of Films* (Hutchinson, 1969), p. 107.
21. Ibid., p. 111.
22. *Los Angeles Examiner*, 10 March 1943.

19. PERFECT STRANGERS

1. André De Toth, *Fragments* (Faber, and Faber, 1994), p. 187.
2. *Evening Standard*, 6 November 1943.
3. Minutes of management meeting of D&P Studios Ltd held on 26 November 1942, Prudential Archive, Box 2347.
4. Minutes of management meeting of D&P Studios Ltd held on 10 June 1943, ibid.
5. Minutes of management meeting of D&P Studios Ltd held on 22 July 1943, ibid.
6. Minutes of management meeting of D&P Studios Ltd held on 22 July 1943, ibid.
7. Ibid.
8. Ibid.
9. Cable from Alexander Korda to Daniel O'Shea, 30 November 1943, David Selzick Collection, Harry Ransom Humanities Research Center, University of Texas at Austin, Box 307, File 2.
10. Kenneth Barrow, *Mr Chips* (Methuen, 1985), p. 159.
11. Glynis Johns, interview with the author, 12 February 2002.
12. Quoted in Michael Burn, *Mary and Richard: The Story of Richard Hillary and Mary Booker* (André Deutsch, 1988), p. 19.
13. David Korda, interview with the author, 8 June 2000.
14. De Toth, *Fragments*, p. 329.
15. Interview, *The Golden Years*, Robert Vas, documentary (*Omnibus*, BBC TV, 1968).
16. *Los Angeles Examiner*, 21 December 1944.
17. *Los Angeles Times*, 27 June 1945.
18. André De Toth, interview with author, 7 June 2000.
19. Joan Fontaine, *No Bed of Roses* (William Morrow & Co), p. 173.
20. *Observer*, 2 September 1945.
21. *Daily Sketch*, 2 September 1945.

22. Proposal submitted to Prudential board, 9 March 1944, Prudential Archive, Box 2350.
23. Sir David Cunynghame, diary, 20 April 1944.
24. Cable from Teddie Carr to Ed Raftery, 3 December 1943, United Artists Collection, State Historical Society of Wisconsin, US Mss 99AN, Series 8B, Gradwell Sears Papers, Box 3, File 6.
25. Cable from Alexander Korda to Ed Raftery, 12 January 1944, ibid.
26. Selznick Collection, Box 805, File 7.
27. Sir David Cunynghame, diary, 20 August 1944.
28. Ibid., 1 September 1944.
29. Ibid., 26 October 1944.
30. Ibid., 21 June 1945.
31. Ibid., 26 June 1945.
32. Ibid., 19 October 1945.

20. FORWARD INTO THE FUTURE

1. *Los Angeles Examiner*, 22 October 1945.
2. Letter from Alexander Korda to Sidney Bernstein, 20 May 1946, London Film Productions Archive, British Film Institute Special Collection.
3. *Sidney Lewis Bernstein* v. *Sir Alexander Korda and London Film Productions Ltd*, writ, 14 June 1946, ibid.
4. *The Times*, 5 June 1946.
5. Letter agreement with Orson Welles, 1 September 1946, London Film Productions Archive, C/128(i), British Film Institute Special Collection.
6. Cable from Alexander Korda to Samuel Goldwyn, 2 January 1946, Samuel Goldwyn Papers, Margaret Herrick Library, Academy of Motion Picture Arts and Sciences, Beverly Hills.
7. Cable from Jenia Reissar to David Selznick, 6 January 1946, David Selznick Collection, Harry Ransom Humanities Center, University of Texas at Austin, Box 557, File 6.
8. Sir David Cunynghame, diary, 29 April 1946.
9. 'London Film Productions Ltd: Periodical Report' by E. H. Lever, 12 September 1938, Prudential Archive, Box 2357.
10. Sir David Cunynghame, diary, 19 June 1946.
11. *Selected Diaries of Cecil Beaton*, ed. Richard Buckle (Pimlico, 1991), p. 190.

12. Ibid.
13. Ibid.
14. Letter from Cecil Beaton to Greta Garbo, 22 June 1947, Cecil Beaton Papers, Hugo Vickers Collection.
15. Letter from Cecil Beaton to Greta Garbo, 15 July 1947, ibid.
16. Norman Spencer, interview with the author, 31 March 1998.
17. Interview with the author, 9 November 2000.
18. *Selected Diaries of Cecil Beaton*, p. 190.
19. Ibid., p. 189.
20. Ibid., 26 March 1947.
21. Ibid., 15 December 1947.
22. *Los Angeles Examiner*, 2 July 1947.
23. Ibid., 13 November 1947.
24. *News Chronicle*, 15 November 1947.
25. *Daily Mail*, 23 January 1948.
26. *News Chronicle*, 24 January 1948.
27. *Daily Mail*, 23 January 1948.
28. *Evening Standard*, 23 January 1948.
29. Cecil Beaton, diary, March 1948, Cecil Beaton Papers, Hugo Vickers Collection.
30. Christine Norden, 'The Champagne Days are Over' (unpublished manuscript, 1978, Michael Thornton Collection), p. 40.
31. Merle Oberon, interview with Michael Thornton, 10 December 1969.
32. Christine Norden, 'The Champagne Days are Over', p. 43.
33. Guy Hamilton, interview wiht the author, 15 October 1997.
34. Christine Norden, ibid., p. 49.
35. Christine Norden, 'The Champagne Days are Over', p. 61.
36. Ibid., p. 42.
37. Ibid., p. 63.
38. Merle Oberon, interview with Michael Thornton, 10 December 1969.
39. Christine Norden, 'The Champagne Days are Over', p. 58.
40. Ibid.

21. NEVER PAY CASH

1. Public Record Office, BT64/2366.
2. A Paper on Film Finance, 26 February 1948, ibid.
3. Interview with the author, 14 November 1994.

4. Finance for Film Production, no date, Public Record Office, BT64/2366.
5. 'A Central Company for Independent British Film Production', undated memorandum, ibid.
6. Ibid.
7. Application by British Lion to FCI for Financial Aid, 14 June 1948, ibid.
8. Letter from Rupert Somervell to Sir Wilfrid Eady, 2 July 1948, ibid.
9. National Film Finance Corporation, First Annual Report, para. 8.
10. Letter from Sir Wilfrid Eady to Rupert Somervell, 19 April 1948, ibid.
11. Ludovico Toeplitz, *Ciak a chi tocca* (Edizioni Milano Nuova, 1964),
    p. 138.
12. Myrna Loy, *Being and Becoming* (Bloomsbury, 1987), p. 231.
13. Ibid., p. 230.
14. Ibid., p. 231.
15. *Weekly Scotsman*, 4 November 1948.
16. Sir David Cunynghame, diary, 10 November 1948.
17. Ibid., 7 December 1948.
18. Quoted in *The British Film Industry* (Political and Economic Planning, 1952), p. 145.
19. Sir David Cunynghame, diary, 17 December 1948.
20. William Macquitty, *A Life to Remember* (Quartet Books, 1991), p. 303.

22. AULD LANG SYNE

1. Memorandum from Pat Duggan to Samuel Goldwyn, 21 May 1948, Samuel Goldwyn Papers, Margaret Herrick Library, Academy of Motion Picture Arts and Sciences, Beverly Hills.
2. Letter from Samuel Goldwyn to Alexander Korda, 28 July 1948, ibid.
3. Cable from Alexander Korda to Samuel Goldwyn, 10 August 1948, ibid.
4. Letter from Alexander Korda to Samuel Goldwyn, 26 August 1948, ibid.
5. Letter from Samuel Goldwyn to Alexander Korda, 31 August 1948, ibid.

6. Michael Powell, *Million Dollar Movie* (Random House, 1995), p. 22.
7. Memorandum from Lynn Farnol, received 15 November 1948, Goldwyn Papers.
8. *Daily Express*, 31 October 1948.
9. Powell, *Million Dollar Movie*, p. 62.
10. Cable from Michael Powell to Max Wilkinson, 27 November 1948, Goldwyn Papers.
11. Cable from Samuel Goldwyn to Michael Powell, 28 November 1948, ibid.
12. Letter from Samuel Goldwyn to Alexander Korda, 8 December 1948, ibid.
13. cable from Alexander Korda to Samuel Goldwyn, 7 March 1949, ibid.
14. 'Summary of Mr Goldwyn's telephone conversation with Sir Alexander Korda (in Rome) on June 23, 1949', ibid.
15. Powell, *Million Dollar Movie*, p. 60.
16. Letter from Max Wilkinson to Michael Powell, 10 November 1948, Goldwyn Papers.
17. *Daily Express*, 27 January 1956.
18. Letter from David Selznick to Milton Kramer, 18 June 1948, David Selznick Collection, Harry Ransom Humanities Research Center, University of Texas at Austin, Box 1439, File 2.
19. Ibid., Box 1439, File 3.
20. Ibid., Box 741, File 4.
21. Letter from David Selznick to Alexander Korda, 16 June 1949, ibid., Box 741, File 5.
22. Memorandum from David Selznick to Alexander Korda, 22 July 1949, ibid., Box 741, File 6.
23. Cable from David Selznick to Jenia Reissar, 17 August 1949, ibid., Box 741, File 7.
24. Memorandum from David Selznick to Jenia Reissar, 19 August 1949, ibid., Box 741, File 7.
25. Letter from Michael Powell to David Selznick, 6 October 1949, ibid., Box 742, File 4.
26. Cable from David Selznick to Jenia Reissar, 2 October 1949, ibid., Box 742, File 4.
27. Cable from David Selznick to Jenia Reissar, 20 October 1949, ibid., Box 916, File 6.
28. Minutes of the Arbitration Hearing, 13 May 1950, ibid., Box 3349, File 3.

29. *New York World-Telegram and Sun*, 11 November 1950.
30. Sir David Cunynghame, diary, 22 August 1950.
31. Ibid., 22 September 1950.
32. Ibid., 3 November 1950.
33. *Hansard*, 14 December 1949, col. 2695.
34. Powell, *Million Dollar Movie*, p. 44.

23. ELSEWHERE

1. Quoted in Paul Tabori, *Alexander Korda* (Oldbourne, 1959), p. 276.
2. Sir David Cunynghame, diary, 28 June 1949.
3. Ibid., 11 June 1942.
4. Ibid., 25 May 1950.
5. David Russell, interview with the author, 1998.
6. Sir David Cunynghame, diary, 15 May 1950.
7. Robin Lowe, interview with the author, 28 May 1998.
8. Sir David Cunynghame, diary, 6 March 1950.
9. Christine Norden, 'The Champagne Days are Over', (unpublished manuscript, 1978, Michael Thornton Collection), p. 59.
10. David Parkinson, ed., *Graham Greene Film Reader: Morning in the Dark* (Carcanet, 1993), p. 467.
11. Ibid., pp. 465–6.
12. Ibid., p. 468.
13. Sir David Cunynghame, diary, 10 October 1951.
14. *British Film Industry* (Political and Economic Planning, 1952), p. 245.
15. Michael Powell, *Million Dollar Movie* (Random House, 1995), p. 137.
16. Sir David Cunynghame, diary, 18 April 1951.
17. Ibid., 30 November 1951.
18. Ibid., 3 December 1951.
19. *Daily Express*, 30 March 1953.
20. *Evening News*, 22 March 1952.
21. Letter from Alexander Korda to Winston Churchill, 13 August 1947, Churchill Papers, Chur 2/151, Churchill Archives Centre, Churchill College, Cambridge.
22. Letter from Alexander Korda to Winston Churchill, 26 May 1950, ibid., Chur 2/171.
23. Norman Spencer, interview with the author, 31 March 1998.

24. Letter from Lady Beatrice Maria Korda to Winston Churchill, 5 November 1951, Churchill Papers, Chur 2/191.
25. Christmas card from Lady Beatrice Maria Korda to Winston Churchill, 23 December 1951, ibid.
26. Letter from Lady Beatrice Maria Korda to Winston Churchill, 28 December 1951, ibid.
27. This 'Preface' was enclosed in a letter from Lady Beatrice Maria Korda to Winston Churchill, 10 January 1952, ibid.
28. Letter from Lady Alexander Korda to Winston Churchill, 3 February 1952, ibid.
29. Letter from Lady Beatrice Maria Korda to Winston Churchill, 7 February 1952, ibid.
30. Letter from Lady Beatrice Korda to Winston Churchill, 7 March 1952, ibid.
31. Letter from Lady Beatrice Korda to Winston Churchill, 27 March, ibid.

24. A HOME AT LAST

1. Michael Korda, *Charmed Lives* (Allen Lane, 1980), p. 287.
2. Christine Norden, 'The Champagne Days are Over', (unpublished manuscript, 1978, Michael Thornton Collection), p. 126.
3. Sir David Cunynghame, diary, 27 May 1953.
4. Quoted in *Variety*, 25 January 1956.
5. *Daily Herald*, 9 May 1953.
6. *Sunday Chronicle*, 31 May 1953.
7. Letter from Alexander Korda to Laurence Olivier, 8 June 1953, Sir Laurence Olivier Collection, British Library.
8. Cable, 8 June 1953, ibid.
9. Sir David Cunynghame, diary, 18 June 1953.
10. Quoted in Paul Tabori, *Alexander Korda* (Oldbourne, 1959), p. 284.
11. Sir David Cunynghame, diary, 20 October 1953.
12. *Hansard*, 20 November 1953.
13. Ibid.
14. Quoted in *Daily Express*, 24 January 1956.
15. Sir David Cunynghame, diary, 27 January 1954.
16. Ibid., 15 April 1955.
17. Ibid., 26 April 1955.
18. David Lewin, interview with the author, 11 July 2000.

19. *Daily Express*, 1 July 1954.
20. Ibid., 24 January 1956.
21. Alexander Korda, 'Sick' ('Betegek'), from *Kórborlások* (Balla, J., Budapest, 1911).
22. David Korda, interview with the author, 8 June 2000.
23. *Daily Express*, 24 January 1956.
24. David Lewin, interview with the author, 11 July 2000.
25. Christine Norden, 'The Champagne Days are Over', p. 162.
26. *Daily Mirror*, 19 May 1956.
27. David Korda, interview with the author, 8 June 2000.

Select Bibliography

Balcon, Michael, *Michael Balcon Presents a Lifetime of Films*, Hutchinson, 1969

Barrow, Kenneth, *Flora*, Heinemann, 1981

—— *Mr Chips*, Methuen, 1985

Billard, Pierre, *L'Age classique du cinema Français*, Flammarion, 1995

Brown, Malcolm, ed., *Letters of T. E. Lawrence*, J. M. Dent & Sons, 1988

Buckle, Richard, ed., *Selected Diaries of Cecil Beaton*, Pimlico, 1991

Burn, Michael, *Mary and Richard: The Story of Richard Hillary and Mary Booker*, André Deutsch, 1988

Callow, Simon, *Charles Laughton: A Difficult Actor*, Methuen, 1987

Dean, Basil, *Mind's Eye: An Autobiography*, Hutchinson, 1973

Dent, Alan, *Vivien Leigh: A Bouquet*, Hamish Hamilton, 1969

De Toth, André, *Fragments*, Faber & Faber, 1994

Feyder, Jacques and Rosay, Françoise, *Le Cinéma, notre métier*, Pierre Cailler, 1946

Fontaine, Joan, *No Bed of Roses*, W. H. Allen, 1978

Fraenkel, Heinrich, *Unsterblicher Film*, Kindler Verlag, 1956

Fresnay, Pierre and Possot, *Pierre Fresnay*, Editions de la Table Ronde, 1975

Gibbs, Anthony, *In My Time*, Peter Davies, 1969

Glancy, Mark H., *When Hollywood Loved Britain: The Hollywood 'British' Film 1939–45*, Manchester University Press, 1999

Graves, Robert, *Broken Images: Selected Letters 1914–1946*, Hutchinson, 1982

Griffith, Richard, *The World of Robert Flaherty*, Gollancz, 1953
Grossmith, George, *G.G.*, Hutchinson, 1933

Higham, Charles and Mosley, Roy *Merle: A Biography of Merle Oberon*, New English Library, 1983
Holden, Anthony, *Olivier*, Weidenfeld & Nicolson, 1988

Kiernan, Thomas, *Laurence Olivier*, Sidgwick & Jackson, 1982
Korda, Alexander, *Kórborlások*, Balla, J., Budapest, 1911
Korda, Maria, 'The Man Called Alexander Korda', unpublished manuscript, British Library, 1957
Korda, Michael, *Charmed Lives: A Family Romance*, Allen Lane, 1980
Kruger, Loren, ed., *Light and Shadows: The Autobiography of Leontine Sagan*, Witwatersrand University Press, 1996
Kulik, Karol, *Alexander Korda: The Man Who Could Work Miracles*, W.H. Allen, 1975

Lanchester, Elsa, *Charles Laughton and I*, Faber & Faber, 1938
Lanchester, Elsa, *Herself*, St. Martins Press, 1983
Loder, John, *Hollywood Hussar*, Howard Baker, 1977
Loy, Myrna, *Being and Becoming*, Bloomsbury, 1987

Macquitty, William, *A Life to Remember*, Quartet Books, 1991
Marshall, Arthur Calder, *The Innocent Eye: The Life of Robert J. Flaherty*, W. H. Allen, 1963.
Massey, Raymond, *A Hundred Different Lives: An Autobiography*, Robson Books, 1979
McFarlane, Brian, ed., *Sixty Voices*, BFI Publishing, 1992
Minney, R. J., *'Puffin' Asquith*, Leslie Frewin Publishers, 1973
Moorehead, Caroline, *Sidney Bernstein: A Biography*, Jonathan Cape, 1984

Nemeskürty, István, *Word and Image: History of the Hungarian Cinema*, Corvina Press, Budapest, 1968
Noble, Peter, ed., *The British Film Yearbook 1947–48*, Skelton Robinson, 1947
Norton, Richard, *Silver Spoon*, Hutchinson, 1954

Pagnol, Marcel, *Confidences: Mémoires*, Juilliard, 1981
Parkinson, David, ed., *The Graham Greene Film Reader: Mornings in the Dark*, Carcanet, 1993

Political & Economic Planning, *The British Film Industry*, 1952

Powell, Michael, *A Life in Movies: An Autobiography*, Heinemann, 1986

Powell, Michael, *Billion Dollar Movie*, Random House, 1995

Romsics, Ignác, *Hungary in the Twentieth Century*, Corvina, Budapest, 1999

Rotha, Paul and Griffith, Richard *The Film Till Now: A Survey of World Cinema*, 2nd edn, Vision, 1951

Rózsa, Miklós, *Double Life*, Midas Books, 1982

Savio, Francesco, *Cinecittà anni trenta*, Bulzoni Editore, 1979

Siepmann, Eric Otto, *Confessions of a Nihilist*, Gollancz, 1955

Smith, David C., ed., *The Correspondence of H. G. Wells*, Pickering & Chatto, 1998

Stockham, Martin, *The Korda Collection: Alexander Korda's Film Classics*, Citadel Press, 1992

Sussex, Elizabeth, *The Rise and Fall of British Documentary*, University of California, 1975

Tabori, Paul, *Alexander Korda*, Oldbourne, 1959

Toeplitz, Ludovico, *Ciak a chi tocca*, Edizioni Milano Nuova, 1964

Vickers, Hugo, *Vivien Leigh*, Hamish Hamilton, 1988

Von Sternberg, Josef, *Fun in a Chinese Laundry*, The Macmillan Company, New York, 1965

Wenden, D.J., *The Birth of the Movies*, E. P. Dutton & Co, 1974

Williams, Emlyn, *Emlyn*, Penguin Books, 1976

Wolfe, Humbert, *Cyrano de Bergerac*, Hutchinson, 1937

Wood, Alan, *Mr Rank: A Study of J. Arthur Rank and British Films*, Hodder & Stoughton, 1952

Zsuffa, Joseph, *Béla Balázs: The Man and the Artist*, University of California Press, 1987

The Films of Sir Alexander Korda

In this list, the nature of Alexander Korda's contribution has been indicated by the following abbreviations: D = Director; S = Screenwriter; P = Producer; EP = Executive Producer. It is important, however, to bear in mind that as a producer he would often make major contributions to a film without taking specific credits.

HUNGARY

1914   *A becsapott újságíró* (*The Duped Journalist*), D
       Örház a Kárpátokban (*Watch-house in the Carpathians*), D

1915   *Tutyu and Totyó* (*Tutyu and Totyo*), D
       Lyon Lea (*Lyon Lea*), D
       A tiszti kardbojt (*The Officer's Swordknot*), D, S

1916   *Fehér éjszakák* (*White Nights*), D, S
       Mesék az írógépröl (*Tales of the Typewriter*), D, S
       A nagymama (*Grandmother*), D, S
       Az egymillió fontos bankó (*The One Million Pound Note*), D, S
       Ciklámen (*Cyclamen*), D
       Vergödö szívek (*Struggling Hearts*), D, S
       Mágnás Miska (*Miska the Magnate*), D

1917   *A gólyakalifa* (*The Stork Caliph*), D
       Mágia (*Magic*), D
       Szent *Péter esernyöje* (*St Peter's Umbrella*), D
       Harrison és Barrison (*Harrison and Barrison*), D

1918   *Faun,* D
       Az aranyember (*The Golden Man*), D
       Marian, D

1919   *Ave Caesar!,* D
       Féher rózsa (*White Rose*), D
       Yamata, D
       Se ki, se be (*Neither In Nor Out*), D
       A 111-es (*Number 111*), D

VIENNA

1920   *Seine Majestät, das Bettelkind* (*The Prince and the Pauper*), D

1922   *Herren der Meere* (*Masters of the Sea*), D
       Eine Versunkene Welt (*A Vanished World*), D
       Samson und Delilah (*Samson and Delilah*), D

BERLIN

1923   *Das unbekannte Morgen* (*The Unknown Tomorrow*), D, S

1924   *Jedermanns Frau* (*Everybody's Woman*), D
       Tragödie im Hause Habsburg (*Tragedy in the House of
          Hapsburg*), D

1925   *Der Tänzer meiner Frau* (*Dancing Mad*), D, S

1926   *Madame wünscht keine Kinder* (*Madame Wants No
          Children*), D

1927   *Eine Dubarry von heute* (*A Modern Dubarry*), D

HOLLYWOOD

1927   *The Stolen Bride*, D
        The Private Life of Helen of Troy, D

1928   *Yellow Lily*, D
        Night Watch, D

1929   *Love and the Devil*, D
        The Squall, D
        Her Private Life, D

1930   *Lilies of the Field*, D
        Women Everywhere, D
        The Princess and the Plumber, D

PARIS

1931   *Rive Gauche/Die Manner um Lucie*, D
        Marius/Zum Golden Anker, D

LONDON

1932   *Service for Ladies* (US title: *Reserved for Ladies*), D
        Women Who Play, D

1933   *Wedding Rehearsal*, D
        Men of Tomorrow, P
        That Night in London (US: *Overnight*), P
        Strange Evidence, P
        Counsel's Opinion, P
        Cash (US: *For Love or Money*), P
        The Girl from Maxim's, D, P
        The Private Life of Henry VIII, D, P

1934   *Catherine the Great*, P
        The Private Life of Don Juan, D, P

The Private Life of the Gannet, P
The Scarlet Pimpernel, P

1935　*Sanders of the River* (US: *Bosambo*), P
Wharves and Strays (short), P
The Ghost Goes West, P

1936　*Miss Bracegirdle Does Her Duty* (short), P
The Fox Hunt (short), P
Things to Come, P
Moscow Nights (US: *I Stand Condemned*), P
Men Are Not Gods, P
Forget-Men-Not (US: *Forever Yours*), P
Rembrandt, D, P

1937　*The Man Who Could Work Miracles*, P
Fire Over England, EP
I, Claudius (unfinished), P
Dark Journey, EP
Elephant Boy, P
Farewell Again (US: *Troopship*), P
Storm in a Teacup, EP
Action for Slander, EP
Knight without Armour, P
The Squeaker (US: *Murder on Diamond Row*), P
The Return of the Scarlet Pimpernel, P
Paradise for Two (US: *The Gaiety Girls*), P

1938　*The Divorce of Lady X*, P
The Drum (US: *Drums*), P
South Riding, EP
The Challenge, EP
Prison without Bars, EP
Q Planes (US: *Clouds Over Europe*), EP

1939　*The Four Feathers*, P
The Rebel Son, EP
The Spy in Black (US: *U-Boat 29*), EP
The Lion Has Wings, P

1940　*Over the Moon*, P
Twenty-one Days (US: *21 Days Together*)

Conquest of the Air, P
The Thief of Baghdad (completed in the United States), P
Old Bill and Son, EP

HOLLYWOOD

1940   *That Hamilton Woman* (UK title: *Lady Hamilton*), P

1941   *Lydia*, P

1942   *To Be or Not to Be*, EP
       Jungle Book, P

LONDON

1943   *The Biter Bit* (short), P

1945   *Perfect Strangers* (US: *Vacation from Marriage*), D, P

1947   *The Shop at Sly Corner*, EP
       A Man About the House, EP
       An Ideal Husband, D, P
       Mine Own Executioner, P

1948   *Night Beat*, EP
       Anna Karenina, P
       The Winslow Boy, EP
       The Fallen Idol, P
       Bonnie Prince Charlie, P

1949   *The Small Back Room*, EP
       That Dangerous Age (US: *If This Be Sin*), EP
       The Last Days of Dolwyn (US: *Woman of Dolwyn*), EP
       Saints and Sinners, EP
       The Third Man, EP

1950   *The Cure for Love*, EP
       The Happiest Days of Your Life, EP

The Angel with the Trumpet, EP
The Bridge of Time (short), EP
My Daughter Joy (US: *Operation X*), EP
State Secret (US: *The Great Manhunt*), EP
The Wooden Horse, EP
Seven Days to Noon, EP
Gone to Earth (US: *The Wild Heart*), EP

1951 *The Elusive Pimpernel* (US: *The Fighting Pimpernel*), EP
The Tales of Hoffman, EP
Lady Godiva Rides Again, EP
The Wonder Kid, EP

1952 *Mr Denning Drives North*, EP
Outcast of the Islands, EP
Home at Seven (US: *Murder on Monday*), EP
Who Goes There? (US: *The Passionate Sentry*), EP
Cry the Beloved Country (US: *African Fury*), EP
Edinburgh (short), EP
Road to Canterbury (short), EP
The Sound Barrier (US: *Breaking the Sound Barrier*), EP
The Holly and the Ivy, EP

1953 *The Ringer*, EP
Folly to be Wise, EP
Twice upon a Time, EP
The Captain's Paradise, EP
The Story of Gilbert and Sullivan (US: *The Great Gilbert and Sullivan*), EP
The Man Between, EP

1954 *The Heart of the Matter*, EP
Hobson's Choice, EP
Belles of St Trinian's, EP
The Teckman Mystery, EP

1955 *The Man Who Loved Redheads*, EP
Three Cases of Murder, EP
The Constant Husband, EP
A Kid for Two Farthings, EP

The Deep Blue Sea, EP
Summer Madness (US: *Summertime*), EP
Storm Over the Nile, EP

1956 *Richard III*, EP
Smiley, EP

Index